IMPROVING PROCEDURAL JUSTICE IN ANTI-DUMPING INVESTIGATIONS

By synthesising both theoretical and empirical insights, this book offers a distinctive perspective on procedural justice within the context of anti-dumping investigations. The book highlights the disjunction between the provisions outlined in the World Trade Organization's Anti-Dumping Agreement (ADA) and the practical encounters faced by stakeholders such as exporters, regulatory bodies and legal experts affiliated with the WTO. Employing a mixed-methods approach, the research encompasses a comprehensive doctrinal analysis of procedural complexities alongside empirical investigations involving key stakeholders such as WTO legal experts, Chinese exporters and investigating authorities. Furthermore, this book underscores the potential for enhancing procedural justice through either a comprehensive reform of the ADA or concrete measures such as a standardized anti-dumping questionnaire. Such improvements offered in the book have the potential to curtail the misuse of anti-dumping investigations, consequently mitigating a substantial number of disputes that might be brought before the WTO's dispute settlement mechanism.

ABDULKADIR YILMAZCAN holds a PhD from the University of Hong Kong, Faculty of Law, and is a former Turkish trade official, currently serving as Trade Compliance Manager at ASELSAN. His academic achievements include LLM degrees in international trade law from the University of Sussex (Jean Monnet Scholar) and maritime law from Ankara University. His research focus encompasses international trade law, maritime law and export controls.

IMPROVING PROCEDURAL JUSTICE IN ANTI-DUMPING INVESTIGATIONS

Lessons from the US and EU Practices against China

ABDULKADIR YILMAZCAN
PhD, The University of Hong Kong

CAMBRIDGE
UNIVERSITY PRESS

CAMBRIDGE
UNIVERSITY PRESS

Shaftesbury Road, Cambridge CB2 8EA, United Kingdom

One Liberty Plaza, 20th Floor, New York, NY 10006, USA

477 Williamstown Road, Port Melbourne, VIC 3207, Australia

314–321, 3rd Floor, Plot 3, Splendor Forum, Jasola District Centre, New Delhi – 110025, India

103 Penang Road, #05-06/07, Visioncrest Commercial, Singapore 238467

Cambridge University Press is part of Cambridge University Press & Assessment, a department of the University of Cambridge.

We share the University's mission to contribute to society through the pursuit of education, learning and research at the highest international levels of excellence.

www.cambridge.org
Information on this title: www.cambridge.org/9781009450881

DOI: 10.1017/9781009450904

First published 2024

A catalogue record for this publication is available from the British Library

Library of Congress Cataloging-in-Publication Data
Names: Yilmazcan, Abdulkadir, author.
Title: Improving procedural justice in anti-dumping investigations : lessons from the US and EU practices against China / Abdulkadir Yilmazcan.
Description: New York, NY : Cambridge University Press, 2024. | Includes bibliographical references and index.
Identifiers: LCCN 2023053949 (print) | LCCN 2023053950 (ebook) | ISBN 9781009450881 (hardback) | ISBN 9781009450928 (paperback) | ISBN 9781009450904 (ebook)
Subjects: LCSH: Antidumping duties. | Antidumping duties–China. | Dumping (International trade) | Dumping (International trade)–China.
Classification: LCC HF1425 .Y55 2024 (print) | LCC HF1425 (ebook) | DDC 382/.50951–dc23/eng/20231229
LC record available at https://lccn.loc.gov/2023053949
LC ebook record available at https://lccn.loc.gov/2023053950

ISBN 978-1-009-45088-1 Hardback

For my father, Mehmet Yılmazcan

CONTENTS

ILLUSTRATIONS

Figures

Tables

ACKNOWLEDGEMENTS

This book is an outcome of my transformative journey at the University of Hong Kong (HKU). From the very beginning, I knew that pursuing my PhD in Hong Kong would bring both challenges and rewards. Today I can clearly say that it has been an immensely fulfilling experience. The opportunity to conduct my studies in the vibrant city of Hong Kong, within the esteemed academic atmosphere of HKU, has been a distinctive privilege. Besides the invaluable knowledge gained, I have cherished the friendships forged, the happy memories created and the cultural engagement I experienced. I am therefore profoundly grateful to the countless individuals who have played a pivotal role in both my PhD journey and the publication of this book. Their solid support and inspiration have been instrumental in shaping my progress as an international trade law scholar and professional.

First and foremost, I am grateful to my supervisor, Professor Kelvin Kwok, for his excellent academic and personal counselling throughout my studies. I would never have advanced this far without his guidance and helpful comments. I am also highly thankful to my co-supervisor, Professor Zhao Yun, for his immense academic support during my four years at HKU. I am greatly indebted to Professor Michael Palmer for his valuable lectures, his insightful comments on my manuscript and his encouragement in publishing my articles. I have to thank Professor Julian Chaisse who contributed to my book with his deep knowledge of international trade law. I am deeply grateful to Cambridge University Press and my editor Joe Ng for his tremendous support during the publication process of this book as well as to peer reviewers for their significant contributions regarding the improvement of my manuscript.

I would also like to thank MOFCOM officials, all the WTO lawyers and exporters for their participation in the survey. Without their comments, I would not be able to conclude this book's empirical findings. Many thanks to my dear friend Brian Huang, who contributed to my manuscript with his remarks.

Special thanks to Dr Agnes Chong for her great guidance from the beginning until the end of my PhD studies. Without her help, it would have been almost impossible for me to adapt and pursue my studies.

I have always felt lucky to have such an encouraging family. I must thank both my family and my wife's family for supporting us wholeheartedly. I deeply appreciate my parents, Mehmet and Nesrin Yılmazcan, for their unquestioning support throughout my life.

And most importantly, I would like to thank my lovely wife, Merve Yılmazcan, without whom this book could not have been written, and my dear twin daughters, Elif and Zeynep, for being so patient and energising from the beginning of my PhD until the publication of this book.

I am truly grateful to all those who have been by my side, offering unwavering support. Thank you for making this journey possible.

ABBREVIATIONS

ACWL	Advisory Centre on WTO Law
AD	anti-dumping
ADA	Anti-dumping Agreement
CPTPP	The Comprehensive and Progressive Agreement for Trans-Pacific Partnership
DS	dispute settlement
DSB	dispute settlement body
DSM	dispute settlement mechanism
DSU	dispute settlement understanding
EU	European Union
FANs	friends of anti-dumping
FTA	Free Trade Agreement
GATT	General Agreement on Tariffs and Trade
GDP	gross domestic product
ICC	International Commerce Centre
MNE	multinational enterprise
MOFCOM	The Ministry of Commerce of the People's Republic of China
MOFTEC	Ministry of Foreign Trade and Economic Co-operation
NGR	Negotiating Group on Rules
RCEP	Regional Comprehensive Economic Partnership
SCM	The Agreement on Subsidies and Countervailing Measures
SOE	state-owned enterprise
TBT	Technical Barriers to Trade
USITC	The United States International Trade Commission
VAT	value-added tax
WTO	World Trade Organization

1

Introduction

1.1 Background to the Problem

This book attempts to clarify the controversial issue of anti-dumping and its relationship with hidden trade protectionism.[1] My interest in this and other anti-dumping issues was initially sparked by my involvement in international trade regulation as a civil servant. I have participated in or directly conducted several trade remedy investigations, including anti-dumping and anti-circumvention, while wondering whether the common use of trade remedies is proportionate, especially regarding complex investigation procedures. Further reading on the issues involved in the international trade law literature encouraged me to offer research and analysis on anti-dumping procedures and procedural justice as a remedy against hidden trade protectionism.

Exporting products with a lower price compared to their normal value in the home market is dumping.[2] Dumping constitutes price discrimination between national markets.[3] Most of these measures are challenged through the Dispute Settlement Mechanism (DSM) under the framework of the World Trade Organization (WTO).[4] For instance, zeroing[5] is the

[1] Some parts of this book was previously published as an article. Yilmazcan, Abdulkadir, 'The Role of Anti-Dumping in the US–China Trade War', China & WTO Rev. 2021, no. 1 (2021), 7–36.

[2] Peter Van den Bossche and Werner Zdouc, *The Law and Policy of the World Trade Organization: Text, Cases and Materials* (Cambridge University Press, 2017), 677.

[3] Raj Krishna, *Anti-Dumping in Law and Practice* (The World Bank, The World Bank E-Library, 1999), 6.

[4] WTO is an international organisation mainly aiming at open and non-discriminatory markets that would increase welfare in all countries. Bernard M. Hoekman and Petros C. Mavroidis, *World Trade Organization (WTO): Law, Economics, and Politics* (Routledge, 2007), 1.

[5] Zeroing is a calculation method that generally leads to a larger dumping margin. This is because, typically, an anti-dumping investigation deals with one or more years as the investigation period, and during this period, some of the transactions may not be subject to dumping. Generally, the average of these transactions should be calculated to find the dumping margin for a specific exporter. However, in the zeroing method, the investigating

single most litigated issue under WTO law.[6] Tariffs and other trade policies are traditionally used by governments to boost domestic industries.[7] One may call this policy *import substitution* and criticise it for protecting inefficient sectors. Therefore, several countries switched to *export promotion* policies with the expectation of international competition in favour of these sectors.[8] Yet, during the negotiations of the General Agreement on Tariffs and Trade (GATT) and the establishment of the WTO, developed countries were especially unwilling to liberalise trade and reduce the tariffs imposed. Temporary trade barriers (anti-dumping, safeguards and countervailing duties) are labelled as the international trade system's safety valves.[9] Without these measures, WTO members would be unwilling to reduce their customs barriers. During the negotiations of the GATT, trade remedies were seen as a small trade-off compared to the larger gains from the liberalisation process. However, the last few decades showed the opposite. Trade remedies can constitute a threat to open and non-discriminatory markets. Trade barriers have proliferated over the years, and among these three trade barriers, anti-dumping is the most popular.[10] Nevertheless, anti-dumping rules divide scholars and policymakers.

The reason for such a persistent debate on dumping and anti-dumping is the controversial causes of dumping. Dumping can occur under particular circumstances: (1) companies endure financial difficulties, go out of business or dissolve their stocks because of overcapacity; (2) companies are subsidised by their government or a third party and (3)

authority omits the transactions without dumping and calculates the dumped transactions, thus reaching a higher dumping margin. The Appellate Body constantly rules that zeroing is not allowed under the ADA.

[6] Thomas J. Prusa and Edwin Vermulst, 'United States – Continued Existence and Application of Zeroing Methodology: The End of Zeroing?', *World Trade Rev.* 10, no. 1 (2011), 45–61. Some examples focusing on the zeroing issue would be DS402, United States – Use of Zeroing in Anti-Dumping Measures Involving Products from Korea, DS350, United States – Continued Existence and Application of Zeroing Methodology or DS322, United States – Measures Relating to Zeroing and Sunset Reviews.

[7] James Brander and Barbara Spencer, 'Tariff Protection and Imperfect Competition', in Gene M. Grossman (ed.), *Imperfect Competition and International Trade* (MIT Press, 1992), 107.

[8] Robert C. Feenstra, *Advanced International Trade: Theory and Evidence* (Princeton University Press, 2015), 209.

[9] Chad P. Bown, *Trade Remedies and World Trade Organization Dispute Settlement: Why Are So Few Challenged?* (The World Bank, 2005), 7.

[10] Chad P. Bown, 'Temporary Trade Barriers Database: Update through 2013', World Bank, accessed June 2023, http://econ.world bank. org/ttbd/.

companies use dumping as a strategy to expand market share.[11] If a firm is capable of discriminating its prices, then it is likely to benefit from a closed home market.[12] A closed market secures the exporters' high-profit margin, enabling the company to discriminate or predate its losses arising from dumping in other markets and cross-subsidise. Closed markets send false price signals and adversely affect firms, possibly resulting in their extinction. Therefore, anti-dumping has become increasingly popular among WTO members and as well as a highly controversial topic under the WTO law.

Almost a hundred years ago, Viner, one of the leading scholars in this field, analysed the motives of the act of dumping in international trade.[13] Viner's two well-known articles focus on the link between industrial reform and dumping practices.[14] The articles highlight how different countries react to dumping practices and also the shift of dumping accusations from England to other countries, such as the United States (US) or Germany. During that period, countries introduced new tariffs or took other measures to prevent dumping just as they do today. The analyses used at that time were based on key modern economic principles, namely economies of scale and comparative advantage. Further studies have signalled the need for other factors to be considered, and economists have structured new models to better understand the dumping phenomenon. Caves and Jones suggest that the theory of monopolistic price discrimination can explain dumping.[15] This means that the monopolist is already enjoying his position in the home market and, therefore, can bear losses resulting from sales below cost and secure a monopolist position in the foreign market. Caves and Jones's model also claims that firms facing dumping do not have a choice to export.[16] However, Brander and Krugman developed and elaborated the earlier model and showed that the opening of trade has positive effects on

[11] Terence P. Stewart, 'US–Japan Economic Disputes: The Role of Anti-Dumping and Countervailing Duty Laws', *Ariz. J. Int'l & Comp. L.* 16 (1999), 698.

[12] Ibid.

[13] Jacob Viner, 'The Prevalence of Dumping in International Trade: I', *J. Pol. Econ.* 30, no. 5 (1922), 655–680; Jacob Viner, 'The Prevalence of Dumping in International Trade: II', *J. Pol. Econ.* 30, no. 6 (1922), 796–826.

[14] Ibid.

[15] Rafael S. Espinosa Ramírez, 'Reciprocal Dumping and Environmental Polices', *Panor. Econ.* 3, no. 6 (2017), 10.

[16] Paul R. Krugman, 'Industrial Organization and International Trade', *Handb. Ind. Organ.* 2 (1989), 1179–1223.

consumer welfare because firms practise 'reciprocal dumping' when they face dumping.[17] The literature is still divided on whether dumping is unfair or whether it should be allowed for consumer welfare purposes.[18]

This book assumes that anti-dumping investigations are directed in such a way that exporters are discouraged from cooperating with the investigating authorities. Once exporters are unable to submit sufficient information, investigating authorities can inflate anti-dumping duties and use this balancing tool for protectionist purposes. Anti-dumping measures have been criticised for being protective. However, this book holds the view that anti-dumping is not protective, provided that it is used to balance market distortions and that procedural justice is secured. But, if the investigating authorities use legal gaps or take advantage of certain provisions and exercise excessively strict procedural rules to set higher duties on imported goods, this creates protectionism.[19]

Strict procedural rules can secure rights if used in the defendants' favour, as in criminal cases.[20] The same applies to anti-dumping rules. Messerlin, for instance, noted that China is negotiating stricter anti-dumping rules under the Anti-dumping Agreement (ADA), which means a restricted field of application for the investigating authorities.[21] China defends the ADA's regulatory reform, including the prohibition of zeroing, limitations on measures to a maximum of five years, and disclosure of more information.[22] In this case, the ADA's stricter rules would limit the discretion of investigating authorities and work in favour of exporting members. In its current form, the ADA leaves room for discretion so that members can enforce complex and burdensome rules during anti-dumping investigations. For the purposes of this book, strict

[17] James Brander and Paul Krugman, 'A "Reciprocal Dumping" Model of International Trade', *J. Int'l Econ.* 15, nos. 3–4 (1983), 320.

[18] Brink Lindsey and Dan Ikenson, *Antidumping 101: The Devilish Details of 'Unfair Trade' Law* (Center for Trade Policy Studies, Cato Institute, 2002), 3; Diane P. Wood, '"Unfair" Trade Injury: A Competition-Based Approach', *Stan. L. Rev.* 41, no. 5 (1989), 1155. In practice, the US labels dumping as unfair. The Antidumping Act of 1921 begins with the following line 'This memorandum deals with the unfair practice of "dumping"'. Similarly, the USITC official website defines dumping and certain subsidies as unfair trade practices.

[19] Yilmazcan, Abdulkadir, 'The Role of Anti-Dumping in the US–China Trade War', China & WTO Rev. 2021, no. 1 (2021), 7–36.

[20] Gemma Daly, 'Should Truth Commissions Be Viewed as Second-Best Alternatives to Prosecutions', *SOAS L.J.* 2 (2015), 188.

[21] Patrick A. Messerlin, 'China in the World Trade Organization: Antidumping and Safeguards', *World Bank Econ. Rev.* 18, no. 1 (2004), 105–130.

[22] Ibid.

procedural rules in anti-dumping are used to create procedural obstacles for exporters. The concept of 'red tape' is relevant within this context.[23] In terms of long questionnaires and detailed verification visits, investigating authorities can be criticised for red tape. Within the scope of this book, strict procedural rules have a broader meaning than red tape or procedural obstacles since the burdens are not limited to requiring excessive information from exporters. Strict procedural rules also cover the procedures followed by the investigating authorities, such as the calculation methods or limited disclosure of the information used for final determinations.

In this context, strict procedural rules constitute a limitation on the right to defend and meaningful participation. Imagine a company exporting its products to overseas markets while selling them to its domestic market at the same time. This company is accused of unfair trade practices by the overseas investigating authorities and has been asked to submit a questionnaire consisting of a hundred pages to supply confidential information such as the costs of raw materials and labour. The company needs to hire lawyers in a foreign jurisdiction to defend itself, which is costly. Most exporters, therefore, choose not to cooperate. So, the long questionnaire or the legal costs would be procedural obstacles, whereas the rules, including the calculation methods governing the anti-dumping investigation, would be strict procedural rules.

Procedural rules can be classified as 'strict' when they unreasonably limit the exporters' right to defend. Within the scope of WTO law, only the Agreement on Rules of Origin states 'unduly strict requirements' as a benchmark.[24] Another formulation of a similar benchmark is 'not be

[23] The excessive use of administrative procedures or bureaucracy is called 'red tape'. Preece S. Lynn and Bart M. McMillan, 'Free Trade Does Not Equal Freedom from Red Tape: Practitioner Thoughts on FTAA Rules of Origin', *Int'l L. Rev.* 1 (2003), 159.

[24] Agreement on Rules of Origin Article 2:

> (c)rules of origin shall not themselves create restrictive, distorting, or disruptive effects on international trade. They shall not pose **unduly strict requirements** or require the fulfilment of a certain condition not related to manufacturing or processing, as a prerequisite for the determination of the country of origin. However, costs not directly related to manufacturing or processing may be included for the purposes of the application of an ad valorem per centage criterion consistent with subparagraph.
>
> (www.wto.org/english/docs_e/legal_e/22-roo_e.htm#2, accessed 30 June 2023)

more trade-restrictive than necessary' as stated under the Technical Barriers to Trade (TBT) Agreement.[25] Equating strictness with trade restrictiveness or protection can be accommodating.[26] The DSM needs to define the scope of strictness case by case. Within the scope of this book, strict procedural rules include, but are not limited to the following examples. The procedures can be classified as strict if the investigating authority: (1) requires exporters to fill long and detailed questionnaires (as in the case of the US with nearly 150 pages), (2) prepares the questionnaires in the local language (not applicable to the US and European Union (EU) as English is one of the WTO's official languages), (3) rejects minor revision requests after submission of the questionnaire, (4) rejects requests to grant an extension, (5) limits the scope of non-confidential summary, (6) limits access to the non-confidential summary, or (7) demands confidential or private information during on-the-spot investigations, such as access to e-mails. All in all, the investigating authority limits the information submitted by exporters and relies on available facts so that the margins are inflated, and inflated margins eventually restrict trade.[27]

[25] TBT Agreement Article 2.2:

> Members shall ensure that technical regulations are not prepared, adopted or applied with a view to or with the effect of creating unnecessary obstacles to international trade. For this purpose, technical regulations shall **not be more trade-restrictive than necessary** to fulfil a legitimate objective, taking account of the risks non-fulfilment would create. Such legitimate objectives are, inter alia: national security requirements; the prevention of deceptive practices; protection of human health or safety, animal or plant life or health, or the environment. In assessing such risks, relevant elements of consideration are, inter alia: available scientific and technical information, related processing technology or intended end-uses of products.
>
> (www.wto.org/english/docs_e/legal_e/17-tbt_e.htm, accessed 30 July 2023)

[26] In the DS400 and DS401, Norway held this view. DS401, European Communities – Measures Prohibiting the Importation and Marketing of Seal Products, accessed 30 June 2023, www.wto.org/english/tratop_e/dispu_e/cases_e/ds401_e.htm.

[27] On the relationship between discretion and strictness, Mitchell, Sornarajah and Voon argue that good faith can ease the strictness of 'overly formalistic application of legal rules'. Therefore, limiting excessive discretion is also associated with the good faith principle. While multilateral agreements require discretionary areas to get signed, the discretionary power of the signatories should not be enjoyed unreasonably and unfairly. Andrew D. Mitchell, Muthucumaraswamy Sornarajah and Tania Voon, eds., *Good Faith and International Economic Law* (Oxford University Press, 2015), 88.

Some examples of strict procedural rules can be tracked through varied procedural requirements for different sorts of economies. In terms of non-market economy status, Chinese exporters receive different questionnaires in almost every jurisdiction. In the EU, exporters who want to be treated as market economy exporters need to fill in an additional questionnaire.[28] The US questionnaires are also different for market economies and non-market economies.[29] Furthermore, some empirical findings in this book suggest that the procedural rules are applied especially strictly to Chinese exporters vis-à-vis other exporters.[30] One WTO lawyer, for instance, notes that there is prejudice against Chinese exporters during anti-dumping investigations. The differentiation of forms between market economies and non-market economies is a natural result of Article 2.2 of the ADA. Furthermore, the strictness of procedures is not a negative practice per se; however, considering objective indicators, such as the length of questionnaires, legal costs, timing or language requirements, this strictness can indicate protectionism by impeding the opportunity to defend interests.

Procedural obstacles may seem like minor problems in global trade. However, given their effects, they should not be disregarded. Anti-dumping as a whole has been long debated. Apart from a few WTO members and academics, the general belief is that anti-dumping is harmful to global trade.[31] The ADA under the WTO is still being

[28] More information on EU investigations can be found at European Commission website 'trade Defence', European Commission, accessed 15 January 2023, https://ec.europa.eu/trade/policy/accessing-markets/trade-defence/actions-against-imports-into-the-eu/anti-dumping/#_templates.

[29] US Anti-dumping questionnaires available at 'Antidumping Questionnaires', US Department of Commerce, accessed 30 June 2023, https://enforcement.trade.gov/questionnaires/questionnaires-ad.html.

[30] Regarding other non-market economies, the questionnaires are the same but, for most non-market economies (Tajikistan, Turkmenistan, Kyrgyzstan, Moldova, Georgia) there have been no or few anti-dumping investigations. Only Vietnam faced a considerable number of investigations (69 between 1995 and 2020). Both the EU and US still do not consider Vietnam as a market economy but as Vietnam has signed FTAs with these economies, it is likely to be considered as a market economy soon. Regardless, more empirical study would be useful to clarify the different treatment faced by Chinese and Vietnamese exporters.

[31] Thomas J. Prusa, 'Anti-dumping: A Growing Problem in International Trade', *World Econ.* 28, no. 5 (2005), 683–700; Inge Nora Neufeld, *Anti-dumping and Countervailing Procedures: Use or Abuse?: Implications for Developing Countries* (United Nations, 2001), 20; Mitsuo Matsushita, Thomas J. Schoenbaum, Petros C. Mavroidis and Michael Hahn, *The World Trade Organization: Law, Practice, and Policy* (Oxford University Press, 2015), 406.

debated, and attempts to revise it have failed. Although the literature suggests abolishing or replacing anti-dumping laws, this is unrealistic at this stage for political reasons.[32] Therefore, this book focuses on the procedural effects of these investigations and argues that before a substantial revision of the ADA, procedural justice must be secured in a way that benefits all WTO Members.

The ADA has little to say on procedural aspects of anti-dumping investigations, and WTO members enforce their own procedural rules in investigations. It has been asserted that anti-dumping investigations constitute a barrier for exporters.[33] As a result, exporters prefer not to cooperate. This, in turn, results in high anti-dumping duties, which defeats the ADA's primary purpose.[34]

This research examines whether or not this phenomenon is real. In order to visualise the common practice, the book focuses on the US's and EU's procedural rules, specifically against China, as it is the top target for several WTO members. Supplementing research to date, this book not only discusses the underestimated effect of procedural obstacles but also offers a new perspective in terms of international trade policy to hidden trade protectionism. To date, procedural justice has not been explicitly proposed in relation to anti-dumping procedures. In this context, this book examines the WTO's DSM and the rules negotiations to establish whether there have been sufficient attempts to limit the misuse of anti-dumping measures. This book also proposes a revision of the ADA under the procedural justice framework. Procedural justice would improve exporters' levels of cooperation and avoid inflated anti-dumping measures. Concrete suggestions, such as a standard anti-

[32] ADA is subject to a single undertaking like other WTO agreements, which means that members must agree the agreements as a whole. Any amendment to an agreement requires a consensus. It is hard to achieve a consensus for a controversial issue like anti-dumping.

[33] David N. Palmeter, 'The Antidumping Law: A Legal and Administrative Nontariff Barrier', in Richard Boltuck and Robert E. Litan (eds.), *Down in the Dumps: Administration of the Unfair Trade Laws* (Brooking Institution, 1991), 65–89; Xiuping Hua, Ying Jiang, Qian Sun and Xinyi Xing, 'Do Antidumping Measures Affect Chinese Export-Related Firms?', *Rev. Quant. Finance Account.* 52 (2019), 1–30, 1; Sarah J. Marsh, 'Creating Barriers for Foreign Competitors: A Study of the Impact of Anti-dumping Actions on the Performance of US Firms', *Strateg. Manag. J.* 19, no. 1 (1998), 25–37, 34; Nam-Ake Lekfuangfu, 'Rethinking the WTO Anti-Dumping Agreement from a Fairness Perspective', *Cambridge Student L. Rev.* 4 (2008), 307.

[34] Abdulkadir Yilmazcan, 'The Role of Anti-Dumping in the US–China Trade War', *China & WTO Rev.* 7, no. 1 (2021), 7–36.

dumping questionnaire for all members, are addressed in order to conceptualise procedural justice during anti-dumping investigations.

1.2 Research Question and Outline

This book's concerns are evaluated through an examination of three specific issues. First, the main interest is to determine to what extent the procedural rules used in anti-dumping investigations can be used to achieve hidden trade protectionism in favour of domestic industries. In answering this question, particular attention is given to the relationships between the US, EU and China as a case study. Second, this research sets out to verify whether the anti-dumping investigation procedures used by the US and EU support the assumption of hidden trade protectionism, particularly against China. Lastly, the book explores to what extent procedural justice would avoid the hidden trade protectionism in anti-dumping investigations.

In seeking answers to these questions, the book is organised as follows. Chapter 1 introduces the research questions and the scope of research; a summary of the relevant literature is also included. Chapter 2 sets out the theories and relevant concepts used in the book. The arguments for and against anti-dumping laws are explained considering efficiency, fairness and political issues. The theories used are interdisciplinary in nature and require a political economy perspective. Also, macro and micro views need to be taken into account because anti-dumping investigations involve both states and firms. Later, the justifiable level of anti-dumping laws is discussed. Anti-dumping laws are ill-defined cures for market distortions; this book suggests that the improvement of procedural justice can reduce the negative reaction to anti-dumping laws by limiting their misuse.

Chapter 3 focuses on WTO disputes about anti-dumping issues. Anti-dumping or, to be more specific, zeroing is the single-most litigated issue under WTO law.[35] Although the Appellate Body has found zeroing method inconsistent with ADA several times, it is still being used with

[35] Prusa and Vermulst, 'United States – Continued Existence and Application of Zeroing Methodology', 45–61. Some examples focusing on the zeroing issue would be DS402, United States – Use of Zeroing in Anti-Dumping Measures Involving Products from Korea; DS350, United States – Continued Existence and Application of Zeroing Methodology or DS322, United States – Measures Relating to Zeroing and Sunset Reviews.

small alterations.[36] Chapter 3 shows that the so-called jewel in the crown[37] is sometimes ineffective. To do so, the role of the DSM in the anti-dumping issue is presented, and anti-dumping cases dealing with procedural issues are analysed. The procedural issues mentioned in this chapter are as follows: calculation methods, transparency, public notice/notification, selection of investigated parties (sampling), submission of evidence and rebuttals, access to non-confidential files, hearings, newcomers and enforcement. Chapter 3 analyses the reasons for revising the ADA. First, not all problems in practice can be challenged before the DSM, and second, the DSM cannot resolve all disputes that come before it due to a lack of explicit rules under the ADA.

Chapter 4 explains the anti-dumping investigation procedures of the US and EU and their differences. China represents a special case for other members with its socialist market economy and a growing impact in the global political arena. Within the scope of this research, China needs to be evaluated in detail as (1) nearly one-quarter of all anti-dumping measures were taken against China,[38] (2) Chinese exporters complain about the anti-dumping investigations both at the domestic level and the WTO DSM, (3) the protectionist policies towards Chinese exporters eventually turn into general policies towards other WTO members since the ADA is silent on some procedural issues. Thus, Chapter 4 describes the trade policies of these top three economies and reveals facts about the ongoing trade war from an anti-dumping perspective. These different procedural rules form a connection with the notion of hidden trade protectionism and anti-dumping.

Chapter 5 is dedicated to the results of the fieldwork on procedural problems in the course of anti-dumping investigations. The chapter notes that some problems with anti-dumping are not mentioned in the literature. The fieldwork attempts to uncover the problems that arise in practice. As China is the top anti-dumping target and the top hunters are the US and EU, the fieldwork focuses first on Chinese exporters who shared their experience of US and EU investigation procedures. In addition, law firms were asked to take part in an online survey about their experience with these two jurisdictions. The questions did not involve confidential information about their clients but focused on

[36] Chad P. Bown and Thomas J. Prusa, US Antidumping: Much Ado about Zeroing, The World Bank Research Working Paper (2010), 3. Also see DS402, DS350, DS322, etc.

[37] Van den Bossche and Zdouc, *The Law and Policy of the World Trade Organization*, 94.

[38] Placing China as the top anti-dumping target amongst all WTO members.

procedural obstacles that inflate anti-dumping margins. Lastly, officials at the relevant public authority in China, the Ministry of Commerce of the People's Republic of China (MOFCOM), were interviewed as they take part in anti-dumping investigations to support their exporters. The officials from MOFCOM believe the US and EU do not treat China equally and fairly. After the procedural problems from the field were identified, additional questions were sent to the investigating authorities in the US and EU. In this part of the book, these complaints and responses are gathered according to empirical data collection methods. Chapter 5 then evaluates the data in these three jurisdictions. The current situation and the inefficiency of the ADA are also highlighted.[39]

Chapter 6 is the final substantial part of the book, explaining the need for a revision of the ADA. There are ongoing negotiations on the ADA but they are without positive outcomes. There are several reasons for this lack of progress, such as deadlock in the Doha Development Round, the mega trade agreements or unwillingness on the part of top users of anti-dumping measures. Still, alternative solutions are proposed to settle the hidden trade protectionism in anti-dumping problems. Normative solutions include a comprehensive reform of the ADA. Such a revision has already been suggested in the literature, but this book departs from most others by prioritising procedural revisions rather than substantive reform. The study proposes changes to procedural justice in anti-dumping procedures. Due to the constraints of a short timescale on substantive ADA reform, other possibilities are also discussed to improve procedural justice, including (1) publishing best practice guidelines; (2) creating a standard questionnaire to be used by all WTO members; (3) reforming and fixing the DSM; (4) raising awareness among exporters that cooperation with investigating authorities may have a significant effect on the anti-dumping measures imposed; (5) improving the accounting systems for Chinese exporters; (6) a support tool for exporters or exporting countries, such as the Advisory Center on WTO Law (ACWL) in Geneva; and (7) software to assist exporters to fill in questionnaires. The boldest suggestion is the standard anti-dumping investigation questionnaire, which may solve most of the procedural problems arising from divergent enforcement. Only with such a standard could an exporter defend itself in different anti-dumping investigations and cooperate effectively with investigating authorities. This chapter aims to

39 Edwin Vermulst, 'Ten Major Problems with the Anti-Dumping Instrument in the European Community', *J. World Trade* 39 (2005), 105.

highlight the current state of the negotiations on the ADA as well as the importance of procedural justice during a possible revision of the ADA and other practical means.

Chapter 7 is the conclusion and consolidates ideas and findings. This chapter calls for and reflects on the possibility of a more transparent and fair anti-dumping system for all WTO members achieved by promoting procedural justice. It also considers the significance of the book's findings for international trade law discourse more generally by relating them to contemporary trade issues such as the US–China trade war, Brexit, the WTO crisis, and mega free trade agreements.

1.3 Scope of the Research

This book focuses on three economies, namely the US, EU and China. From a macroeconomic perspective; these three economies are the world's 'dominating powerhouses'.[40] In 2022, the US produced around 15.5 per cent of global GDP, while the EU accounted for 14.9 per cent.[41] China, on the other hand, had 18.6 per cent of global GDP alone, placing itself at the top.[42] This also means that these three economies are generating almost half of the global GDP, so trade policies between these three economies significantly impact the global economy.

From the perspective of anti-dumping investigations, limiting the scope of the book to the US, EU and China seems helpful. These members represented more than 25 per cent of the anti-dumping measures enforced between 1995 and 2022(6) and more than 50 per cent of the global exports in 2021.[43] China is the top country for both the EU and the US in terms of anti-dumping measures. The US and EU are the first- and fourth-ranked targets in terms of measures enforced by China.[44]

As mentioned above, China is a special case in this comparison. For some three decades, China implemented gradual reforms to transform

[40] Ralph Wrobel, '"The China Effect": Changes in International Trade Patterns as Reasons for Rising Anti-Globalism'. No. 2020-1. Ordnungspolitische Diskurse (2020).

[41] Ibid. GDP based on PPP, share of world, IMF Datamapper, accessed 17 June 2023, www.imf.org/external/datamapper/PPPSH@WEO/OEMDC/ADVEC/WEOWORLD.

[42] Ibid.

[43] Ibid.

[44] Anti-dumping Measures: Reporting Member vs Exporter, WTO, accessed 17 June 2023, www.wto.org/english/tratop_e/adp_e/adp_e.htm.

into a market-driven economy. Agricultural production was the first stage supported by manufacturing and exports.[45] The growth model is unique as the socialist market economy carries Chinese characteristics. Three main features of China's socialist market economy were highlighted by Jiang Zemin:

> First, concerning the ownership structure, it keeps the public sector in the dominant position, supplements it with a private sector that includes individually owned enterprises and other sectors... Second, concerning distribution, it retains distribution according to work in the dominant position, supplements it with other modes, permits and encourages some localities and individuals to prosper first, gradually achieves prosperity for all and prevents polarization. Third, concerning economic operating mechanisms, it achieves the long-term, organic integration of the planned economy and market economy; makes full use of the advantages of both.[46]

Together with accelerated export growth, these features also make China the first target of anti-dumping measures. Especially after 2001, China's accession to the WTO affected its trading partners' attitude towards Chinese competition. Other members of the WTO were obliged to convert WTO-inconsistent import restrictions against China into WTO-consistent measures such as anti-dumping.[47] However, while using the so-called WTO-consistent anti-dumping measures, WTO members are likely to overprotect their domestic industries. Regarding the scope of this book, China is the main concern along with the US and EU because, as mentioned, China's WTO membership prevents other members from enforcing China-specific import restrictions. Therefore, WTO members, specifically the US and EU, seek alternative ways to restrict imports from China as much as they can. The investigation procedures allow WTO members to inflate anti-dumping measures.

The first aspect of the possible misuse of anti-dumping measures is the excessive application of non-market economy status. US law defines a

45 Shenggen Fan, Ravi Kanbur, Shang-Jin Wei and Xiaobo Zhang, eds., *The Oxford Companion to the Economics of China* (Oxford University Press, 2014), 7.

46 Xun Gong and Corinne Cortese, 'A Socialist Market Economy with Chinese Characteristics: The Accounting Annual Report of China Mobile', *Account. Forum* 41, no. 3 (2017), 206–220.

47 Chad P. Bown, 'China's Market Economy Status and Antidumping: A $100 Billion, $10 Billion, or $1 Billion Dispute? Part 2', Peterson Institute for International Economics (8 June 2016), accessed 1 June 2022, https://piie.com/blogs/trade-investment-policy-watch/chinas-market-economy-status-and-antidumping-100-billion-10-0.

non-market economy as one without the market principles of cost or pricing structures resulting in an unfair value of goods.[48] China argues that if China were not treated as a non-market economy, dumping margins would be lower.[49]

> On a trade-weighted basis, less than 1.5 per cent of China's total goods exports to the US were subject to a US-imposed antidumping import restriction in 2000. By 2015 US imposed antidumping import restrictions affected roughly 7 per cent (about $35 billion) of China's annual exports to the United States. The significant uptick after 2007 is consistent with research indicating that import restrictions tend to increase during macroeconomic slowdowns – e.g., the Great Recession – and periods of the sharp appreciation of the real exchange rate. To the extent that China believes that its exports to the United States have been limited because of its treatment under NME status, it is clear why China is concerned about its NME status.[50]

This 7 per cent may seem negligible, but it is high compared to other countries.[51] Furthermore, in terms of value, 7 per cent corresponds to nearly $100 billion USD.

Second, the procedural rules are designed to discourage exporters from cooperating with investigating authorities. The outcome is the excessive use of the 'facts available' provision. Thus, investigating authorities are able to calculate higher anti-dumping duties than needed. The parties need to cooperate to be exempted or subjected to a lower duty in the context of the anti-dumping investigations. However, procedural obstacles might be burdensome, such that the cost of non-cooperation might outweigh the benefits of cooperation. This book analyses whether these procedures are protective policy tools against exporting firms and other members. Then, revealing these different and burdensome procedures in different members, it is easier to discuss whether there is a need for a renegotiation of the ADA and see whether the Negotiating Group on Rules (NGR) is taking sufficient initiative.

Combining these two side effects, rather than being a minor trade-off to liberalise markets, anti-dumping creates tension between the US, EU and China. There are internal and external factors placing China as the

48 19 USC § 1677(18)A, accessed 17 June 2023, www.law.cornell.edu/uscode/text/19/1677.

49 Chad P. Bown, 'Should the United States Recognize China as a Market Economy?' The Peterson Institute for International Economics, Policy Brief No. PB16–24 (2016), 3.

50 Ibid., 4.

51 United States 1.3 per cent, South Korea 3.9 per cent or India 2.7 per cent. Bown, ibid.

top anti-dumping target, which are further elaborated in Chapter 4. It is worth noting that the practices against China inevitably turn into general policies because members cannot explicitly apply different rules to China. Strict procedures to increase the level of protection from China become a general restrictive trade policy against each and every WTO member.

Therefore, these economies represent a substantive part of the problem. The solution applicable to these three economies is also applicable to other WTO members. This solution is based on the application of procedural justice into the anti-dumping investigation procedures.

Rawls's classification of procedural justice is based on three categories: perfect, imperfect, and pure.[52] Perfect procedural justice always leads to just outcomes whereas imperfect procedural justice cannot guarantee just outcomes.[53] Pure procedural justice seeks agreeable outcomes. Coin flipping or traffic lights are some examples of pure procedural justice.[54] The collective consent in pure procedural justice creates a notion of justice.[55] In general, legal proceedings are a form of imperfect procedural justice as there is no guarantee that the outcome will be just. However, without imperfect procedural justice, the outcome cannot be just.

At this juncture, procedural justice is a requirement for substantive equality.[56] There are four widely recognised components of procedural justice, namely trustworthiness, respectful treatment, neutrality and voice.[57] According to another categorisation, procedural justice improves accuracy, cost-balancing and meaningful participation.[58] Like neutrality, accuracy means that substantive laws are applied in the same way at any time. Accuracy also secures predictability while avoiding discretion. Cost-balancing requires a comparison of the benefits of accuracy against its costs. Meaningful participation is required to provide procedural justice independent of accuracy and cost-balancing. Relevant parties to

[52] Filippo Fontanelli and Paolo Busco, 'The Function of Procedural Justice in International Adjudication', *Law Pract. Int'l Court. Trib.* 15, no. 1 (2016), 1–23.

[53] Ibid.

[54] Ibid.

[55] Ibid.

[56] Paul Stancil, 'Substantive Equality and Procedural Justice', *Iowa L. Rev.* 102 (2016), 1649.

[57] Trustworthiness means acting honestly and considering the public interest. Respectful treatment means behaving politely and professionally. Neutrality means following the same procedures for everyone, every time. Voice means allowing individuals to express their interests and opinions during the decision-making process. Julie M. Barkworth and Kristina Murphy, 'Procedural Justice Policing and Citizen Compliance Behaviour: The Importance of Emotion', *Psychol. Crime & L.* 21, no. 3 (2015), 254–273.

[58] Stancil, 'Substantive Equality and Procedural Justice'.

a dispute may defend their interests only by meaningful participation.[59] In this context, two categorisations overlap in being objective and transparent while allowing meaningful participation for the parties. Therefore, procedural justice can reduce the misuse and overly protectionist effects of anti-dumping measures by ensuring enhanced transparency, less discretion on the part of investigating authorities and more predictable investigation procedures for all members.[60] In such circumstances, exporters would have more opportunity to express their position.

At this point, it is also notable that due process is a relevant and similar concept to procedural justice.[61] In other words, due process covers two essential elements: impartiality of the court and the juridical equality of parties to the trial.[62] So the main application of due process is within court proceedings. Due process generally points to 'procedural due process', which means that the predetermined procedures should be followed when life, liberty or property of citizens are restricted by the state.[63] Therefore, procedural due process deals with the notice and hearing process during government actions as well as court proceedings. 'Substantive due process' requires just reasons for the government to deprive one's life, liberty or property.[64] Substantive procedural justice is a controversial concept as some argue the origin of due process only covers procedural due process.[65] When the term is used in its single format as 'due process', it mostly points to procedural due process. In adjudicative procedures, due process is often referred to as 'minimum procedural standards' or 'fundamental procedural norms'.[66]

[59] Ibid.

[60] Procedural justice also consists of other elements such as the authorities' motivation, honesty, ethicality, and the opportunities for representation; the quality of the decisions; the opportunities for error correction, the authorities' bias. Another approach is grouping these elements under three main groups; effort to be fair, ethicality and consistency. Tom R. Tyler, 'What Is Procedural Justice-Criteria Used by Citizens to Assess the Fairness of Legal Procedures', *Law & Soc'y Rev.* 22 (1988), 131.

[61] *Due process*: the conduct of legal proceedings according to established rules and principles for the protection and enforcement of private rights, including right to a fair hearing before a tribunal with the power to decide the case. Bryan A. Garner, *Black's Law Dictionary* (West Group, 1999), 516.

[62] John P. Gaffney, 'Due Process in the World Trade Organization: The Need for Procedural Justice in the Dispute Settlement System', *Am. U. Int'l L. Rev.* 14 (1998), 1179.

[63] Erwin Chemerinsky, *Constitutional Law* (Aspen, 2019), 813.

[64] Ibid.

[65] Ibid.

[66] Gaffney, 'Due Process in the World Trade Organization'.

Due process under the WTO adjudication is more concerned with the DSM. Article 12 of the Dispute Settlement Understanding (DSU) has determined the general framework of due process in dispute settlement proceedings.[67] Panel and Appellate Body reports also interpret the concept of due process within the DSM. In DS371, the Appellate Body highlights the role of due process within the DSM as:

> Due process is intrinsically connected to notions of fairness, impartiality, and the rights of parties to be heard and to be afforded an adequate opportunity to pursue their claims, make out their defences, and establish the facts in the context of proceedings conducted in a balanced and orderly manner, according to established rules. The protection of due process is thus a crucial means of guaranteeing the legitimacy and efficacy of a rules-based system of adjudication.[68]

In this context, due process and procedural justice can both be applied to the DSM in terms of impartiality of the tribunal and juridical equality of the parties to the dispute.[69] However, it should be kept in mind that despite the similarities, due process and procedural justice are different concepts. Due process does not guarantee that the outcome is just.[70] At the same time, the lack of due process results in unjust treatment.[71] Subsequently, procedural justice is a broader concept than due process. In terms of the scope of this book, due process remains closely related, but the main focus is the procedural justice in anti-dumping investigations rather than the due process in WTO's DSM.

Another issue out of the scope of this book is the justification of unfair trade practices conducted by Chinese exporters. Apart from being the top anti-dumping target, there is sound evidence that the majority of Chinese exporters are subsidised and controlled by the central government and are thus able to dump in overseas markets.[72] However, the main argument of the book is that even if Chinese exporters conduct unfair trade

[67] Dispute Settlement: Legal Text, Understanding on Rules and Procedures Governing the Settlement of Disputes, accessed 16 July 2023, www.wto.org/english/tratop_e/dispu_e/dsu_e.htm#12.

[68] DS371, Thailand – Customs and Fiscal Measures on Cigarettes from the Philippines, Appellate Body Report, WT/DS371/AB/R (2011).

[69] Gaffney, 'Due Process in the World Trade Organization', 1195.

[70] David Resnick, 'Due Process and Procedural Justice', *NOMOS: Am. Soc'y Pol. Legal Phil.* 18 (1977), 206.

[71] Ibid.

[72] For more details see Trade Policy Review Report by the Secretariat China, WTO, 2018, WT/TPR/S/375, accessed 16 July 2023, https://docs.wto.org/dol2fe/Pages/SS/directdoc.aspx?filename=q:/WT/TPR/S375.pdf&Open=True; Edwin Vermulst and Brian Gatta,

practices, procedural justice is needed for the sake of international trade overall because, if the importing members adopt overprotective measures against unfair trade practices utilising overly complicated anti-dumping investigations, the circumvention risk arises and protectionism spreads among WTO members, slashing the welfare gains from trade. Therefore, the book does not discuss whether Chinese exporters actually export with dumped prices or not.

1.4 Conclusion

This book examines how anti-dumping procedures can be used to overprotect domestic industries and considers whether procedural justice would avoid this misuse, and the case studies and empirical findings highlight the need for a revision of the ADA. The different procedures or burdensome exercises by the US and EU against Chinese exporters comprise a significant proportion of these disputes and/or lead to a low level of cooperation. Therefore, the ADA needs revision.

Other studies have proposed the revision of the ADA in terms of addressing procedural issues as well as substantive ones.[73] Yet, there is no explicit proclamation that investigating authorities are using strict procedural rules in a protective manner. This book attempts to discover whether or not the authorities are using strict procedural rules, and the anti-dumping investigations by the US and EU against China represent a coherent case study. Also, if the answer is positive, then the relationship between strict procedural rules and protective outcomes of anti-dumping investigations can be conceptualised as the 'procedural effect', and procedural justice is promoted as providing an improved legal framework. Unlike this book, the literature on procedural justice focuses on the DSM in the WTO context.[74] This book applies procedural justice to anti-dumping investigation procedures to avoid its misuse.

In addition, the NGR is discussing a consolidated text of the ADA and SCM, but these proposals do not explicitly suggest applying the concept of procedural justice into anti-dumping investigations. Improved

'Concurrent Trade Defense Investigations in the EU, the EU's New Anti-subsidy Practice against China, and the Future of Both', *World Trade Rev.* 11 (2012), 527.

[73] Vermulst, '10 Major Problems with the Anti-Dumping Instrument in the European Community', 105.

[74] Adam S. Chilton and Ryan W. Davis, 'Equality, Procedural Justice, and the World Trade Organization', *Intercultural Hum. Rts. L. Rev.* 7 (2012), 277.

procedural justice brings greater participation of exporters during investigations, which would reduce the discretion of investigating authorities in calculating anti-dumping duties. Eventually, procedural justice would reduce the anti-dumping measures in force as well as the duty rates. Thus, disputes arising from anti-dumping measures would decrease. This book, therefore, suggests revising the ADA by means of procedural justice but also proposes alternative solutions, such as a standard questionnaire for use by all WTO members or low-cost legal assistance to exporters. By drawing more attention to procedural justice in anti-dumping investigations rather than the DSM prioritising procedural justice, this book attempts to contribute to existing literature and steer trade negotiations. Mega FTAs offer the potential for partial revision of global anti-dumping practices. If positive results are achieved through these FTAs, similar provisions could be extended to the ADA to provide a uniform practice.

2

A Theoretical Framework for Evaluating Anti-dumping Laws

> Whenever a theory appears to you as the only possible one, take this as a sign that you have neither understood the theory nor the problem which it was intended to solve.[1]

2.1 Introduction

This chapter presents the arguments for and against anti-dumping laws. The book holds the view that none of these arguments is satisfactory on its own. Arguments for anti-dumping laws are vague or inconsistent with national practices. Arguments against anti-dumping laws are more reliable in determining the side effects of these measures. The latter arguments also suggest that anti-dumping laws are protectionist and should be abolished. Instead of advocating one side over the other, this book focuses on the fact that anti-dumping laws are not well designed.[2] Anti-dumping laws cannot completely avoid unfair trade or level the playing field. Nonetheless, anti-dumping laws play a balancing role against market distortions and constitute a safety valve in the political arena. They helped developed countries liberalise in favour of developing countries, and anti-dumping laws later turned into a popular trade policy tool used by both developed and developing countries. For political reasons, anti-dumping laws cannot be abolished as a whole or replaced with other mechanisms. The optimum solution would be to find the reasons for existing defects and suggest achievable revisions.

To propose an accurate solution, the problem should be clearly defined. The proliferation of anti-dumping measures is a concern for the WTO's agenda, and negotiations on the ADA are deadlocked. In addition, anti-dumping measures are the most frequently challenged

[1] Karl Popper quotes, accessed 16 July 2023, www.brainyquote.com.
[2] Prusa, 'Anti-dumping: A Growing Problem in International Trade'.

issue requiring WTO adjudication.[3] These facts show the need for a revision of this ill-defined trade remedy. The arguments against anti-dumping laws label anti-dumping as protectionist. This book diverges from these arguments in a sense that anti-dumping is not protectionist per se; rather the lack of procedural justice constitutes the major problem of over-protectionism.

Procedural theorists question why the procedures matter and what their goals should be.[4] A sound answer is that procedures enable substantive laws to be implemented in an objective, fair and predictable way.[5] However, procedures have two implications. On the one hand, the rights of defendants can be secured if the gap between substantive and procedural rules is small (assuming that substantive rules grant rights to defendants). On the other hand, if substantive laws are silent on some issues, administrative bodies may use strict procedures to limit the right to defend. In this context, procedural justice based on the principles of neutrality, transparency and respect for rights, supplements substantive laws.[6]

If applied to anti-dumping investigations, procedural justice would also improve equality, transparency and uniformity while leaving less room for discretion. These functions are linked to the principles of fairness, especially non-discriminatory fairness, which is also the basis of the WTO. Compliance with the principles of procedural justice does not mean compliance with the legal norms in force. The authorities may conduct an investigation in conformity with the relevant regulations; however, if there is room for discretion or a lack of transparency, there would still be a violation of the principles of procedural justice.

Therefore, a lack of procedural justice encourages investigating authorities to take advantage of the legal gaps in the ADA. Strict procedural rules limit exporters from having a full opportunity to defend themselves; this results in lower levels of cooperation, allowing investigating authorities to misuse the gaps in the ADA. If an exporter cannot cooperate with the investigating authorities, then the dumping margin is

[3] Over 4,412 measures in force and 142 disputes on anti-dumping. WTO Statistics, accessed 16 July 2023, www.wto.org.

[4] Robin J. Effron, 'Reason Giving and Rule Making in Procedural Law', *Ala. L. Rev.* 65 (2013), 685.

[5] Ibid.

[6] Stancil, 'Substantive Equality and Procedural Justice', 1649; Rebecca Hollander-Blumoff and Tom R. Tyler, 'Procedural Justice and the Rule of Law: Fostering Legitimacy in Alternative Dispute Resolution', *J. Disp. Resol.* 2011 (2011), 1.

calculated according to the facts available. The outcome is the inflated anti-dumping margins of over-protectionism. The improvement of procedural justice, in contrast, would allow exporters to have meaningful participation. A higher level of cooperation results in less discretion, more transparency and lower anti-dumping measures. The improvement of procedural justice is the main suggestion of this book, as it would limit the misuse of anti-dumping laws. Rather than using the facts available, investigating authorities would be able to calculate the actual level of market distortion. This would support the equality of anti-dumping laws and reduce conflict.

To address these issues, the following questions were posed to structure the theoretical framework of the whole book: What are the justifications for the anti-dumping laws? What are the arguments against anti-dumping laws? To what extent are anti-dumping laws needed? What is the justifiable level of anti-dumping protection? The following two sections introduce and criticise the arguments for and against anti-dumping laws, and then the justifiable level of anti-dumping laws is discussed. This book suggests that none of these theories alone are satisfactory. Therefore, this book suggests that improving procedural justice can reduce the negative reaction against anti-dumping laws by limiting their misuse.

In this context, rationales for and against the anti-dumping laws are explained as a whole regardless of their relationship to procedural justice. Still some arguments such as predatory pricing are linked to procedural justice in the forthcoming sections. Furthermore, the section on the justifiable level of anti-dumping laws connects procedural justice with the theoretical framework of anti-dumping laws (Table 2.1).

2.2 Arguments for Anti-dumping Laws

The justifications for anti-dumping laws presented in the literature are based on national concerns and principles of fairness. As national concerns can be linked to economic and political factors, this book categorises the arguments into three main groups: efficiency arguments, political arguments and fairness arguments.

2.2.1 Efficiency Arguments

It has been argued that anti-dumping laws can improve economic efficiency as long as these measures are not used for protectionist purposes. Economic efficiency is also linked to the notion of distributive fairness,

Table 2.1 *Summary of arguments for and against anti-dumping laws*

Arguments for Anti-dumping Laws			Arguments against Anti-dumping Laws		
Efficiency arguments	Fairness arguments	Political arguments	Efficiency arguments	Fairness arguments	Political arguments
International price discount	Unfair trade	Economic nationalism	Distortion of competition and welfare	Public interest	Public choice
Predatory pricing	Subsidies	Safety valve	Domestic protection and cartelisation	Rights theory	Liberalisation and WTO
Foreign direct investment	Level playing field		Misallocation of resources	Abuse of investigation procedures	
Infant industry			Circumvention		

which is expected to lead to greater equality of income, wealth, opportunities, capabilities or other factors.[7] To sustain efficiency, the neoliberalist argument supports public intervention.[8] Anti-dumping measures are argued to be suitable public interventions for these purposes. Dumping is regarded as a strategic market distortion and a type of unfair trade practice.[9] The distortion of a domestic market is condemned by Viner, who claims that dumped prices are abnormal and provide only temporary cheapness.[10]

There are challenges in applying economic efficiency theory to anti-dumping laws. The first problem is the level of intervention in the market. According to Posner, 'efficiency means exploiting economic resources in such a way that value – human satisfaction as measured by aggregate willingness to pay for goods and services – is maximized'.[11] By definition, market efficiency is beneficial for all actors in the market, including consumers and competitors. However, anti-dumping laws are not triggered by consumer welfare; instead, they protect domestic industries, which constitute a smaller interest group. Besides, the deadweight loss effect of anti--dumping measures would be a decrease in imports, which negatively affects foreign welfare.[12] As anti-dumping laws do not prioritise consumers or foreign welfare, the restoring effect on market efficiency is limited.

Second, the problem with this argument is that not all kinds of dumping are harmful to market efficiency. Chaisse and Chakraborty assert that '[e]conomic considerations suggest that dumping facilitates lower prices to consumers, greater competition in the market, and improved performance of the domestic industry. It also acts as an anti-inflationary mechanism of price control.'[13] Instead of combatting each kind of dumping, it would be more effective to take action against the types that are injurious. Intermittent (short-term) or sporadic (occasional) dumping is considered more harmful to the domestic economy

[7] Steven M. Suranovic, 'A Positive Analysis of Fairness with Applications to International Trade', *World Econ.* 23, no. 3 (2000), 290.

[8] Pierce Lee, 'Rethinking the Rhetoric of Anti-dumping: A Response to Mark Wu's Reform Proposal', *Ga. J. Int'l & Comp. L.* 42 (2013), 457.

[9] Ibid.

[10] Julien Chaisse and Debashis Chakraborty, 'Normative Obsolescence of the WTO Anti-dumping Agreement: Topography of the Global Use and Misuse of Initiations and Measures', *Asian J. Int'l L.* 6, no. 2 (2016), 253.

[11] Stephen E. Margolis, 'Two Definitions of Efficiency in Law and Economics', *J. Legal Stud.* 16, no. 2 (1987), 471–482.

[12] Chung-Fu Lai and Xi-Tsz Lee, 'The Effects of Anti-dumping Duties in a New Open Economy Macroeconomics Model', *Int'l J. Econ. Fin. Issues* 6, no. 3 (2016), 838.

[13] Chaisse and Chakraborty, 'Normative Obsolescence of the WTO', 261.

and market efficiency. Intermittent and sporadic dumping is more likely to occur where a company needs to dispose of an oversupply of perishables, specifically agricultural products.[14] Continuous or long-term dumping, on the other hand, does not negatively affect consumer welfare as in the case of intermittent or sporadic dumping. Long-term dumping would have a negative impact if the prices were unreasonably low or predatory. Long-term dumping without predation could even be positive for consumer welfare.

Third, the level of public intervention suggested by the neoliberalist argument to improve market efficiency would be problematic. A weak intervention would encourage anti-competitive practices, while a strong intervention would discourage foreign investment and affect overall welfare. Argentina would be a good example of a protectionist economy that nevertheless suffered from economic crises.[15] In this context, economic models suggest that lower anti-dumping duties have limited effects, while higher anti-dumping duties significantly restrict imports.[16] This book argues that anti-dumping laws should aim to eliminate market distortions rather than be used as protective measures. The justifiable level of anti-dumping laws also leads to the correct level of public intervention. A transparent, fair and uniform set of procedural rules applicable to anti-dumping investigations can contribute to determining the justifiable level of anti-dumping laws, thus defining the optimum level of public intervention.

So, in theory, economic efficiency is a justifiable rationale for anti-dumping laws, assuming that dumping causes imbalances such as short-term or occasional low prices in the market. However, these laws are not the right tool to sustain market efficiency in their current form. Anti-dumping laws should be improved in a way that takes overall welfare into consideration. Some efficiency arguments are presented below.

2.2.1.1 International Price Discrimination

A popular argument for anti-dumping laws is price discrimination. The price of an identical product is expected to be the same or higher in the foreign market because of the risks of international trade. Companies aim

14 Robert Howse and Michael Trebilcock, *The Regulation of International Trade* (Routledge, 2005), 279.

15 Andres Gallo, 'Trade Policy and Protectionism in Argentina', *Econ. Affairs* 32, no. 1 (2012), 59.

16 Lai and Lee, 'The Effects of Anti-dumping Duties', 837.

at profit maximisation, which makes dumping questionable. Exercising price discrimination in favour of a foreign market is abnormal from the importing country's perspective. In addition, price discrimination shows that the exporter has the market power to discriminate. So, the first problem is that price discrimination signals the potential for an upcoming monopoly. Monopolies are prohibited under competition laws because they create inefficiency, which covers limited choice for consumers, high prices and a shortage of supply.[17] In the end, customers are forced to search for lower-priced markets or to consume less. Thus, an efficient market will fail because of price discrimination. This theory applies the same reasoning to anti-dumping laws.

However, this argument is not convincing. First, price discrimination can be an efficient strategy for firms in terms of profit maximisation. Firms may offer discounts during certain periods or to select customers, which is acceptable in a free market. Increasing market share, dissolving stocks while going out of business, or dissolving to invest more in a new product would be examples of other justifiable reasons for international price discrimination.[18]

Second, an actionable anti-competitive practice occurs when the firm uses its dominant position and charges higher prices by discriminating against other customers or different areas. However, the situation is the opposite in anti-dumping laws. If the exporter is not charging a low price in one market but instead charging a high price in its home market, this still counts as price discrimination. Anti-dumping laws allow a response against any kind of price discrimination, as Deardorff states:

> To see this, consider the effects of a prohibition against price discrimination. This would lead the monopolist to reduce price in one market and raise it in the other. One group of consumers will benefit, the other will lose, and the profits of the firm will also decline. It is possible that the gains to the first group of consumers from the lower price will be large enough to offset the losses to others, but this outcome is by no means necessary. It appears that such a prohibition could easily lower or raise welfare.[19]

A welfare loss occurs in the exporter's home market, whereas low prices create a welfare gain in the importing market. As the anti-

[17] Ibid.

[18] Wentong Zheng, 'Reforming Trade Remedies', *Mich. J. Int'l L.* 34 (2012), 160.

[19] Alan V. Deardorff, 'Economic Perspectives on Dumping Law', in John H. Jackson and Edwin A. Vermulst (eds.), *Anti-dumping Law and Practice: A Comparative Study* (The University of Michigan Press, 1989).

dumping duties are paid by importers, domestic consumers bear the additional costs of a potential monopoly operating abroad. By the enforcement of anti-dumping measures, the importing country collects the duties that constitute a positive output for the government, but this would not directly create a benefit for consumers. Instead, the additional costs incurred by importers are passed on to consumers. Therefore, from a consumer perspective, anti-dumping laws do not constitute an efficient solution.

Last, anti-dumping laws have a limited effect on the market strategy of a monopoly because there are other ways for a monopoly to increase its market power, such as a merger and acquisition or circumvention. In the case of an anti-dumping measure, the exporter would pursue a merger and acquisition strategy that would improve market power as the local firm would already have been operating. After the merger, the exporter would benefit from the local firm's distribution channels, reputation or clientele. Details of the circumvention of anti-dumping duties are discussed thoroughly below. However, for the purposes of this part, it is noted that circumvention is prohibited or actionable in most jurisdictions, but governments are late to notice and slow to react. Until a measure is taken against circumvention, a firm could destroy the competition in the market and take a dominant position.

2.2.1.2 Predatory Pricing (Avoidance of Monopoly)

Predatory pricing is one of the most popular efficiency arguments supporting anti-dumping laws.[20] In the case of predatory dumping, exporters are forcing domestic producers in the importing country out of business. The motive behind this behaviour is that if the prices are unreasonably low, there is little chance of domestic producers surviving. Afterwards, the exporter increases its prices and enjoys the privilege of a monopoly.[21] This makes predatory pricing a market strategy where the predator suffers in the short term but benefits in the long term as it aims to gain a dominant position.[22] This practice is argued to be a paradox by some economists who stress that the ultimate aim of competition laws is to reduce consumer prices, and predatory pricing ensures this

[20] Matsushita et al., *The World Trade Organization*, 376; Zheng, 'Reforming Trade Remedies', 161.

[21] Patricia Wruuck, *The Political Economy of Anti-dumping Protection* (Springer, 2015), 48.

[22] Gaudin Germain and Despoina Mantzari, 'Margin Squeeze: An Above-Cost Predatory Pricing Approach', *J. Comp. L. & Econ.* 12, no. 1 (2016), 151–179.

happens.[23] However, the problem is the short duration of the low price, which creates instability, as mentioned by Edlin.[24] The two elements of predatory pricing standards are price discrimination and below-cost sales, which are also analysed during an anti-dumping investigation.[25] However, selling below cost is not a requirement for anti-dumping measures. If the price is above cost but below the normal value in the home market, anti-dumping can be enforced. The calculation methods for these factors have long been debated under WTO jurisprudence, but members such as the US are constantly using alternative methods to inflate the dumping margins.[26]

There are concerns about the justification for the predatory pricing argument. First, the theory has normative force but lacks positivity. In this sense, predatory pricing cannot justify the extreme number of anti-dumping measures in force. The mismatch between the rationale and the real outcomes of anti-dumping laws can be traced back to the US and Canada almost a century ago. These anti-dumping laws were intended to avoid international predatory pricing or monopolies, but they became tools to limit imports.[27] Just like anti-dumping laws, competition laws were also designed to combat monopolies.[28] Their aim is the same; however, the rhetoric of anti-dumping laws favours limiting imports rather than combatting the threat of foreign monopolies.[29] Prusa explains:

> A century ago, one could plausibly argue that predatory dumping was more of a problem than anti-dumping. The same cannot be said today. WTO-sanctioned use of AD surely causes more injury than any reasonable person's notion of economically harmful dumping. Today AD is a bigger problem for international trade than economically meaningful dumping.[30]

The number of anti-dumping measures in force and the disputes handled by the WTO DSM support the fact that anti-dumping is being abused – it is overused and beyond its original purpose.[31] These misuse

[23] Robert H. Bork, *The Antitrust Paradox* (Basic Books, 1978).
[24] Aaron S. Edlin, 'Stopping Above-Cost Predatory Pricing', *Yale L. J.* 111, no. 4 (2002), 952.
[25] Morgan Clarisse, 'Competition Policy and Anti-dumping', *J. World Trade* 30 (1996), 61.
[26] See DS294, DS350, DS471, DS515 or DS535.
[27] Lee, 'Rethinking the Rhetoric of Anti-dumping', 472.
[28] Ibid.
[29] Ibid.
[30] Prusa, 'Anti-dumping: A Growing Problem in International Trade', 683–700.
[31] See note 3.

practices were also spread from developed countries to developing countries, as a result of learning by suffering.[32]

In addition, empirical studies show that predatory dumping rarely occurs in practice.[33] Pushing other competitors out of the market is not an easy task. One reason is that the domestic producers are entitled to challenge exporters on unfair trade practices, so they are not unarmed against predatory pricing. Another reason is that an average competitor may not bear the costs of predatory pricing for an extended period. A company needs to have more than one-third of the market share to sustain such a strategy.[34] Third, some standards have been developed to test whether or not consumer interest or well-being is being harmed. As Areeda and Turner highlight, the profit sacrifice test limits the scope of predatory pricing:

> [P]redation in any meaningful sense cannot exist unless there is a temporary sacrifice of net revenues in the expectation of greater future gains.... Thus, predatory pricing would make little economic sense to a potential predator unless he had (I) greater financial staying power than his rivals, and (II) a very substantial prospect that the losses he incurs in the predatory campaign will be exceeded by the profits to be earned after his rivals have been destroyed.[35]

In this context, the predator needs to believe that if the company sacrifices its profits then it will recover the losses in the long term. The US Supreme Court cited the test in the *Matsushita* case (1986) focusing on the recoupment requirement, which is the estimation of the predator's profit gain.[36] Only a limited number of companies can go this far and bear the risk of selling below cost, which is counted as a method of dumping according to Article 2.2 of the ADA. In addition, even if domestic competitors are pushed out, it is possible for other competitors to enter the market by means of mergers and acquisitions or other

32 Chaisse and Chakraborty, 'Normative Obsolescence of the WTO', 235.

33 Claude d'Aspremont, David Encaoua and Jean-Pierre Ponssard, 'Competition Policy and Game Theory: Reflections Based on the Cement Industry Case', in George Norman (ed.), *Market Structure and Competition Policy: Game Theoretical Approaches* (Cambridge University Press, 2000), 9–30, 71.

34 Kelvin Kwok, 'The New Hong Kong Competition Law: Anomalies and Challenges', *World Comp.* 37, no. 4 (2014), 553.

35 Phillip Areeda and Donald F. Turner, 'Predatory Pricing and Related Practices under Section 2 of the Sherman Act', *J. Reprints Antitrust L. & Econ.* 6 (1975), 219, 698.

36 Herbert Hovenkamp, 'The Areeda–Turner Test for Exclusionary Pricing: A Critical Journal', *Rev. Indust. Org.* 46, no. 3 (2015), 225. See *Matsushita Elec. Ind. Co. v. Zenith Radio Corp.*, 475 US 574 (1986), 588–593.

pricing strategies. This makes predatory pricing a risky strategy. However, the opposite is also possible as there may be other barriers to enter a market. The main concern of the contestable theory is that players should enter and exit markets without obstacles.[37] This is beneficial in terms of competition because if the player(s) in a market increases prices, then it is easy for foreign competitors to enter the market. When the previous players reduce the prices to their original level, latecomers will exit the market without experiencing difficulties. Overall, prices will not be determined by a few companies in this situation.

The contestable market, in that sense, is related to predatory pricing and anti-dumping theories. Morgan emphasises that:

> The idea is that, if the higher-priced market is non-contestable, the price discriminators will be able to reap supracompetitive prices in that market, and use the proceeds to underwrite (or cross-subsidize, in an economic sense) lower-priced sales in another market. If, on the other hand, the argument goes, the higher-priced market is open to competition, or 'contestable', the existence or simply the possibility of competition will ensure that prices in that market, even if higher than in the second market, will not be sustainable at a supracompetitive level. Any attempt at supracompetitive pricing would simply attract additional competitors, and this competition would drive prices back down.[38]

In a contestable market, predatory dumping is less likely to occur because the price is already balanced. Predation aims to push other competitors out of business and benefit from the monopoly position. The ultimate aim, therefore, is high prices, but in contestable markets, competitors may not be able to sustain unreasonably low prices for a long time. Other competitors are able to enter the market when the prices rise. Predatory dumping in this context would require (1) significant market power, (2) requisite intent, (3) price-below-cost calculation, and (4) injury to competition.[39]

The second concern about the predatory pricing argument is that it is hard for a government to accurately distinguish between predation and price discrimination. This matters because simple price discrimination is likely to increase welfare, whereas predatory pricing may cause a loss in

[37] Mark Williams, *Competition Policy and Law in China, Hong Kong and Taiwan* (Cambridge University Press, 2005), 29.

[38] Morgan, 'Competition Policy and Anti-dumping', 62.

[39] Ying Bi, 'Is Dumping Still Harmful? New Thinking on Anti-dumping in the Global Free Trade', *JE Asia & Int'l L.* 6 (2013), 29.

welfare. If the government sets the predatory pricing standards rigidly, then efficient competitors without any anti-competitive intention would be punished. On the other hand, lax standards can lead to unpunished predators and leave consumers with fewer options.[40]

Given the reasons above, predatory pricing is a normative justification, but the positive justifications are weak. As Hoekman and Mavroidis explain:

> In practice, most analysts and even most practitioners would agree that predation is no longer a motivating force for AD, if it ever was AD is simple protectionism. However, this is the only conceptually valid rationale for AD.[41]

Therefore, the target of anti-dumping laws should be limited to predation. Compared to simple price discrimination, predation is a much more serious threat to importing countries. Price discrimination increases competition between firms, whereas predation aims to destroy it. To deal with the challenge, Willig suggests a simple classification: non-monopolising and monopolising dumping.[42] As monopolising dumping is harmful to an importing country as well as to other economies, this should be actionable, unlike non-monopolising dumping.[43] However, differentiating between these two is not as practical as it seems. Such a classification would bring additional procedural burdens on exporters and non-transparency in the use of greater discretion when calculating the normal value and dumping margin. Therefore, without procedural justice, hidden trade protectionism cannot be cured.

Overall, the predatory pricing argument applies to only a few cases. Procedural justice during the investigations can eliminate many of the problems mentioned above by forcing members to be more objective and transparent in terms of calculation methods. This would not only reduce the total number of anti-dumping measures but would also change the focus from simple price discrimination into predatory pricing. In this sense, the improvement from procedural justice would contribute to scrutiny of the argument and enhance efficiency.

40 Bruce Yandle and Elizabeth M. Young, 'Dumping, Anti-dumping and Efficiency', World Bank Internal Discussion Paper, 1987, accessed 12 September 2023, http://documents.worldbank.org/curated/en/163311468914400721/pdf/multi0page.pdf.

41 Hoekman and Mavroidis, *World Trade Organization (WTO): Law, Economics, and Politics*, 49.

42 Bi, 'Is Dumping Still Harmful', 29.

43 Ibid.

2.2.1.3 Foreign Direct Investment

In theory, the imposition of trade barriers attracts foreign direct investment. This is the phenomenon of tariff jumping by foreign competitors to eliminate tariffs and other trade barriers.[44] Scholars such as Haaland and Wooton suggested that anti-dumping measures increase foreign direct investment and have a positive impact on employment.[45]

The foreign direct investment argument has little applicability in practice. The argument is weak because, first, the decision to undertake foreign direct investment is not dependent on trade barriers. Companies evaluate several factors before deciding to invest abroad. Tax structure, FTAs with other countries, political and economic stability, the legal system, and connectivity are elements to consider before tariffs. Second, anti-dumping measures would have a limited effect on foreign direct investment because anti-dumping measures are enforced for five years in principle. Tariffs, on the other hand, are indefinite, so tariff jump motivation would be limited with respect to anti-dumping measures.

2.2.1.4 Infant Industry

This theory suggests that protective trade barriers are useful before a domestic industry has reached full economies of scale or the state of perfect competition.[46] The infant industry theory aims to create a more efficient and competitive market. It is also linked to strategic trade theory, as mentioned by Howse:

> [G]overnments can promote their national interests by assisting firms to establish pre-emptive, first-mover, positions in markets, and to realize learning-curve advantages, in part by maintaining entry barriers to potential competitors. Again, this is a highly controversial aspect of modern international trade theory.[47]

However, the scope of an infant industry is obscure, and it may lead to misuse. The edge of government protection is not clear. There is no objective measuring method for the industry to determine whether it is still at an infant stage. Because of rent-seeking and lobbying activities,

[44] Laura Rovegno, 'Trade Protection and Market Power: Evidence from US Anti-dumping and Countervailing Duties', *Rev. World Econ.* 149, no. 3 (2013), 443–476.

[45] Mathew P. K. Tharakan, 'Is Anti-Dumping Here to Stay?', *World Econ.* 22, no. 2 (1999), 179–206.

[46] Seo Dong Woo, 'Material Retardation Standard in the US Anti-dumping Law', *Law & Pol'y Int'l Bus.* 24 (1992), 835–914, 867.

[47] Howse and Trebilcock, *The Regulation of International Trade*, 10.

protection will continue, and so the competitiveness of the industry will decline. If objective rules can be enforced to limit infant industry protection, this would be a more convincing argument. Without these control mechanisms, infant industry protection would ultimately create inefficiency. Therefore, it should not be a justification for anti-dumping laws.

2.2.2 Fairness Arguments

A systemic approach to detect unfairness would be possible by focusing on the principles of fairness.[48] Fairness arguments are blurred given that defining fairness is a challenging task. Before discussing fairness arguments on anti-dumping, it would be helpful to focus on fairness itself. Within the context of this book, policies aiming at the maximum benefit for the maximum number of people or companies without discriminating and harming others are constituted as fair and efficient. Reciprocity fairness would suggest that harmful acts should be responded to with

48 **Distributive fairness or justice** means policies creating more equality, income, wealth opportunities, etc.

Non-discriminatory fairness means making decisions irrespective of the differences. WTO's core principles such as the most favoured nation or national treatment principles are good examples of non-discriminatory fairness.

Golden rule fairness is one of the oldest and most basic moral principles and has been the subject of attention by many philosophers. Kant explains that if one does not accept an action applied on himself, then he should not act in the same way to others. The rationale can also be explained as doing no harm to others. In this sense, predatory pricing is seen unfair due to the aim of pushing other competitors out of the market.

Reciprocity fairness is another way of looking at golden rule fairness. Reciprocity fairness can be summarised as 'do onto others as they do onto you'. In terms of anti-dumping laws, it can be argued that if the exporters dump and injure the domestic producers, then there should be a reaction which is the anti-dumping measures. Another interpretation of reciprocity fairness is about the fair value a product. It is argued that the fair price of a good is around the cost of the product. If the price is significantly over or under the cost, then it is not fair.

Maximum benefit fairness (communitarian) occurs in a situation where several actions with positive outcomes are available, the action generating the maximum benefit should be chosen according to this theory. Where all the options have negative outcomes, the one having the minimum negative output should be chosen.

Samuel V. Bruton, 'Teaching the Golden Rule', *J. Bus. Ethics* 49, no. 2 (2004), 179–187; Suranovic, 'A Positive Analysis of Fairness', 294.

harmful acts that expand the scope of the previous evaluation. This motivation would justify anti-dumping measures against predatory dumping and other market distortions.

2.2.2.1 Unfair Trade

The WTO defines its core objective as the promotion of fair trade rather than free trade.[49] The promotion of fair trade implies the objection to unfair trade, and it has long been claimed that dumping is unfair.[50] This argument is popular among politicians rather than economists.[51] Still, the argument is based on two fairness principles.

First, in terms of non-discriminatory fairness, dumping is discriminatory as exporters determine different prices for the same product.[52] Discrimination causes a distortion of competition. The anti-competitive effects of dumping create a loss in the overall welfare by harming domestic industries. Another approach is that, as other markets may be distorted by government interventions, anti-dumping laws mediate between social, economic and structural differences.[53] In this sense, anti-dumping laws serve as quasi-safeguard measures to balance the differences between markets.[54] On the other hand, enforcement of anti--dumping measures also constitutes an exception to the basic principle of non-discrimination of the WTO.

Second, anti-dumping measures can be justified under reciprocity fairness. If an exporting country is artificially increasing the competitiveness of its exporters by means of subsidies or protectionism, then imposing measures on the products is fair to balance the competitiveness of domestic firms.[55] The exact reciprocity would require implementing similar subsidies to domestic firms, but this would also decrease the competitiveness of these firms. Therefore, rather than implementing subsidies, anti-dumping measures remain a better approach for reciprocating.

One weakness to this argument is the lack of a clear definition of unfairness. This deficiency affects both the arguments mentioned above. If all WTO members can agree on the definition of unfair trade, then the

49 Understanding the WTO: Basics, WTO, accessed 16 July, 2023, www.wto.org/english/thewto_e/whatis_e/tif_e/fact2_e.htm.
50 Zheng, 'Reforming Trade Remedies', 165.
51 Wood, '"Unfair" Trade Injury', 1155.
52 Suranovic, 'A Positive Analysis of Fairness', 288.
53 Wood, '"Unfair" Trade Injury', 1155.
54 Bi, 'Is Dumping Still Harmful?', 29.
55 Suranovic, 'A Positive Analysis of Fairness', 294.

application of anti-dumping measures would be smooth. Although there are several approaches to define fairness and unfairness, none universally applies. In *DS162*, Japan recalls debates in US Congress discussing the 1916 Act. According to the minutes, Representative Denison objected to the bill and argued that:

> I consider as childish that provision of this bill prohibiting what is called 'unfair competition': it is commonly referred to as 'anti-dumping', and pretends to protect American industries . . .. The democratic leader . . . in making his statement to the House said that the Republicans should support this bill because this provision against unfair competition is a protective measure and is a Republican policy.[56]

The US, on the contrary, noted that, according to the Japan Fair Trade Commission, refusal to deal, discriminatory pricing, dumping and resale price maintenance constitute unfair trade practices.[57] This proves that WTO members are using the same concepts but have different understandings. WTO adjudication also cannot provide a solution that works in all circumstances. Rather, the rulings in several cases such as *Egypt – Rebar*, *US – Orange Juice* or *EC – Bed Linen* show that fairness analysis must be on a case-by-case basis.[58] The way of defining unfair trade significantly changes the application of anti-dumping laws.

The elusive nature of the definition of unfair trade causes another dilemma. While neoclassical economic theories suggest using anti-dumping only against predatory pricing, the level playing field[59] allows each kind of dumping to be remedied.[60] This means that a choice is made between the welfare of producers over that of consumers.[61] If the welfare of consumers is considered, dumping would not be classified as an unfair trade practice. The ADA, on the contrary, is designed in favour of domestic producers. Therefore, it is unclear why the welfare of producers should overcome the welfare of consumers.

56 DS162, United States — Anti-Dumping Act of 1916, Report of the Panel, 37 (2004).
57 Ibid.
58 Chios Carmody, 'Fairness in International Economic Law and Relations', SSRN (13 February 2013), https://ssrn.com/abstract=2161623, 12.
59 Level playing field is a situation where each player has an equal chance to succeed. Cambridge Dictionary, 'a level playing field', accessed 16 July, 2023, https://dictionary.cambridge.org/dictionary/english/a-level-playing-field.
60 Lee, 'Rethinking the Rhetoric of Anti-dumping', 480.
61 Ibid.

2.2.2.2 Subsidies

As discussed above, there are three main trade remedies regulated under the WTO law: anti-dumping, countervailing measures and safeguards. The relationship of subsidies to the research question is that exporters are more likely to and capable of predating if they receive subsidies.[62]

The Agreement on SCM regulates subsidies under the WTO framework and prohibits certain types of subsidies under Articles 3 and 5 while defining others as non-actionable.[63] The reason for this restriction is the market inefficiency created by subsidies because subsidised products are more likely to be sold below cost, which increases demand.[64] Another

[62] Article 1.1 of The Agreement on Subsidies and Countervailing Measures defines subsidy as 'a financial contribution by a government or any public body within the territory of a Member . . . or . . . there is any form of income or price support in the sense of Article XVI of GATT 1994; and . . . a benefit is thereby conferred'.

[63] Article 3:

> 3.1 Except as provided in the Agreement on Agriculture, the following subsidies, within the meaning of Article 1, shall be prohibited:(a) subsidies contingent, in law or in fact, whether solely or as one of several other conditions, upon export performance, including those illustrated in Annex I; (b) subsidies contingent, whether solely or as one of several other conditions, upon the use of domestic over imported goods.
>
> 3.2 A Member shall neither grant nor maintain subsidies referred to in paragraph 1,

Article 5:

> No Member should cause, through the use of any subsidy referred to in paragraphs 1 and 2 of Article 1, adverse effects to the interests of other Members, i.e.:
>
> (a) injury to the domestic industry of another Member;
>
> (b) nullification or impairment of benefits accruing directly or indirectly to other Members under GATT 1994 in particular the benefits of concessions bound under Article II of GATT 1994;
>
> (c) serious prejudice to the interests of another Member.
>
> This Article does not apply to subsidies maintained on agricultural products as provided in Article 13 of the Agreement on Agriculture.
>
> (Full text of the SCM Agreement, accessed 16 July, 2023 www.wto.org/english/docs_e/legal_e/24-scm_01_e.htm)

[64] Eleanor M. Fox, 'Competition Law and the Agenda for the WTO: Forging the Links of Competition and Trade', *Pac. Rim L. & Pol'y J.* 4 (1995), 1.

criticism of this argument is that the firms receiving subsidies become ineffective; they come to depend on subsidies after a while and lose their motivation to improve competitiveness. Subsidies have a distorting effect on both importing and exporting markets.[65] Therefore, as Denton concludes:

> The trade regime that one constructs must . . . rule out artificial comparative advantage arising from interventions such as subsidies and protection. It must equally frown upon dumping, insofar as it is a technique used to secure an otherwise untenable foothold in world markets.[66]

The roots of anti-dumping and countervailing measures are connected in the sense that they combat artificial comparative advantage. They are generally regulated in the same piece of legislation.[67] The countervailing measures taken against subsidised goods are based on the same merits as anti-dumping and have similar objectives.[68] They both aim to protect infant industries and prevent monopolies and unfair trade practices. Therefore, subsidies are regarded as unfair practices, and they can be combatted by anti-dumping or countervailing measures in accordance with reciprocity fairness.

One could question the reason for countervailing measures not being used as much as anti-dumping measures. According to WTO statistics, between 1996 and 2022(6), anti-dumping measures were used nearly twelve times more than countervailing measures by WTO members.[69] From a practical point of view, it is harder to prove subsidies compared to dumping, because subsidy programmes are generally confidential, concealing instances where exporters and governments are cooperating to increase market share abroad. Nevertheless, the determination of injury in domestic industry is similar in anti-dumping investigations, although the calculation of countervailing measure procedures is different. Finally, subsidies are more likely to increase tension between two

[65] Andrew Green and Michael Trebilcock, 'Enforcing WTO Obligations: What Can We Learn from Export Subsidies?', *J. Int'l Econ. Law* 10, no. 3 (2007), 660.

[66] Ross Denton, '(Why) Should Nations Utilize Anti-Dumping Measures', *Mich. J. Int'l L.* 11 (1989), 224.

[67] See Tariff Act 1930. Joseph Francois, 'Subsidies and Countervailing Measures: Determining the Benefits of Subsidies', in Kyle W. Bagwell, George A. Bermann and Petros C. Mavroidis (eds.), *Law and Economics of Contingent Protection in International Trade* (Cambridge University Press, 2009).

[68] Ivo Van Bael and Jean-François Bellis, *EU Anti-Dumping and Other Trade Defence Instruments* (Kluwer Law International, 2011).

[69] WTO Statistics.

countries than dumping because of the direct accusation levelled at a government. However, anti-dumping investigations only cover the exporters.

Another possibility would be the initiation of an anti-subsidy investigation that terminates with an anti-dumping measure. The EU, for instance, terminates many anti-subsidy investigations with anti-dumping measures.[70] The final measures are greater in the case of anti-dumping.[71] There are also cases where both anti-dumping and countervailing measures are imposed together.[72] In that sense, reciprocity fairness would justify some anti-dumping measures if there was clear evidence of a government subsidy.

2.2.2.3 Level Playing Field or Undistorted Competition

A definition of a 'level playing field' would be the situation where each player has an equal chance to succeed.[73] Trade or competition is fair only when all the conditions are equal.[74] However, similar conditions rarely exist between markets. First, there are economic and social differences between markets that affect the overall competitiveness, but this is a natural outcome. Second, environmental, labour or tax policies create favourable conditions for domestic producers.[75] Third, while attempting to maximise their interests, firms may distort competition, as in the case of predation.

Therefore, competition or anti-dumping laws are used to balance these distortions. Level playing field arguments can be correlated with reciprocity fairness as they suggest acting against market distortion caused by other governments or exporters. So, in the case of dumping, there is an artificial advantage supplied by the government of exporting countries that the importing country needs to balance by way of the conditions of competition between the exporters and the domestic producers. However, the argument for the level playing field can be twofold. In the *DS136* case, the US submits to the Panel that:

[70] Jørgen Drud Hansen and Jørgen Ulff-Møller Nielsen, 'The Puzzle of Simultaneous Anti-dumping and Anti-subsidy Measures', draft, at 4 (2011), www.etsg.org/ETSG2011/Papers/Nielsen.pdf.

[71] Ibid.

[72] Ibid.

[73] Cambridge Dictionary, 'a level playing field'.

[74] Robert E. Hudec, 'Differences in National Environmental Standards: The Level-Playing-Field Dimension', *Minn. J. Global Trade* 5 (1996), 21.

[75] Lee, 'Rethinking the Rhetoric of Anti-dumping', 474.

> The United States argues that anti-dumping rules are a practical, albeit indirect, response to these trade-distorting policies. The anti-dumping rules allow Members to respond through the imposition of offsetting duties when confronted with one harmful result of these policies, namely, injurious dumping in export markets by the producers that benefit from these policies. From this perspective, the anti-dumping rules represent an effort to maintain a 'level playing field' among producers in different countries. Anti-dumping duties are designed to offset, quantitatively, the artificial advantages realized by the exporting country's producers so that producers in the importing country may compete, at least in the importing country's market, on an equal footing with the exporting country's producers.[76]

This argument favours anti-dumping measures based on reciprocity. However, the same argument is used in the opposite way by Hong Kong as a third-party submission in *DS234*. The delegation notes:

> We also submit that the *CDSOA* (Continued Dumping and Subsidy Offset Act) is inconsistent with the *object* and *purpose* of the ADA and ASCM. We all note that the aim of anti-dumping and countervailing duties is to restore a level playing field by removing the injury to the relevant domestic industry. By distributing anti-dumping and countervailing duties to the domestic producers, the *CDSOA* provides them with an additional and WTO-inconsistent layer of protection and therefore destroys the level playing field.[77]

Therefore, the level playing field argument is controversial. There is no evidence to indicate that anti-dumping laws secure a competitive market.[78] Rather, a level playing field argument can be used as a cover for hidden trade protectionism.

2.2.3 Political Arguments

2.2.3.1 Economic Nationalism

Economic nationalism is not in favour of free trade. It is about positioning national interests over the gains from trade. The three components of economic nationalism would oppose 'free trade and economic

[76] DS136, United States – Anti-Dumping Act of 1916, Report of the Panel, 33 (2004).

[77] DS234, United States – Continued Dumping and Subsidy Offset Act of 2000, Third Party Submissions and Oral Statements, 23 (2004).

[78] Prusa, 'Anti-dumping: A Growing Problem in International Trade', 695.

isolationism; laissez-faire on domestic economic issues; and a strong nationalist stance' as explained by Colantone and Stanig.[79]

The reason for the popularity of economic nationalism is that the gains from liberalisation are difficult to realise in the short term. Lower tariffs generally create pressure on domestic industries, which impacts governments. Following tariff liberalisation, firms that are not competitive enough go out of business, resulting in increased unemployment. Rather than bearing these risks, politicians tend to use the nationalism argument to support domestic businesses artificially. This artificial support results in a clash of interests between domestic producers and consumers. As Rodrik argues, some benefit from free trade and some cannot.[80] So, trade becomes a source of conflict. The optimum policy should balance free trade and domestic social norms.[81] Without this balance, anti-dumping laws become misused policy tools.

2.2.3.2 Safety Valve

The safety valve argument on anti-dumping laws evolves from political reality. The GATT/WTO negotiations included significant concessions so that liberalising members requested exceptions to the rules.[82] Although not clearly stated as an exception by the WTO, anti-dumping laws constitute a deviation from the Most Favoured Nation Principle. The reason behind this is that there are advantageous rules for developing and least developed countries under the WTO agreements. Developed countries need safety valves to protect their domestic industries from external shocks. Developing countries, supported by the favourable rules of the WTO, can gain advantages and dominate the competition in developed countries. Therefore, one of the main supporters of anti-dumping rules was the US during the GATT 47 negotiations. Without the anti-dumping rules, the US was unwilling to agree on tariff cuts.[83]

The safety valve is a tricky argument for anti-dumping laws. As mentioned before, anti-dumping may not be the right tool to combat

[79] Italo Colantone and Piero Stanig, 'The Trade Origins of Economic Nationalism: Import Competition and Voting Behavior in Western Europe', *Am. J. Pol. Sci.* 62, no. 4 (2018), 936–953.
[80] Dani Rodrik, 'Has Globalization Gone Too Far?', *Challenge* 41, no. 2 (1998), 85.
[81] Ibid.
[82] Zheng, 'Reforming Trade Remedies', 116.
[83] Tania Voon, 'Eliminating Trade Remedies from the WTO: Lessons from Regional Trade Agreements', *Int'l & Comp. L. Q.* 59, no. 3 (2010), 625–667.

anti-competitive trade practices. It is rather a protective tool to support domestic industries. However, the burden is on consumers. A regression model by Moore and Zanardi claims that countries using anti-dumping measures do less to liberalise trade.[84] Furthermore, countries liberalising their economies are rewarded with higher income, lower inflation and better institutions.[85] Some argue that the safety valve argument does not support countries in liberalising their economies.[86] For instance, an empirical study by Fingers and Nogues covering interviews with Latin American officials argues that the anti-dumping mechanism provides more room for trade liberalisation.[87] However, the econometric models cannot decisively prove that the GATT/WTO would not be established without anti-dumping provisions. GATT 47[88] successfully contributed a significant tariff cut when it was signed. According to WTO statistics, the average tariffs of the US fell from 5.5 to 3.5 per cent since 1996.[89] Even if it is assumed that the WTO has no effect on tariff cuts, the WTO is still necessary for the smooth operation of international trade.

The general view of anti-dumping is that it is protectionist and misused.[90] However, taking the safety valve function into account, anti--dumping laws are necessary evils of international trade to prosper from the positive effects of trade.[91] This book contends that anti-dumping measures can be justified given their political economic benefits. The Uruguay Round of negotiations led to a dramatic decline in tariffs globally, promoting free trade. The contribution of the anti-dumping mechanism to liberalisation therefore outweighs the risk of protectionism. Furthermore, without anti-dumping measures, liberalisation does not seem possible while it is possible to limit the misuse of anti-dumping investigations through improved procedural justice.

[84] Michael O. Moore and Maurizio Zanardi, 'Does Anti-dumping Use Contribute to Trade Liberalization in Developing Countries?' *Can. J. Econ./Rev. Can. écon.* 42, no. 2 (2009), 492.

[85] Ibid.

[86] Ibid.

[87] Ibid.

[88] The General Agreement on Tariffs and Trade (GATT 1947). Full text available at www.wto.org/english/docs_e/legal_e/gatt47_01_e.htm, accessed 16 July 2023.

[89] WTO Tariff Analysis Online system, accessed 16 July 2023, http://tao.wto.org/.

[90] Prusa, 'Anti-dumping: A Growing Problem in International Trade', 334; Chaisse and Chakraborty, 'Normative Obsolescence of the WTO'.

[91] Gunnar Niels and Adriaan Ten Kate, 'Anti-dumping Protection in a Liberalising Country: Mexico's Anti-dumping Policy and Practice', *World Econ.* 27, no. 7 (2004), 967–983.

2.3 Arguments against Anti-dumping Laws

The arguments against anti-dumping laws are more prominent than the arguments for anti-dumping. Still, it is doubtful whether anti-dumping laws will ever be replaced by other rules such as competition laws.

2.3.1 Efficiency Arguments

Anti-dumping laws are criticised in the literature.[92] Economists argue that anti-dumping measures are used as substitutes for import tariffs.[93] Cann suggested questioning conventional theory to find a balance between effective manufacturers and consumer welfare.[94] Cann points out that politically biased anti-dumping laws are not beneficial to economies.[95] This book also argues that political considerations result in strict procedural rules in anti-dumping investigations. The misuse of anti-dumping laws also creates adverse economic outcomes. However, it is not possible to abolish anti-dumping laws in the short term. Instead, the negative effects of anti-dumping laws can be reduced by improving procedural justice.

2.3.1.1 Distortion of Competition and Welfare

Distortion of competition and welfare is the primary efficiency argument against anti-dumping laws. Porter's theory of competitive advantage connects international trade and competition. There are several elements of competitive advantage, namely demand conditions, related and supporting industries, firm strategy structure and rivalry.[96] Some argue that neither state interventionism nor the free market is efficient. Instead, the state should act as a catalyst to support the industries to achieve competitiveness.[97] Porter also notes that companies need to achieve

92 Tharakan, 'Is Anti-Dumping Here to Stay?'; Prusa, 'Anti-dumping: A Growing Problem in International Trade', 334; Chaisse and Chakraborty, 'Normative Obsolescence of the WTO'.

93 Nandini Bandyopadhyay, 'Anti-dumping Investigation in Agriculture: Issues of Trade Diversion-Named vs Non-named Countries', LSU Master's Theses (2008), 2.

94 Wesley A. Cann, 'Internationalizing Our Views toward Recoupment and Market Power: Attacking the Anti-dumping/Antitrust Dichotomy through WTO-Consistent Global Welfare Theory', *U. Pa. J. Int'l Econ. L.* 17 (1996), 69.

95 Ibid.

96 Michael Porter, *Competitive Advantage of Nations: Creating and Sustaining Superior Performance*, Vol. 2 (Simon & Schuster, 2011), 73.

97 Ibid., 87.

competitiveness in order to survive. Some suggest that pressure creates innovation, supporting competition and globalisation.[98] If a firm prioritises political connections instead of productivity or innovation, then efficiency is limited.[99] Thus, anti-dumping distorts the competitiveness of domestic firms.

Second, many economists agree that price discrimination is the natural result of competition.[100] Anti-dumping laws disregard the essence of competition. Zheng, states: 'International price discrimination, however, is a rational, generally pro-competitive response of a producer facing an overseas market'.[101] Price discrimination is a justifiable market strategy and is not forbidden within a domestic market. Therefore, it should not be per se actionable in the case of international price discrimination.[102]

In addition, low pricing would be a proper market strategy aimed at improving market share.[103] In the case of anti-dumping measures, low prices are eliminated. Anti-dumping laws do not distinguish between pro-competitive and anti-competitive strategies.[104] Low price is the desired outcome of competition laws, whereas anti-dumping laws involve action against low prices with no further evaluation. The conventional view is that below-cost prices constitute a monopolising strategy.[105]

In addition, dumping creates asymmetry in the domestic market in terms of market power and information. Therefore, anti-dumping measures should be used as corrective mechanisms. However, because of the misuse of anti-dumping laws, domestic producers are overprotected, which creates another asymmetry. Due to the increase in the market power of domestic producers, consumers are left with few choices and higher prices.

Consequently, it is argued that enforcement of anti-dumping measures only benefits a small group such as domestic producers.[106] Some argue

98 Ibid., 92.

99 Ibid.

100 Christopher F. Corr, 'Trade Protection in the New Millennium: The Ascendancy of Anti-dumping Measures', *Nw. J. Int'l L. & Bus.* 18 (1997), 49.

101 Zheng, 'Reforming Trade Remedies', 160.

102 Ibid.

103 Stewart, 'US–Japan Economic Disputes', 697.

104 Corr, 'Trade Protection in the New Millennium', 49.

105 Robert D. Willig, 'Economic Effects of Antidumping Policy', in Robert Z. Lawrence (ed.), *Brookings Trade Forum* (Brookings Institution Press, 1998), 57–79, 66.

106 Pandey Sanjay Kumar and Mansi Bahal, 'International Trade: Dumping and Its Impact on Competition', Competition Commission of India (2012).

that dumping has positive effects on consumer welfare, so anti-dumping measures are not beneficial to consumers.[107]

2.3.1.2 Domestic Protection and Cartelisation

Cartelisation also constitutes a distortion of competition, but this argument is more specific as it involves collusion between businesses. The argument is that domestic firms are encouraged to act together in the case of dumping, which may lead to cartelisation. According to Article 4.1 of the ADA, the domestic industry covers the producers of like products in addition to the identical product subject to investigation.[108] Article 5.1 requires a written application by the domestic industry before the initiation of the anti-dumping investigation. Firms manufacturing most of the domestic goods, including like products, need to act together and express their intent to the government.

Therefore, the structure of the ADA encourages domestic industry to act together, which is not acceptable in terms of competition laws. The architecture of the ADA results in domestic cartels moving together against foreign competitors. Messerlin finds that anti-dumping laws create cartels, and even if fines are imposed on these cartels, the members of the cartel gain more and so can bear the risk of being fined.[109] Therefore, the ADA creates a new problem while attempting to deal with international price discrimination. Moreover, compared to international price discrimination, which can be pro-competitive, cartelisation has a more detrimental effect on competition. In this context, anti-dumping laws give rise to a polarisation between domestic and foreign competitors.

2.3.1.3 Misallocation of Resources

This argument is a variation of the theory of comparative advantage. Comparative advantage theory requires that relative economic efficiency

[107] Zheng, 'Reforming Trade Remedies', 160.

[108] Article 4.1 states, 'For the purposes of this Agreement, the term "domestic industry" shall be interpreted as referring to the domestic producers as a whole of the like products or to those of them whose collective output of the products constitutes a major proportion of the total domestic production of those products…'; Article 5.1 states, 'Except as provided for in paragraph 6, an investigation to determine the existence, degree and effect of any alleged dumping shall be initiated upon a written application by or on behalf of the domestic industry'. Full text of the ADA available at www.wto.org/english/docs_e/legal_e/19-adp_01_e.htm, accessed 16 July 2023.

[109] Patrick A. Messerlin, 'Anti-Dumping Regulations or Pro-Cartel Law? The EC Chemical Cases', *World Econ.* 13, no. 4 (1990), 465–492.

should direct specialisation between nations. If countries grant subsidies to industries, this creates a false advantage over other markets. The public interventions creating artificial advantages constitute a misallocation of resources.

If anti-dumping laws are as popular as they are today, again, the protected industries will enjoy false or artificial advantages compared to other markets.[110] In addition, due to the anti-dumping measures, jobs and businesses move from one country to another, creating a contrast to the natural comparative advantage.[111] Empirical evidence supports this argument by showing that uncompetitive industries receive more protection but create less efficiency,[112] thus, resulting in higher costs to consumers, which also constitutes misallocation of resources.[113]

Another issue is the impact of anti-dumping measures on downstream industries. Bown et al. find that additional tariffs have negative effects on downstream industries by increasing production costs and decreasing investment, employment, wages and sales.[114] They also find that if the US had not imposed anti-dumping measures on Chinese products between 1988 and 2016, 4.8 per cent more jobs would have been created in the US economy.[115]

2.3.1.4 Circumvention

Circumvention of anti-dumping measures is a threat that impairs the expected outcomes from anti-dumping laws. Companies can change strategies before a government effects measures, so high anti-dumping duties end up with leaks and tax fraud. Here, the overall aim is lost again as the domestic producers do not see the expected outcome from anti-dumping. Therefore, anti-dumping measures are inefficient in solving the asymmetry created by dumping.

Also, anti-dumping measures may cause instability if overused or misused. Procedural burdens can quickly drive exporters away from

110 Stewart, 'US–Japan Economic Disputes', 689.

111 Cann, 'Internationalizing Our Views', 88.

112 Stefanie Lenway, Randall Morck and Bernard Yeung, 'Rent Seeking, Protectionism and Innovation in the American Steel Industry', *Econ. J.* 106 (1996), 410–421, 420.

113 Corr, 'Trade Protection in the New Millennium', 49.

114 Chad Bown, Paola Conconi, Aksel Erbahar and Lorenzo Trimarchi, 'Trade Protection along Supply Chains: The Negative Effects of Tariffs on Downstream Sectors', USApp – American Politics and Policy, 2021, accessed 16 July 2023, http://eprints.lse.ac.uk/109194/1/usappblog_2021_02_10_trade_protection_along_supply_chainshow.pdf.

115 Ibid.

cooperating with the authorities. The considerable discretion of investigating authorities results in inflated final measures. This turns a balancing tool into a protective policy measure, thus provoking importers and exporters to circumvent the measure. Furthermore, as there are no uniform rules of anti-circumvention under WTO agreements, firms are better off circumventing the duties. Even though this argument lacks normative power, it helps to clarify a deficiency in anti-dumping laws.

Therefore, circumvention represents one of the most crucial and practical drawbacks to the enforcement of anti-dumping measures. Apart from responding to lobbying activities by domestic industries and creating inefficiency, investigating authorities should also consider the circumvention risk before adopting high anti-dumping duties. In the case of circumvention, importers would classify products under false HS codes and pay even less tax or declare the origin of the goods wrong so that anti-dumping duties are not collected. It is certain that investigating authorities are aware of these risks, so continuing to adopt high anti-dumping duties would imply that decision-makers are more interested in political support from local industries than economic efficiency.

2.3.2 Fairness Arguments

2.3.2.1 Public Interest

According to the ADA, there is no requirement to take into account public interest before the initiation of an anti-dumping investigation.[116] The lack of such a condition has been debated in the literature as it disregards consumer welfare. Also, the Canadian Anti-Dumping regulation is welcomed as a good practice since the regulation covers public interest before the initiation of an anti-dumping investigation.[117] This is also the case for EU investigations. An article by Leclerc evaluates the effects of such a provision in terms of consumer welfare.[118] First, the efficiency rationales for anti-dumping measures are discussed, namely predatory pricing or sporadic dumping. Then, it is concluded that anti-dumping measures do not prevent predatory pricing or sporadic dumping. I agree with this idea because governments are slow compared

[116] Matsushita et al., *The World Trade Organization*, 410.

[117] See the Article 45 (1) of Special Import Measures Act of Canada, accessed 16 July 2023, http://laws-lois.justice.gc.ca/PDF/S-15.pdf.

[118] Jean-Marc Leclerc, 'Reforming Anti-dumping Law: Balancing the Interests of Consumers and Domestic Industries', *McGill L.J.* 44 (1998), 111.

to companies. Hence, if exporters wish to apply predatory pricing policy in a foreign market, exporters may circumvent these duties. In addition, the effect of sporadic dumping is trivial in big markets, so anti-dumping duties would be late and ineffective. Lecrerc then analyses non-efficiency rationales for anti-dumping laws. It is suspected that anti-dumping laws are not driven by communitarianism or fairness according to a study by Hutton and Trebilcock.[119] Cases under the public interest provision are also discussed to establish whether this is a useful approach for balancing the interests of producers and consumers. However, this provision is found to be nearly useless due to the narrow interpretation by the Canadian anti-dumping authority.[120] Finally, the main motivation behind anti-dumping laws seems to be nothing more than protectionism according to Lecrerc, and the only hope is to overcome the problem through regional trade agreements, as in the EU, where members cannot enforce anti-dumping duties against each other. The article is quite useful because the Canadian anti-dumping regulation is commonly praised in the literature, and this article shows its disadvantages by taking consumer welfare into account. Thus, even one of the most liberal systems is working for the sake of producers rather than consumers.

To avoid the shortcomings of anti-dumping, Wu proposed a revision of the ADA involving a fairness test.[121] However, according to Bhagwati, the notion of fair trade based on reciprocity or a level playing field is a threat to trade liberalisation.[122] Bhagwati warns that it is possible in almost every single case to interpret public policies in a way that they are regarded as subsidies. This results in retaliatory anti-dumping measures.[123] Within this context, a fairness test would transform anti-dumping into a more complex and abusive tool.[124] Because of the disagreement on the definition of unfair dumping, the legal standards of anti-dumping are lax.[125] The ease and common use of anti-dumping generates imbalances rather than level playing fields. Hudec summarises the problem as:

[119] Susan Hutton and Michael Trebilcock, 'An Empirical Study of the Application of Canadian Anti-Dumping Laws: A Search for Normative Rationales', *J. World Trade* 24 (1990), 124.

[120] Ibid., 139.

[121] Mark Wu, 'Anti-dumping in Asia's Emerging Giants', *Harv. Int'l L.J.* 53 (2012), 1.

[122] Lee, 'Rethinking the Rhetoric of Anti-dumping', 473.

[123] Ibid.

[124] Ibid.

[125] Ibid.

> If politics were completely rational, there would be little reason to be concerned about level-playing-field claims against imports from countries with weak environmental standards. Policy debate cannot completely answer these fairness complaints because the normative concepts that underlie the notions of fairness in this debate are simply not coherent when applied to international trade relations. No one knows whether any playing field is truly level, nor does anyone know how to make it level. Instead, the present system of unfair trade laws seems to be held in check by nothing more than a rather vague sense of restraint.[126]

This means that most of the anti-dumping measures in force might be against the public interest while contradicting the maximum benefit fairness principle. Hence, anti-dumping laws increase the welfare of a few actors. Domestic industries directly enjoy the anti-dumping measures while they support politicians and government officials. On the other hand, importers, exporters and consumers suffer. Even so, an objective public interest test is challenging and would create additional problems.

2.3.2.2 Rights Theory

Rights theory rejects any intervention that would restrict personal rights.[127] The theory argues that anti-dumping measures violate the rights of contract and property and are therefore not acceptable.[128] The foreign exporter and importer should have the right to contract and change the property of the goods under consideration, and anti-dumping duties limit these rights to some extent.

Also, investigations incur high costs for exporters to defend themselves. The costs could reach one million USD for a company defending itself before the US authorities. Even for large firms, defence in a foreign jurisdiction is practically and financially challenging. The same applies to developing countries because, according to a study by the World Bank, developing countries only have 55 per cent of the legal capacity of developed countries.[129] This reality also takes away an equal chance for exporters and governments during an anti-dumping investigation. These outcomes show that anti-dumping measures have adverse effects on the

[126] Hudec, 'Differences in National Environmental Standards', 28.

[127] Robert McGee, 'Some Ethical Aspects of Anti-dumping Laws', SSRN (2000), 20, available at https://ssrn.com/abstract=242412, accessed 16 July 2023.

[128] Ibid.

[129] Alessandro Romano, and Peachya Thammapitagkul, 'Anti-dumping: A Public Interest Not So Much in the Public Interest', *Manchester J. Int'l Econ. L.* 10 (2013), 76.

rights of the firms to trade, particularly if they are located in developing countries.

This theory is weak in the sense that public intervention is almost inevitable in international trade. Countries naturally have the authority to control or impose tariffs on imported goods. In terms of product safety regulations, for instance, the welfare of consumers is prioritised over that of firms. Therefore, rights theory is in a vacuum but still useful to highlight the restrictive effects of anti-dumping laws.

2.3.2.3 Abuse of Investigation Procedures

There is a mismatch between the architecture of international trade law and its enforcement. Dani Rodrik notes:

> Perhaps no other area of economics displays such a gap between what policy-makers practice and what economists preach as does international trade. The superiority of free trade is one of the profession's most cherished beliefs, yet international trade is rarely free.[130]

The general provisions of the ADA encourage members to take advantage of using investigation procedures as a tool for protectionism. Calculation of dumping margin, using unsatisfactory evidence, non-transparent procedures and burdensome requests from exporters are examples of the abusive use of the gaps in the ADA.[131]

The abuse of the investigation procedures argument is the central focus of this book. Some argue the lack of procedural justice results in excessive protectionism. Debroy and Chakraborty highlight the problem at the macro level by stating:

> While industrial tariff reform in developed countries enhance the level of market access, increased usage of protectionist policies like anti-dumping investigations, especially through back-to-back investigations on the same product totally nullifies that.[132]

Furthermore, Raju accurately adds that 'although designed as a corrective mechanism against unfair trade, it has currently been hijacked for

[130] Dani Rodrik, 'Political Economy of Trade Policy', in Gene M. Grossman and Kenneth Rogoff (eds.), *Handbook of International Economics*, Vol. 3 (Elsevier Science BV, 1995), 1458.

[131] OECD, Competition Policy, 'General Distribution OCDE/GD (96) 59' (OECD, 1996).

[132] Bibek Debroy and Debashis Chakraborty, eds., *Anti-Dumping: Global Abuse of a Trade Policy Instrument* (Academic Foundation, 2007), 24.

protectionist purposes'.[133] 'Trade protectionism' is the opposite of the free-trade doctrine. In other words, it involves restricting imports by tariffs, non-tariff barriers or other monetary measures. These tools, such as high customs tariffs or complex administrative burdens benefit domestic industries and subsidise their market share. Almost all economists defend the idea of free trade, but governments are inclined to enforce protectionist policies.[134]

This book argues that the abuse of investigation procedures constitutes a form of 'hidden trade protectionism'. The rationale behind hidden trade protectionism can be explained by the following motivations in the light of the public choice theory.[135] According to Skyes:

> The public choice perspective on international trade agreements begins with the observation that trade agreements are compacts not among nations, but among their self-interested political officials. These officials are typically interested in maximizing their political fortunes measured by such things as votes, campaign contributions, and government revenues that can be spent in various ways to secure political support.[136]

Therefore, the decision to effect protectionism is a reflection of well-organised lobbying and does not reflect the general will.[137] As government officials or politicians cannot explicitly protect the lobbying groups, alternative ways are being used. One way of doing this is by exercising strict procedural rules against exporters. The WTO members tend to abuse the procedures during anti-dumping investigations to protect domestic manufacturers. Chaisse and Chakraborty point out,

> As discussions have proven, the present investigative procedures favour domestic protectionist bias, declaring the whole regime as a non-tariff

[133] K. D. Raju, 'India's Involvement in Anti-Dumping Cases in the First Decade of WTO', in Bibek Debroy and Debashis Chakraborty (eds.), *Anti-Dumping: Global Abuse of a Trade Policy Instrument* (Academic Foundation, 2007), 31–47.

[134] Robert Falkner, *International Political Economy* (University of London Press, 2005), 24.

[135] The social choice theory dates back to 1785 when the mathematician Marquis de Condorcet first put forward the voting paradox. However, the name of the theory is given by Kenneth Arrow in 1951. The theory briefly deals with the problem when a group of people need to choose between more than one alternative. Under these circumstances, Arrow suggests that without being dictatorial it is impossible to find a voting system to satisfy each subgroup's interests. Ulle Endriss, 'Logic and Social Choice Theory', *Log. Philos. Today* 2 (2011), 335.

[136] Alan O. Sykes, 'Regulatory Protectionism and the Law of International Trade', *Univ. Chi. L. Rev.* 66 (1999), 24–25.

[137] David Quartner, 'Public Choice Theory, Protectionism and the Case of NAFTA', *Econ. Aff.* 26, no. 1 (2006), 59.

> barrier (NTB). The ADA has provided numerous loopholes and leeway for manipulation at both the substantial and procedural levels.[138]

The loopholes under the ADA allow investigating authorities to create procedural burdens on exporters. If exporters cannot cooperate with the investigating authorities, investigations are steered by the investigating authorities and the domestic industries, resulting in higher levels of protection.

This book argues that the abuse of investigation procedures is the most plausible theory discussed in this chapter. Anti-dumping laws are highly controversial, and both the arguments for and against anti-dumping laws have some valid points. Besides, as mentioned, anti-dumping laws cannot be replaced by other mechanisms. Consequently, several suggestions have been made to revise the ADA. The reason for the deadlock at the WTO level is due to the coupling of procedural and essential issues. Unlike most other views, this book argues that before substantial reform, procedural justice needs to be secured. Also, procedural reform is more acceptable for both developed and developing countries. Unlike the early years of the WTO, anti-dumping measures are now being used by developing members. Improving transparency and limiting the discretion of investigating authorities is therefore beneficial for all members of the WTO. Furthermore, improvements from procedural justice would result in lower anti-dumping duties, which would reduce the tension between members. Overall, short-term reforms should be aimed at avoiding abusive investigation procedures.

2.3.3 Political Arguments

2.3.3.1 Public Choice Theory

Public choice theory seeks to explain politics by using economics.[139] The theory argues that politicians and government officials act in their own interest rather than the public interest. The Nobel Prize–winning economist James Buchanan is one of the key figures who developed the theory of public choice.[140] Buchanan demonstrates the need for a constitutional framework to harmonise the resources and self-interests of politicians.

[138] Chaisse and Chakraborty, 'Normative Obsolescence of the WTO', 253.

[139] Jorgen Ulff-Moller Nielsen and Gert Tinggaard Svendsen, 'EU Lobbying and Anti-Dumping Policy', *J. World Trade* 46 (2012), 193.

[140] James D. Gwartney, Richard L. Stroup, Russell S. Sobel and David A. Macpherson, *Economics: Private and Public Choice* (Cengage Learning, 2014), 128.

Without this framework, government actions are deemed to fail.[141] Public choice economists argue that the government and its actions should be guaranteed to correct market failures.[142] The reason is that all players in the political arena involving government officials mostly choose to act in favour of themselves rather than the public interest.

Regarding anti-dumping laws, policymakers and government officials defend the interests of a small group, domestic industries, rather than pursue public interest. Lobbying and rent-seeking activities by these small groups return better gains for politicians and government officials. Therefore, anti-dumping laws leave discretion to politicians and government officials, which makes this instrument biased and inefficient. Without this discretion, anti-dumping duties would be lower. However, lobbying activities result in abusive investigation procedures and higher anti-dumping duties. That brings the need for procedural justice to limit the investigation procedures being more objective.

Lindsey and Ikenson focus on the US anti-dumping policies triggered by 'energetic and well-organised protectionist lobbies'.[143] Other studies show that rent-seeking firms or lobbies are older, less profitable, and less innovative, and their CEOs receive higher salaries compared to non-rent seekers.[144] In other words, rent-seeking firms are generally corrupt, yet, they are well-organised. With political support, the US investigating authorities apply complex procedures, and in contrast to Horlick's perfectionism evaluation, many scholars such as Lindsey and Ikenson believe the reason is protectionism.[145]

Imagine a case where rent-seeking pushchair producers claim that their products are more expensive because of higher quality. Government officials would protect them through anti-dumping measures. However, public choice theory would suggest the avoidance of anti-dumping measures so that consumers could have more options with lower prices. In this sense, public choice theory suggests that anti-dumping investigations can be used in an abusive manner.

141 Ibid.

142 Romano and Thammapitagkul, 'Anti-dumping: A Public Interest', 67.

143 Lindsey Brink and Daniel Ikenson, 'The Rhetoric and Reality of US Anti-dumping Law', in Bibek Debroy and Debashis Chakraborty (eds.), *Anti-dumping: Global Abuse of a Trade Policy Instrument* (Academic Foundation, 2007), 101.

144 Lenway et al., 'Rent Seeking, Protectionism and Innovation', 410–421.

145 Gary Horlick, 'Ten Major Problems with the Anti-Dumping Instrument in the United States', *J. World Trade* 39 (2005), 169; Brink and Ikenson, 'The Rhetoric and Reality of US Anti-dumping Law'.

Table 2.2 *Global GDP and export ratios of developed and developing countries*

	Number of countries included in the group		Global GDP (%)		Global exports of goods and services (%)	
	1990	**2022**	**1990**	**2022**	**1990**	**2021**
Developed	23	39	62.5	41.2	75	53
Developing	130	155	37.5	58.8	20.3	47

Sources: Prepared by the Author by using the data from IMF Data Mapper, accessed 17 June 2023, www.imf.org/external/datamapper/datasets/WEO and TradeMap accessed 17 June 2023, www.trademap.org/

2.3.3.2 Liberalisation and the WTO

As mentioned, anti-dumping measures are seen as safety valves in the liberalisation process. According to this perspective, anti-dumping plays an important role. However, it is still a deviation from the core principles of the WTO/GATT. Given the reality that anti-dumping laws are being widely used, they threaten the ideals of WTO and liberalisation. Like all exceptions, anti-dumping laws should be used carefully to avoid any loss of the gains from trade. Statistics also show that anti-dumping is the top issue causing disputes between WTO members.[146]

Within this context, the liberalisation and the WTO argument need a macro perspective. Economic indicators were against developing countries during the 1990s. Currently, the previous concessions granted to developing countries may be seen as burdensome because, following the liberalisation era, manufacturing has shifted from developed to developing countries. Table 2.2 visualises the transformation in favour of the developing countries.

Developing countries are gaining dominance in the global economy and developed countries, consequently, are trying to withdraw the concessions they gave in different ways. Mega trade agreements such as the RCEP[147] or rising tariffs up to bound rates are some examples of these

[146] Between 1995 and 2022, there were 142 cases on anti-dumping and 136 on subsidies and countervailing measures out of 616 cases. The list is available at www.wto.org/english/tratop_e/dispu_e/dispu_e.htm, accessed 16 July 2023.

[147] The Regional Comprehensive Economic Partnership, signed in November 2020 among fifteen countries; Brunei, Cambodia, Indonesia, Laos, Malaysia, Myanmar, the Philippines, Singapore, Thailand, Vietnam, Australia, China, Japan, New Zealand and Republic of Korea. For more information please visit https://rcepsec.org/.

reactions. In addition, anti-dumping measures are justifiable under the WTO agreements since dumping is traditionally labelled as an unfair trade practice. Americans and Europeans shaped the international framework of anti-dumping law.[148] There was an advantage for these countries to use anti-dumping measures against developing countries.[149] The disregard of developing countries during the drafting of the ADA may be one reason for anti-dumping being the most controversial topic in the WTO. ADA comprises legal gaps that allow investigating authorities to enjoy discretion. Once the gaps are discovered, they spread rapidly. That is why more and more developing countries are also using anti-dumping measures against others. This phenomenon is referred to as 'learning-by-suffering'.[150] Because of blurry anti-dumping rules, investigating authorities might enforce strict procedures, and this constitutes hidden trade protectionism.

Although almost all developing countries and Japan contend that anti-dumping laws are excessively discretionary, efforts to revise the ADA have been unsuccessful.[151] The discretion and lack of transparency, therefore, seem helpful for developed WTO members as they result in overprotective anti-dumping measures. This also explains the ongoing negotiations on the ADA and their deadlock.

2.4 Justifiable Level of Anti-dumping Laws

After the evaluation of the arguments above, it is noteworthy that the theories are controversial. Determination of the justifiable level of anti-dumping laws is therefore challenging. From a fairness-based market efficiency perspective, dumping is arguably a market distortion.[152] Therefore, anti-dumping laws can be justified on limited grounds. These include (1) eliminating predatory dumping and thus monopolisation; (2) functioning as a measure to balance between different economic structures and government distortions; and (3) playing a safety valve role.[153]

148 Wu, 'Anti-dumping in Asia's Emerging Giants'.
149 Ibid.
150 Chaisse and Chakraborty, 'Normative Obsolescence of the WTO', 235.
151 Ian Wooton and Maurizio Zanardi, 'Trade and Competition Policy: Anti-Dumping versus Anti-trust' Working Papers (2002/6) Business School – Economics, University of Glasgow, revised October 2002 .
152 Lee, 'Rethinking the Rhetoric of Anti-dumping', 472.
153 Bi, 'Is Dumping Still Harmful?', 29.

Predatory dumping is regarded as an actionable practice. Predation is different from simple price discrimination in the sense that the predator aims to drive away other competitors and then enjoy a monopoly. Therefore, anti-dumping measures are justifiable in the case of predatory dumping. The problem is that the theory cannot explain the vast number of anti-dumping measures in force as empirical studies prove that predation rarely exists. Price discrimination, however, is not a harmful behaviour per se, and it is insufficient to justify anti-dumping laws.

Anti-dumping laws can also be justified on limited grounds in terms of protecting domestic industries from government distorted industries. Exporters can dump overseas if they receive government subsidies or their home market is overprotected. Anti-dumping laws can be used to avoid these distortions. The economic theory of GATT highlights the role of reciprocity as a vital concept to benefit from trade.[154] Trading partners prosper when they allow trade to grow and reduce barriers mutually. However, when one party protects its domestic market or grants subsidies, trade partners retaliate by enforcing other protective measures. Therefore, subsidies and other strategic market distortions result in more anti-dumping measures while restricting international trade. The EU, for instance, has amended its trade defence legislation recently. According to the new method, the EU does not consider whether or not the country under investigation is a market economy. Instead, the Commission focuses on undistorted prices based on the country and sector-specific reports and considers social and environmental standards.[155] Since China's non-market economy status is controversial, this amendment expands the discretion of the EU to apply higher anti-dumping measures. The non-market economy status also restricts the meaningful participation of Chinese exporters.

Analysis of the safety valve argument requires a political economy approach. Within this context, the legal framework of the WTO embodies various sets of rules, each serving different purposes. As Van Den Bossche explains, there are six groups of basic rules and principles under WTO law:

> [T]he principles of non-discrimination; the rules on market access, including rules on transparency; the rules on unfair trade; the rules on

[154] Chios Carmody, 'A Theory of WTO Law', *J. Int'l Econ. L.* 11, no. 3 (2008), 527–557.

[155] Report from the Commission to the European Parliament and the Council, European Commission, 31 July 2018, accessed 17 July 2023, https://eur-lex.europa.eu/LexUriServ/LexUriServ.do?uri=COM:2018:0561:FIN:EN:PDF.

> conflicts between trade liberalisation and other societal values and interests; the rules on special and differential treatment for developing countries; and a number of key institutional and procedural rules relating to decision making and dispute settlement.[156]

The classification above asserts that the main emphasis of WTO law is not only free trade but also fair trade for all members. Fair trade also supports a balanced global economy. One of the fundamental principles of the WTO requires non-discrimination. GATT/WTO framework considers the development level of its members. This would be advantageous to developing and least developed countries; first, to avoid the side effects of liberalisation and, second, to allow them to enjoy the benefits of the liberalisation process. However, as a precaution, developed countries insisted on some exceptions to the rules to protect their domestic industries. Therefore, the current three-layer structure has been formed in terms of anti-dumping measures: non-discrimination and market access as the basic rule; differential treatment for developing members as the booster of trade; and trade remedies (anti-dumping, countervailing, safeguards) as the safety valves for the developed countries.

On the other hand, arguments against anti-dumping laws sound more plausible. Anti-dumping laws aim to avoid market distortions. However, the justifications mentioned above are hard to achieve through anti-dumping laws. As mentioned in the World Bank report:

> A perfect anti-dumping action will identify the long-run competitive domestic price, determine the expected long-run production costs of the alleged predatory firm, and demonstrate that the predator is pricing below cost. Every dimension of the problem is difficult.[157]

Complying with this formula is a challenge, and as the ADA has legal gaps, members are encouraged to abuse anti-dumping laws for overly protectionist purposes. In the current legal framework, members fill these gaps with domestic laws and procedural rules. As argued by the public choice theory, these procedural rules favour domestic interest groups rather than consumers. Abusive procedural rules end up with high anti-dumping duties constituting a form of hidden trade protectionism. The inflation of the dumping margins creates inefficiency for all market actors. First, the domestic lobbying producers become reluctant to

156 Van den Bossche and Zdouc, *The Law and Policy of the World Trade Organization*, 39.
157 Yandle and Young, 'Dumping, Anti-dumping and Efficiency'.

relinquish protection. Second, consumers are left with higher prices and fewer options. Last, exporters lose market power.

In its current form, anti-dumping laws are not designed to avoid market distortions completely. High anti-dumping duties encourage firms to circumvent. Yet, anti-dumping measures are restricting trade. As mentioned by Prusa:

> AD law has nothing to do with economically harmful practices; rather, AD is just a cleverly designed form of protectionism. In other words, not only is too much medication being administered but the medication has nothing to do with the disease it is supposedly intended to be addressing.[158]

Anti-dumping is indeed an inadequate policy and a faulty safety valve.[159] Trebilcock and Howse correctly argue that anti-dumping laws are inadequate for identifying and punishing international predatory pricing.[160] This is because anti-dumping measures penalise non-predatory prices more than predatory prices.[161] Commentators suggest replacing anti-dumping laws with competition laws, given that they both prohibit predatory pricing.[162] However, there are also other views that anti-dumping laws cannot be replaced with competition laws.[163]

This book agrees with that view since there are more differences than similarities. These two disciplines derive from the same origins, but they diverge in terms of their objectives and even contradict each other in some respects. For instance, price undertakings are prohibited under competition laws, but the ADA allows these arrangements. So, the contradiction is that competition laws aim to achieve lower consumer prices, whereas anti-dumping laws force exporters to increase prices. Price discrimination is not illegal per se under competition laws, while it is prohibited by anti-dumping laws.[164] Competition laws aim to secure consumer welfare, whereas anti-dumping laws protect domestic producers. One is competition oriented, while the other prioritises the competitor. Again, a big difference between competition and anti-dumping

158 Prusa, 'Anti-dumping: A Growing Problem in International Trade', 683–700.

159 Zheng, 'Reforming Trade Remedies', 151.

160 Howse and Trebilcock, *The Regulation of International Trade*, 282.

161 Ibid.

162 Bernard Hoekman, *Competition Policy and the Global Trading System: A Developing-Country Perspective* (The World Bank, 1999), 4.

163 Matsushita et al., *The World Trade Organization*, 406.

164 Owais Hasan Khan, 'Interface between Antidumping and Competition Law: A Critical Analysis', *Interface* 123 (2016), 133.

laws is the sanctions. The investigating authorities may collect anti-dumping duties if dumping is found under the ADA. Under the US antitrust law, however, the sanctions are criminal fines and imprisonment. EU competition law imposes fines based on annual sales. With predatory dumping, it is hard for any jurisdiction to enforce criminal sanctions against exporters in another country. Only the importer operating in the domestic market could be sentenced, but this would not avoid the threat of monopoly. Also, in many competition cases, offenders are well-known companies with recognised brands. The subjects are service suppliers such as banks, airlines or software companies. Therefore, in the case of an investigation, these firms try to cooperate with the relevant authorities to protect their reputation. However, in the case of predatory dumping, the reputation of exporters is low. Within all anti-dumping measures in force, the top three sectors are base metals, chemicals and plastics, respectively.[165] Compared to reputable brands, these exporters would not need to comply with anti-dumping laws or even competition laws. When anti-dumping measures are enforced, these exporters may find circumventing methods to continue to predate. As an alternative, they may lower the prices more than the anti-dumping measure so that the consumer price would remain around the same levels. Also, there are more efficient ways of gaining monopoly power in a foreign market, such as mergers and acquisitions.[166] Within this context, competition laws would not avoid predatory dumping.

Another major problem with replacing anti-dumping laws with competition laws is the lack of universal competition law. Attempts to regulate competition law internationally failed in the 2003 WTO ministerial meeting in Cancun.[167] Despite some efforts by the EU for an agreement on competition law, the negotiations were blocked. Therefore, members enforce their competition laws, which raise a challenging issue on its extraterritorial enforcement. As stated in the OECD report:

> [c]oncerning coverage, competition policies control only practices over which jurisdiction can be enforced and which affect the domestic economy. They do not address practices of domestic enterprises which have

[165] Anti-dumping Measures by Sector, WTO, accessed 17 July 2023, www.wto.org/english/tratop_e/adp_e/adp_e.htm.
[166] William A. Kerr, 'Dumping-One of Those Economic Myths', *Estey Centre J. Int'l L. Trade Pol'y* 2, no. 2 (2001), 217.
[167] Williams, *Competition Policy and Law in China, Hong Kong and Taiwan*, 7.

> effects only in other countries, they cannot easily tackle restraints affecting the domestic economy which occur abroad, and jurisdictions may clash over the behaviour of multinational firms. Moreover, there is considerable uncertainty about the proper competition-policy means to achieve overall efficiency. Over the years, anti-trust practices have shifted away from intervention towards 'rules of reason' based policies. It is now considered appropriate, in some circumstances, to allow many forms of collaboration, other than price collusion, output, allocation and market sharing, because they reduce transaction costs, strengthen competition and improve efficiency.[168]

Neither the extraterritorial application nor a multilateral agreement appears feasible. Instead, a non-binding multilateral agreement or bilateral agreements would be more practical as in the case of the US–EU, US–Japan or US–Canada agreements.[169] The bilateral competition agreements cover notification and information exchange requirements, unlike anti-dumping laws.[170] Even some new-generation agreements include harmonisation of competition laws whereas, in the case of anti-dumping laws, there is no such cooperation between countries.[171]

In this context, replacing anti-dumping laws with competition laws does not seem possible for now. It should be noted that without anti-dumping measures, global trade liberalisation would not succeed. However, because of the political disagreement between developed and developing countries (plus Japan), anti-dumping laws are not likely to be abolished, replaced or even revised substantively. There have been unsuccessful attempts to revise the ADA. Commentators have nonetheless argued that enhancing transparency and the limitation of discretion should be a priority.[172]

In its current form, anti-dumping measures are used without giving exporters enough opportunities to defend themselves. Procedural justice supports the equality of substantive laws by improving accuracy, cost and participation. Lawrence notes that:

[168] Trade and Competition: Frictions after the Uruguay Round, OECD Economics Department Working Papers No. 165 (1996), 8, accessed 17 July 2023, www.oecd-library.org/docserver/448346818265.pdf?expires=1614743590&id=id&accname=guest&checksum=09E0B528B657F096315B9466E2760DE4.

[169] Mitsuo Matsushita, 'Basic Principles of the WTO and the Role of Competition Policy', *Wash. U. Global Stud. L. Rev.* 3 (2004), 384.

[170] Taylor D. Martyn, *International Competition Law: A New Dimension for the WTO?* (Cambridge University Press, 2006), 116.

[171] Ibid., 117.

[172] Chaisse and Chakraborty, 'Normative Obsolescence of the WTO'.

> procedural justice is deeply entwined with the old and powerful idea that a process that guarantees rights of meaningful participation is an essential prerequisite for the legitimate authority of action-guiding legal norms. Meaningful participation requires notice and opportunity to be heard, and it requires a reasonable balance between cost and accuracy.[173]

Procedural justice requires the participation of the relevant parties, which completes substantive legal norms. If the rules on anti-dumping procedures are standardised, then members can monitor investigations more easily. The same applies to exporters because defending a case in different jurisdictions would be less costly and more transparent. In this sense, procedural justice would reduce the tension between WTO members.

This book holds the view that investigation procedures play a significant role in terms of the final duty. The procedural effects cause many of the problems debated above. Therefore, improvements in procedural justice of anti-dumping laws would eliminate concerns. Under international law, procedural justice is traditionally applied to international tribunals.[174] The due process of the WTO DSM is also discussed as WTO has regulated the procedures of the panel and Appellate Body proceedings under the DSU.[175] However, this book is unique in proposing the application of procedural justice to anti-dumping investigations. Procedural justice is also easier to agree on compared to the substantial reform proposals during WTO negotiations. Therefore, before fairness or a public interest test, procedural justice needs to be secured to avoid the misuse of anti-dumping laws.

2.5 Conclusion

The GATT was structured from the perspective of free trade. After the Second World War, liberalisation was the primary concern, with the goal of reaching a better level of global welfare. The WTO was designed to improve global welfare through liberalisation and trade. The concept of the level playing field was used to give each member an equal chance to gain from trade. Besides, as developing and least developed countries

173 Lawrence B. Solum, 'Procedural Justice', *S. Cal. L. Rev.* 78 (2004), 183.

174 Gates Garrity-Rokous and Raymond H. Brescia. 'Procedural Justice and International Human Rights: Towards a Procedural Jurisprudence for Human Rights Tribunals', *Yale J. Int'l L.* 18 (1993), 559.

175 Chilton and Davis, 'Equality, Procedural Justice, and the World Trade Organization', 277.

have benefited from preferential treatment, developed countries needed safety valves for their domestic industries.

In this sense, anti-dumping is a necessary evil in the WTO framework. It is the top issue brought before the WTO DSM and has been long-debated in the NGR. As both developed and developing economies commonly use this tool, it is not realistic to abolish anti-dumping or completely replace it with competition law. Within this context, anti-dumping law has a balancing role in the international trade framework. It functions as an unshaped keystone in the WTO structure. The problem with the negotiations is that substantial and procedural rules are discussed together. It would be better to start with procedural justice where there is more chance for consensus, as it would be beneficial to all members. Then, substantial matters could be discussed with the long term in mind.

Turning from the political perspective to anti-dumping investigation procedures, the main argument of this research is that there are hidden motives behind the strict rules applied by investigating authorities. The process may be triggered by the subsidy granted to an exporter by a government. Then, with or without subsidy, the exporting company pursues predation in foreign markets. There may be other reasons for exporting at a lower price, but this book assumes that the main goal of predating exporters is to push domestic manufacturers out of the market and benefit a dominant position. Empirical evidence suggests that real predation rarely exists. Yet, domestic industry seeks protection in any case. In most instances, the local industries lobbying for production are ineffective and not competitive. The government of the importing country generally acts in accordance with the interests of local industries. Thus, anti-dumping measures are used widely as they are allowed under the ADA.

The actual rationale behind anti-dumping measures is balancing unfair trade. Dumping is claimed to be unfair because it harms competition. Dumping has a direct effect on domestic industries and an indirect effect on consumer welfare. Anti-dumping measures should be applied to protect the competition, not just domestic producers. Competition aims to protect consumer welfare, but the perspective of championing consumer welfare is limited in the literature. However, this needs to be brought to the forefront of policymakers' decisions.

There is currently no binding rule for the investigating authorities to consider regarding the concept of consumer welfare. Article 6.12 of the ADA only states that industrial users or consumer organisations are able to submit their opinions.[176] As mentioned, only a few members, such as the EU and Canada, have regulated public interest as a condition in their domestic anti-dumping regulations. Because domestic industries are better organised compared to consumer groups, politicians and government officials tend to stand by domestic producers and overprotect them by using gaps in the ADA. The procedural rules create an opportunity for investigating authorities to overuse anti-dumping measures as tools for excessive protectionism.

Given the political realities of the WTO framework, anti-dumping laws cannot be abolished entirely. The arguments for anti-dumping laws are not totally convincing, and the arguments against have stronger economic, fairness and political aspects. However, the solution lies in the determination of a justifiable level of anti-dumping laws.

This book offers improvements via procedural justice as a remedy. Procedural justice limits the discretion of investigating authorities and secures transparency, which would also allow standard procedures in different jurisdictions and guarantee improved opportunities for companies to defend themselves. Greater participation in anti-dumping procedures would enhance the principles of fairness and reduce the political tension between members. This would also reduce the number of disputes on anti-dumping before WTO adjudication. If a different approach is chosen, then reciprocity, retaliation, and strict procedural rules will cause increased protectionism. Consequently, the gains from trade may not be achieved with over protectionism.

[176] Article 6.12 states, 'The authorities shall provide opportunities for industrial users of the product under investigation, and for representative consumer organizations in cases where the product is commonly sold at the retail level, to provide information which is relevant to the investigation regarding dumping, injury and causality.'

3

WTO Disputes on Anti-dumping Procedures

3.1 Introduction

The foundations of the DSM evolved under the GATT 1947s Articles XXII and XXIII.[1] GATT 94 affirms the application of these two articles. The DSM as a whole was established with GATT 94 under the Uruguay Round Understanding on Rules and Procedures Governing the DSU.

Before the DSM, country-specific trade issues, such as export quotas on cotton or safeguard measures on textiles, were discussed at the ministerial level. With the establishment of the system, the negotiation agenda was cleared from this kind of trade disputes. Therefore, the DSM contributes to the negotiation process as well as assisting members in solving disputes in an efficient way. Furthermore, some economists argue that the WTO is an 'incomplete contract' and DSB completes the agreement by its rulings.[2]

The legal basis for the DSM is also linked with the 'single undertaking' approach that, in the context of WTO law, defines the rules regulating anti-dumping investigations. This term is explained in the introductory part of the Uruguay Round Final Act as follows:

> While the WTO is not a successor organization to the GATT, contracting parties to the GATT 1947 will automatically become Members of the WTO if they assume the obligations provided for in the agreements on goods, services and intellectual property protection, and submit schedules of concessions covering trade in goods (including both market access and subsidy commitments in the case of agricultural products) and services. This ensures a 'single undertaking' approach to the results of the Uruguay Round, since membership in the WTO will entail accepting all the results of the Round without exception.[3]

[1] World Trade Organization, *A Handbook on the WTO Dispute Settlement System* (Cambridge University Press, 2017).

[2] Bernard M. Hoekman and Michel M. Kostecki, *The Political Economy of the World Trading System: The WTO and Beyond* (Oxford University Press, 2009).

[3] Legal Texts: Uruguay Round Final Act, WTO, accessed 17 July 2023, www.wto.org/english/docs_e/legal_e/ldc2_512.htm.

With the principle of the single undertaking, all members of the WTO are obliged to comply with GATT 94 and its annexes, such as the ADA. The DSM mechanism ensures all members comply with WTO law within the scope of the single undertaking.

This chapter focuses on WTO disputes on anti-dumping. The DSM plays a key role under WTO law. This mechanism is widely credited as the 'jewel in the crown'.[4] However, there are also some problems reducing the overall efficiency of the system. The average duration of a dispute from initiation until the issuance of a Panel and Appellate Body reports takes around three years.[5] Also, the retaliation system is ineffective, so WTO members may choose not to comply with DSM reports. Therefore, scholars have suggested reforms to improve timelines and enforceability.[6]

This chapter demonstrates DSM outcomes in terms of anti-dumping cases. According to WTO statistics, more than 4,412 anti-dumping measures were in force between 1995 and 2022(6).[7] During this period, 142 cases came before the WTO DSM regarding ADA. These two figures place anti-dumping as the first enforced and challenged trade remedy amongst safeguards and countervailing measures. In other words, anti-dumping is the single-most litigated issue under WTO law.[8] Although the Appellate Body and Panels handle the rules on anti-dumping procedures, problems remain. Thus, this chapter demonstrates that DSM is sometimes ineffective. To highlight the deficiencies, the DSM's role in the anti-dumping issue is presented. Then, anti-dumping cases dealing with procedural issues are individually analysed.

3.2 Functioning of the WTO Dispute Settlement Mechanism

There are three major stages in the dispute settlement process, namely consultations, panel and appellate review proceedings, and implementation of rulings.[9] The flowchart below shows the details of the DSM proceedings.

Compared with other mechanisms in international law, the WTO's DSM is the most efficient rule-based system. The compliance rate is

[4] Van den Bossche and Zdouc, *The Law and Policy of the World Trade Organization*, 94.

[5] Kyle Bagwell, Chad P. Bown and Robert W. Staiger, 'Is the WTO Passé?', *J. Econ. Lit.* 54, no. 4 (2016), 1125–1231.

[6] William J. Davey, 'The WTO and Rules-Based Dispute Settlement: Historical Evolution, Operational Success, and Future Challenges', *J. Int'l Econ. L.* 17, no. 3 (2014), 679–700.

[7] 'Anti-dumping', WTO, accessed 30 June 2023, www.wto.org.

[8] Prusa and Vermulst, 'United States – Continued Existence and Application of Zeroing Methodology'. Some examples focusing on the zeroing issue would be DS402, United States – Use of Zeroing in Anti-Dumping Measures Involving Products from Korea, DS350, United States – Continued Existence and Application of Zeroing Methodology or DS322, United States – Measures Relating to Zeroing and Sunset Reviews.

[9] Van den Bossche and Zdouc, *The Law and Policy of the World Trade Organization*.

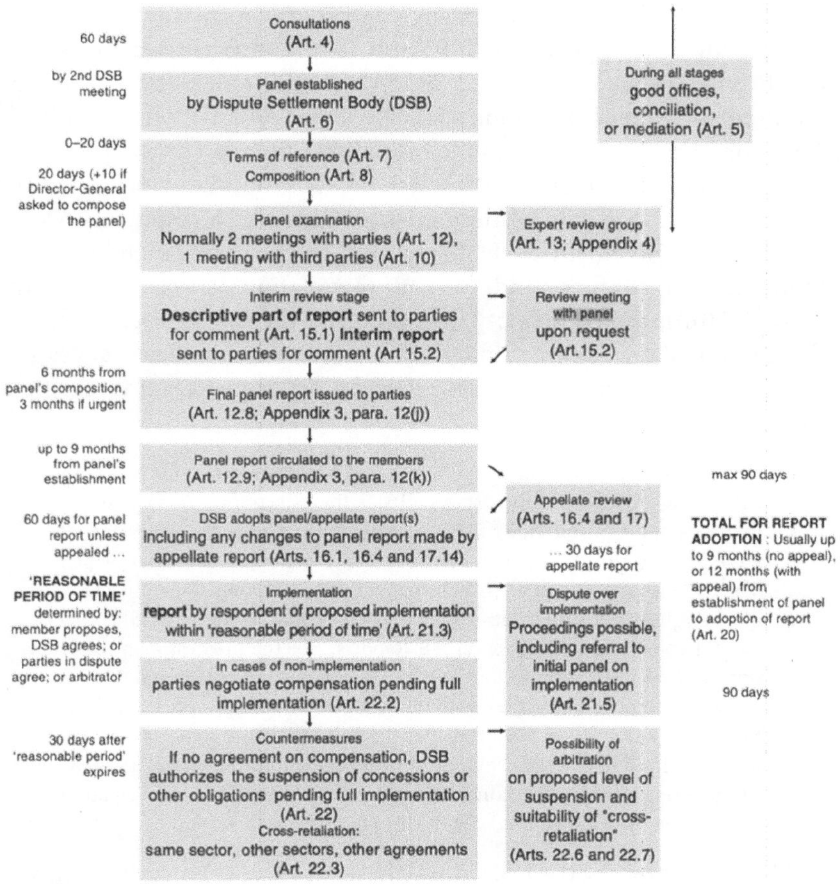

Figure 3.1 Flowchart of DSM proceedings.
Source: World Trade Organization[10]

around 80 per cent, showing that members widely respect the system.[1011] Nonetheless, there are problems with the mechanism. In the context of this study, the first risk is that it takes a long time to settle a dispute and exporters are adversely affected during these procedures. Firms facing procedural barriers primarily need to persuade their government to initiate dispute settlement procedures. As seen from Figure 3.1, the circulation of reports takes nine months without an appeal and twelve

[10] 'The Process – Stages in a Typical WTO Dispute Settlement Case', WTO, accessed 30 June 2023, www.wto.org/english/tratop_e/dispu_e/disp_settlement_cbt_e/c6s1p1_e.htm.

[11] Arie Reich, 'The Effectiveness of the WTO Dispute Settlement System: A Statistical Analysis', in Toshiyuki Kono, Mary Hiscock and Arie Reich (eds.), *Transnational Commercial and Consumer Law* (Springer, 2018), 18.

months with an appeal. However, in reality, the average was twenty-three months for disputes between 1995 and 1999 and twenty-eight months for disputes between 2007 and 2011.[12] In addition, there is a period required for implementation, which is also around fifteen months.[13] Therefore, DSM can be late in the resolution of market access problems. Second, there is no guarantee that the member found in violation of the agreement will conform to the measure. Out of 616 disputes, 36 were about the enforcement of DSM rulings; in 33 cases, members were found not to conform and were thus violating Article 21.5 of the DSU.[14] Third, the complexity and the need for the legal capability of the DSB make it more difficult for developing or least-developed members to challenge measures taken by developed trading partners. According to Reich:

> It should be noted that although developed countries constitute less than 25% of all WTO member states (161), they account for 57% of all Requests for Consultations, 56.7% of all Panel Requests, 58.5% of all Panel Reports, and 62.7% of all AB Reports. Developing countries, which constitute about 53% of all WTO member states, account for only 42.7% of all Requests for Consultations, 43.3% of all Panel Requests, 41.5% of all Panel Reports, and 37.3% of all AB Reports. But the greatest disproportion we find in relation to LDCs. Although they constitute about 22% of all WTO member states, they account for only about 0.17% of all Requests for Consultations, and 0% of all Panel Requests, Panel Reports and AB Reports. In other words, except for one single case where an LDC submitted a request for consultations, we have seen no participation whatsoever of LDCs in the WTO's dispute settlement system.[15]

These figures show the DSM does not serve all WTO members equally. Thus, this part demonstrates the general functioning of the DSM before delving into the details of WTO disputes.

3.2.1 Main Institutions of the Dispute Settlement Mechanism

The DSM consists of the DSB, Panels, the Appellate Body, the WTO Secretariat, arbitrators, experts and other institutions. The first three are explained below, as they are central to dispute settlement procedures.

[12] Ibid.
[13] See Figure 3.1.
[14] Reich, 'The Effectiveness of the WTO Dispute Settlement System'.
[15] Ibid.

3.2.1.1 Dispute Settlement Body (DSB)

Article 2 of the DSU establishes the DSB to administer dispute settlement procedures under the WTO. The Article also entitles the DSB to 'establish panels, adopt panel and Appellate Body reports, maintain surveillance of implementation of rulings and recommendations, and authorise the suspension of concessions and other obligations under the covered agreements'.[16] DSB is political in that the General Council of the WTO acts as the DSB in a separate session with the participation of all members. The General Council generally meets once a month as the DSB.

3.2.1.2 Panels

In cases where the consultations between members do not end positively, parties may ask the DSB to establish Panels. Panels serve as the first-instance tribunals for the settlement of disputes with three or, exceptionally, five ad hoc members.[17] Article 8 of the DSU regulates the composition of panels. According to the Article, panel members should be well-qualified governmental or non-governmental individuals as long as they are independent of the members. All WTO members are entitled to suggest names periodically to the WTO Secretariat. In addition to these names, the Secretariat also lists suitable panellists and appoints them to disputes according to their expertise. Parties to the dispute may reject the panellist if there is a compelling reason. According to Articles 11 and 19, after reviewing the dispute, the Panel makes recommendations to the DSB in case any violation is found. Panels need to interpret WTO agreements. However, if there is a similar case ruled by the Appellate Body, Panels should follow these.[18] The Appellate Body reverses Panel findings when it is against a previous Appellate Body ruling; failing to follow Appellate Body rulings would undermine the consistency and predictability of the DSM.[19]

3.2.1.3 Appellate Body

If members are not satisfied with the outcome of the Panel report, they may appeal the case before the Appellate Body. The Appellate Body is a

[16] Article 2 of the DSU. Full text available at https://www.wto.org/english/docs_e/legal_e/28-dsu_e.htm.

[17] World Trade Organization, *A Handbook on the WTO Dispute Settlement System*.

[18] Hoekman and Kostecki, *The Political Economy of the World Trading System*.

[19] Ibid.

permanent tribunal and the final stage of WTO adjudication.[20] One reason to introduce the Appellate Body was that the DSU changed the previous system of GATT adjudication, where consensus was needed to make the final report binding. This system was changed to a 'negative consensus' method where all members need to reject the Panel report to reverse it.[21] Reverse consensus hastened the adoption of Panel reports, with the Appellate Body as the safety mechanism for members, providing consistency and predictability in WTO adjudication.

The appointment of Appellate Body members is regulated under Article 17.2 of the DSU. The DSB appoints seven members of the Appellate Body for four years, and they can be renewed for another term.[22] The members of the Appellate Body are independent of their governments and any other organisations.[23] The members are generally professors, government officials, lawyers or judges.[24] However, the Appellate Body has not functioned since 2019 due to the blockade of Appellate Body member appointments.

According to Article 17.6, the appeal procedure shall not go beyond the legal matters discussed in the panel proceedings. Thus, factual findings by the panel are outside of the scope of the Appellate Body.[25] The Appellate Body may uphold, reverse or modify the panel rulings. However, in some disputes, it has gone further and made legal analysis.[26] This is because the Appellate Body does not have remand authority. Rather than leaving some aspects of the dispute unclear, the Appellate Body makes a legal analysis.[27] Within thirty days of commencing its circulation, the Appellate Body report becomes binding unless all members reject it.[28]

3.2.2 *Key Features of Dispute Settlement Mechanism*

The DSM serves as a vital element of a well-functioning WTO system. In this context, DSM has several features to provide security and

[20] World Trade Organization, *A Handbook on the WTO Dispute Settlement System.*
[21] Ibid.
[22] Van den Bossche and Zdouc, *The Law and Policy of the World Trade Organization.*
[23] Ibid.
[24] World Trade Organization, *A Handbook on the WTO Dispute Settlement System.*
[25] Van den Bossche and Zdouc, *The Law and Policy of the World Trade Organization.*
[26] Ibid.
[27] Ibid.
[28] Ibid.

predictability to the WTO system. The functions of the system are described here to clarify the scope and limitations of the DSM. Also, some statistical data is presented to demonstrate hot disputes, top complainants, top respondents, etc.

The first feature of DSM is that it ensures the rights of members. Parties may bring a case before the DSM when there is a dispute under the scope of WTO agreements. The design of the DSM encourages mutual agreement; otherwise, the case goes through the Panel and Appellate Body stages. If the respondent is found to be violating particular articles of the WTO agreement, DSM would allow compensation and retaliation as a measure.[29] The judicial system also enables WTO agreements to be interpreted. In addition to Article IX:2 of the WTO Agreement, allowing the Ministerial Conference and the General Council of the WTO to adopt interpretations, Article 3.2 of the DSU also authorises the dispute settlement system to interpret the provisions of the WTO Agreement.[30]

Another feature of the DSM is that specific procedures are set in the DSU to resolve disputes promptly.[31] DSU regulates procedures for consultation, panel and appellate review and adoption of reports. Article 20 of the DSU sets the maximum time for panel and appeal procedures as twelve and sixteen months, respectively. Arbitration, under Article 25, is also an alternative to the typical panel and Appellate Body proceedings which became relevant after the Appellate Body ceased to function.

The existence of the DSM also prohibits members from taking unilateral actions against other members. Otherwise, the gains from the Uruguay Round would be lost. The judicial system allows members to complain about a specific measure by others instead of retaliating unilaterally, which would lead to protectionism. The DSM is also exclusive and compulsory in that members cannot settle WTO law-related disputes under different mechanisms. Similar dispute settlement mechanisms are regulated under mega-FTAs, such as RCEP, so these may be challenged in the near future. RCEP excludes trade remedy related disputes, so these issues will be solved by the WTO's DSM. Also, under the DSU, there are some advantageous provisions to support developing and least-developed countries.[32]

[29] Ibid.

[30] Ibid.

[31] Ibid.

[32] Ibid.

Another notable aspect of WTO's DSM is that the standard of review for Panel and Appellate Body is neither 'de novo' nor 'total deference' under Article 11 of the DSU.[33] Rather, the obligation of the Panels and Appellate Body is to conduct an objective assessment of the factual and legal matters before them. De novo review means that the Panel acts as if it is the Member state and makes its own findings whereas, in total deference, the Panel does not evaluate substantive findings by members but only reviews procedures.[34] The framework of the concept of objective assessment is however questionable.[35] In terms of anti-dumping cases, there is a special standard of review provisions under the ADA. Article 17.6 requires the panel to evaluate the facts of the matter and interpret relevant provisions in accordance with customary rules of public international law.[36] As highlighted by the Appellate Body in *DS184*, these rules are defined under Articles 31 and 32 of the Vienna Convention on the Law of Treaties.[37] Some tests have been developed regarding the application of law to the facts, such as the reasonableness test.[38] Croley and Jackson note that some Panel reports, such as *DS29*, evaluate reasonableness as a very narrow concept in good faith with Article 31 of the Vienna Convention.[39] Article 32 of the Vienna Convention also prohibits interpretations leading to unreasonable results. Therefore, determining the limit of competency of the Panel and Appellate Body is a challenging task that requires careful consideration. This is also a reason why the US blocks the appointment of Appellate Body members and blocks the DSM. The US accuses the Appellate Body of going beyond its authority.

[33] Claus-Dieter Ehlermann and Nicolas Lockhart, 'Standard of Review in WTO Law', *J. Int'l Econ. L.* 7, no. 3 (2004), 491–521.

[34] Matthias Oesch, 'Standards of Review in WTO Panel Proceedings', *J. Int'l Econ. L.* 6, no. 3 (2005), 635–659.

[35] Ehlermann and Lockhart, 'Standard of Review in WTO Law'.

[36] Article 17.6 of the ADA available at www.wto.org/english/docs_e/legal_e/19-adp_02_e.htm#articleXVII, accessed 17 July 2023.

[37] DS184, United States – Anti-Dumping Measures on Certain Hot-Rolled Steel Products from Japan, Vienna Convention is available at https://legal.un.org/ilc/texts/instruments/english/conventions/1_1_1969.pdf, accessed 16 July 2023.

[38] Holger Spamann, 'Standard of Review for World Trade Organization Panels in Trade Remedy Cases: A Critical Analysis', *J. World Trade* 38 (2004), 509.

[39] Steven P. Croley and John H. Jackson, 'WTO Dispute Procedures, Standard of Review, and Deference to National Governments', *Am. J. Int'l L.* 90, no. 2 (1996), 193–213.

As of 2023, the DSM held 616 cases regarding WTO agreements.[40] The top four agreements referred to during these cases are (1) the ADA, (2) Subsidies and Countervailing Measures Agreement, (3) Agriculture and (4) Safeguards.[41] The top complainants are the US (138), EU (109) and Canada (40).[42] The top respondents are the US (168), EU (102) and China (49).[43]

3.3 Disputes on Procedural Matters

This part distinguishes procedural and essential issues and examines disputes on procedural matters. More emphasis is on the cases where the EU and the US are respondent parties in accordance with the study's research questions.

As mentioned, the DSM has processed 616 cases since its foundation. Within these, 142 cases related to provisions of the ADA.[44] These cases are analysed in this part. Before the analysis, one could question the scope of procedural matters in anti-dumping investigations. This question does not have a clear-cut answer. In Black's Law Dictionary, the word 'procedure' is defined as '1. A specific method or course of action. 2. The Judicial rule or manner for carrying on a civil lawsuit or criminal prosecution'.[45] In terms of the legal framework, procedural and substantive law are defined as follows, respectively: 'The rules that prescribe the steps for having a right or duty judicially enforced, as opposed to the law that defines the specific rights or duties themselves'[46] and '[t]he part of the law that creates, defines, and regulates the rights, duties, and powers of parties'.[47] Therefore, procedural issues on anti-dumping cover issues regarding the investigation methods. However, a broad interpretation of the law would find no difference in substantive and procedural issues as they all affect the essence and the outcome:

[40] Chronological List of Disputes Cases, available at www.wto.org/english/tratop_e/dispu_e/dispu_status_e.htm, accessed 16 July 2023.
[41] Disputes by Agreement, WTO, available at www.wto.org/english/tratop_e/dispu_e/dispu_agreements_index_e.htm, accessed 16 July 2023.
[42] Disputes by Member, available at www.wto.org/english/tratop_e/dispu_e/dispu_by_country_e.htm, accessed 16 July 2023.
[43] Ibid.
[44] Disputes by Agreement, WTO.
[45] Garner, *Black's Law Dictionary*, 1221.
[46] Ibid.
[47] Ibid., 1443.

> The distinction between substance and procedure might be understood as purely nominal. A nominalist theory of procedure would hold that a given legal rule is procedural if and only if we call it 'procedural.' If it is the case that the two sets of legal rules (substance and procedure) are nothing more than names given to arbitrary collections, then it should follow that there can be no adequate theory of procedural justice.[48]

It is not possible to distinguish between procedural and substantive issues precisely, but it is a necessity for an in-depth legal analysis. The ADA consists of procedural and substantive rules, but some of the areas are left to member states to regulate, and the procedural rules are easy to use against exporters to discourage cooperation. Also, procedural rules are underestimated, so this study attempts to demonstrate the overall effect of procedural practices. In this context, the study tries to classify matters related to anti-dumping investigations into two groups: procedural and substantive. Substantive issues associated with anti-dumping investigations are: dumped price, injury analysis, causation analysis, representation of the domestic industry, good cause, like product, and the evidence to justify initiation. On the other hand, procedural rules cover calculation methods (zeroing), transparency, public notice/notification, hearing, submission of evidence and rebuttals, access to non-confidential files, selection of investigated parties (sampling), missing documents in the non-confidential file, absence of non-confidential summary, newcomer, translation and standard of review.

Procedural and substantive matters are discussed in the Panel and Appellate Body reports, and these reports together create a vast volume of information. Within the context of this study, a brief content analysis has been applied to determine some trends and patterns in these documents.[49] Content analysis is a systematic, replicable method to analyse long texts.[50] The dataset to be reviewed consists of documents related to 142 cases on anti-dumping measures. The reports range from 90 to 500 pages excluding the annexes, which include third-party submissions, responses of parties and communications. Some of the cases were terminated by a mutually agreed solution without a report.[51] The content

48 Solum, 'Procedural Justice', 181.

49 Steve Stemler, 'An Overview of Content Analysis', *Pract. Assess. Res. Eval.* 7, no. 17 (2001), 137–146.

50 Ibid.

51 DS479, DS404, DS344, DS313, DS281, etc.

analysis covers almost 600 documents where a word frequency query has been conducted.[52] The result of the query brings some suggestions:

- The US and EU are the top two WTO members in terms of word count within these documents, China follows these two.
- Inconsistency is more frequent than consistency.
- The word 'transparency' has been mentioned so rarely in the documents that it does not appear in the word frequency table.
- The frequency of terms such as confidential, notice, due process, questionnaire or extension is relatively lower than terms such as facts available, submission, determination, agreement, article or evidence.
- Apart from zeroing, other procedural issues are not mentioned frequently.

The context analysis shows that this study is correct in choosing the US, EU and China as focus countries. Also, the query result supports the view that procedural issues regarding investigations are underestimated. In this context, procedural issues regarding anti-dumping investigations are examined below.

3.3.1 Calculation Methods

The calculation of anti-dumping duty relies on calculation of the dumping margin. Article 9.3 states: 'The amount of the anti-dumping duty shall not exceed the margin of dumping as established under Article 2.' However, there is no single calculation methodology to be applied by all members. The ADA allows members to adopt different methodologies while calculating the dumping margin.[53] To apply anti-dumping measures, investigating authorities must calculate the dumping margin, export price, normal value and adjustments. The formula of dumping margin is:

$$\text{Dumping Margin} = \text{Normal Value} - \text{Export Price}$$

To calculate the amount of anti-dumping duties to adopt, the following formula should be applied:[54]

52 For the query, NVivo software has been used.

53 Judith Czako, Johann Human and Jorge Miranda, *A Handbook on Anti-dumping Investigations* (Cambridge University Press, 2003), 97.

54 Gennady G. Mokrov, Raisa V. Kamanina, Valentina V. Pavlova, Katerina V. Isaeva and Leonid D. Bashkatov, 'Antidumping Investigation: Calculation of the Dumping Margin', *Indian J. Sci. Technol.* 9, no. 42 (2016), 7.

$$\text{Dumping Margin} = \frac{(\text{Normal Value} - \text{Export Price}) \times 100}{\text{CIF Value}}$$

The calculation method for the above formula changes the result of the adopted anti-dumping duty. Article 2.4.2 of the ADA[55] enables three different methodologies for calculating the normal value and export price: weighted average to weighted average (W–W), transaction to transaction (T–T), and exceptionally weighted average normal value to individual export transactions (W–T).[56] Regarding how to compare the normal value and export price, the third sentence of Article 2.4 provides five criteria to take into consideration: sale, taxation, levels of trade, quantities and physical characteristics.[57] The Panel in DS179 states:

> Nor does Article 2.3 itself contain any guidance regarding the methodology to be employed in order to construct the export price. Rather, the only rules governing the methodology for construction of an export price are set forth in Article 2.4 of the AD Agreement.[58]

While providing a general framework, ADA does not provide specific and detailed guidelines for the calculation of dumping margin or the

55 Article 2.4.2 reads

> Subject to the provisions governing fair comparison in paragraph 4, the existence of margins of dumping during the investigation phase shall normally be established on the basis of a comparison of a weighted average normal value with a weighted average of prices of all comparable export transactions or by a comparison of normal value and export prices on a transaction-to-transaction basis. A normal value established on a weighted average basis may be compared to prices of individual export transactions if the authorities find a pattern of export prices which differ significantly among different purchasers, regions or time periods, and if an explanation is provided as to why such differences cannot be taken into account appropriately by the use of a weighted average-to-weighted average or transaction-to-transaction comparison.

56 For the details of these calculation methods see Edwin Vermulst and Daniel Ikenson, 'Zeroing under the WTO Anti-Dumping Agreement: Where Do We Stand?', *Glob. Trade Cust. J.* 2, no. 6 (2007), 232.

57 ADA Article 2.4, third sentence is as follows: 'Due allowance shall be made in each case, on its merits, for differences which affect price comparability, including differences in conditions and terms of sale, taxation, levels of trade, quantities, physical characteristics, and any other differences which are also demonstrated to affect price comparability.'

58 DS179, United States – Anti-dumping Measures on Stainless Steel Plate in Coils and Stainless Steel Sheet and Strip from Korea, Report of the Panel, p. 34.

injury margin,[59] leaving investigating authorities with considerable discretion. Similarly, in *DS219*, the Panel states:

> An investigating authority must act in an unbiased, even-handed manner and must not exercise its discretion in an arbitrary manner. This obligation also applies where an investigating authority confronts practical difficulties and time constraints. We do not find, in Article 2.4, or in any other relevant provision in the Agreement, any specific rules governing the methodology to be applied by an investigating authority in calculating adjustments. In the absence of any precise textual guidance in the Agreement concerning how adjustments are to be calculated, and in the absence of any textual prohibition on the use of any particular methodology adopted by an investigating authority with a view to ensuring a fair comparison, we consider that an unbiased and objective authority could have applied this methodology applied by the European Communities and calculated this adjustment on the basis of the actual data in the record of this investigation.[60]

In this context, there is only a general framework provided by the ADA regarding the comparison of prices. As seen in the Panel report above, it is hard to prove that the investigating authority is unfair in comparing the normal value and export prices. One method used in the transaction-to-transaction and weighted average-to-export transaction is highly controversial. In the case of zeroing, sales with negative dumping margins are omitted so that only dumped transactions are calculated. Zeroing is a calculation method that generally leads to a higher dumping margin.[61] Generally, an anti-dumping investigation deals with one or more years as the investigation period and, during this period, some of the transactions may not be subject to dumping. Usually, the average of these transactions should be calculated to find the dumping margin for a specific exporter. However, in the zeroing method, the investigating authority omits transactions without dumping and only calculates the dumped transactions, thus reaching a higher dumping margin. For instance, if there are ten export transactions where the exporter sells goods below the home market price in five of these shipments, and if the

[59] Training Module on the WTO Agreement on Anti-Dumping, UNCTAD, available at https://unctad.org/system/files/official-document/ditctncd20046_en.pdf, accessed 16 July 2023.

[60] DS219, European Communities – Anti-Dumping Duties on Malleable Cast Iron Tube or Pipe Fittings from Brazil, Panel Report, Appellate Body Report, WT/DS219/R, p. 55.

[61] Yilmazcan, 'The Role of Anti-Dumping in the US–China Trade War', 16.

average of those ten shipments are taken into consideration, then the final anti-dumping measure will be lower.[62] However, with the zeroing methodology, only the five dumped transactions are considered to find the average dumping margin; consequently, this method results in higher anti-dumping duties.[63,64] The US, in several disputes, was found to be in violation of the ADA due to use of the zeroing methodology. However, zeroing has not been completely abandoned by Commerce. Thus, zeroing remains a controversial issue. Also, the classification of zeroing is problematic. The literature is divided on whether zeroing is a procedural or substantial issue.[65] In any case, zeroing is the 'most single litigated' issue under the DSM.[66]

Regarding cases on zeroing, even the Panels and Appellate Body decisions were contradictory at the beginning of WTO adjudication.[67] The Appellate Body overturned Panel reports; Panels refused Appellate Body decisions; and, after several disputes, the nonconformity of zeroing was accepted in the DSM.[68] The main criticism of zeroing is related to the fair comparison obligation under Article 2.4.2. In *DS141*, for instance, the Appellate Body agrees with the Panel that by zeroing those transactions without dumping, the investigating authority is changing the entirety of the prices and inflating the dumping margin.[69] Simple zeroing, therefore, violates the fair comparison principle under Article 2.4.2 of the ADA. However, investigating authorities find other ways of zeroing that aim to comply with previous reports and still inflate the dumping margins. Zeroing can be applied to three kinds of calculation methods: 'transaction to transaction zeroing, weighted average to weighted average zeroing, or weighted average normal value to individual export price

62 Ibid.
63 Ibid.
64 Yilmazcan, Abdulkadir, 'The Role of Anti-Dumping in the US–China Trade War', China & WTO Rev. 2021, no. 1 (2021), 7–36.
65 Horlick classifies calculation methods as a procedural issue whereas Vermulst calls zeroing as a substantive matter. Horlick, 'Ten Major Problems in the United States', 173; Vermulst, 'Ten Major Problems with the Anti-Dumping Instrument in the European Community', 107.
66 Prusa and Vermulst, 'United States – Continued Existence and Application of Zeroing Methodology'.
67 Petros C. Mavroidis, Patrick A. Messerlin and Jasper M. Wauters, *The Law and Economics of Contingent Protection in the WTO* (Edward Elgar, 2008), 65.
68 Ibid.
69 Vermulst and Ikenson, 'Zeroing under the WTO Anti-Dumping Agreement', 236.

transaction zeroing'.[70] However, the DSM mostly finds any kind of zeroing inconsistent with the ADA. Apart from those simple zeroing methods, there is another type of zeroing called 'model zeroing'. With the model zeroing calculation method, investigating authorities make a model-based comparison for an individual exporter and disregard models without dumping. For instance, an exporter ships five types of products under the same HS code, but the investigating authority determines that some models are not being dumped so these models are disregarded. Thus, the remaining models constitute a base for the dumping margin determination that is higher than the average of all the products together. Regarding model zeroing, the Appellate Body also rejected the view that investigating authorities cannot specifically target model zeroing by focusing only on some models and omitting others.[71] According to the Appellate Body, if negotiators had wanted targeted dumping to be handled separately, they would have drafted the Article accordingly.[72] As there is no specific rule under the Article or the ADA, investigating authorities should take into consideration whole models together for an individual exporter. Otherwise, investigating authorities can identify the model with dumped prices and omit others to determine the dumping margin, which is a violation of the fair comparison principle. In *DS264*, the Appellate Body ruled that zeroing is a violation of the ADA.[73] The legal basis for this ruling is that Article 2.4.2 requires all comparable transactions to be taken into account.[74] Thus, omitting transactions without dumping leads to unfair comparisons and results. By referring to the practice of Commerce of applying zeroing to softwood lumber imports from Canada, the Appellate Body showed that this method inflates the 'all others rate' that is applied to non-cooperating companies. Consequently, the US's zeroing practice was found inconsistent with the ADA.[75]

In *DS219*, Brazil complained that the EU had violated the ADA by practising zeroing while calculating the dumping margin. The Panel

70 Njeri Mwathi, Types of Zeroing Methods in Dumping Margin Calculations, LinkedIn, accessed 17 June 2023, www.linkedin.com/pulse/types-zeroing-methods-dumping-margin-calculations-njeri-mwathi/.

71 Ibid.

72 Ibid.

73 DS264, United States – Final Dumping Determination on Softwood Lumber from Canada.

74 Ibid.

75 Ibid.

found that the EU acted inconsistently with its obligations under Article 2.4.2 ADA.[76]

In *DS294*, the EC complained about US use of the zeroing methodology. The Panel distinguished between simple and model zeroing.[77] According to the Panel, simple zeroing is the standard practice of omitting the transactions without dumping.[78] Model zeroing means comparing weighted average prices on a model-by-model basis and omitting models without a negative dumping margin.[79] The Panel ruled that the US acted inconsistently by applying zeroing in the original investigation and did not decide on model zeroing for judicial economy purposes.[80] The Appellate Body holds its position that model zeroing has already been found to be inconsistent with Article 2.4.2 of the ADA and confirmed that the Panel was right to avoid this argument.[81,82]

In *DS322*, Japan brought the same arguments against Commerce's practice of model zeroing.[83] The Panel found the Commerce's practice of model zeroing inconsistent with the ADA but did not find simple zeroing to be inconsistent. According to the Appellate Body, disregarding models with negative dumping margin results in an unfair comparison since the product as a whole is not evaluated. Thus, model zeroing is inconsistent with the ADA. Furthermore, the Appellate Body reversed the Panel's decision on simple zeroing and found it also inconsistent with a T–T comparison, as all transactions need to be covered to achieve a fair comparison.[84,85]

In *DS464*, Korea challenged the Differential Pricing Methodology (DPM) used by Commerce.[86] This method aims at 'targeted dumping',

[76] DS219, European Communities – Anti-Dumping Duties on Malleable Cast Iron Tube or Pipe Fittings from Brazil, 36.
[77] Yilmazcan, 'The Role of Anti-Dumping in the US–China Trade War', 17.
[78] Ibid.
[79] Vermulst and Ikenson, 'Zeroing under the WTO Anti-Dumping Agreement', 235.
[80] DS294, United States – Laws, Regulations and Methodology for Calculating Dumping Margins (Zeroing), Appellate Body Report.
[81] Ibid.
[82] Yilmazcan, Abdulkadir, 'The Role of Anti-Dumping in the US–China Trade War', China & WTO Rev. 2021, no. 1 (2021), 7–36.
[83] DS322, United States – Measures Relating to Zeroing and Sunset Reviews; Yilmazcan, 'The Role of Anti-Dumping in the US–China Trade War'.
[84] Ibid.
[85] Yilmazcan, Abdulkadir, 'The Role of Anti-Dumping in the US–China Trade War', China & WTO Rev. 2021, no. 1 (2021), 7–36.
[86] DS464, United States – Anti-Dumping and Countervailing Measures on Large Residential Washers from Korea.

which involves different prices for different purchasers, regions or periods. This type of dumping is hard to determine compared to ordinary dumping, so the US applies the W-T calculation together with 'zeroing' to uncover this practice. Korea challenged the calculation method on the basis that not enough evidence was disclosed by the US, demonstrating that Korean export prices differed between purchasers, regions or periods.[87] Furthermore, Korea argued that the US did not explain why other methods identified under Article 2.4.2 of the ADA were not used. The Appellate Body found that the calculation method was inconsistent, although one member of the Appellate Body expressed an opposing view.[88] The Appellate Body ruling is remarkable in the sense that even in the exceptional calculation method, zeroing is not allowed.[89]

In a more recent case, *DS534*, on targeted dumping, the Panel found zeroing permissible.[90] Thus, the zeroing issue became hot again as the Panel did not follow past Appellate Body rulings. However, the problem in practice is that given the US's strategy of blocking new appointments to the Appellate Body, the appeal procedure for this Panel report is fruitless. The Appellate Body is not able to work since new members have not been appointed.[91]

In the Committee on Anti-Dumping Practices meeting held in 2017, the EU expressed its concerns about a US investigation where two EU members constituted only 1 per cent of imports but were still included in the calculation in order to inflate the final anti-dumping measure as a way of targeted dumping.[92] Investigating authorities were unable to calculate dumping margins for each exporter during the anti-dumping investigations. Apart from calculations for cooperating companies, non-cooperating companies or companies excluded from the sampling may be subject to an 'all others rate'. In *DS184*, Japan argued that the US

[87] Ibid.

[88] Ibid.

[89] Kim Kyounghwa and Dukgeun Ahn, 'To Be or Not to Be with Targeted Dumping', *J. Int'l Econ. L.* 21, no. 3 (2018), 597.

[90] DS534, United States – Anti-Dumping Measures Applying Differential Pricing Methodology to Softwood Lumber from Canada, accessed on 16 December 2023, https://docs.wto.org/dol2fe/Pages/FE_Search/FE_S_S009-DP.aspx?language=E&CatalogueIdList=237961&CurrentCatalogueIdIndex=0&FullTextHash=371857150&HasEnglishRecord=True&HasFrenchRecord=True&HasSpanishRecord=True.

[91] Yilmazcan, Abdulkadir, 'The Role of Anti-Dumping in the US–China Trade War', China & WTO Rev. 2021, no. 1 (2021), 7–36.

[92] Minutes of the Regular Meeting, The Committee of Anti-dumping Practices, 2017, WTO document G/ADP/M/52.

inflated the 'all others rate', which is inconsistent with Article 9.4 of the ADA prohibiting the 'all others rate' exceeding the weighted average margin of selected exporters or constructed normal values. The US regulation allows Commerce to use any reasonable method to calculate the 'all others rate' by including margins based on the facts available. The Panel agrees with Japan that Commerce inflated dumping margins while calculating the 'all others rate'.[93] The EU, as a third party, states that it is not possible to calculate the 'all others rate' without relying on the facts available, and Article 9.4 does not prohibit the calculation based partially on facts available.[94] The Appellate Body mentions that Article 9.4 identifies the ceiling for those exporters who were not asked to cooperate, thus finding that the US regulation exceeds the limit.[95] In this context, calculating the 'all others rate' based on the facts available is found to be inconsistent by the Appellate Body.

In *DS414*, for instance, the Panel ruled that the facts available mechanism is designed for completing the investigation on time. The Panel states:

> In our view, the purpose of the facts available mechanism is not to punish non-cooperation by interested parties. As explained by the Appellate Body, the purpose of Article 12.7 of the SCM Agreement is rather to 'ensure that the failure of an interested party to provide necessary information does not hinder an agency's investigation,' in the sense that 'the provision permits the use of facts on record solely for the purpose of replacing information that may be missing'.[96]

Updegraff focuses on Commerce's use of facts available and adverse facts available. While interpreting the ruling by the WTO adjudication such as the *DS414*, Updegraff argues that even if the facts available is claimed not to be a punitive mechanism, 'adverse facts available' used by the Commerce naturally results in punitive outcomes.[97] Adverse facts available is a customised policy that has more negative outcomes than facts available.[98] The method has been criticised for resulting in

93 DS184, United States – Anti-Dumping Measures on Certain Hot-Rolled Steel Products from Japan, Panel Report.

94 Ibid.

95 Ibid.

96 Report of the Panel, China – Countervailing and Anti-Dumping Duties on Grain Oriented Flat-Rolled Electrical Steel from the United States, WT/DS414/R, 2014, 74.

97 Ragan Updegraff, 'Striking a Balance between Necessity and Fairness: The Use of Adverse Facts Available in Dumping and Subsidies Investigations', *Geo. J. Int'l L.* 49 (2017), 789.

98 Chad P. Bown, Bernard Hoekman and Caglar Ozden, 'The Pattern of US Antidumping: The Path from Initial Filing to WTO Dispute Settlement', *World Trade Rev.* 2, no. 3 (2003), 362.

predetermined and inflated dumping margins. Thus, the facts available appears to be pressuring firms to cooperate, but if strict procedural rules are enforced, investigating authorities benefit from facts available and conclude higher dumping margins. Updegraff also takes this view and calls for a revision of the ADA to limit the use of facts available and adverse facts available.[99] Moore conducts an empirical analysis of the use of facts available and compares the pre-WTO era to the post-WTO era. Moore concludes that both the usage of facts available and dumping margins were increased in the post-WTO era.[100]

In *DS471*, China also challenged the application of a single rate against Chinese firms.[101] China argued that the application of a single rate presumption for all non-market entities is inconsistent with Articles 6.10 and 9.2 of the ADA.[102] The Panel agreed with China based on previous Appellate Body reports interpreting the above-mentioned articles as obliging investigating authorities to calculate dumping margins individually.[103] In terms of the non-market economy situation, exporters should have the chance to prove that they are not operating under government control.

DS471 is also a remarkable case in the sense that when the Panel was discussing the methodologies used, the US shifted from targeted dumping to another methodology so that the US claimed that the measure was in conformity when the report was published.[104] Also, the Appellate Body's ruling on allowing investigating authorities to calculate average prices to reach a pattern and not requiring investigating authorities to disclose explanations for the pattern may result in new targeted dumping disputes.[105] The calculation methodology used by the US investigating authorities is biased in that the actual prices are ignored in almost all cases.[106]

99 Updegraff, 'Striking a Balance between Necessity and Fairness', 788.

100 Michael O. Moore, 'US Facts – Available Antidumping Decisions: An Empirical Analysis', *Eur. J. Pol. Econ.* 22, no. 3 (2006), 648.

101 DS471, United States – Certain Methodologies and Their Application to Anti-Dumping Proceedings Involving China, Panel Report, accessed 15 July 2023, www.wto.org/english/tratop_e/dispu_e/cases_e/ds471_e.htm, 120.

102 Ibid.

103 Ibid.

104 Thomas J. Prusa and Edwin A. Vermulst, 'United States – Certain Methodologies and Their Application to Anti-Dumping Proceedings Involving China: Nails in the Coffin of Unfair Dumping Margin Calculation Methodologies', *World Trade Rev.* 18, no. 2 (2019), 2.

105 Ibid.

106 Ibid.

In *DS179*, Korea argues that Article 2.4 requires a fair comparison of export price and normal value. In that regard, the US practice of double-conversion of local sales from USD to Korean Won and back to USD again creates an inflated normal value. Thus, the US practice of double-conversion of local sales inflates the dumping margin and unfairly penalises Korean exporters. Consequently, the Panel found the US practice to be inconsistent with Article 2.4 of the ADA.[107]

3.3.2 Transparency

If the parties subject to investigation are not capable of accessing relevant evidence, they cannot defend their interests. Transparency is a general concept, and specific matters related to transparency are handled separately in the following parts.

EU anti-dumping procedures have been criticised for non-transparency in several ways, such as complaints being kept confidential until the initiation of the investigation, non-confidential versions of responses to questionnaires not including enough information, the Commission's investigation guidelines are not publicly available, calculation formulas are treated as confidential, verification reports are not provided to parties, hearings are *ex parte*, etc.[108]

The US system allows access to more information. For instance, importers and exporters have a chance to see the complaint before initiation and to comment on the arguments. Also, the parties receive the non-confidential submissions and access the full file upon request. While no party can access confidential information in the EU system, the US investigating authorities allow parties' lawyers to access the information. However, there is a criminal liability while using this information, such as leaking documents to unauthorised parties.[109] The US authorities also allow access to verification reports, unlike the EU. So, compared to the EU, the US system is relatively more transparent. However, there are also complaints against the US practice.

In *DS179*, Korea complains about US anti-dumping measures at the first submission by stating:

[107] DS179, United States – Anti-Dumping Measures on Stainless Steel Plate in Coils and Stainless Steel Sheet and Strip from Korea.

[108] Vermulst, 'The 10 Major Problems with the Anti-dumping Instrument in the European Community', 105–113.

[109] Administrative Protective Order, accessed 16 July, 2023, www.usitc.gov/secretary/apo_forms_and_redbook.htm.

> Because anti-dumping laws clearly fall within the scope of Article X:1, their administration must comport with the 'minimum standards' of fairness established by Article X:3(a). The requirements of procedural fairness in anti-dumping investigations are further amplified by the explicit requirements of the Anti-Dumping Agreement. Thus, Articles 6.1, 6.2, and 6.9 of the Anti-Dumping Agreement establish a broad requirement that the administering authorities inform the parties of the 'essential facts' of the case in a manner that allows them a 'full' and 'ample opportunity' to defend their interests. In the same vein, Article 12.2 of the Anti-Dumping Agreement requires publication of 'the findings and conclusions reached on all issues of fact and law considered material by the investigating authorities' in both preliminary and final determinations, including: (1) 'a full explanation of the reasons for the methodology used in the establishment and comparison of the export price and the normal value', (2) 'all relevant information on the matters of fact and law and reasons which have led to the imposition of final measures', and (3) 'the reasons for the acceptance or rejection of relevant arguments or claims made by the exporters and importers'.[110]

Korea, therefore, complains about the non-disclosure of a calculation methodology that violates the right to defend. Also, as highlighted by Korea, access to the essential facts constitutes a requirement for procedural justice. However, the Panel found that the US did not act inconsistently with Article 12.2 of the ADA, which requires sufficiently detailed findings to be sent to parties regarding determinations.[111]

Criticisms about non-transparency are not only levelled at the US or EU. China also does not allow access to confidential information; therefore, the Chinese anti-dumping system has been criticised for being non-transparent.[112] Furthermore, the calculation method used by Chinese officials is almost impossible to determine from the files disclosed. MOFCOM's anti-dumping manual is not accessible, nor is the decision-making process.[113] In *DS460*, the US, as a third party, contends that Article 6.5 of the ADA does not include any exception, including the WTO's DSM proceedings.[114] Thus, according to this view, the information submitted to the investigating authorities as confidential cannot

110 DS179, United States – Anti-Dumping Measures on Stainless Steel Plate in Coils and Stainless Steel Sheet and Strip from Korea.

111 Ibid.

112 Tian Yu, 'The 10 Major Problems with the Anti-dumping Instrument in the People's Republic of China', *J. World Trade* 39, no. 1 (2005), 97–103.

113 Ibid.

114 DS460, China – Measures Imposing Anti-Dumping Duties on High-Performance Stainless Steel Seamless Tubes ('Hp-Ssst') from the European Union, Report of Panel.

even be submitted to the Panel or Appellate Body without the consent of the owner of that information. However, the problem with Article 6.5 is its vagueness.[115] The determination of naturally confidential information differs from member to member. Thus, the scope of the definition can be arbitrarily used by the investigating authorities to expand the amount of classified information. In *DS425*, the EU claims that China violated Article 6.9 of the ADA by not providing essential facts for consideration.[116] In its third-party submission, Norway highlights the correlation between transparency, procedural justice and fairness.

> In Norway's view, the mere structure of Article 6.5.1 indicates that the statement needs to be public. Norway reiterates the serious effects anti-dumping investigations may have, and the corresponding need to ensure that the investigation follows certain rules of procedural justice and fairness. When information is kept confidential, it is thus of great importance to ensure that this is done for the right reasons. If the investigating authority is not required to make public statements containing the reasons why summarisation of confidential information is not possible, the potential for abuse would be significant.[117]

The lack of information creates a barrier to determining the methodology used to calculate the dumping margin.[118] The Panel refers to a previous Appellate Body report and notes that investigating authorities are not obliged to disclose all facts but only essential facts. The Panel

[115] Article 6.5 reads:

> Any information which is by nature confidential (for example, because its disclosure would be of significant competitive advantage to a competitor or because its disclosure would have a significantly adverse effect upon a person supplying the information or upon a person from whom that person acquired the information), or which is provided on a confidential basis by parties to an investigation shall, upon good cause shown, be treated as such by the authorities. Such information shall not be disclosed without specific permission of the party submitting it.
>
> (www.wto.org/english/docs_e/legal_e/19-adp_01_e.htm#articleVI, accessed 15 July 2023)

[116] DS425, China – Definitive Anti-Dumping Duties on X-Ray Security Inspection Equipment from the European Union. Article 6.9 reads: 'The authorities shall, before a final determination is made, inform all interested parties of the essential facts under consideration which form the basis for the decision whether to apply definitive measures. Such disclosure should take place in sufficient time for the parties to defend their interests' (www.wto.org/english/docs_e/legal_e/19-adp_01_e.htm#articleVI, accessed 15 July 2023).

[117] Ibid., Report of Panel, Addendum.

[118] Ibid.

partly agrees with the EU's claim that MOFCOM should have disclosed the average unit values and price data as the basis for its calculation of the dumping margin.[119]

Practices by other members are also subject to WTO adjudication. In *DS122*, Poland complains about Thailand's practice that:

> a party has no opportunity to properly defend itself if it does not have access to the proof and evidence by which a foreign government proposes to foreclose future sales in its territory. Transparency is lost, and respondents appropriately believe that conclusions were pre-ordained, regardless of actual evidence.[120]

However, the Panel did not evaluate the arguments under Article 6 due to unclarity. Still, the Panel finds that Article 3.1[121] of the ADA requires investigating authorities to make the documents available to the relevant parties and the evidence should be discernible from these.[122] The Appellate Body reversed the Panel's finding because Article 3.1 allows investigating authorities to make an injury determination based on all relevant information rather than disclosed information.[123] In DS189, the Panel decides:

> We are aware that, for the purpose of transparency, Article 6.5.1 obliges an authority to require the parties providing confidential information to furnish non-confidential summaries which shall be in sufficient detail to permit a reasonable understanding of the substance of the information submitted in confidence. We consider that this is an important element of the AD Agreement which reflects the balance struck by the Agreement between the need to protect the confidentiality of certain information, on the one hand, and the need to ensure that all parties have a full opportunity to defend their interests, on the other. However, we see nothing in Article 6.5.1, nor elsewhere in Article 6.5, that authorizes a Member to disregard

[119] Ibid., 111.

[120] DS122, Panel Report, WT/DS122/R.

[121] Article 3.1 states,

> A determination of injury for purposes of Article VI of GATT 1994 shall be based on positive evidence and involve an objective examination of both *(a)* the volume of the dumped imports and the effect of the dumped imports on prices in the domestic market for like products, and *(b)* the consequent impact of these imports on domestic producers of such products.

[122] Ibid., para 7.143.

[123] DS122, Appellate Body Report, WT/DS122/AB/R, 35.

> confidential information solely on the basis that the nonconfidential summary of that information contains insufficient detail to permit authorities to calculate normal value, export price and the margin of dumping.[124]

The Panel also adds that while transparency is ensured, investigating authorities may rely on confidential information for the final determination provided that parties receive non-confidential summaries to defend their interests.[125] Therefore, the general interpretation of the transparency obligation under the ADA is not unlimited access to information by all parties. Instead, it is balanced transparency to allow interested parties to defend themselves while protecting the rights of the owners of the information. Otherwise, commercially confidential information would be disclosed to all parties. The investigating authorities need to balance these interests by taking procedural justice into account, which is a challenging task.

Another issue regarding transparency is the procedures at the DSM. According to Article 13 of the DSU, Panels have the right to seek information regarding the dispute.[126] Fact-finding and confidentiality together may create a dilemma when the relevant member refuses to provide information based on the confidentiality argument.[127] According to the Appellate Body report in *DS70*, if a member refuses to provide information, the matter shall be considered in favour of the other party.[128] On the other hand, the information provided to the DSM shall be accessible unless it contains business confidential information.[129] Business confidential information would cover 'pricing practices, sales volumes, profit margins, utilisation of capacity, cash flow, inventories, wages, and ability to raise capital'.[130] Article 17.7 of the ADA reads as follows:

124 DS189, Argentina – Definitive Anti-Dumping Measures on Carton-Board Imports from Germany and Definitive Anti-Dumping Measures on Imports of Ceramic Tiles from Italy, Panel Report, 174.

125 Ibid.

126 Article 13 of the DSU available at www.wto.org/english/tratop_e/dispu_e/dsu_e.htm#13, accessed 15 July 2023.

127 Olivier Prost, 'Confidentiality Issues under the DSU: Fact-Finding Process versus Confidentiality', in Refus Yerxa and Bruce Wilson (eds.), *Key Issues in WTO Dispute Settlement* (Cambridge University Press, 2005), 190–203.

128 Ibid.

129 Ibid.

130 Graham Cook, 'Confidentiality and Transparency in the WTO's Party-Centric Dispute Settlement System', in J. Huerta-Goldman and Marco Tulio Molina-Tejeda (eds.), *Practical Aspects of WTO Litigation* (Kluwer, 2019), 1–23.

> Confidential information provided to the panel shall not be disclosed without formal authorization from the person, body or authority providing such information. Where such information is requested from the panel but release of such information by the panel is not authorized, a non-confidential summary of the information, authorized by the person, body or authority providing the information, shall be provided.[131]

Therefore, the confidential information submitted to the Panel during an anti-dumping case cannot be disclosed without the formal authorisation of the relevant party. This is another limitation for the relevant parties because the confidential information consists of prices, which is essential information for a fair comparison as required by Article 2.4. It is also notable that the scope of Article 17.7 is limited to the information submitted by a person, body or authority, whereas Article 18.2 covers information submitted by a member.[132] Therefore, after requesting relevant information from the parties, Panels should consider the nature of the information and classify it accordingly. However, as there is no specific guideline on how to balance due process against confidentiality, a dilemma remains with the current legal framework.[133] In this context, improved transparency is an essential need both for investigation procedures and DSM proceedings.

3.3.3 Public Notice/Notification

According to Article 12 of the ADA, the initiation of an anti-dumping investigation should be announced by public notice.[134] The notice should contain at least the following: product involved, name of exporting country, date of initiation, basis on which dumping is alleged, addressing the representation by interested parties, a summary of factors on which the allegation of injury is based, and deadlines for submitting views.[135] If this notice's content lacks essential information or the relevant parties are not notified about the investigation properly, the right to defence is injured.

131 Article 17.7 of the ADA available at www.wto.org/english/docs_e/legal_e/19-adp_02_e.htm#articleXVII, accessed 16 July 2023.

132 DS454, China – Measures Imposing Anti-Dumping Duties on High-Performance Stainless Steel Seamless Tubes ('HP-SSST') from Japan, Report of the Panel.

133 Prost, 'Confidentiality Issues under the DSU', 195.

134 Article 12 Public Notice and Explanation of Determinations.

135 Czako et al., *A Handbook on Anti-dumping Investigations*, 38.

In *DS219*, Brazil argued that the EU did not disclose its findings in the public notice regarding domestic producers' export performance.[136] Brazil mentioned that the public record of investigation does not contain an 'evaluation of productivity; return on investments; cash flow; wages; margin of dumping; and ability to raise capital and that the European Communities' purported evaluation of these factors'.[137] These factors are used to determine the market price, and so constitute a basis for the comparison between importing and exporting markets and the determination of the dumping margin. Consequently, the Panel found the EU to be violating Articles 12 and 12.2 as the injury factors mentioned under Article 3.4 have not been published.

In *DS471*, China claimed that Commerce failed to notify relevant exporters subject to investigation.[138] China also claimed the usage of 'facts available' and 'adverse facts available' violates the ADA as the exporters are willing to submit information. However, Commerce did not attempt to collect information and did not treat the firms individually. The Panel found that in thirty determinations, Commerce has applied the single rate presumption, which is a violation of the ADA.

After collecting evidence and deciding on final determinations, the investigating authorities need to issue another public notification. According to Article 12.2.2 of the ADA, this notification should include at least the following: summary of arguments by parties, and explanations of acceptance or rejection of the arguments.[139] In addition, concerning confidential information, public notices should include a description of the good, the names of the exporters, dumping margins and the methodology used, considerations on injury determination, and an explanation of determinations.[140]

In *DS488*, the public notice of final determinations was questioned. In Korea's submission to the WTO, it was claimed that Commerce violated Article 12.2.2 of the ADA by failing to disclose the reasons for rejecting relevant arguments by Korean exporters and US importers.[141]

136 DS219, European Communities – Anti-Dumping Duties on Malleable Cast Iron Tube or Pipe Fittings from Brazil.

137 Ibid.

138 DS471, United States – Certain Methodologies and Their Application to Anti-Dumping Proceedings Involving China.

139 Czako et al., *A Handbook on Anti-dumping Investigations*, 74.

140 Ibid.

141 DS488, United States – Anti-Dumping Measures on Certain Oil Country Tubular Goods from Korea, Panel Report, accessed 15 July 2023, www.wto.org/english/tratop_e/dispu_e/cases_e/ds488_e.htm.

Korean exporters argued that a Korean exporter subject to investigation is not affiliated with another company.[142] Affiliation affects the dumping margin as two companies are then regarded as a single entity.

3.3.4 Selection of Investigated Parties (Sampling)

Investigating authorities can select a limited number of exporters to calculate the dumping margin based on the footnote to Article 5.4 of the ADA.[143] However, there is no explicit rule stating which companies should be selected. Therefore, the selection of exporters can affect the outcome of the investigation. Companies submit information as being included in the sample group or are treated individually.

Article 5.10[144] of the ADA defines the maximum duration of an anti-dumping investigation. Including too many exporters would cause an infringement of this article. Although Article 6.10 allows the investigating authority to limit the examination, sampling procedures can also be complicated and challenged before the DSM as in *DS337*, where Norway challenged the EU for selecting samples inconsistently.

In this case, 'Norway argues that the EC violated Article 6.10 because it: included only three out of the ten largest exporters and producers in its sample. The sample, therefore, does not account for the "largest percentage of the volume of exports that can reasonably be investigated"'.[145] The Panel also found that the EU acted inconsistently as one of the companies mentioned should have been included in the sample. Also, the rejection of information submitted by companies and the usage of 'facts available' was found to violate the ADA.[146] Another point made by the Panel was that a fixed amount of anti-dumping duty was imposed on

142 Ibid.

143 'In the case of fragmented industries involving an exceptionally large number of producers, authorities may determine support and opposition by using statistically valid sampling techniques', accessed 15 July 2023, www.wto.org/english/docs_e/legal_e/19-adp_01_e.htm#fntext-13.

144 Article 5.10 states, 'Investigations shall, except in special circumstances, be concluded within one year, and in no case more than 18 months, after their initiation.' See Anti-dumping Agreement, WTO, accessed 30 June 2023, www.wto.org/english/res_e/publications_e/ai17_e/anti_dumping_e.htm.

145 DS337, European Communities – Anti-Dumping Measure on Farmed Salmon from Norway, Panel Report, Adopted on 17 November 2007, accessed 30 June 2023, www.wto.org/english/tratop_e/dispu_e/cases_e/ds337_e.htm.

146 Ibid.

non-investigated cooperating companies, which is regarded as a violation.[147]

The EU was also accused of using arbitrary and unfair sampling methods in the *DS141*. According to the EU calculation, 86 per cent of Indian exports were dumped, but India argues that companies in this calculation represent 47 per cent of the companies so the conclusion by the EU investigating authorities creates an inconsistency with the ADA. Japan as a third party submitted the following comment:

> Japan finds support in the Appellate Body Report in US – Hot-Rolled Steel for its argument that the European Communities' position would dilute the requirement established in Article 3.1 that a determination of injury be based on 'positive evidence' and an 'objective examination.' Japan submits that the European Communities' methodology is inconsistent with the requirement that the evidence 'must be of an affirmative, objective and verifiable character, and that it must be credible'. In addition, Japan alleges that by using the data of the sampled producers in a biased and unfair manner, the European Communities failed to comply with the requirement that a determination of injury must involve an objective examination – that is, that the 'examination' process must conform to the dictates of the basic principles of good faith and fundamental fairness.[148]

The EU argues that it is consistent to treat non-cooperating exporters as 'dumped' since there are no specific rules under the ADA on unexamined exporters. Also, the data from examined exporters can be used to determine the dumping margin for unexamined exporters under Article 6.10.[149] This is one issue that requires further clarification. As there are no specific procedural rules, sampling methodology can be arbitrary and non-transparent. The current legal framework creates a risk for exporters that are willing to cooperate but cannot do so due to the sampling methodology. These companies, even if they do not dump, may face the duty applicable to the highest dumping margin, which does not represent the average. Consequently, the Appellate Body reversed the ruling of the Panel and found that the investigating authorities cannot treat all unexamined exporters as dumped and decided that the EU acted inconsistently with Articles 3.1 and 3.2.[150]

147 Ibid.

148 DS141, European Communities – Anti-Dumping Duties on Imports of Cotton-Type Bed Linen from India, Appellate Body Report.

149 Ibid.

150 Ibid.

In *DS471*, China contends that Commerce's sampling method violates Article 9.4 of the ADA.[151] The Article prohibits investigating authorities from applying higher anti-dumping duties than the weighted average of the dumping margin based on the sampling groups. China argued that Commerce assigned a PRC-wide rate based on a fictional entity, meaning that the margin was higher than it would be for separate rate respondents.[152] The Panel did not make any determination due to judicial economy as the Panel found the single rate presumption of the US inconsistent with Articles 6.10 and 9.2 of the ADA.[153] The Appellate Body also did not evaluate China's claim under Article 9.4.

In *DS405*, China objected to the sampling method used by the EU, arguing that any information was provided in terms of (1) the geographical spread of sampled firms; (2) factual data used during the selection of this sample; (3) business models of complainants; (4) the ratio of the sampled firms' sales to the total sales and (5) selection criteria for ten complainants.[154] The EU holds that the information required to determine the sampling methodology is confidential under Article 6.5.[155] However, the Panel found the EU acting inconsistently with 6.5.1 of

[151] Article 9.4 reads

> When the authorities have limited their examination in accordance with the second sentence of paragraph 10 of Article 6, any anti-dumping duty applied to imports from exporters or producers not included in the examination shall not exceed:
>
> (i) the weighted average margin of dumping established with respect to the selected exporters or producers or,
> (ii) where the liability for payment of anti-dumping duties is calculated on the basis of a prospective normal value, the difference between the weighted average normal value of the selected exporters or producers and the export prices of exporters or producers not individually examined,

provided that the authorities shall disregard for the purpose of this paragraph any zero and de minimis margins and margins established under the circumstances referred to in paragraph 8 of Article 6. The authorities shall apply individual duties or normal values to imports from any exporter or producer not included in the examination who has provided the necessary information during the course of the investigation, as provided for in subparagraph 10.2 of Article 6.

[152] DS471, United States – Certain Methodologies and Their Application to Anti-Dumping Proceedings Involving China, Appellate Body Report, 17.

[153] Ibid., 164.

[154] DS405, European Union – Anti-Dumping Measures on Certain Footwear from China, Panel Report, 297.

[155] Ibid.

the ADA, which requires the investigating authorities to ask for a non-confidential version of the information submitted. Furthermore, if the non-confidential version cannot be made available to interested parties, investigating authorities should clarify the reasons.[156]

In another case, *DS488*, Korea argued that Commerce violated Articles 6.10 and 6.10.2 of the ADA by not providing a reasonable basis to explain why only two exporters were selected as mandatory respondents, and additional voluntary respondents were rejected.[157] The Panel decided that the methodology used by Commerce leads to the selection of two companies with the largest percentage of exports to the US. The Panel also recalls *DS405* and finds it impractical to examine all exporters.[158]

3.3.5 *Submission of Evidence and Rebuttals*

Article 6 of the ADA sets rules on evidence, stating that investigating authorities need to provide ample opportunity to present counter-evidence and rebuttals. Limiting this right is disadvantageous for exporters.

In *DS397*, China argued that the EU violated Article 6 of the ADA by not allowing exporters to defend themselves during the investigation. The Appellate Body agreed that the exporters did not have a timely opportunity to access the information about the product types that the normal value calculation was based upon.[159] Consequently, exporters were not allowed to defend their interests properly. The Appellate Body evaluated this as a violation of Article 6.2 of the ADA. This decision is remarkable in the sense that the concept of due process is mentioned regarding the anti-dumping investigations:

> Whenever information [submitted in the course of an anti-dumping investigation] is treated as confidential, transparency and due process concerns will necessarily arise because such treatment entails the withholding of information from other parties to an investigation. Due process requires that interested parties have a right to see the evidence submitted

156 Ibid.

157 DS488, United States – Anti-Dumping Measures on Certain Oil Country Tubular Goods from Korea.

158 Ibid., 78.

159 Report of the Appellate Body, European Communities – Definitive Anti-Dumping Measures on Certain Iron or Steel Fasteners from China, WT/DS397/AB/R.

> or gathered in an investigation, and have an adequate opportunity for the defence of their interests.[160]

Due process is generally a concern of the DSU or the DSM adjudication, but, in this case, the Appellate Body acknowledged that due process is also applicable to anti-dumping investigations.

In *DS99*, Korea argued that the US violated Article 2.2.1.1[161] of the ADA because the investigating authority disregarded an economic analysis of the Dynamic Random-Access Memory Semiconductors (DRAMs) market and the cost data submitted by respondents.[162] Flamm, as Hyundai's consultant, offered an econometric study on the cost trend for DRAMs and found that prices were on a declining trend between 1992 and 1996, arguing that Korean exporters were not dumping. Korea also asserted that the data submitted by the petitioner was not verified; therefore, this discriminatory treatment of data caused a violation of Article 6.6[163] of the ADA. The Panel rejected these arguments as unconvincing. Nearly two years later, parties notified DSU that they had reached a mutually agreed solution.[164]

[160] Ibid.; also see Repertory of Appellate Body Reports, Due Process, available at www.wto.org/english/tratop_e/dispu_e/repertory_e/d2_e.htm#D.2.1, accessed 15 July 2023.

[161] Article 2.2.1.1 states,

> For the purpose of paragraph 2, costs shall normally be calculated on the basis of records kept by the exporter or producer under investigation, provided that such records are in accordance with the generally accepted accounting principles of the exporting country and reasonably reflect the costs associated with the production and sale of the product under consideration. Authorities shall consider all available evidence on the proper allocation of costs, including that which is made available by the exporter or producer in the course of the investigation provided that such allocations have been historically utilized by the exporter or producer, in particular in relation to establishing appropriate amortization and depreciation periods and allowances for capital expenditures and other development costs. Unless already reflected in the cost allocations under this sub-paragraph, costs shall be adjusted appropriately for those non-recurring items of cost which benefit future and/or current production, or for circumstances in which costs during the period of investigation are affected by start-up operations.

[162] DS99, United States – Anti-Dumping Duty on Dynamic Random Access Memory Semiconductors (DRAMS) of One Megabit or above from Korea, Panel Report.

[163] Article 6.6 states, 'Except in circumstances provided for in paragraph 8, the authorities shall during the course of an investigation satisfy themselves as to the accuracy of the information supplied by interested parties upon which their findings are based.'

[164] DS99, United States – Anti-Dumping Duty on Dynamic Random-Access Memory Semiconductors (DRAMS) of One Megabit or above from Korea.

In *DS471*, China claimed that in treating China as a non-market economy, WTO members did not give companies sufficient opportunity to defend their interests.[165] The US argued that Chinese exporters did not respond to the first questionnaire, so they were regarded as non-cooperating companies. The US also pointed out that this is why non-cooperating companies were not asked for further information.[166] The panel found that Commerce's determination of a PRC-wide rate was inconsistent under Articles 6.10 and 9.2 of the ADA.

3.3.6 Access to Non-confidential Files

This part is also related to transparency, as restricting the accession of non-confidential files impedes meaningful participation. Article 6 of the ADA also mentions the obligation of the investigating authorities to provide opportunities to access non-confidential files. Missing documents in the non-confidential file is another issue that has been argued in cases such as *DS405*.[167]

In *DS405*, China argues that the EU failed to comply with Article 6.2 of the ADA due to the violation of Article 6.5. China claims that some of the essential files are missing from the investigation file. Regarding Article 6.5.2, China claims that the following information is treated as confidential without showing a good cause: (1) the names of complainant EU producers and other EU producers of the like product; (2) information pertaining to the selection of the sample of the domestic industry, adjustments for differences affecting price comparability, the non-confidential questionnaire response of one sampled EU producer, and missing declarations of support; (3) certain information in the complaint and a Note for the File dated 6 July 2005; and (4) certain information in the non-confidential versions of the questionnaire responses of the sampled EU producers. Therefore, the non-confidential file did not contain enough information for interested parties. The Panel finds that China made a general argument and evaluates the facts accordingly,[168] concluding that "Article 6.5.2 does not impose any affirmative obligation

[165] DS471, United States – Certain Methodologies and Their Application to Anti-Dumping Proceedings Involving China, Panel Report, 130.

[166] Ibid., 132.

[167] DS405, European Union – Anti-Dumping Measures on Certain Footwear from China, Report of Panel.

[168] Ibid., 282.

on investigating authorities to examine whether or not confidential treatment is warranted, but addresses what actions investigating authorities may take if they 'find that a request for confidentiality is not warranted'".[169] Thus, the Panel finds that the EU did not violate Article 5.6.2.[170] On the other hand, Panel finds the EU violating Article 6.5.1 as the Article obliges investigating authorities to ask for non-confidential summaries to the interested parties who submit confidential information.[171] Thus, even if the investigating authorities have discretion in determining the scope of confidential information, the non-confidential summaries should be requested and made available to other interested parties.

In *DS337*, Norway challenges the EU's practice under Articles 6.2 and 6.4. The argument is based on the fact that the EU did not disclose non-confidential information about the investigation.[172] The documents that are missing from the non-confidential version of files include: (1) sampling forms and questionnaires; (2) responses to questionnaires; (3) all submissions of Norwegian Government and Norwegian Seafood Federation and (4) submissions of sampled Norwegian exporters.[173] The Panel accurately rules that unless the information is rejected, it should be included in the investigation file and, if it is not confidential and used by the investigating authority, it should be shared with interested parties. This is to provide ample opportunities for parties to defend themselves. Therefore, the Panel found that the EU's practice was a violation of Article 6.4. As mentioned, the EU has been criticised for not being transparent enough to provide opportunities to interested parties to defend themselves.

3.3.7 Hearings

Article 6.2 allows parties to present their case orally. There are cases where hearing procedures are challenged, as in *DS488*. In this case, Korea argued that a Korean exporter's oral submissions were not taken into consideration by Commerce.[174] The Panel, however, concluded that

[169] Ibid., 311.
[170] Ibid.
[171] Ibid.
[172] DS 337, European Communities – Anti-Dumping Measure on Farmed Salmon from Norway, Panel Report.
[173] Ibid.
[174] DS488, United States – Anti-Dumping Measures on Certain Oil Country Tubular Goods from Korea, Panel Report.

Korean respondents had been given sufficient opportunities to submit their views and defend their interests by written submissions as well as attending oral hearings.[175] Therefore, Korea's claim was rejected.

In *DS184*, Japan complained about the hearing procedures of the USITC. Japan accused the USITC of accepting information submitted by US producers after the hearing and almost a month later than the response deadline.[176] A hearing is already at a late stage of the investigation to submit information. The information presented orally should be submitted in writing and made available to other interested parties.[177] Japan argued that even after this stage, the USITC accepted new information by US producers. Japan claimed that together with other contradictions, this practice constitutes a violation of Article X:3 (a) of the GATT 94.[178] The Article obliges members to administer regulations in a uniform, impartial and reasonable manner. This is an indirect argument as each contradiction should have been addressed to a specific Article of the ADA. The Panel rejected this argument mainly because Japan centred its argument on Article X:3, and no particular ADA provision is mentioned.[179]

3.3.8 Newcomers

After the termination of an investigation, there may be new firms that export from the country that are subject to anti-dumping measures. As anti-dumping duties are specific to firms, newcomers need to be handled individually. Newcomers apply to the investigating authorities and try to prove that they are not dumping so that they may request an exemption or lower duties. If the investigating authority is not satisfied with the evidence submitted, the newcomer will be subject to 'all others rate'.

[175] Ibid.

[176] DS184, United States – Anti-Dumping Measures on Certain Hot-Rolled Steel Products from Japan, First Submission by Parties.

[177] Article 6.3 of the ADA.

[178] Article reads: 'Each contracting party shall administer in a uniform, impartial and reasonable manner all its laws, regulations, decisions and rulings of the kind described in paragraph 1 of this Article.' Available at www.wto.org/english/docs_e/legal_e/gatt47_01_e.htm, accessed 15 July 2023.

[179] DS184, United States – Anti-Dumping Measures on Certain Hot-Rolled Steel Products from Japan, Panel Report, 78.

Article 15 of the ADA addresses the matter of developing countries during anti-dumping investigations.[180] In *DS141*, India highlighted that the EU did not consider this Article for newcomers. When exporters are sampled, EU anti-dumping law does not allow newcomer review.[181] This leads to unfair outcomes for newcomers as they are subject to high anti-dumping duties. Therefore, the EU has been criticised for not considering 'constructive remedies' rather than adopting anti-dumping duties. The 'constructive remedies' would be lesser duties or price undertakings for the purposes of Article 15 of the ADA.[182] The EU defended its approach on the basis that Indian exporters are given the opportunity to offer price undertakings; however, the Panel concludes that the term 'explore' requires members to examine actively other alternatives for developing members.[183] Therefore, the Panel decided that the EU acted inconsistently in terms of Article 15 of the ADA.[184]

3.3.9 *Enforcement*

Enforcement of anti-dumping measures is another issue that needs to comply with the ADA. In *DS132*, the Panel ruled that the extension of the provisional measure by Mexico is inconsistent with Article 7.4 of the ADA. The retrospective application of the anti-dumping measure covering the provisional measure period violated Article 10.2.[185] The late release of bonds or cash deposits constitutes another inconsistency with Article 10.4 of the ADA.[186]

In *DS136*, the EU challenged the Act 1916 of the US. The Panel made some determinations on the Act and ruled that some procedural rules are missing. Some examples are the lack of notification requirements to the importing country and verification of information before the initiation of an investigation or the requirement that measures should not be

180 DS141, European Communities – Anti-Dumping Duties on Imports of Cotton-Type Bed Linen from India, Panel Report.

181 World Trade Organization, *Dispute Settlement Reports 2001: Volume 8, Pages 3303–4047*, Vol. 8 (Cambridge University Press, 2004), 2341.

182 DS141, European Communities – Anti-Dumping Duties on Imports of Cotton-Type Bed Linen from India, Panel Report, 66.

183 Ibid., 67.

184 Ibid.

185 DS132, Panel Report, WT/DS132/R.

186 Ibid.

retroactive.[187] Two years after the Panel and Appellate Body reports, the EU sought authorisation to suspend concessions under Article 22.2 of the DSU.[188]

In *DS379*, China brought several issues before the WTO DSM. The Panel ruled in favour of the US that China was not able to establish the issue of double remedies.[189] The Appellate Body, however, reversed the Panel's decision on the basis that imposition of both anti-dumping measures and countervailing measures constitute a violation of the SCM Agreement.[190] Double remedies offset the same subsidisation twice and therefore overprotect local industries in the importing countries. The US in this case had four sets of measures adopted at the same time; the Appellate Body required the US to make its measures consistent with the SCM Agreement.[191,192]

In *DS471*, China challenged the US regarding the general and prospective application of the adverse facts available method as a violation of Article 6.10 and 9.2 of the ADA.[193] General and prospective applications demonstrate that the exercise in question is a rule or norm.[194] Rule or norms can be challenged, whether they are in a written or unwritten form. Adverse facts available is considered as a general application by the

187 DS135, Panel Report, WT/DS136/R.

188 Article 22.2 of the DSU states that

> If the Member concerned fails to bring the measure found to be inconsistent with a covered agreement into compliance therewith or otherwise comply with the recommendations and rulings within the reasonable period of time determined pursuant to paragraph 3 of Article 21, such Member shall, if so requested, and no later than the expiry of the reasonable period of time, enter into negotiations with any party having invoked the dispute settlement procedures, with a view to developing mutually acceptable compensation. If no satisfactory compensation has been agreed within 20 days after the date of expiry of the reasonable period of time, any party having invoked the dispute settlement procedures may request authorization from the DSB to suspend the application to the Member concerned of concessions or other obligations under the covered agreements.

189 Yilmazcan, 'The Role of Anti-Dumping in the US–China Trade War', 17.

190 DS379, United States – Definitive Anti-Dumping and Countervailing Duties on Certain Products from China, Appellate Body Report, accessed 15 July 2023, https://docs.wto.org/dol2fe/Pages/SS/directdoc.aspx?filename=Q:/WT/DS/379ABR.pdf&Open=True.

191 Ibid.

192 Yilmazcan, Abdulkadir, 'The Role of Anti-Dumping in the US–China Trade War', China & WTO Rev. 2021, no. 1 (2021), 7–36.

193 Prusa and Vermulst, 'United States – Certain Methodologies'.

194 Appellate Body Reports DS244, DS294.

Appellate Body since it applies to an unidentified number of companies.[195] The adverse facts available method was also considered as a prospective application by the Appellate Body as there was certainty in the application of the norm.[196] This is mentioned at the Appellate Body report:

> Rather, where prospective application is not sufficiently clear from the constitutive elements of a rule or norm, it may be demonstrated by a number of factors. These include: the existence of an underlying policy that is implemented by the rule or norm; the systematic application of the challenged rule or norm; the design, architecture, and structure of the rule or norm; the extent to which the rule or norm provides administrative guidance for future conduct; and the expectations it creates among economic operators that the rule or norm will be applied in the future.[197]

The analysis of the Appellate Body is remarkable in the sense that underlying policies are taken into consideration by the Appellate Body as unwritten norms. In that sense, procedural burdens avoiding cooperation can be challenged before the DSM as general and prospective applications to improve procedural justice.

3.4 Effectiveness of the Dispute Settlement Mechanism

This part evaluates the effectiveness of the DSM based on the basis of the WTO disputes above and the literature. The DSM considers procedural issues, but it is uncertain whether the members strictly comply with these reports. The US, for instance, insists on using a zeroing methodology despite several rulings by the DSM.

The WTO's DSM is respected as many disputes are settled through the proceedings or even before the establishment of the panels. On the other hand, members attempting to benefit from the DSM face serious burdens, especially developing members who do not have legal capacity to make sound arguments. According to the DSU, the Panels and the Appellate Body are bound by the arguments made by the parties.[198]

[195] Prusa and Vermulst, 'United States – Certain Methodologies', 14.

[196] Ibid.

[197] DS471, United States – Certain Methodologies and Their Application to Anti-Dumping Proceedings Involving China, Appellate Body Report, WT/DS471/AB/R, 55.

[198] Article 7.2 of the DSU reads: 'Panels shall address the relevant provisions in any covered agreement or agreements cited by the parties to the dispute.' Article 17.12 of the DSU reads: "The Appellate Body shall address each of the issues raised in accordance with paragraph 6 during the appellate proceeding.' Available at www.wto.org/english/tratop_e/dispu_e/disp_settlement_cbt_e/c10s2p1_e.htm, accessed 15 July 2023.

In other words, the complainant would be right in arguing that the respondent violated the WTO agreements, but the Panel or the Appellate Body does not accept the claim if the respondent referred to the wrong article. DSM also does not make ex officio determinations, so the legal capacity of the complaining party affects the outcome of the dispute. Also, within the growing jurisprudence of the DSM, it is a challenging task for trade officials to master the substantive and procedural aspects of WTO law and accurately prepare arguments.[199] Many studies have focused on the per capita income or the number of representatives in Geneva to assess legal capacity. Michalopoulos shows that many developing countries lack representatives at the WTO to track cases actively.[200] Busch, Reinhardt and Shaffer surveyed the legal capacity of the WTO members and find that other factors, such as bureaucratic organisation, experience in WTO matters, and involvement in WTO litigation, also affect legal capacity.[201] Another implication is that the legalisation of international trade poses new challenges to developing countries.[202]

Turning back to the effectiveness of the DSM, some parameters need to be considered, namely time, cost and enforceability. In terms of the timing of the proceedings, Article XX of the DSU reads that Panel reports should be circulated within no more than nine months.[203] If the report is appealed, the report should be adopted by the DSB within 12 months.[204] However, in practice, the process takes longer than the timeframe:

> The average (not the maximum!) duration from consultations request to adoption was much longer than the maximum 15–19 months prescribed by the DSU for a process including an AB appeal, namely: 23.21 months for disputes that started between 1995–1999, and 28 months for those that started between 2007–2011. Keep in mind that this average includes also cases that did not go to appeal, where the maximum duration was prescribed to be shorter.[205]

Thus, even the average duration of the procedures is longer than expected. The statistics have not been updated, but the current situation

[199] World Trade Organization, *A Handbook on the WTO Dispute Settlement System*, 109.

[200] Constantine Michalopoulos, *Developing Countries' Participation in the World Trade Organization* (The World Bank, 1999), 19.

[201] Marc L. Busch, Eric Reinhardt and Gregory Shaffer, 'Does Legal Capacity Matter? A Survey of WTO Members', *World Trade Rev.* 8, no. 4 (2009), 559–577.

[202] Ibid.

[203] Article 12.9 of the DSU.

[204] Article 20 of the DSU.

[205] Reich, 'The Effectiveness of the WTO Dispute Settlement System'.

is more worrisome. In terms of the enforceability of DSB rules and recommendations, *DS471* is notable. The Panel was established in early 2014 in this case between China and the US. The Appellate Body report was circulated in May 2017 ruling that the US had violated several provisions under the ADA.[206] As the case covers thirty-eight anti-dumping duty determinations, the implementation of the decision is complex. Consequently, the US announced that a reasonable period of time is needed to comply with the Appellate Body report.[207] China requested that the reasonable period of time needs to be determined by a binding arbitrator under Article 21.3(c) of the DSU.[208] The Arbitrator determined the reasonable period of time at the upper limit as fifteen months under Article 21 3 (c) of the DSU based on the complexity of the case.[209] The expiry date of the arbitration award was due in August 2018. Under Article 22 of the DSU, China requested the suspension of consultations or other remedies around $7 billion USD for twenty-five products subject to anti-dumping duties.[210] In November 2019, the Arbitrator circulated the award that China may request authorisation from the DSB to retaliate to the effect of $3.5 billion USD annually.[211] Under Article 21.6 of the DSU, the DSB monitors the implementation of rulings and recommendations until the dispute is resolved.[212] The US did not implement the award by the end of 2020. This means that, for at least six years, the dispute has not been solved and economic operators are adversely being affected.

Second, the WTO dispute settlement procedures are also costly. WTO lawyers in Brussels and Washington charge between $500 and $1,000 USD per hour, which means complex cases cost millions.[213] Also, some

[206] DS471, United States – Certain Methodologies and Their Application to Anti-Dumping Proceedings Involving China.

[207] Ibid.

[208] Ibid.

[209] United States – Certain Methodologies and Their Application to Anti-Dumping Proceedings Involving China, Award of the Arbitrator, WT/DS471/RPT*, accessed 15 July 2023, https://docs.wto.org/dol2fe/Pages/SS/directdoc.aspx?filename=q:/WT/DS/471RPT.pdf&Open=True.

[210] DS471, United States – Certain Methodologies and Their Application to Anti-Dumping Proceedings Involving China.

[211] Ibid.

[212] Article 21, DSU, available at www.wto.org/english/tratop_e/dispu_e/dsu_e.htm#21, accessed 15 July 2023.

[213] Baoqing Han, 'Analyzing China's Litigation Costs in the WTO: Problems and Solutions', *J. WTO China* 3, no. 4 (2013), 121.

instances require experts to be consulted, which increases legal costs. The survey conducted by Busch, Reinhardt, and Shaffer shows that more than half of the trade diplomats at the WTO feel that due to the high cost of litigation, members chose to participate as third parties rather than file their cases before the DSM.[214]

The last parameter of efficiency is the enforceability of the Panel and Appellate Body reports. The desired outcome of the DSM is agreement by parties after the consultation stage. If the consultations fail, the parties request establishment of the Panel, which can be appealed. Thus, the other outcomes of the DSM are the report of the Panel and the Report of the Appellate Body.

> Although DSU requires the parties of the dispute to comply with the recommendations or rulings of the DSB promptly, such prompt compliance is extremely rare. Instead, the parties to the dispute often resort to arbitration to decide the reasonable time of implementation. Usually, the respondent will be given 15 months' grace, thereby postponing the dispute resolution. Finally, the party violating the rules can utilize such a long period to attain his protection purpose. Therefore, these lengthy periods contribute to some member's wilful offense in a bid to pursue short-term interests. However, the complainant sustains irretrievable loss.[215]

In other words, direct enforceability is not common in practice. Immediate compliance is the priority, but if this is not possible, the respondent member is required to comply with the Panel or Appellate Body report within a reasonable period of time. Under Article 21, the reasonable time can be offered by the respondent and approved by the DSB, mutually agreed by the parties within forty-five days after the recommendations and rulings or determined by the arbitrator provided that it does not exceed fifteen months.

Among these solutions, the most desired is mutual agreement during the consultation stage. Otherwise, the DSB requires the respondent member to withdraw the measure in question. If an immediate withdrawal is impractical, Article 3.7 of the DSU allows compensation,[216] which should also be agreed upon bilaterally. If the parties to the dispute cannot agree the level of compensation, the complainant can approach the DSB in order to receive authorisation for 'suspending concessions or

214 Busch et al., 'Does Legal Capacity Matter', 567.

215 Han, 'Analyzing China's Litigation Costs in the WTO'.

216 DSU full text available at www.wto.org/english/tratop_e/dispu_e/dsu_e.htm#7, accessed 15 July 2023.

other obligations under the covered agreements' under Article 22.2 of the DSU. An example of the suspension of concessions is the removal of tariff reductions from the respondent member. Suspension of WTO obligations subject to DSB approval means countermeasures or retaliation against the respondent. These countermeasures typically constitute a violation of WTO agreements, but under Article 22.2 of the DSU, this is justifiable for the complaining party. Some members believe responding to a trade barrier with another trade barrier is against the philosophy of the WTO as it harms both sides.[217]

Another problem with the remedies of the DSM is the lack of retrospective measures. The respondent member is not obliged to compensate for past damage to the complainant under the DSU.[218] In other words, the primary deficiency is that DSU remedies are conditional and prospective.[219] This remedial gap encourages members to violate WTO agreements as members learn how to act strategically.[220] Therefore, the lack of retrospective measures harms the flow of trade and, even if DSM recommendations are fulfilled, trade cannot be quickly restored as it shifts to other countries.

The disputes mentioned in this chapter focus on the procedural barriers put up by investigating authorities. However, the concept of procedural justice is not the primary focus of the literature. Rather, the literature highlights procedural justice under DSM proceedings. Gaffney seeks the normative basis of procedural justice in the WTO in the shift from a 'power-oriented GATT approach' into a 'rule-oriented WTO system'.[221] Still, the author urges for public hearings under the WTO DSM, which is a point that the US vigorously defends.[222] Schneider highlights the contribution of the DSM in terms of procedural justice, allowing less powerful countries to challenge powerful countries.[223] Procedural justice, however, is also needed during the original investigation, as argued in this study.

217 World Trade Organization, *A Handbook on the WTO Dispute Settlement System*.

218 Claus D. Zimmermann, 'The Neglected Link between the Legal Nature of WTO Rules, the Political Filtering of WTO Disputes, and the Absence of Retrospective WTO Remedies', *Trade L. & Dev.* 4, no. 1 Summer (2012), 253.

219 Rachel Brewster, The Remedy Gap: Institutional Design, Retaliation, and Trade Law Enforcement, *Geo. Wash. L. Rev.* 80, no. 1 (2011), 104, available at SSRN https://ssrn.com/abstract=2146121, accessed 15 July 2023.

220 Ibid.

221 Gaffney, 'Due process in the World Trade Organization', 1185.

222 Ibid., 1205.

223 Andrea Kupfer Schneider, 'Not Quite a World without Trials: Why International Dispute Resolution Is Increasingly Judicialized', *J. Disp. Resol.* 2006 (2006), 119.

It is incorrect to label DSM as a complete success or failure considering that Chaisse and Chakraborty state:

> It can be concluded that, in its first two decades of working, the DSB has proved to be highly successful in the settlement of AD disputes in the WTO. However, the panels and AB have acted with caution and have sometimes shied away from legal analysis, without going on to examine the political implications of their findings.[224]

Rather, DSM is a successful mechanism for dealing with trade disputes between WTO members. However, procedural justice during anti-dumping investigations cannot be guaranteed through DSM proceedings.

Above all, there is currently another problem faced by the WTO DSM. The US has blocked the appointment of new Appellate Body Members for a long time. Normally, the Appellate Body operates with seven members.[225] As of December 2019, the number of Appellate Body Members dropped to one and in November 2020, the last member's term ended without renewal.[226] This eventually paralysed the DSM, meaning that the Panel reports cannot be appealed. To overcome the crisis, the EU proposed 'Interim Appeal Arbitration Pursuant to Article 25 DSU', aimed at settling disputes until Appellate Body members can be appointed.[227] The proposal became effective with the signature of the multi-party interim appeal arbitration arrangement (MPIA) by the nineteen WTO members in April 2020.[228,229] Currently, there are twenty-six

224 Chaisse and Chakraborty, 'Normative Obsolescence of the WTO'.

225 Yilmazcan, Abdulkadir, 'The Role of Anti-Dumping in the US–China Trade War', China & WTO Rev. 2021, no. 1 (2021), 7–36.

226 The US mainly complains of three issues on the Appellate Body; AB outlawed zeroing while it is permissible under the Article 17.6 of the ADA, AB expanded its evaluations beyond the scope of appeal in several cases, AB did not comply with the timeframes determined by the DSU. Bernard Hoekman and Petros C. Mavroidis, 'Burning Down the House? The Appellate Body in the Centre of the WTO Crisis', The Appellate Body in the Centre of the WTO Crisis (1 July 2019). Robert Schuman Centre for Advanced Studies Research Paper No. RSCAS 56 (2019), 1.

227 Rajesh Sharma, 'WTO Appellate Body at Cross Roads: Options and Alternatives' in Chang-fa Lo, Junji Nakagawa and Tsai-fang Chen (eds.), *The Appellate Body of the WTO and Its Reform* (Springer, 2020), 239–54.

228 Interim Appeal Arrangement for WTO Disputes Becomes Effective, accessed 15 July 2023, https://trade.ec.europa.eu/doclib/press/index.cfm?id=2143.

229 Yilmazcan, Abdulkadir, 'The Role of Anti-Dumping in the US–China Trade War', China & WTO Rev. 2021, no. 1 (2021), 7–36.

signatories including EU, China and Japan, but the crisis remains since the US is not a signatory of the interim appeal.[230]

3.5 Conclusion

This chapter identifies the role of the DSM in anti-dumping investigations. DSM is well respected as it enables members to solve trade disputes. Anti-dumping is the top issue to be challenged before the DSM. The reason is that the ADA is silent on some aspects of anti-dumping investigations and members try to overprotect domestic industries by excessive use of anti-dumping measures. This chapter focused on disputes related to 142 anti-dumping cases heard by the DSM.

In the context of these cases, the study classifies ten procedural issues: calculation methods, transparency, public notice, selection of investigated parties, submission of evidence and rebuttals, access to non-confidential files, hearing, newcomers and enforcement. In some disputes, these procedural issues were addressed by the Panels and the Appellate Body and inconsistencies were found. However, the concept of procedural justice in anti-dumping investigations is mentioned in only a few cases, such as *DS425*.

This chapter also shows that the DSM in some regard lacks effectiveness. Anti-dumping is the single-most litigated issue, and cases regarding the ADA evidence the issues. In terms of duration, DSM proceedings take longer than expected. It is also costly to effectively pursue cases. There are organisations, such as ACWL, to support the legal needs of developing countries, but nonetheless, the majority of WTO members prefer to pursue cases as third parties and reserve their rights. Also, even when the Panel or Appellate Body report is in favour of the complainant, enforcement is difficult since other procedures need to be followed before retaliation. Therefore, non-compliance with WTO agreements can be advantageous from a strategic point of view.

Reviewing the reports of Panels and the Appellate Body shows that the DSM cannot effectively secure procedural justice. First, the Panels and Appellate Body are bound by the claims and relevant articles. The DSM cannot adopt ex officio determinations for the purposes of judicial economy. Second, the standard of review is another issue to be addressed

[230] EU Welcomes Japan Joining Dispute Settlement Arrangement, accessed 15 July 2023, https://policy.trade.ec.europa.eu/news/eu-welcomes-japan-joining-dispute-settlement-arrangement-2023-03-10_en.

in terms of DSM and its effectiveness. Standard of review refers to the procedures applied by a higher court while examining the decision of a lower court.[231] Gaffney notes that, unlike the International Court of Justice, the Appeal Process of the Appellate Body is limited by Article 11 of the DSU.[232] Thus, a review by the Appellate Body is limited to the legal arguments covered in Panel reports. Third, as required by Article 17.7 of the ADA, confidential information acquired by the Panel during a review of an anti-dumping case cannot be disclosed without formal authorisation by the relevant party.[233] This also limits the evaluation of the Panel's reports as determinations that are based on confidential information cannot be appealed. Fourth, as the legal capacity of members is limited, particularly developing countries, all the procedural problems cannot be brought before the DSM. Furthermore, even if these issues are discussed through the DSM, parties violating the ADA or other GATT provisions do not comply with the reports. Procedural justice requires transparent and predictable anti-dumping proceedings, and DSM's role to guarantee procedural justice is limited.

Also, the literature on procedural justice in anti-dumping investigations is incomplete. Gaffney calls for improved procedural justice in the DSM rather than in the anti-dumping investigations. Ruttley, MacVay and Weisbergerger also focus on due process in WTO Dispute Settlement.[234] Horlick and Vermulst highlight the procedural problems of the US and EU.[235] Bouët and Métivier argue that legal capacity and retaliation capacity directly affect the motives of developing countries in bringing cases before the DSM.[236]

For these reasons, this chapter contributes to the research question in the sense that anti-dumping procedures can be used as a form of hidden trade protectionism. The safety mechanism of proper enforcement of WTO agreements is the DSM. Anti-dumping is the top issue to be

231 Gaffney, 'Due Process in the World Trade Organization', 1173.

232 Ibid.

233 Article 17.7 of the ADA, available at www.wto.org/english/docs_e/legal_e/19-adp_02_e.htm#articleXVII, accessed 15 July 2023.

234 Philip Ruttley, Iain Macvay and Marc Weisberger, *Due Process in WTO Dispute Settlement* (Cameron May, 2001).

235 Gary Horlick and Edwin Vermulst, 'Ten Major Problems with the Anti-Dumping Instrument: An Attempt at Synthesis', *J. World Trade* 39 (2005), 67.

236 Antoine Bouët and Jeanne Métivier, 'Is the Dispute Settlement System, "Jewel in the WTO's Crown", Beyond Reach of Developing Countries?', *Rev. World Econ.* 156 (2019), 1–38.

discussed through this mechanism. However, this chapter demonstrates that procedural issues are addressed through the DSM, and in most of these cases, the US and the EU are respondents while China is the complainant. The overall evaluation of the DSM reports is that anti--dumping investigations lead to complex dispute settlement cases, and members such as the US find ways to circumvent the rulings of the Panels or the Appellate Body. Zeroing is the most prominent issue that the DSM could not solve. After several Appellate Body rulings finding zeroing inconsistent with the ADA, the US has now blocked the appointment of new members. The US is pursuing a rigid foreign trade policy to overprotect US industries, but it exceeds the limits of the WTO agreements, particularly of the ADA. The chapter is helpful in demonstrating that the DSM is not a perfect guarantee of procedural justice in anti-dumping investigations; therefore, the study pursues two more steps in the following chapters. In Chapter 5, the study examines other procedural problems than those discussed before the DSM by conducting empirical research. In Chapter 6, the study focuses on the ongoing negotiations at the WTO to revise the ADA and examines whether there are alternatives to secure procedural justice.

4

Procedures of the US, EU and the Position of China under the Anti-dumping Investigations

4.1 Introduction

As a rule, domestic regulations by WTO Members should not violate WTO agreements.[1] In this regard, local anti-dumping laws should not contradict the ADA. However, the ADA does not touch every aspect of anti-dumping investigations. The investigating authorities of different WTO members, through regulations or guidelines, address procedural issues or leave them untouched, creating room for discretion while turning cooperation into a painful process for exporters.

Discretion is generally exercised in favour of domestic manufacturers and against foreign competitors. For exporters, strict procedural rules have a restricting effect on trade because challenging these rules is time-consuming and costly. In most cases, the ADA sets the general framework and leaves discretion to members. According to the Panel in *DS219*, while using discretion, the investigating authorities should be unbiased and even-handed without arbitrary practices.[2] In *DS211*, the Panel notes that the ADA covers two types of procedural obligations: 'those that are stipulated explicitly and in detail, and which have to be performed in a particular way in every investigation, and, on the other hand, those that establish a certain due process or procedural principles, but leave to the discretion of the investigating authority exactly how they will be performed'.[3] For the second type of procedural issue, investigating authorities need to show a significant degree of effort in providing opportunities to the relevant parties to defend themselves.[4] Referring to *US-Hot Rolled*

[1] Article XVI:4 of the Marrakesh Agreement states, 'Each Member shall ensure the conformity of its laws, regulations and administrative procedures with its obligations as provided in the annexed Agreements.'

[2] DS219, European Communities – Anti-Dumping Duties on Malleable Cast Iron Tube or Pipe Fittings from Brazil, 55.

[3] DS211, Egypt – Definitive Anti-Dumping Measures on Steel Rebar from Turkey, Report of the Panel, 4.

[4] Ibid.

Steel Case (*DS184*), the Panel comments that cooperation is a two-way process and needs effort from investigating authorities. Failing to provide opportunities in this sense may be an improper exercise of discretion.

Therefore, investigation procedures need to be analysed in detail before suggesting that procedural justice would bring anti-dumping laws to a justifiable level. In this context, this chapter describes the anti-dumping investigation procedures of the US and the EU, as well as their differences. From an exporter's point of view, anti-dumping investigations are burdensome, especially if each member applies different procedural rules. Thus, this chapter highlights these differences by focusing first on China's position in anti-dumping investigations as the top target and then explaining the procedures of the two primary users, the US and EU. The chapter describes the trade policies of these selected economies highlighting the correlation between the room for discretion granted to WTO members and the level of protection. Furthermore, focusing on the anti-dumping procedures of the selected economies also casts light on the ongoing trade war and its effects[5] Therefore, examining the investigation procedures clarifies the need for improving procedural justice in anti-dumping proceedings.

4.2 Position of China in Anti-dumping Investigations

China is the top target for most anti-dumping measures. Between 1995 and 2022(6), China faced 1,542 anti-dumping initiations, of which 1,156 ended with final measures.[6] On the other hand, compared to the EU and the US, the number of anti-dumping measures adopted by China is remarkably low.[7] Also, China is more likely to comply with Panel or Appellate Body Reports.[8]

[5] Regarding the reason of the trade war, the US accuses China of IP violations and market distortions resulting in a large trade deficit in favour of China but on the other hand the US is criticised of not complying with the WTO DSB decisions and blocking the appointment of new Appellate Body Members. Yongding Yu, 'Can China and the United States Avoid a Full-Blown Trade War?', in Ha Jiming and Adam S. Posen (eds.), *US–China Economic Relations: From Conflict to Solutions* (PIIE, 2019), 41–57.

[6] WTO Statistics, available at https://www.wto.org/english/tratop_e/adp_e/adp_e.htm, accessed 15 July 2023.

[7] Between 1995 and 2022(6) China enforced 293 anti-dumping measures while the US had 855 and EU 545. WTO Statistics, ibid.

[8] In cases such as DS414, China – GOES, DS425, China – X-Ray Equipment, DS427, China – Broiler China complied with the reports and calculated the margins again. Weihuan Zhou and Shu Zhang, 'Anti-dumping Practices and China's Implementation of WTO Rulings', *China Quart.* 230 (2017), 512–527.

The US and EU have special policies for the growing exports from China. Also, the Chinese economy has unique features inspired by socialism that directly affect its market economy status. This part presents an overview of the Chinese position in the context of the anti-dumping investigations.

4.2.1 *Chinese Economy*

China has a highly resilient culture. As once noted, 'Chinese history featured many periods of civil war, interregnum, and chaos. After each collapse, the Chinese state reconstituted itself as if by some immutable law of nature'.[9] China's Great Leap Forward campaign to move to an industrial economy in 1958 ended up with a scarcity of food supplies in a few years.[10] In 1970, the Chinese economy was entirely under the control of the government, but the transformation started gradually. On average, 60 per cent of the GDP is being produced by the private sector in China.[11] The private sector employs 80 per cent and makes more than 60 per cent of the investment. Also, the share of exports has exceeded 50 per cent.[12] Today, even though there is political and economic tension with the US, China is improving in its place as a global economy with its 1.3 billion population and $21 trillion GDP (purchasing power parity).[13] China is currently the second economy globally and is expected to overtake the US around 2030.[14]

Despite the rapid growth, there are concerns about the Chinese economy and its integration into the global markets. The restrictions on foreign banks in China create distress. Only a limited number of banks can acquire the licence for the renminbi business, and yet they cannot find enough funding in the Chinese currency.[15]

9 Henry Kissinger, *On China* (Penguin Press, 2012).

10 Dennis Tao Yang, 'China's Agricultural Crisis and Famine of 1959–1961: A Survey and Comparison to Soviet Famines', *Comp. Econ. Stud.* 50, no. 1 (2008), 1–29.

11 Edward Cunningham, What Is the Future of China's Private Sector? Harvard Kennedy School, accessed 15 July 2023, www.hks.harvard.edu/faculty-research/policy-topics/international-relations-security/what-future-chinas-private-sector.

12 China December Trade Data Bad, But Likely to Get Worse This Year, accessed 15 July 2023, www.scmp.com/economy/china-economy/article/2181951/china-trade-data-worse-expected-bad-news-economy.

13 As of 2016, China is the largest economy globally. China, The World Factbook, accessed 15 July 2023, www.cia.gov/library/publications/the-world-factbook/geos/ch.html.

14 Stephen G. Brooks and William C. Wohlforth, 'The Once and Future Superpower: Why China Won't Overtake the United States', *Foreign Aff.* 95 (2016), 91.

15 John D. Langlois Jr, 'The WTO and China's Financial System', *China Quart.* 167 (2001), 610–629.

Another main issue is the State-Owned Enterprises (SOEs). The Chinese Central Government appoints the top managers of SOEs in strategic sectors.[16] The so-called revolving door system allows high-ranking government officials to SOEs or vice versa. It is questionable whether these top managers follow the orders from the central government. As these managers pursue the rise in the profitability of the SOEs, they lobby the government and sometimes clash with other SOEs' interests. An example is that some SOEs seek anti-dumping protection while other SOEs lobby against anti-dumping duties if they rely on imported materials.[17] Although the growth of the private sector is sharp, the largest Chinese companies are generally SOEs operating in capital-intensive sectors such as transportation, energy, telecoms, heavy industries or military equipment.[18]

Some figures on the SOEs highlight the size of government involvement in the Chinese market. There are more than 150,000 SOEs worth around $16.8 trillion USD which is almost 150 per cent of the GDP in China. The central government controls almost one-third of these SOEs.[19] This structure of the Chinese economy also creates concerns while deciding on the market economy status.

Another factor affecting the market economy status is China's currency policies. To make the renminbi reliable for foreign investors, China enforces a managed exchange rate instead of a floating currency.[20] Foreign investment in China was dramatically high during the 1990s, and the depreciation in the renminbi would constitute a risk. Instead, the renminbi was required to be low enough to keep Chinese exports relatively competitive and to be stable in the long term.[21] This also affects the anti-dumping petitions because as multinational companies invest in low-currency countries such as China, they do not participate in anti-dumping filings in their home markets.[22]

One criticism of the Chinese economy is that, according to statistics, China has export-based growth; however, most of these exports are made by multinational enterprises (MNE). Nearly half of Chinese exports and

16 Arthur R. Kroeber, *China's Economy: What Everyone Needs to Know®* (Oxford University Press, 2016), 104.

17 Ibid.

18 Ibid., 89–94.

19 Ibid., 99.

20 Ibid., 142.

21 Ibid.

22 Bradford J. Jensen, Dennis P. Quinn and Stephen Weymouth, 'The Influence of Firm Global Supply Chains and Foreign Currency Undervaluations on US Trade Disputes', *Int'l Org.* 69, no. 4 (2015), 941.

70 per cent of high-tech exports are made by foreign firms, whereas in countries such as Japan, the US and Germany, these goods are produced and exported by domestic firms.[23] Thus, the value-added exports are relatively low. In contrast, China has been enforcing a national IP strategy since 2008.[24] As of 2011, China has been first in terms of patent applications.[25] The quality of these applications can be studied but it seems that China is showing efforts to increase the technological contribution for its domestic exporters.

An international accounting system assures transparency and predictability for foreign firms. This also applies to the firms on the stock exchange. The full implementation of the International Financial Reporting Standards is still an ongoing process,[26] and the accounting profession is still under government control.[27] For instance, government control can be seen in the annual report of China Mobile, a company which is traded on the Hong Kong Stock Exchange.[28] The concern about the report is that there are differences between the versions available on Mainland China's and Hong Kong's websites.[29] The first one reflects the connections with the Communist Party of China while the latter obscures. In addition, issues related to the accounting techniques make the figures questionable.

4.2.2 China's Protocol of Accession to the WTO[30]

China first applied to become a WTO member in 1986, and after fifteen years, in 2001, the accession protocol was put in force.[31] Being seen as a threat to domestic industries, China faced reservations from other

23 Kroeber, *China's Economy: What Everyone Needs to Know®*, 238.

24 Wenting Cheng and Peter Drahos, 'How China Built the World's Biggest Patent Office: The Pressure Driving Mechanism', *Int. Rev. Intellect. Prop. Compet. L.* 49, no. 1 (2018), 15.

25 Ibid., The World Bank Data, accessed 15 July 2023, https://data.worldbank.org/indicator/IP.PAT.RESD?name_desc=false&view=map&year=2020.

26 Who Uses IFRS Standards? accessed 15 July 2023, www.ifrs.org/use-around-the-world/use-of-ifrs-standards-by-jurisdiction/china/.

27 Gong and Cortese, 'A Socialist Market Economy with Chinese Characteristics'.

28 Ibid.

29 Ibid.

30 This section was previously published as Yilmazcan, Abdulkadir, 'The Role of Anti-Dumping in the US–China Trade War', China & WTO Rev. 2021, no. 1 (2021), 7–36.

31 Jeffrey M. Telep and Richard C. Lutz, 'China's Long Road to Market Economy Status', *Geo. J. Int'l L.* 49 (2017), 693.

members, which slowed the negotiations. The accession process was held in two independent tracks. The Working Party directed the multilateral track on China's Resumption of GATT Membership, which was established in 1987.[32] The group then changed into the WTO Working Party on the Accession of China, where forty-three members discussed the draft protocol.[33] There were also bilateral talks especially with the US on specific issues such as China's non-market economy status.

The non-market economy status is discussed in a forthcoming part, but at this time it should be noted that the controversial Article 15 of the Accession Protocol was heavily drafted and integrated into the protocol of the bilateral track with the US.[34] It is controversial whether the expiry of Article 15 1 (ii) shifts the burden of proof from the Chinese exporters to the investigating authorities or domestic industries.[35] The textual analysis of the article does not explicitly mention the burden of proof or the records of these negotiations, thus leaving the issue contentious.

The acceptance of China as a WTO member was not easy compared to other members. The Protocol includes WTO-plus conditions for China such as:

- –the requirement that China liberalises the right to import and export goods for all enterprises in China (Article 5.1 of the Accession Protocol);
- –the restriction on the Chinese Government from influencing or directing SOEs in import purchasing procedures (Article 6.1 of the Accession Protocol);
- –the obligation to ensure "prices for traded goods and services in every sector to be determined by market forces" (Article 9.1 of the Accession Protocol);
- –the agreement that subsidies granted to SOEs are deemed to be specific (Article 10.2 of the Accession Protocol);
- –the obligation to eliminate all export taxes and charges (Article 11.3 of the Accession Protocol);

32 Weihuan Zhou and Delei Peng, 'EU–Price Comparison Methodologies (DS516): Challenging the Non-Market Economy Methodology in Light of the Negotiating History of Article 15 of China's WTO Accession Protocol', *J. World Trade* 52, no. 3 (2018), 505–533, 518.

33 Accessions, China, WTO, accessed 15 July 2023, www.wto.org/english/thewto_e/acc_e/a1_chine_e.htm.

34 Ibid.

35 Jorge Miranda, 'Implementation of the "Shift in Burden of Proof" Approach to Interpreting Paragraph 15 of China's Protocol of Accession', *Glob. Trade Cust. J.* 11, no. 10 (2016), 447–453.

–the commitment to ensure that all SOEs and state invested enterprises 'make purchases and sales based solely on commercial considerations', and that the Chinese Government does 'not influence, directly or indirectly, commercial decisions' of these enterprises (paragraph 46 of the Working Party Report);
–the undertaking that price controls are not used 'for purposes of affording protection to domestic industries or services providers' (paragraph 62 of the Working Party Report); and
–a range of obligations on the publication of laws and regulations to ensure transparency (paragraphs 324–336 of the Working Party Report).[36]

These are challenging concessions included in the Accession Protocol related to market access to goods, market access to services, agriculture, subsidies, transparency, non-market economy status in anti-dumping investigations, and safeguard investigations.[37] Still, China has accepted those conditions because remaining outside of the WTO costs more than the concessions given during the negotiations for China.[38] Besides, Chinese leaders evaluate the WTO as a driving force for reforms. The economic, legal and political implications of the accession to WTO should be noted.

In the context of economic implications, China has taken several steps, such as reducing the tariffs on agricultural products from 31.5 to 14.5 per cent as well as reducing the tariffs on industrial products from 35 to 17 per cent until 2004.[39] According to World Bank statistics, the weighted average of tariffs applied by China fell from 14.5 per cent (2001) to 3.4 (2017).[40] Foreign banks are allowed to operate in China and offer services in the renminbi. Foreign companies were allowed to offer accounting and consultancy services. The investment banking industry also played a crucial role in economic growth and reforming SOEs into market-driven entities.[41]

WTO accession also contributed positively in terms of legal implications. Legal reforms for the WTO accession elevate the rule of law while

[36] Zhou and Peng, 'EU–Price Comparison Methodologies (DS516)', 533.

[37] Karen Halverson, 'China's WTO Accession: Economic, Legal, and Political Implications', *BC Int'l & Comp. L. Rev.* 27 (2004), 327; Yilmazcan, 'The Role of Anti-Dumping in the US-China Trade War', 15.

[38] Halverson, 'China's WTO Accession', 332.

[39] Gregory Chow, 'The Impact of Joining WTO on China's Economic', Legal and Political Institutions 80 (2001), 3, accessed 15 July 2023, http://econwpa.wustl.edu.

[40] The World Bank Data, accessed 15 July 2023, https://data.worldbank.org/indicator/TM.TAX.MRCH.WM.AR.ZS?locations=CN.

[41] Kam C. Chan and Hung-gay Fung, eds., *China's Capital Markets: Challenges from WTO Membership* (Edward Elgar, 2007), 141.

limiting the one-party rule.[42] Another guarantee of the rule of law is the constitution, but the Chinese constitution is silent on the direct enforcement of international agreements such as the WTO accession.[43] Still, substantive legal reforms were undertaken such as foreign trade law, customs law, technical regulations and IP law.[44] As IP is the main concern for other WTO members, China revised major IP laws such as the Patent Law, the Trademark Law and the Copyright Law and other regulations.[45] Specific IP crimes were also added to Chinese criminal laws.[46] Still, IP remains one of the main concerns for foreign companies doing business in China.

Thus, China liberated its market more than any other major developing member. China also regulated its trade remedy legislation before its accession. Anti-dumping regulations were promulgated in 1997 and safeguard regulations in 2001.[47] In this context, China initiated 293 anti-dumping investigations between 1995 and 2022(6).[48] Two hundred and sixty-five of these initiations were terminated with a measure.[49] The top target of Chinese anti-dumping investigations are the US, Japan, Korea and the EU, respectively. Compared to WTO agreements, China's trade remedy regulations are undetailed.[50]

In terms of political implications, WTO provides a forum for its members to discuss trade-related matters. It functions as a quasi-judicial legal process of interpretation by allowing members to negotiate national regulatory regimes and omit restrictive trade measures.[51] Within this context, China's influence on the global economy is increasing. WTO membership also improves transparency and predictability. On the other hand, to promote global integration, China announced new policies such

42 Chow, 'The Impact of Joining WTO on China's Economic', 9.

43 Julia Ya Qin, 'Trade, Investment and Beyond: The Impact of WTO Accession on China's Legal System', in Perry Keller (ed.), *Law and the Market Economy in China* (Routledge, 2017), 271.

44 Ibid., 272.

45 Ibid., 284.

46 Ibid.

47 Ibid., 274.

48 WTO, Antidumping Statistics, accessed 15 July 2023, www.wto.org/english/tratop_e/adp_e/adp e.htm.

49 Ibid.

50 Qin, 'Trade, Investment and Beyond', 274.

51 David Kennedy and Joseph E. Stiglitz, eds., *Law and Economics with Chinese Characteristics: Institutions for Promoting Development in the Twenty-First Century* (Oxford University Press, 2013), 65.

as the Belt and Road or the Greater Bay Area Initiatives. The Belt and Road Initiative (BRI) is one of the most significant regional economic development programmes triggered by China since 2013.[52] Trade, investment, financial services and innovation are some areas to be enhanced through the implementation period. The Greater Bay Area Initiative aims to improve the socio-economic progress within southern China and create a solid starting point for the BRI.[53]

4.2.3 Non-market Economy Status[54]

The basis of non-market economy status can be traced back to GATT 47, which is a part of GATT 94. Annex 1's notes and the supplementary notes on Article VI of the GATT 47 reads as follows:

> It is recognized that, in the case of imports from a country which has a complete or substantially complete monopoly of its trade and where all domestic prices are fixed by the State, special difficulties may exist in determining price comparability for the purposes of paragraph 1, and in such cases importing contracting parties may find it necessary to take into account the possibility that a strict comparison with domestic prices in such a country may not always be appropriate.[55]

The Article VI assumes that markets operate at reliable prices.[56] The explanatory note above acknowledges that there may be cases where domestic prices do not reflect the actual costs which mislead the investigating authorities during the determination of the dumping margin.[57] So, in the case of a non-market economy, the highest comparable price of the like product will be considered for determining the dumping margin. A higher comparable price leads to a higher dumping margin and more anti-dumping protection. Therefore, being treated as a non-market

52 Yun Zhao, ed., *International Governance and the Rule of Law in China under the Belt and Road Initiative* (Cambridge University Press, 2018).

53 Greater Bay Area Overview, accessed 15 July 2023, www.bayarea.gov.hk/en/about/overview.html.

54 This section was previously published as Yilmazcan, Abdulkadir, 'The Role of Anti-Dumping in the US–China Trade War', China & WTO Rev. 2021, no. 1 (2021), 7–36.

55 The General Agreement on Tariffs and Trade (GATT 1947), Annexes, accessed 15 July 2023, www.wto.org/english/docs_e/legal_e/gatt47_03_e.htm#annexi.

56 André J. Washington, 'Not So Fast, China: Non-Market Economy Status Is Not Necessary for the Surrogate Country Method', *Chi. J. Int'l L.* 19 (2018), 262.

57 Yilmazcan, 'The Role of Anti-Dumping in the US-China Trade War', 15.

economy or market economy directly affects the export performance of any WTO member.[58]

The Accession Protocol of China had two substantive consequences in terms of the non-market economy status.[59] First, the protocol implies that China can be treated as a non-market economy, and Chinese exporters need to prove that they are operating under market conditions.[60] Second, Article 15 (d) sets the condition for China to be treated as a market economy based on the criteria of the importing members' national laws.[61] This structure of the protocol leaves a large room for discretion in favour of members other than China. The same sector may be considered as a market economy by a member while treated as a non-market economy by another.

According to Chinese officials, China's non-market economy status terminated in 2016.[62] However, members such as the EU are still finding alternative ways to treat China as a non-market economy. The US also continues to treat China as a non-market economy. This status inflates the anti-dumping margins and causes the anti-dumping laws to be over protectionist.[63] Vermulst and Sud analyse the contradictory trade policies of the EU, which uses certain criteria to determine market economy status, including (1) low degree of public intervention, (2) transparent and non-discriminatory company law covering international accounting standards, (3) IP rights and bankruptcy regime, and (4) independent financial sector.[64] The authors note that the EU granted market economy

58 Ibid.

59 Ibid.

60 Laura Puccio, 'Granting Market Economy Status to China: An Analysis of WTO Law and of Selected WTO Members' Policy', European Parliamentary Research Service, November-PE 571 (2015), 5.

61 Article 15 (d): Once China has established, under the national law of the importing WTO Member, that it is a market economy, the provisions of subparagraph (a) shall be terminated provided that the importing Member's national law contains market economy criteria as of the date of accession. In any event, the provisions of subparagraph (a)(ii) shall expire 15 years after the date of accession. In addition, should China establish, pursuant to the national law of the importing WTO Member, that market economy conditions prevail in a particular industry or sector, the non-market economy provisions of subparagraph (a) shall no longer apply to that industry or sector.

62 Weihuan Zhou, 'China's Litigation on Non-Market Economy Treatment at the WTO: A Preliminary Assessment', *Chin. J. Comp. L.* 5, no. 2 (2017), 346.

63 Weihuan Zhou and Andrew Percival, 'Debunking the Myth of "Particular Market Situation" in WTO Antidumping Law', *J. Int'l Econ. L.* 19, no. 4 (2016), 865.

64 Edwin Vermulst, and Juhi Dion Sud, 'The New Rules Adopted by the European Union to Address "Significant Distortions" in the Anti-Dumping Context', in Marc Bungenberg,

status to economies similar to China such as Russia and the Ukraine, even before they became WTO members, and so the decision to classify China seems political rather than economic.[65] As noted by Smith and Pan, the US relies on classifying China as a non-market economy due to matters such as IP, subsidised exports, an undervalued currency and unfair harm to US producers.[66]

In general, the concerns over the Chinese market are the subsidies, cheap financing and other benefits in favour of the SOEs.[67] It is also discussed that these subsidies create inefficient SOEs.[68] Other policies that affect China's market economy status are 'export credits and export credit insurance; public information services; assistance for exporters to explore international markets; setting up institutions to promote trade by developing foreign trade relations, sponsoring exhibitions, providing information and advisory services; and facilitating exports by small and medium-sized enterprises'.[69]

After the termination of Article 15 (a) (ii) of the Accession Protocol, China carried the matter before the WTO DSM. China requested consultations under the *DS515* against the US and *DS516* against the EU. The consultations are still ongoing in terms of the *DS515*.[70] The Panel had been composed for *DS516* but lapsed in 2020.[71]

4.2.4 *Why the Top Target?*

As mentioned above, China is the top member of the WTO facing anti-dumping measures. Within the 1,156 measures against China between 1995 and 2022(6), 211 of the measures are enforced by India,

Michael Hahn, Christoph Herrmann and Till Müller-Ibold (eds.), *The Future of Trade Defence Instruments* (Springer, 2018), 67.

65 Ibid., 67.

66 Stephen C. Smith and Yao Pan, 'US–China Economic Relations', in Shenggen Fan, Kanbur Ravi, Shang-Jin Wei and Xiaobo Zhang (eds.), *The Oxford Companion to the Economics of China* (Oxford University Press, 2014), 121.

67 Kroeber, *China's Economy: What Everyone Needs to Know®*, 241.

68 Ibid.

69 Bin Xu, 'Trade Policy Reform and Trade Reform', in Shenggen Fan, Kanbur Ravi, Shang-Jin Wei and Xiaobo Zhang (eds.), *The Oxford Companion to the Economics of China* (Oxford University Press, 2014), 157.

70 DS515, United States – Measures Related to Price Comparison Methodologies, accessed 15 July 2023, www.wto.org/english/tratop_e/dispu_e/cases_e/ds515_e.htm.

71 DS516, European Union – Measures Related to Price Comparison Methodologies, accessed 15 July 2023, www.wto.org/english/tratop_e/dispu_e/cases_e/ds516_e.htm; Yilmazcan, 'The Role of Anti-Dumping in the US-China Trade War', 16.

163 by the US and 111 by the EU.[72] There are external and internal factors placing China as the top anti-dumping target.

The first external factor is related to multinational enterprises (MNEs). MNEs create foreign direct investment into countries with lower costs. China ranked second in terms of foreign direct investment as of 2018.[73] For hi-tech goods, the majority of the exports are made by MNEs.[74] Also, almost half of the total exports are made by MNEs.[75] These companies have different effects on Chinese manufacturers. If the local manufacturers have market power in the domestic market, MNEs lobby against these producers in the overseas markets through anti-dumping petitions; for instance, a TV manufacturer MNE investing in China would be unhappy with a domestic manufacturer. In this case, the MNE files anti-dumping petitions against the domestic producer in order to cut the exports of the domestic TV manufacturer. Another issue with the MNEs is that they sometimes subcontract to local manufacturers. In this case, local manufacturers do not have bargaining power and export with the prices imposed by the NME. The reason is that small and medium-sized domestic manufacturers rely on the demands of NMEs.[76] Thus, they face anti-dumping investigations.

Another external factor is the manufacturers in the importing country. The lobbying activity of the manufacturers ends up with anti-dumping measures. During the petitions, the manufacturers claim to create more jobs, but retailers or importers accuse the manufacturers of moving the production to other low-cost countries.[77] Hence, anti-dumping measures divert trade rather than protect the domestic industries.

One external factor derives from trade liberalisation. Due to immediate market access to developing countries, developed markets use trade remedies such as anti-dumping to harass developing countries such as China.[78] Developed markets such as the EU try to prevent Chinese

[72] WTO, Antidumping Statistics.

[73] UNCTAD, World Investment Report 2018, accessed 15 July 2023, https://unctad.org/en/PublicationsLibrary/wir2018_en.pdf.

[74] Kroeber, *China's Economy: What Everyone Needs to Know®*, 238.

[75] Tom Hancock, 'China's Relentless Export Machine Moves Up the Value Chain', *Financial Times*, accessed 15 July 2023, www.ft.com/content/cdc53aee-bc2e-11e8-94b2-17176fbf93f5.

[76] Yuefen Li, 'Why Is China the World's Number One Anti-Dumping Target?', *China in a Globalizing World* (2005), 85.

[77] Ibid., 86.

[78] Ibid., 87.

exports from suppressing domestic manufacturers, as in the case of the steel industry, where China benefited from its overcapacity.[79] Developing countries such as India have similar reasons to enforce anti-dumping measures against China. The average rate of tariffs in India fell from 128 per cent to 35 shortly after the WTO was established.[80] Also, all non-tariff barriers were eliminated in order to integrate with other markets.[81] As a result, India has been one of the top three anti-dumping users since 1995.[82]

In terms of internal factors, China is the top anti-dumping target, and the fast growth of exports is notable. As of 2020, China is the top exporting country capturing nearly 13 per cent of global merchandise exports.[83] China's top importing partners were Taiwan, Korea, Japan, and the US respectively in 2021.[84] In the same year, China's top export markets were the US, Hong Kong, Japan and Korea. China exported nearly $580 billion USD to the US and $470 billion USD to the EU.[85]

Apart from the increased exports, as government control over the market gradually diminishes, the private sector made duplicate investments that resulted in overcapacity problems.[86] Between 1995 and 2022 (6), the top three sectors that China faces anti-dumping measures in are base metals, chemicals and machinery.[87] The first two sectors are labour-intensive and low value-added sectors. Therefore, low-cost exports become the main advantage for competition but also the main reason for China to be the top target of anti-dumping investigations.

As mentioned previously, the provision of the non-market economy status puts China in a disadvantaged position. Even though Article 15 (ii) expired in 2016; the issue is still contentious because as long as China is treated as a non-market economy, it is an easy target for anti-dumping

79 Sherzod Shadikhodjaev, 'Non-Market Economies, Significant Market Distortions, and the 2017 EU Anti-Dumping Amendment', *J. Int'l Econ. L.* 21, no. 4 (2018), 886.
80 Aradhna Aggarwal, 'Trade Effects of Anti-dumping in India: Who Benefits?', *Int'l Trade J.* 25, no. 1 (2010), 112–158.
81 Ibid.
82 Ibid.
83 World Trade Statistical Review 2021, Statistics on Anti-Dumping, 11, accessed 15 July 2023, www.wto.org/english/res_e/statis_e/wts2021_e/wts2021_e.pdf.
84 TradeMap, available at www.trademap.org/, accessed 15 July 2023.
85 Ibid. China–EU – International Trade in Goods Statistics, available at https://ec.europa.eu/eurostat/statistics-explained/index.php?title=Main_Page, accessed 17 June 2023.
86 Li, 'Why Is China the World's Number One Anti-Dumping Target?', 92.
87 Anti-dumping Gateway, WTO, accessed 15 July 2023, www.wto.org/english/tratop_e/adp_e/adp_e.htm.

investigations because the investigation procedures are much easier against a non-market economy compared to a market economy. The investigating authority does not need to rely on exporters' submissions on the costs of the exporters. Instead, the costs are calculated based on the comparable prices of like products in the third country or by adding a reasonable amount for administrative, selling and general costs and for-profits to the cost of production in the country of origin.[88] Due to the capability of generalisation of the dumping margin calculation in non-market economy cases, investigating authorities do not need to conduct on-the-spot verifications or calculate dumping margins for all Chinese exporters individually.

Another factor resulting in high anti-dumping duties against China would be the lack of legal capacity of Chinese exporters. In the beginning, Chinese exporters were unaware of the outcomes of anti-dumping investigations.[89] They were also reluctant to cooperate with investigating authorities, especially when they realised the costs of foreign law firms in jurisdictions such as the US or EU. After facing several investigations, Chinese law firms began to advise on anti-dumping investigations. Also, MOFCOM is coordinating the cooperation procedures during the investigations. Regarding the low-priced exports of Chinese industries, a low level of technology, low production costs and a weak position in the global value chain contributes to the likelihood of anti-dumping investigations.[90] Anti-dumping remains a severe threat to the Chinese market as more FTAs are being signed between other markets.[91] Therefore, while other markets are liberalising, Chinese exporters are being suppressed by additional duties such as anti-dumping.[92] This also negatively affects the improvement of technology among Chinese manufacturers as low price remains the main advantage of Chinese exports. To support research and development, the Chinese Government initiated subsidy programmes that contributed to sustaining lower prices but at the same time resulted in more anti-dumping investigations.[93]

[88] WTO ADA, Article 2.2.

[89] Li, 'Why Is China the World's Number One Anti-Dumping Target?', 99.

[90] Xiaosong Wang, Zhexi Liu, Yue Lu and Chunming Zhao, 'Trade Barriers and Participation in the Global Value Chain: An Empirical Study Based on Anti-dumping toward China', *China World Econ.* 27, no. 2 (2019), 86–106.

[91] Ibid.

[92] Ibid.

[93] Ibid.

Finally, China has a unique VAT scheme with two components. The VAT is applied differently in domestic and international transactions.[94] If a company exports goods overseas, this transaction is exempted from VAT whereas domestic sales are subject to VAT.[95] This policy supports export-oriented growth objectives. An empirical study shows that China's export VAT rebate scheme is substantially supporting China's exports.[96] This, in return, creates pressure in markets abroad and domestic manufacturers lobby against Chinese exports for anti-dumping protection.

Listing all these factors, China has alternative options to respond. Bown highlights possible options for China: (1) ignoring and accepting the trade barriers, (2) using anti-dumping as a retaliatory tool, (3) using WTO DSM, and (4) negotiation.[97] Since 2018, the trade war between the US and China has escalated, affecting $550 billion USD to China and $185 billion USD to the US.[98] As well as retaliation from both sides, the WTO DSM was used intensively, with six disputes since March 2018.[99] On the trade war, Liu and Woo assert that 'economic disputes are a systemic feature of the present uncoordinated multipolar political order'.[100]

4.2.5 Role of MOFCOM in Anti-dumping Investigations

MOFCOM reflects China's trade policy and an understanding of the role of this government body would contribute to research questions. China's anti-dumping legal framework has three layers, namely Foreign Trade

94 John Whalley and Jing Wang, 'Using Tax-Based Instruments for Innovative China's Trade Rebalancing', in Shenggen Fan, Kanbur Ravi, Shang-Jin Wei and Xiaobo Zhang (eds.), *The Oxford Companion to the Economics of China* (Oxford University Press, 2014), 146.

95 KPMG, *China: Country VAT Essentials Guide* (2017), 20.

96 Chien-Hsun Chen, Chao-Cheng Mai and Hui-Chuan Yu, 'The Effect of Export Tax Rebates on Export Performance: Theory and Evidence from China', *China Econ. Rev.* 17, no. 2 (2006), 226–235.

97 Chad P. Bown, 'Antidumping and Other Trade Disputes', in Shenggen Fan, Kanbur Ravi, Shang-Jin Wei and Xiaobo Zhang (eds.), *The Oxford Companion to the Economics of China* (Oxford University Press, 2014), 117.

98 Richard Fuchs, Peter Alexander, Calum Brown, Frances Cossar, Roslyn C. Henry and Mark Rounsevell, 'Why the US–China Trade War Spells Disaster for the Amazon', *Nature* 567, no. 7749 (2019), 451.

99 Chronological List of Disputes Cases, WTO.

100 Tao Liu and Wing Thye Woo, 'Understanding the US–China Trade War', *China Econ. J.* 11, no. 3 (2018), 319–340.

Law, Anti-dumping Regulations and departmental rules.[101] MOFCOM play a central role in this framework. In terms of anti-dumping, the main functions of MOFCOM are conducting anti-dumping investigations and defending the interests of the Chinese exporters. While facing many anti-dumping investigations, China had two alternatives to cope with. First, following the other developing markets such as India and retaliating with new anti-dumping investigations, and second, improving the ways to defend the interests of the Chinese exporters.[102] One study argues that China is not using anti-dumping investigations in retaliatory manners like the US.[103] Another study suggests, 'It seems that some retaliatory response is less likely against wealthier instigator countries, but given some response, a WTO DSU case is more likely the wealthier the instigator country is.'[104] So China opted for the second alternative to protect its exports-based growth. Until now, China pursued twenty cases at the WTO DSM only against two members: the US and EU with sixteen and five cases, respectively.[105] That also illustrates the conflict between these two trading blocks. Within this context, rather than the anti-dumping investigations conducted by MOFCOM, this study focuses on the MOFCOM's participation in the anti-dumping investigations against China.

Before China's accession to WTO, rules on 'Response to Anti-dumping Charges Raised by Foreign Countries against Chinese Export Commodities' were in force to respond to anti-dumping investigations from other countries.[106] According to this regulation, the Chambers of Importers & Exporters Associations had the primary responsibility to coordinate the response against the anti-dumping investigations while

[101] Yusong Chen, 'Laws and Implementation in China: A 16 Years Review after Accession to the WTO', in Marc Bungenberg, Michael Hahn, Christoph Herrmann and Till Müller-Ibold (eds.), *The Future of Trade Defence Instruments* (Springer, 2018), 283–294.

[102] Yan Luo, *Anti-Dumping in the WTO, the EU, and China: The Rise of Legalization in the Trade Regime and Its Consequences*, Vol. 69 (Kluwer Law International, 2010), 157.

[103] Xiaohua Bao and Larry D. Qiu, 'Is China's Antidumping More Retaliatory than that of the US?', *Rev. Int'l Econ.* 19, no. 2 (2011), 386.

[104] Robert M. Feinberg and Kara M. Reynolds, 'How Do Countries Respond to Anti-dumping Filings? Dispute Settlement and Retaliatory Anti-dumping', The World Economy 41, no. 5 (2018), 1251–1268.

[105] WTO, Dispute Settlement: The Disputes, accessed 15 July 2023, www.wto.org/english/tratop_e/dispu_e/find_dispu_cases_e.htm.

[106] Le Thi Thuy Van and Sarah Y. Tong, 'China and Anti-dumping: Regulations, Practices and Responses', East Asia Institute. National University of Singapore Working Paper 149 (2009), 16.

keeping MOFTEC[107] informed about the process.[108] During this period, Chinese exporters rarely cooperated with the investigating authorities due to a lack of legal capacity and high costs.[109]

After the accession to the WTO, MOFTEC promulgated the 'Provisions on Responding to Actions of Anti-dumping of Export Products' in 2001.[110] The detailed guidance of the regulation positively contributed to the cooperation process. In 2006, the regulation was amended giving MOFCOM a more active role. Article 2 of the regulation obliges exporters to respond to the anti-dumping investigations actively.[111] Utilising trade associations, MOFCOM is required to determine effective policies to respond to anti-dumping investigations.[112] Trade associations are actively used in order to protect the interests of the small-to-medium-sized exporters.[113]

The process of responding to an investigation starts with the announcement of MOFCOM. Then the related business association such as the Chamber of Commerce notifies its members.[114] The Chamber of Commerce and MOFCOM guides the exporters to prepare the submission to the investigating authority. MOFCOM also supports the foundation of ad hoc business associations such as China's shoe alliance against raising almost half a million USD to appeal the decision of the EU Commission.[115]

4.3 US Investigation Procedures

This part evaluates the basics of the US anti-dumping proceedings. Between 1995 and 2023(6), the US has initiated 891 anti-dumping investigations of which 628 were terminated with a measure. China is by far the top target with 163 measures.[116] The second and third targets

107 Ministry of Foreign Trade and Economic Co-operation, State Economic and Trade Commission (SETC) and the State Development Planning Commission (SDPC) merged into MOFCOM in 2003.

108 Van and Tong, 'China and Anti-dumping: Regulations, Practices and Responses'.

109 Ibid.

110 Ibid., 17.

111 MOFCOM, Decree No 12, 2006, Promulgating the Provisions on Responding to Actions of Anti-dumping of Export Products, http://english.mofcom.gov.cn/.

112 Luo, *Anti-Dumping in the WTO, the EU, and China*, 158.

113 Ibid.

114 Ibid.

115 Van and Tong, 'China and Anti-dumping: Regulations, Practices and Responses', 20.

116 WTO Statistics.

are Korea and Chinese Taipei with 43 and 32 measures, respectively.[117] The US anti-dumping measures cover around 4 per cent of its imports, which means around $114 billion USD.[118]

Anti-dumping procedures can be evaluated in four main phases: pre-initiation, investigation, determination and enforcement, and judicial review. These phases are focused in detail in the context of ADA, the US anti-dumping regulations,[119] guidelines and other government sources.

The foundation of anti-dumping laws and the Commission dates back to 1916.[120] However, modern USITC was established with the Trade Act of 1974.[121] In 1979, the Tariff Act of 1930 was amended to authorise USITC to conduct anti-dumping investigations.[122]

Apart from the USITC, the US Department of Commerce's Import Administration (Commerce) is involved in anti-dumping proceedings. The Commerce decides on the initiation of an anti-dumping investigation and determines the existence and amount of the dumping.[123] Meanwhile, USITC reviews the injury information and determines the material injury caused by imports.[124]

To free the USITC from politics, its members are appointed for nine years without a chance to be re-elected, and they cannot be removed except in certain cases such as misbehaviour.[125] That is why politically fruitful cases were rejected by the USITC before. Also, the USITC decides on the injury and causation within the first forty-five days of the petition, which is before the initiation of the investigation.[126] Therefore, some cases are rejected before the official initiation of the investigation. Still, the US is one of the top users of anti-dumping investigations as a trade policy and having two institutions makes the process more complicated and costly for the exporters.

117 Ibid.

118 Chad P. Bown and Y. Zhang, 'Measuring Trump's 2018 Trade Protection: Five Takeaways', Technical Report, Peterson Institute for International Economics (2019), 4.

119 The Tariff Act of 1930.

120 John Benedetto, Lauren Gamache, James Holbein and Craig Thomsen, 'Summary of the US International Trade Commission Centennial Proceedings', *J. Int'l Com. & Econ.* 2017 (2017), 11.

121 Ibid.

122 Ibid.

123 Horlick, 'Ten Major Problems in the United States', 169.

124 Ibid.

125 Ibid.

126 Ibid.

4.3.1 *Pre-initiation*

Before the official initiation of an anti-dumping investigation, the domestic industry needs to prepare a petition. This section focuses on the procedures before the initiation of the anti-dumping investigation. Pre-initiation starts with the application of the domestic industry until the notice of initiation. The application should be in a written format by or on behalf of the domestic industry.[127] The application must include specific information on the goods (including the Harmonized Tariff Schedule of the United States), industry, importers, exporters, prices and injury.[128] Also, the differences should be specified between the imported and domestic products under consideration.[129] The statistical information on the injury should be submitted separately for each firm as well as the whole industry.[130] Article 5.2 of the ADA also clarifies the minimum information that needs to be submitted to the investigating authorities.[131] This includes the increase in imports, like products, price undercutting, depressed prices and the impact of imports on the industry. After receiving the application and relevant evidence, Commerce decides to accept or reject the petition within twenty days. If the Commerce decides in favour of the initiation, USITC is informed, and within twenty-five days USITC conducts the preliminary injury and causation determination.[132] Therefore, the preliminary stage cannot exceed forty-five days in total.

4.3.2 *Investigation*

As mentioned above, there are two government bodies in the US responsible for anti-dumping investigations: Commerce and the USITC. Commerce determines the dumping and the dumping margin. Later, the investigation on the determination of injury is conducted by the USITC:

127 Czako et al., *A Handbook on Anti-dumping Investigations*, 21.

128 US International Trade Commission, *Antidumping and Countervailing Duty Handbook*, 14th ed. (2015), I-5.

129 Ibid., p. I-8.

130 Ibid.

131 Czako et al., *A Handbook on Anti-dumping Investigations*, 23.

132 USITC, 'Understanding Antidumping & Countervailing Duty Investigations', accessed 15 July 2023, www.usitc.gov/press_room/usad.htm.

> The USITC is the agency of the US Government that, amongst other things, conducts injury inquiries for contingent remedy cases on safeguards, anti-dumping, and countervailing ... The USITC initiates an inquiry on the basis of a private petition. It holds a public hearing on the question of injury. If it finds that increased imports are a substantial cause of serious injury or threat thereof to an industry in the US, it then holds a public hearing on the question of remedy.[133]

The anti-dumping investigation conducted by the US authorities has five stages: (1) initiation by the Commerce, (2) the preliminary phase of the USITC's investigation, (3) the preliminary phase of Commerce's investigation, (4) the final phase of the Commerce's investigation, and (5) the final phase of the USITC's investigation.[134] Each of these stages needs to be finished within certain time limits: initiation in 20 days after the filing, preliminary determination of the USITC within 45 days after the filing, preliminary determination of the Commerce 115 days after the USITC's preliminary determination, final determination of the Commerce within 75 days of the preliminary determination of the Commerce, final determination of the USITC within 120 days of the Commerce's preliminary determination or 45 days after the USITC's final determination.[135]

In terms of the chronology of events, after the petition of an anti-dumping case, Commerce examines whether the petition is legally satisfactory or not.[136] If the Commerce does not reject the petition, USITC initiates the preliminary investigation and sends questionnaires to importers, purchasers, producers and foreign producers. After receiving the answers, the USITC may send additional questionnaires as well. USITC also holds public briefs, and if there is a negative determination, the investigation is terminated. Otherwise, the Commerce starts the preliminary investigation to determine the 'sales at less than fair value'.[137] If the findings of the Commerce are affirmative, provisional anti-dumping measures can be imposed. After a negative determination or a provisional measure, the Commerce conducts the final investigation to

[133] DS178R United States – Safeguard Measure on Imports of Fresh, Chilled or Frozen Lamb from Australia.

[134] US International Trade Commission, *Antidumping and Countervailing Duty Handbook*, II-3.

[135] Ibid., II-5.

[136] Flow Chart of US' Anti-dumping Proceedings, accessed 15 July 2023, www.tid.gov.hk/english/trade_relations/ad/files/ad_flowchart_usa.pdf.

[137] Ibid.

determine 'sales at less than fair value' through verifications, public hearings and briefs. If there is affirmative determination after the final investigation of the Commerce, provisional anti-dumping duties may be imposed. Afterwards, USITC's final investigation on the injury is held. During the final investigation, the second set of questionnaires is used. Also, hearings and briefs are held before a negative or positive determination of dumping.

As the two agencies have their own procedures, some parts of the overall procedure overlap. Another result of having two agencies is that the USITC and the Commerce have questionnaires around 15 to 150 pages.[138] Also, they have a separate set of questionnaires in accordance with the phase of the investigation. This creates complexity and makes it challenging for the exporters to cooperate from beginning to end. Mentioning the length of the questionnaires, it is also notable to highlight the density of the information required through the questionnaires. The questionnaire of Commerce consists of five sections: (1) Organization, Accounting Practices, Markets and Merchandise; (2) Sales in the Home Market or to a Third Country; (3) Sales to the United States; (4) Cost of Production and Constructed Value; and (5) Cost of Further Manufacture or Assembly Performed in the United States.[139] Some general guidelines for the submission of the questionnaires include:

> Include an original and translated version of all pertinent portions of non-English language documents that accompany your response, including financial statements.
>
> Please respond to each question. If a particular question does not apply, please state so and explain why in your response. Failure to do so could lead to the use of adverse inferences for that particular question.
>
> All monetary amounts should be shown in the currency in which they were originally denominated, and in the currency in which they are registered in your accounts (if the two are different). Also, report the actual exchange rate used for a particular conversion. For all values adjusted for inflation, please provide the data in both nominal and adjusted terms and explain how these values were adjusted.[140]

[138] USITC, Generic Questionnaires, available at www.usitc.gov/trade_remedy/question.htm, accessed 15 July 2023; Commerce Questionnaires, available at https://enforcement.trade.gov/questionnaires/questionnaires-ad.html, accessed 15 July 2023.

[139] Ibid.

[140] Ibid., G-4.

In addition to the strict rules on how to respond to the questions, some parts require almost all information about the business's commercial activities:

> Describe your agreement(s) for sales in the United States and the foreign market (e.g., long-term purchase contract, short-term purchase contract, purchase order, order confirmation). Provide a copy of each type of agreement and all sales-related documentation generated in the sales process (including the purchase order, internal and external order confirmation, invoice, and shipping and export documentation) for a sample sale in the foreign market and US market during the POI.[141]
>
> Describe how you used your normal cost and financial accounting records to compute each of the following cost elements:
>
> a. production quantity;
> b. direct materials;
> c. internal taxes (including value added taxes (VAT)) and import duties on materials purchases. State whether you were exempted from paying or were rebated these taxes and duties on imported raw materials used to produce the merchandise under consideration;
> d. direct labour;
> e. variable production overhead (provide a list of the cost categories that comprise your submitted variable overhead cost figures);
> f. fixed production overhead (provide a list of the cost categories that comprise your submitted fixed overhead cost figures);
> g. research and development costs;
> h. general and administrative (G&A) expenses (provide a list of the cost categories that comprise your submitted G&A costs); and,
> i. net interest expense (include a list of all interest income and expense items and other financing amounts used to compute net interest expense).[142]

So almost every question requests all the information available under the review period accompanied by supporting documents, which make for an average response of well above 500 pages. Considering the USITC questionnaire and other additional questionnaires, complying with the US investigating authorities is challenging, especially for SMEs.

Anti-dumping measures are specific to exporters and products. This means that under normal circumstances, anti-dumping duties should be specific to the manufacturer of a particular product. However, it is usual for the US investigating authorities to have almost sixty companies in an

141 Ibid., A-9.
142 Ibid., D-11.

anti-dumping investigation.[143] Even if all of these exporters attempt to cooperate, Commerce has the discretion to select a few exporters as mandatory respondents. The individual dumping margins are used for the mandatory respondents, and the weighted average of these margins is used as the 'all others rate' for the remaining exporters.[144] Other exporters may request individual calculations, but the Commerce has broad discretion since there are no rules on the requirements to satisfy the demand or on the criteria for the selection of mandatory respondents.[145] In practice, the Commerce chooses the top two exporters and avoids other demands that also overshadow the representability of the 'all others rate'.[146] This is because the weighted average of two companies can be applied to fifty different exporters in practice, which does not accurately represent the real case. Therefore, due to the grey areas of the ADA and local regulations, the US investigation authorities enjoy discretion that results in stricter determination and enforcement.

4.3.3 Determination and Enforcement

The first issue regarding determination and enforcement is the decision on the non-market economy status and the use of facts available provision. For example, the choice of the analogue country where the investigating country practises a high level of discretion creates a considerable difference regarding the final measure. Furthermore, in terms of the decision on market or non-market economy status, the US authorities have a large room for discretion. Moreover, once a decision is made in favour of the non-market economy, it is unlikely to be revoked. Section 1677 (18) of the US Tariff Act 1930 states:

> (i) Any determination that a foreign country is a nonmarket economy country shall remain in effect until revoked by the administering authority.
> (ii) The administering authority may make a determination under subparagraph (A) with respect to any foreign country at any time.[147]

143 Adam Williams, 'What a Dump! The Current State of Antidumping Duty Calculations in Non-Market Economy Cases', *Emory Int'l L. Rev.* 32 (2017), 440.

144 Ibid. The Tariff Act of 1930 19 USCS § 1677 35 (B), defines weighted average dumping margin as 'the percentage determined by dividing the aggregate dumping margins determined for a specific exporter or producer by the aggregate export prices and constructed export prices of such exporter or producer'.

145 Williams, 'What a Dump!', 440.

146 Ibid.

147 19 USC § 1677(18).

There are six main factors to be taken into account while deciding on the non-market economy status: (1) currency manipulation, (2) determination of wages regarding the free labour market forces, (3) market access for joint ventures and foreign investments, (4) the government control over the industries, (5) the government control over the allocation of resources, and (6) other specific and relevant factors about the country.[148] These are customary criteria rather than written rules.[149] The last criterion transforms this evaluation from an economic perspective into a political one.

Second, although the 'facts available' concept is designed for completion of the investigation on time by pressuring the companies, it is exercised as a punishment.[150] Commerce's practice of 'facts available', and especially the 'adverse facts available', results in higher anti-dumping measures than the actual dumping amount. Therefore, strict procedural rules and discretion of the investigating authorities lower the level of cooperation.

Furthermore, there are four specific items where Commerce may inflate the margins. First, Commerce has the discretion to avoid below-cost sales while comparing US prices.[151] In other words, employing only above-cost sales results in a higher calculation of the normal value. This increases the dumping margin. Second, Commerce can rely on constructed value rather than the price information submitted by the party under investigation.[152] In the case of a non-market economy such as China, the Commerce does not rely on the prices of the exporters. To determine the price, the Commerce examines surrogate countries taking into account the level of economic development.[153] There are no additional criteria for Commerce while determining the calculated normal value.[154] Taking into account the Chinese industries of scale, surrogate country prices are likely to be higher. Some scholars suggest that surrogate country prices may also be used to eliminate currency

148 Puccio, 'Granting Market Economy Status to China', 18.

149 Ibid.

150 Moore, 'US Facts-Available Antidumping Decisions', 45.

151 'An Introduction to Anti-Dumping Law of EU and US as It Applies to Seafood', 24, accessed 14 June 2022, www.hambreyconsulting.co.uk/Documents/Course-handbook-eng.pdf.

152 Ibid.

153 Williams, 'What a Dump!', 441.

154 Ibid.

devaluation.[155] However, anti-dumping measures are specific to firms and even the product models, whereas currency devaluation affects the entire economy and export competitiveness. Therefore, anti-dumping is not the right tool to combat a macroeconomic policy. Turning back to surrogate country prices, by using this method, the normal value increases, thus the gap with the Chinese exports also grows. This results in higher anti-dumping measures. The third factor is also related to constructed value. The Commerce can rely on the profit ratios of the domestic industries, which would be particularly higher than exporters' margins. Commerce traditionally uses high-profit margins.[156] Finally, Commerce uses the zeroing methodology in order to increase the dumping margin. Although there are several WTO rulings against the US zeroing practice, the outcome of anti-dumping investigations remains the same. Commerce, therefore, manipulates the actual data on prices to overprotect US manufacturers.

After the preliminary determinations, customs authorities require a cash deposit or bond to cover possible definitive anti-dumping measures.[157] This also increases the financial burden for the importers, thereby depressing the ongoing trade. The decrease in imports after the initiation of an anti-dumping investigation is explained by an economic model named the 'investigation effect'.[158] There are also procedures to correct the Ministerial errors within five days of disclosure of materials.[159] Rather than methodological errors, copying and calculation errors are taken into consideration for correction. The correction can be made in the preliminary and final determination phases. If the USITC finds that there is a material injury on the domestic industry, the Department of Commerce issues an anti-dumping order to enforce the measure.[160] This determination can be made 120 days after the Commerce's preliminary determination or 45 days after the Commerce's final determination. The anti-dumping duty rates are determined by the International Trade

[155] Chen Yu, 'Currency Manipulation and WTO Laws: Should the Anti-Dumping Mechanism Be Entirely Dumped?', *J. World Invest. Trade* 20, no. 6 (2019), 891–915.

[156] Williams, 'What a Dump!'.

[157] 'An Introduction to Anti-Dumping Law of EU and US as It Applies to Seafood', 6.

[158] Robert W. Staiger and Frank A. Wolak, *Measuring Industry Specific Protection: Anti-Dumping in the United States*, No. W4696 (National Bureau of Economic Research, 1994).

[159] 'An Introduction to Anti-Dumping Law of EU and US as It Applies to Seafood', 6.

[160] USITC, 'Understanding Antidumping & Countervailing Duty Investigations'.

Administration of the Commerce. Also, after the determination, if provisional measures are in force, those are turned into final measures.

Wang, Hou and Lin developed an economic model on the political factors behind USITC rulings.[161] They reached three critical conclusions: (1) political factors are the most important determinants of material injury; (2) USITC rulings are biased against China; (3) economic factors did not play a substantial role in USITC rulings against China.[162]

4.3.4 *Judicial Review*

A judicial review of the anti-dumping measures can be at domestic and international levels. The role of the WTO DSM is discussed in detail in the following chapter. This part focuses on the domestic legal remedies. Under the US judicial system, decisions of the Commerce and USITC can be appealed. The US Court of International Trade is the first instance court, and the decisions can also be appealed before the US Court of Appeals for the Federal Circuit (CAFC). The US Supreme Court handled only a few cases, while the CAFC had more.

One crucial question is whether domestic legal remedies are accessible by exporters subject to an anti-dumping investigation. Challenging a decision of the Commerce or USITC would be costly. Studies assert that developing countries are less likely to challenge a decision on anti-dumping investigations due to limited legal capacity.[163] Similarly, escalating the issue before the WTO DSM is a challenging task for a developing country. The domestic legal order would demonstrate the difficulty of challenging the level of discretion during the investigation procedures. The US Court admits the large room for discretion enjoyed by the USITC due to the lack of clear regulations:

> Plaintiff 'COGSI argued that the Commission erred by starting the POI in the year of the BP Oil Spill' when it should have started the POI a year earlier to compensate for the significant one-time disruption to data trends caused by the spill. The court emphasized that there is 'no statutory requirement for a POI so the ITC has broad discretion' to choose the POI. The only statutory requirement is that the ITC must 'evaluate all relevant

[161] Xiaosong Wang, Jack Hou and Faqin Lin, 'ITC Antidumping toward China Rulings: Is Political Factor Overwhelming?', *Bull. Econ. Res.* 74, no. 1 (2021), 1–17.
[162] Ibid.
[163] Feinberg and Reynolds, 'How Do Countries Respond to Anti-dumping Filings?'.

economic factors … within the context of the business cycle and conditions of competition that are distinctive to the affected industry'.[164]

Hence, there are no clear rules about the determination of the period of investigation, which may change the outcome of the investigation substantially. For example, there are several export transactions, and in the first year, exporters had lower export prices whereas in the second, around the normal value of the exporting market. If the USITC determines these two years as the period of investigation, the dumping margins will reflect an overall average. However, if only the first year is selected, then the dumping margins and consequently the anti-dumping duties would be much higher. Although the US courts acknowledge discretion, many cases against anti-dumping decisions are rejected. The CAFC upheld a decision of the US Court of International Trade in 2018 while rejecting the claims by Vietnamese exporters regarding the final determinations of the Commerce.[165]

In *Sichuan Changhong Electric Co., Ltd. v. the United States*, USITC was challenged for violation of due process purposes that limited time was granted to parties to comment on new factual information.[166] The parties were given only four days to comment on new factual information that was gathered during a hearing.[167] Thus, Sichuan Changhong argued that four days is not enough to analyse the new facts and develop adequate comments. The Court noted that more time would improve the quality of comments by parties, but did not find USITC in violation of due process.[168] The dismissal of the case constitutes a limitation to the right to defend and to meaningful participation.

In *Connecticut Steel Corp. v. United States*, one of the domestic producers revised its questionnaire response after the preliminary injury determination, changing the first data submitted.[169] This second data was also

[164] Shara L. Aranoff, Sonam Patel and Molly J. Doggett, 'A Review of the Court of International Trade's 2015 Decisions Addressing Trade Remedy Determinations of the US International Trade Commission and the Court's Decisions Pursuant to 28 USC 1581 (i)', *Geo. J. Int'l L.* 48 (2016), 19.

[165] Toan Dao, 'US Court of Appeals Upholds Anti-dumping Duties on Shrimp from Vietnam', 2018, available at www.seafoodsource.com/news/supply-trade/us-court-of-appeals-upholds-anti-dumping-duties-on-shrimp-from-vietnam, accessed 15 July 2023.

[166] Valerie A. Slater and Lisa W. Ross, 'Judicial Review of the International Trade Commission's Determinations in Antidumping and Countervailing Duty Proceedings: An Overview of Decisions in 2006', *Geo. J. Int'l L.* 39 (2007), 82.

[167] Ibid.

[168] Ibid.

[169] Ibid., 83.

submitted after the deadline for revisions.[170] USITC has taken this data into account while blocking the opportunity for the other parties to comment before a negative determination.[171] Although statutory provisions require parties to be granted a final opportunity to comment, the Court ruled that parties are not needed to comment on all information during preliminary determination due to a tight timetable.[172]

Another notable issue is the enforcement of countervailing duties for non-market economies. The Commerce decided that it is almost impossible to determine the financial contribution of governments to the companies, especially in non-market economies.[173] In 2006, Commerce received a petition on Coated Free Sheet Paper and considered applying countervailing duties against China. After that, the Commerce initiated countervailing and anti-dumping investigations simultaneously, which resulted in Chinese exporters challenging the decision.[174] The so-called GPX Litigation ended with the court decision that, under the current legislation, it is not possible to conduct countervailing duty investigations against non-market economies.[175] Therefore, the US enacted the 'GPX Legislation' in 2012 allowing the Commerce to initiate countervailing duty investigations against non-market economies. This time China challenged the issue before the WTO DSM by arguing that the US failed to avoid enforcement of double remedies in several investigations between 2006 and 2012. The Panel found that the GPX Legislation violates Articles 10, 19.3 and 32.1 of the Agreement on Subsidies and Countervailing Measures in several investigations due to double remedies.[176] In this context, the judicial review mechanism in the US does not fully supporting procedural justice in anti-dumping investigations.

4.4 Investigation Procedures of the EU

This part evaluates the basics of the EU's anti-dumping proceedings. Between 1995 and 2023(6), the EU has initiated 548 anti-dumping

170 Ibid.
171 Ibid.
172 Ibid.
173 Mostafa Beshkar and Adam S. Chilton, 'Revisiting Procedure and Precedent in the WTO: An Analysis of US–Countervailing and Anti-dumping Measures (China)', *World Trade Rev.* 15, no. 2 (2016), 375–395.
174 Ibid.
175 Ibid.
176 WTO, DS449, US – Countervailing and Anti-Dumping Measures (China), one page summary, accessed 15 July 2023, www.wto.org/english/tratop_e/dispu_e/cases_e/1page sum_e/ds449sum_e.pdf.

investigations in which 363 were terminated with a measure. China is by far the top target with 112 measures.[177] The second and third targets are Russia and India with 25 and 23 measures, respectively.[178] EU imports almost 2 trillion euros each year and nearly 2.5 per cent of this import is subject to trade remedies, specifically anti-dumping duties.[179] Moreover, the actual effect of these measures can be seen by trade diversion.[180] On average, almost half of the EU's imports diverts to other countries after the enforcement of trade remedies.[181] According to the EU Trade Defence Report 2019:

> At the end of 2019, the EU's 137 antidumping and anti-subsidy measures were shielding from unfair competition circa 343,000 direct EU jobs. Measures imposed in 2019 contributed to an increase of the number of jobs benefitting from TDI measures by 23,000.[182]

The relevant body for anti-dumping investigations is the Directorate General for Trade as a part of the Commission. Furthermore, if the anti-dumping duties are evaded, the European Anti-Fraud Office (OLAF) conducts circumvention investigations. DG Trade is supported by a committee consisting of the EU Members' representatives.

The EU has amended its trade defence legislation as of 2018. The basic anti-dumping regulation of the EU is Regulation 2016/1036, which also had been amended in 2017 by the Regulation 2017/2321 and in 2018 by the Regulation 2018/825:[183]

> The EU anti-dumping system has been reformed in two ways. In track one, the Commission, the European Parliament, and the Council agreed to modernize the existing EU procedures to make them faster, more

177 WTO Statistics.

178 Ibid.

179 Arnoud R. Willems and Matilda J. Brolin, 'The Unhappy Marriage of Customs and Anti-Dumping Legislation: Tensions Relating to Product Description and Origin', *Leg. Issues Econ. Integration* 45, no. 3 (2018), 230.

180 Trade diversion occurs when there is an intervention such as FTA, Trade remedies or tariff liberalisation. In cases of trade remedies, after the enforcement of a trade remedy, trade from other countries increase.

181 Willems and Brolin, 'The Unhappy Marriage of Customs and Anti-Dumping Legislation', 230.

182 European Commission, Report from the Commission to the European Parliament and the Council, 2019, accessed 15 July 2023, https://trade.ec.europa.eu/doclib/docs/2020/may/tradoc_158733.PDF.

183 Full text of the consolidated version of the Regulation 2016/1036, available at https://eur-lex.europa.eu/legal-content/EN/TXT/?qid=1556980299597&uri=CELEX:02016R1036-20180608, accessed 15 July 2023.

> transparent, and efficient in dealing with unfair trade. In track two, the 'trialogue' discussions resulted in the amendment of the Basic Regulation's provisions on NMEs, effective as of 20 December 2017 (hereinafter the '2017 amendment'). These two tracks represent 'the first major overhaul' of the EU trade defence instruments in the last two decades.[184]

The amendments aim to react faster against unfair trade practices. Therefore, the amendments authorise the Commission to issue country and sector-specific reports on whether there is a significant level of distortion and use country-specific methodologies to calculate the normal value. The new method allows the EU to determine sector-specific decisions. The report on China handles particular types of market distortions such as land, energy, capital, raw materials and labour. The report also examines steel, aluminium, chemicals and ceramic sectors from a market distortion perspective.[185] The level of discretion in that regard is significant. Based on the information published by the EU, the average anti-dumping amount is around 10 per cent when the normal value is used with typical calculation methods.[186] On the other hand, the average reaches around 40 per cent when surrogate methods are applied.[187]

4.4.1 Pre-initiation

The European producers need to submit a complaint to the Commission in order to trigger the process. A complaint needs to satisfy certain conditions:

- contain allegations that a product originating in a country (or countries) outside the EU is being exported to the EU at dumped prices, and that these imports are causing injury to the EU industry;
- contain evidence (e.g., invoices, price offers, publications in specialised press, official statistics, etc.) to support the allegations made;

[184] Shadikhodjaev, 'Non-Market Economies, Significant Market Distortions, and the 2017 EU Anti-Dumping Amendment'.

[185] Country Report on China, accessed 15 June 2022, http://trade.ec.europa.eu/doclib/docs/2017/december/tradoc_156474.pdf.

[186] 'Calculation of Dumping Margins: EU and US Rules and Practices in Light of the Debate on China's Market Economy Status', European Parliament, accessed 30 June 2023, www.europarl.europa.eu/RegData/etudes/IDAN/2016/583794/EPRS_IDA(2016)583794_EN.pdf.

[187] Liu Yong and Xie Yiyi, 'Analysis of the EU's New Surrogate Country System for External Anti-Dumping and Its Illegality', *J. WTO & China* 10 (2020), 52.

- be supported by a significant share of EU production (companies accounting for at least 25% of total EU production of the product); and
- not be opposed by EU companies accounting for a larger production volume than the complainants.[188]

Also, it is expected and encouraged that complainants contact other producers in the EU to receive support, which would lead to anti-competitive behaviours as explained in Chapter 2.

4.4.2 Investigation

The new trade defence legislation allows the EU to determine sector-specific decisions. The recent legislation and the report on China are a unique resource for this part.[189] During the investigation, the Commission and Council have different roles, and the procedure is finished within certain time limits. Basically, the investigation is conducted by the Commission. Definitive duties, on the other hand, are adopted by the Council.[190]

The process starts with a complaint by the EU industries. The Commission decides whether the evidence is sufficient or not. If the decision is affirmative, Commission initiates an investigation that is announced in the *Official Journal of the European Union*. Then questionnaires are sent to exporters, importers and EU producers. These questionnaires are around twenty-five to fifty pages long.[191] The questionnaire for exporters consists of ten sections, and they are as follows:

(1) General information, (2) product description, (3) operating statistics, (4) domestic sales of like products, (5) export sales to EU, (6) cost of production, (7) profitability, (8) allowances, (9) computerised information and (10) certification.[192] Similar to the US questionnaire, the EU

[188] Anti-Dumping Complaints, European Commission, accessed 30 June 2023, https://policy.trade.ec.europa.eu/enforcement-and-protection/trade-defence/anti-dumping-measures/anti-dumping-complaints_en.

[189] Country Report on China .

[190] Piet Eechout, 'Administrative Procedures in EU External Trade Law', accessed 10 July 2023, www.europarl.europa.eu/RegData/etudes/note/join/2011/432758/IPOL-JURI_NT(2011)432758_EN.pdf.

[191] European Commission, Anti-dumping, accessed 15 July 2023, http://ec.europa.eu/trade/policy/accessing-markets/trade-defence/actions-against-imports-into-the-eu/anti-dumping/#_templates.

[192] Ibid.

requires detailed information on the costs and other commercial information:

> Demonstrate with supporting evidence how the full costs associated with the production and sale of the product under investigation are reasonably and correctly reflected in the records of your company. Such information should be provided in particular for the following items, and should include a description of any domestic price control mechanism and actual domestic price schedules set up for the item concerned:
>
> - main raw materials
> - natural gas
> - oil
> - electricity
> - transport costs[193]

Also in the computerised information section, exporters are required to submit Excel files such as turnover, sales, sales value, production and capacity, stocks, employment, investments, total exports, purchases, sales in the domestic market, export sales to the EU to independent customers, and export sales to the EU to related parties.[194] The information to be submitted covers all transactions within the investigation period.

The Commission is entitled to sample if there are many requests for cooperation.[195] Facts available provisions apply to non-cooperating companies. The Commission can then conduct on-site verifications to cross-check the information submitted. This is possible only if the exporters are willing to cooperate and the exporting country's government does not object. If the Commission finds injurious dumping, it may enforce provisional measures in the first place. Later, definitive measures can be enforced if the exporters do not undertake undumped prices. Definitive measures are also announced in the *Official Journal of the European Union*. There are detailed provisions on the disclosure of underlying facts of the definitive measures upon request.[196]

Regarding the timelines, within forty-five days of the complaint, the Commission needs to decide on the initiation. Investigations need to be terminated within fifteen months of the initiation. Also, provisional measures can be adopted within nine months. After the initiation of

[193] Ibid.
[194] Ibid., 35.
[195] Eechout, 'Administrative Procedures in EU External Trade Law'.
[196] Ibid.

the investigation, relevant parties can submit their views and request to be included in sampling within fifteen days. Exporters and producers may request to receive market economy treatment by filling a form within twenty-one days after the announcement of sample companies. Exporters, importers and producers must reply to questionnaires within thirty-seven days upon receipt, and all interested parties may submit views. After receiving the questionnaires, the Commission conducts on-site verifications and announces provisional findings. The Commission, at that stage, may impose provisional measures as well. Within thirty days of the announcement of the provisional findings, relevant parties may submit their comments. The next stage is the announcement of the definitive findings. Parties have ten days to comment before the findings are adopted as definitive measures.

4.4.3 Determination and Enforcement

At the end of the investigation, if it is found that a material injury is made to the domestic industry, then a definitive anti-dumping duty is enforced.[197] In case the dumping margin is found to be 2 per cent or lower, the EU may dispense anti-dumping measures. Before Regulation 2016/1036, Regulation No 1225/2009 was in force.[198] Article 2.7 (b) stated that only if the exporters from China, Vietnam and Kazakhstan and other non-market economies satisfy specific requirements, then they would be granted a market economy status. The underlying motivation behind this classification is that domestic costs and prices in non-market economies cannot be reasonably compared to market economy costs and prices so non-market economies require other methodologies for the calculation of normal value.[199] The criteria listed in Article 2.7 (c) of the Regulation No 1225/2009 are (1) decisions of firms on price, cost, input, raw material, labour etc. reflecting the supply and demand conditions rather than government intervention; (2) accounting records compatible with international accounting standards; (3) financial records are not distorted due to former non-market economy system; (4) firms are subject to bankruptcy laws; (5) exchange rates are driven by market

197 'An Introduction to Anti-Dumping Law of EU and US as It Applies to Seafood', 8.

198 Council Regulation (EC) No 1225/2009, accessed 15 July 2023, https://publications.europa.eu/en/publication-detail/-/publication/81daf628-e6ca-49e6-a41c-05aebdf017fe/language-en.

199 Vermulst and Sud, 'The New Rules Adopted by the European Union', 240.

forces.[200] It is a challenging task to prove these, but when a company receives market economy treatment, they face lower anti-dumping duties or even exemptions.[201] Commission had a large room for discretion in granting companies market economy status.[202] Given that the EU granted market economy status to economies similar to China, such as Russia and Ukraine, even before they became WTO members, the decision to classify China seems political rather than economic.[203] Although the EU officials argue that the non-market economy status is a technical decision, it is linked to democracy, human rights, the rule of law and good governance.[204] In order to receive market economy status, Chinese companies need to submit additional forms during the anti-dumping investigations within twenty-one days.[205] This is a short time for defending the companies interests given that the form requires submission of extremely detailed documents as well as commercial secrets such as "Minutes of Board of Directors meeting (the latest one and others should be available for the verification visit)" since the company formation.[206] This is a procedural burden preventing Chinese exporters to meaningfully participate in the investigation. In 2016, China brought a non-market economy treatment case before the WTO DSM (*DS516*). However, the Panel informed the DSB on two occasions that due to the complexity of legal issues, the Panel needs more time.[207]

Currently, the determination of dumping is regulated in Article 2 of Regulation 2016/1036. The amendment in 2017 abandoned the market economy/non-market economy distinction.[208] In case the sector-specific report on a country mentions the significant market distortion, instead of exporters' price data, undistorted prices or benchmarks from other

200 Council Regulation (EC) No 1225/2009.

201 Vermulst and Sud, 'The New Rules Adopted by the European Union', 240.

202 Ibid.

203 Ibid.

204 For a detailed mixed macro politics-economics-rule-oriented analysis arguing that the non-market economy decision is political rather than economic, see Lingliang Zeng, 'Non-market Economy Issues in Sino-EU Relations: A Purely Technical Matter or Beyond?', in An Chen (ed.), *Contemporary International Law and China's Peaceful Development* (Springer, 2021), 577–597.

205 Silke Melanie Trommer, 'Special Market Economy: Undermining the Principles of the WTO?', *Chin. J. Int'l L.* 6, no. 3 (2007), 565–599.

206 Form for Completion by Companies Claiming Market Economy Treatment, European Commission, accessed 15 July 2023, https://trade.ec.europa.eu/doclib/docs/2013/december/tradoc_151933.pdf\.

207 DS516, European Union – Measures Related to Price Comparison Methodologies.

208 Full text of the consolidated version of the Regulation 2016/1036.

countries are used.[209] Although the wording of the 'non-market economy' concept disappeared, the 2017 amendment follows the previous method to replace non-market prices with market prices.[210] A new criterion is environmental standards.[211] Environmental standards are not explicitly stated as a factor for determining the significant distortions; however, the Commission considers environmental standards while selecting surrogate countries. This selection can allow the Commission to increase the normal value and result in higher anti-dumping duties.[212] From another perspective, market distortions should be handled through subsidy investigations governed by the SCM Agreement.

Regarding the country-specific reports, the EU, by now, had published two reports on China and Russia. The report on China states:

> ... this report finds that China's 'socialist market economy' is characterized by 'a dominant state-ownership ..., an extensive and sophisticated economic planning system, an interventionist government policy in the economy'. These attributes, the report says, demonstrate the existence of tight State control on the economy leading to 'non-market-based resource allocations' and 'the creation of overcapacities in many sectors'.[213]

In other words, the report supports the view of the EU's previous practices by positioning China as a non-market economy. The report also highlights state control over the land, energy, capital, material inputs and labour.[214] Furthermore, the third part of the report is allocated to

[209] Regulation 2016/1036 Article 2 6a

> In case it is determined, when applying this or any other relevant provision of this Regulation, that it is not appropriate to use domestic prices and costs in the exporting country due to the existence in that country of significant distortions within the meaning of point (b), the normal value shall be constructed exclusively on the basis of costs of production and sale reflecting undistorted prices or benchmarks, subject to the following rules.

[210] Shadikhodjaev, 'Non-Market Economies, Significant Market Distortions, and the 2017 EU Anti-Dumping Amendment'.

[211] 2016/1036 Article 2 6a 'The sources the Commission may use include: corresponding costs of production and sale in an appropriate representative country with a similar level of economic development as the exporting country, provided the relevant data are readily available; where there is more than one such country, preference shall be given, where appropriate, to countries with an adequate level of social and environmental protection.'

[212] Shadikhodjaev, 'Non-Market Economies, Significant Market Distortions, and the 2017 EU Anti-Dumping Amendment', 898.

[213] Ibid., 897.

[214] Ibid.

distortions in specific sectors namely steel, aluminium, chemical and ceramic sectors.[215] So, for these sectors, EU industries may rely on the report that China would be treated as a distorted market.[216] In other words, the report on China in specific sectors constitutes a piece of evidence for the EU industries. For instance, the part on the steel industry is evaluated as a distorted market as follows:

> The overarching control of the government prevents free market forces from prevailing in the steel sector in China. The current problem of overcapacity is arguably the clearest illustration of the implications of the government's policies and the distortions resulting therefrom. The current situation of overcapacity triggered a surge of low-priced Chinese exports; causing a depression of steel prices globally and having a negative impact on, inter alia, the financial situation of steel producers worldwide. Consequently, the number of trade defence investigations against Chinese steel imports in different jurisdictions continues to rise (see Section 14.4). While the government has committed to address the overcapacity problem, in particular through the 13th FYP for Steel, it remains to be seen whether this and other targets for the sector are successfully met.[217]

This approach shows that anti-dumping is being used beyond its original purposes. Connecting the overcapacity problem with market distortion and assuming that the exports are low-priced does not seem consistent with the ADA. The design of the ADA is that to adopt an anti-dumping measure, the investigating authority needs to compare the normal value in the exporting country and the export price. However, the country report assumes that due to overcapacity, Chinese exports are low-priced and EU industries can rely on this report to file an investigation. That means Chinese exporters need to prove that the steel market is not distorted. Additionally, they also need to prove the normal value so that the dumping margin can be calculated accordingly.

For the other sectors, there is no explicit provision on Regulation 2016/1036, but it is highlighted at the last subparagraph of Article 6 (a), that all parties shall have ten days to comment on the relevant sources that the Commission intends to use.[218] Moreover, Article 6 (b)

[215] On Significant Distortions in the Economy of the People's Republic of China for the Purposes of Trade Defence Investigations, Commission Staff Working Document, accessed 15 June 2022, http://trade.ec.europa.eu/doclib/docs/2017/december/tradoc_156474.pdf.

[216] Regulation 2016/1036, Article 6 a (d).

[217] Country Report on China.

[218] Regulation 2016/1036, Article 6 (a).

provides a non-exclusive list of significant distortions showing a sign of substantial government intervention. These factors are:

- –the market in question being served to a significant extent by enterprises which operate under the ownership, control or policy supervision or guidance of the authorities of the exporting country;
- –state presence in firms allowing the state to interfere with respect to prices or costs;
- –public policies or measures discriminating in favour of domestic suppliers or otherwise influencing free market forces;
- –the lack, discriminatory application or inadequate enforcement of bankruptcy, corporate or property laws;
- –wage costs being distorted; and
- –access to finance granted by institutions which implement public policy objectives or otherwise not acting independently of the state.[219]

Thus, in these cases, the Commission does not rely on the costs and prices of the exporters but applies different calculation methodologies to reach the normal value where the market is not distorted. In this context, Regulation 1225/2009 and 2016/1036 follow a similar philosophy in replacing non-market prices with market prices.[220]

Like product is another issue causing conflicts. According to Article 2 of the ADA, exported goods can be compared with like products. However, as there is no clear definition of like product at the ADA, WTO's DSM interprets this term. One report mentions that like products should be directly competitive and substitutable, adding that market-based factors should be taken into account.[221] As the determination of like products directly affects the scope of the investigation, investigating authorities can determine more expensive like products so that the difference between the like product and the exported product increases. Alternatively, this determination may result in the broader application of anti-dumping measures. In a recent case, EU customs authorities are collecting anti-dumping duties against e-bike parts while the Chinese exporters are complaining that the original measure is against ordinary bike parts.[222] It is a challenging task to determine which parts are

[219] Ibid., Article 6 (b).

[220] Shadikhodjaev, 'Non-Market Economies, Significant Market Distortions, and the 2017 EU Anti-Dumping Amendment', 895.

[221] DS8, Japan – Taxes on Alcoholic Beverages; Marco Broncken and Natalie McNelis, 'Rethinking the "Like Product" Definition in WTO Antidumping Law', *J. World Trade* 33, no. 3 (1999), 90.

[222] Claims Are Made That Parts for E-bikes Imported from Mainland China Face Unwarranted Anti-dumping Tariffs, HKTDC Research, accessed 15 July 2023,

exclusively designed for e-bikes, so the authorities are aiming at the avoidance of circumvention. This in return, creates unnecessary protection for the e-bike producers. Also, the product-specific rules of origin adopted by the Commission are criticised. The Commission once adopted a negative rule of origin for the photocopiers in order to enforce anti-dumping measures.[223] The rules mention a specific production step that does not confer origin to the product thus determination of circumvention of anti-dumping is easier.

Another issue during the determination is non-cooperation. The Commission calculates the dumping margin based on the facts available when the exporters do not cooperate. Facts available lead to higher anti-dumping duties, so exporters and importers attempt to cooperate, but it is not an easy task to fulfil all the Commission's requirements. After the determination of the dumping margins, the Commission sends its findings to the Council. The Council then rejects or publishes the definitive anti-dumping measures in the *Official Journal of the European Union.*

Regarding politics, the structure of the EU is criticised by Erixon,[224] who contends that the voting mechanism in the Council is set to protect domestic industries. Furthermore, if a state is preparing for parliamentary elections, it is likely to seek to protect the local interest rather than the general interest. Erixon further alleges that price discrimination is beneficial for EU consumers if prices in the EU are lower.[225]

4.4.4 *Judicial Review*

The result of an affirmative investigation is the adoption of anti-dumping measures by regulations or decisions. Interested parties can take these legal acts before the Court of First Instance (CFI) and the Court of Justice of the European Communities (ECJ).[226]

https://hkmb.hktdc.com/en/1X0AH7IX/hktdc-research/Claims-Are-Made-That-Parts-for-E-bikes-Imported-from-Mainland-China-Face-Unwarranted-Anti-dumping-Tariffs.

223 Willems and Brolin, 'The Unhappy Marriage of Customs and Anti-Dumping Legislation', 244.

224 Fredrik Erixon, 'Anti-dumping in the European Union', in Debroy Bibek and Chakraborty Debashis (eds.), *Anti-Dumping: Global Abuse of a Trade Policy Instrument* (Academic Foundation, 2007), 119–32.

225 Ibid.

226 Legal Basis, European Commission, accessed 15 July 2023, http://trade.ec.europa.eu/doclib/docs/2013/april/tradoc_151035.pdf.

The EU's new methodology on sector-specific determinations is questionable because anti-dumping is an exporter-specific measure.[227] These sector-specific reports constitute a piece of evidence in favour of the EU industries, and Chinese exporters need to prove that the market is not distorted by government intervention. One of the recent judgements on market distortion is the *European Commission v. Xinyi PV Products (Anhui) Holdings Ltd.*[228] However, this case deals with an anti-dumping investigation initiated in 2013.

Regarding the old legislation, granting the market economy status was an actionable decision. The judgement in 2006 regarding the ferro molybdenum exporters from China is a good example. The complainant Chinese exporter challenges the decision of the Commission that it was granted the market economy status at the provisional measure, but the Council then revoked the decision at the definitive measure stage due to circumvention of the duty. The complainant claims that the right to defence was violated and the non-market economy treatment cannot be revoked by the Council as the Commission granted the market economy treatment. The CIF rejected the applicants' claims because Community Institutions are entitled to analyse new evidence and decide accordingly. Also, as the applicant was given the opportunity to comment, their right to defence was not violated, according to the Court.[229]

In the case regarding compact disc producers from Taiwan against the EU, the applicants claimed that rather than using the actual prices, the Commission used zeroing methodology and incorrectly found targeted dumping margins.[230] The Court dismissed the claims because the zeroing methodology does not distort the prices in this case.[231]

In another case, Chinese para-cresol exporters challenged the EU's decision as the investigating authority did not consider the deduction of by-product while calculating the normal value.[232] Without the deduction

[227] Vermulst, '10 Major Problems with the Anti-Dumping Instrument in the European Community', 77.

[228] *European Commission v. Xinyi PV Products (Anhui) Holdings Ltd*, Judgement of the Court, available at http://curia.europa.eu/juris/document/document.jsf?docid=199765&mode=req&pageIndex=1&dir=&occ=first&part=1&text=distortion%2Bchina&doclang=EN&cid=698897#ctx1, accessed 15 July 2023.

[229] Legal Basis, European Commission.

[230] Ibid.

[231] Ibid.

[232] People's Republic of China – of the European Union: Judgment of 13 July 2006 (C 224, 16.09.2006, 35), ibid.

of the by-products normal value is found to be higher so that the dumping margin is artificially increased. The Court of First Instance, therefore, annulled the definitive measures based on this calculation.[233]

In another case *Shanxi Taigang Stainless Steel Co. Ltd v. European Commission*, the Chinese exporter argues that ADA and EU Basic Regulation Article 2(7)(a) require a fair comparison of prices and as China is not recognised as a market economy, a proper analogue country such as Taiwan should have been selected rather than the US.[234] The Court rejects the appeal based on the following findings:

> [I]t is apparent from that case-law, first, that the choice of analogue country falls within the broad discretion enjoyed by the EU institutions in the sphere of the common commercial policy, by reason of the complexity of the economic and political situations which they have to examine.[235]

Overall, EU anti-dumping measures are subject to judicial review, but the success rate for the exporters is relatively low. This constitutes another obstacle to secure procedural justice in anti-dumping proceedings.

4.5 Differences between the US and EU Anti-dumping Investigation Procedures

After examining the basics of the US and the EU anti-dumping procedures, this part determines the fundamental differences between these jurisdictions. Some of these issues are questionnaires, data verification, transparency, timing, price undertakings, lesser duty rule, public interest, non-market economies and zeroing. The more there are differences between these two major anti-dumping users, the more challenging it is to cooperate with the investigating authorities. From the exporters' point of view, it is almost impossible to cooperate with two investigating authorities at the same time. Assuming the investigation procedures are the same in all WTO Members, the exporters would then be able to cooperate with different investigating authorities.

The first difference between these two jurisdictions is that the EU assesses the injury and dumping in detail whereas the injury threshold

[233] Ibid.

[234] *Shanxi Taigang Stainless Steel Co. Ltd v. European Commission*, Judgement of the Court (Tenth Chamber) of 29 July 2019, accessed 15 July 2023, https://eur-lex.europa.eu/legal-content/EN/TXT/?uri=CELEX%3A62018CJ0436.

[235] Ibid.

is lax.[236] Second, the Commission is stricter in terms of evidence on prices that parties are required to submit invoices. On the other hand, the Commerce and the USITC are more flexible on these kinds of documentary evidence. The US investigating authorities face more complaints regarding the compliance of evidence and legalistic procedures.[237] Furthermore, the EU has a later review of injury arguments, while the US process of injury review is held during the initial forty-five days. Regarding the questionnaires, the EU requires a single questionnaire to be submitted whereas the USITC and the Commerce have different questionnaires. Also, the USITC or the Commerce may require additional questionnaires to be filled.[238]

In terms of legal procedures and costs, hiring lawyers is not a must in the EU's anti-dumping investigations, whereas it is a requirement for US investigations. Therefore, the investigation by the US is likely to be costly for the exporter.[239] Yet, in practice, hiring a lawyer for the EU investigations is also essential so the costs are near in both jurisdictions. Data verification is made for all complainants by the Commerce, whereas the USITC generally verifies only the largest manufacturers. Also, the EU is faster in the verification process and more tolerant of errors compared to Commerce. On the other hand, the EU is less transparent in allowing parties to access confidential information or the calculation method.[240] It is not clear until the first nine months of the EU investigation whether the provisional measures will be adopted or not. On the other side, USITC's preliminary determination after the first twenty-five days generally includes a decision on provisional measures.[241]

Regarding price undertakings, the EU tends to terminate anti-dumping investigations with price undertakings. Since 2001, 40 per cent of the EU investigations resulted in price undertakings regardless of the exporters' consent.[242] Compared to anti-dumping measures, price undertakings are in favour of the exporters because it requires an increase in the export price. Anti-dumping measures, on the contrary, are increasing the revenues of the importing country. Currently, the *ex officio* use of

[236] 'An Introduction to Anti-Dumping Law of EU and US as It Applies to Seafood', 31.
[237] Ibid.
[238] Ibid.
[239] Ibid.
[240] Ibid.
[241] Ibid.
[242] Armin Steinbach, 'Price Undertakings in EU Anti-dumping Proceedings – An Instrument of the Past?', *J. Econ. Integr.* 29, no. 1 (2014), 166.

price undertakings by the Commission is in decline. The latest Commission's decisions to accept price undertaking offers were in 2013, such as for solar panels. Since 2013, the Commission has generally rejected price undertaking offers from exporters based on circumvention risk. On the other hand, there are only a few price undertaking cases in the US.[243]

After calculating the final measures, investigating authorities are allowed to apply lower duties when these are enough to remove the injury.[244] This is called the *lesser duty rule* and is regulated under Article 9.1 of the ADA.[245] The EU applies this rule more frequently than the US.[246]

One other difference is regarding the continuation of the measures. Article 11 of the ADA sets the duration for the measures and review mechanisms. The normal duration of the measure is five years. Before the termination of the five years, investigating authorities can initiate a sunset review to decide on the continuation of the measure for another five years. The EU keeps the measures in force during the sunset reviews at almost half of the cases, whereas the rate for the US measures is higher, reaching almost 90 per cent.[247]

The decision on non-market economy status also differs in the US and the EU. By the latest amendment to the anti-dumping regulation, the EU dismissed the wording of 'non-market economy'. Instead, the EU now handles significant distortions and publishes country-specific reports as in the case of China. Significant distortions are evaluated as a whole for a

[243] 'An Introduction to Anti-Dumping Law of EU and US as It Applies to Seafood', 32.
[244] Czako et al., *A Handbook on Anti-dumping Investigations*, 75.
[245] The Article read as

> The decision whether or not to impose an anti-dumping duty in cases where all requirements for the imposition have been fulfilled, and the decision whether the amount of the anti-dumping duty to be imposed shall be the full margin of dumping or less, are decisions to be made by the authorities of the importing Member. It is desirable that the imposition be permissive in the territory of all Members, and that the duty be less than the margin if such lesser duty would be adequate to remove the injury to the domestic industry.
>
> (Available at www.wto.org/english/docs_e/legal_e/19-adp_02_e.htm#articleXV, accessed 15 July 2023)

[246] 'An Introduction to Anti-Dumping Law of EU and US as It Applies to Seafood', 32.
[247] Ibid.

country or on a sector-based approach.[248] The US, on the other hand, decides whether to treat the whole country as a market economy or not. Moreover, this decision is valid until another countrywide decision revokes it. The exporters in the US anti-dumping investigations may request individual treatment, but even this is accepted, non-market economy methodologies will be used.[249]

In terms of zeroing, the EU is more compatible with the ADA, whereas the US regularly violates the agreement despite several Panel or Appellate Body reports.[250] The cases related to zeroing are assessed in Chapter 5.

Public interest is not a mandatory condition to adopt anti-dumping measures in terms of the ADA. Therefore, the majority of the members, such as the US, do not consider the public interest. During the US investigations, consumers and users of the good in question can comment but they cannot access confidential information as other parties. On the contrary, Union Interest is the fourth requirement for the European Commission before adopting an anti-dumping measure. Article 21 of the Regulation 2016/1036 allows 'Union producers, trade unions, importers and their representative associations, representative users and representative consumer organisations' to comment on the case and access to information. They may also request to be heard.[251] This is a positive aspect of the EU anti-dumping investigations as it limits the overprotection of domestic industries. In the US however, there are no checks and balances against lobbying activities.

Overall, the EU's anti-dumping investigations are conducted by a single agency. DG Trade of the Commission is responsible for the whole procedures. At the end of the investigation, Council adopts or rejects the Commission's findings. However, due to the involvement of the EU Member States, the process is also complicated.[252] The EU's system is advantageous in terms of allowing relevant parties such as consumers to submit views so that public interest is considered. Also, unlike the US, the EU more frequently uses lesser duty rules. However, the EU is criticised

[248] 37th Annual Report from the Commission to the Council and the European Parliament on the EU's Anti-Dumping, Anti-Subsidy and Safeguard Activities and the Use of Trade Defence Instruments by Third Countries Targeting the EU in 2018, EU Commission, available at http://trade.ec.europa.eu/doclib/docs/2019/march/tradoc_157810.pdf, accessed 17 June 2022.

[249] 'An Introduction to Anti-Dumping Law of EU and US as It Applies to Seafood', 32.

[250] Ibid.

[251] Regulation 2016/1036, Article 21.

[252] 'An Introduction to Anti-Dumping Law of EU and US as It Applies to Seafood', 32.

for being less transparent in allowing parties to access information about the investigation.[253]

4.6 Conclusion

This chapter is devoted to the anti-dumping investigation procedures of the US and the EU and a discussion on their differences. Before that, the position of China was discussed as it is the main target of anti-dumping measures. China is a unique case in terms of anti-dumping investigations. The phenomenon may be summarised by the following words: a socialist market economy with Chinese characteristics. For several reasons, Chinese exports are seen as a threat to domestic industries by other WTO members. Therefore, China was unable to receive market-economy status after the expiry of Article 15 (d) of the Accession Protocol. Furthermore, the EU revised its anti-dumping regulation and removed the wording on 'non-market economy status' while replacing it with the 'significant market distortion'. This methodology also allows the EU to reject Chinese exporters' data and calculate higher anti-dumping margins.

The ADA sets the general framework for anti-dumping investigations. However, there are many undefined concepts or articles allowing members to enjoy discretion. Also, the unregulated areas, such as the public interest, constitute threats to exporters or consumers. Even within the regulated areas of the ADA, there is room for discretion on the part of investigating authorities. Due to different procedures, it is hard for exporters to cooperate with different anti-dumping investigations at the same time. Although the ADA sets a general framework, investigation procedures substantially differ from one jurisdiction to another. The questionnaires used by the US and EU are good examples of such differentiation. This constitutes a limitation for procedural justice as the legal capacity of exporters, and especially SMEs, is insufficient for cooperation with divergent anti-dumping investigations.

Therefore, this chapter shows that while China is the main anti-dumping target, it is not being treated in the same way by the US and EU due to different anti-dumping procedures. This does not mean that Chinese exporters do not engage in dumping practices. China is the top anti-dumping target for other countries as well, so there is a factual basis

253 Ibid.

for the accusations against China. The study deals with the US and EU investigations against China as it frames the larger part of the problem. The point is that Chinese exporters may be receiving subsidies and be capable of dumping overseas but, due to differences in anti-dumping procedures, the anti-dumping measures adopted would be higher than the actual dumping margins. The EU's market distortion approach and linking the overcapacity problem in China to anti-dumping may be hard to justify considering the design of the ADA. Even the domestic legal review mechanism is not sufficient to secure procedural justice in all cases. In other words, the ADA is being enforced in different ways by different members. There is room for discretion in the anti-dumping procedures of the US and the EU. Especially in the case of China, strict procedures may be used to inflate the final measures.

5

The Fieldwork and Its Findings

5.1 Introduction

The foundation of this book rests in a chain of causal relations. First, the blurred and unregulated issues with the ADA allow WTO members to enforce strict procedural rules. Even if these domestic rules and regulations do not contradict the ADA, they create a significant burden on exporters. However, some of these domestic rules have been found to be inconsistent in Panel or Appellate Body reports and, as explained in Chapter 3, the DSM is not able to solve all of the issues. Second, the strict procedural rules exercised explicitly by the EU and the US during anti-dumping investigations are assumed to decrease the level of cooperation by exporters, especially from China. Finally, the low levels of cooperation enable greater discretion on the part of the investigating authorities in calculating the dumping margins. In other words, low levels of cooperation lead to high anti-dumping duties or overprotection of domestic industries.

If there is sound evidence showing that strict procedures lead to lower levels of cooperation, then it is also arguable that investigating authorities benefit from strict procedural rules to overprotect domestic industries. Therefore, the main focus of this chapter is to find some empirical evidence showing the causal relationship between the two variables, strict procedural rules and over protectionism of local industries using anti-dumping measures. This does not mean that there are no other factors encouraging the investigating authorities' use of strict procedural rules in anti-dumping investigations. The empirical findings of this chapter on anti-dumping investigations can only support the central argument that hidden trade protectionism is behind the investigation procedures. In other words, rather than proving the point, these findings can support the view that hidden trade protectionism leads to a low level of cooperation, high final duties and overprotection of local industries.

In this context, this chapter primarily relies on fieldwork through surveys of exporters, WTO law firms, and investigating authorities. The first target the Chinese exporting firms subject to anti-dumping investigations were surveyed online and by phone. Their answers guided the determination of the correlation between the procedural burdens and the level of cooperation. Second, WTO lawyers and practitioners all around the world were questioned about the different procedures used by the EU and the US as they have a deep investigative experience and can compare the processes used by different WTO Members. To ensure a satisfactory level of participation, confidentiality was guaranteed and the purpose of the study was presented to the participants. Last, the public authorities responsible for the anti-dumping investigations were contacted. Among the public authorities, MOFCOM was approached first. MOFCOM shared their experience of the procedural obstacles faced by Chinese exporters and what kind of action is taken to secure due process. Starting consultations or requesting the establishment of panels under the DSB might be examples of these actions. The survey for MOFCOM was similar to the previous groups. Also, questions for the two other public authorities, the EU and the US, were shaped after the examination of data collected through the previous empirical research.

This data enables the reader to better understand the clues to hidden trade protectionism and the overuse of anti-dumping procedures, and thus, the need for improving procedural justice becomes more evident.

5.2 Research Methodology

The methodology used in this chapter is empirical research, which requires a systematic collection of information, with evaluation of this data through recognised methods.[1] The sources of the data can include documents, reporting systems, observations, experiments, and events or surveys and interviews, as in this study.[2] In this chapter, a qualitative data analysis method was used. Surveys with open-ended questions and semi-structured interviews were used to collect evidence. These tools allow the researcher to examine a legal phenomenon and reach a 'logical saturation point'.[3] However, while achieving that point, a simple quantitative analysis is also needed. The technique, called 'quasi-statistics', is applied to

1 Peter Cane and Herbert Kritzer, eds., *The Oxford Handbook of Empirical Legal Research* (Oxford University Press, 2010), 5.

2 Ibid.

3 Marilyn Lichtman, *Qualitative Research for the Social Sciences* (SAGE Publications, 2013), 339.

clarify overall trends.[4] Therefore, empirical research is conducted, covering elements of qualitative and quantitative research methods.

The data collection method of this study is also mainly qualitative, where surveys or interviews are conducted. Individual interviews are useful in the sense that they allow the researcher to examine a legal phenomenon and receive insights into the legal profession.[5]

In terms of content analysis methods, there are three commonly used methods.[6] Classical content analysis is used to analyse texts, such as articles, reports or interview transcripts, by evaluating the frequency of specific concepts and themes.[7] Discourse analysis is an extremely detailed approach focusing on the language, grammar, pauses, repetitions, etc.[8] Grounded theory is based on developing a new theory from scratch as if the researcher does not know anything about the subject matter. In this context, the last two methods are impractical for this study. Discourse analysis can mislead as the surveys should be completed in English, while most of the participants are not native speakers. Therefore, evaluating the linguistic details of non-native speakers would not guide the reader properly. Grounded theory is also not applicable because the study has already adopted a hypothesis. This chapter utilises classical content analysis methods for the surveys and interviews to test the hypothesis.

> Qualitative content analysis does not produce counts and statistical significance; instead, it uncovers patterns, themes, and categories important to a social reality. Presenting research findings from qualitative content analysis is challenging. Although it is a common practice to use typical quotations to justify conclusions (Schilling, 2006), you also may want to incorporate other options for data display, including matrices, graphs, charts, and conceptual networks (Miles & Huberman, 1994). The form and extent of reporting will finally depend on the specific research goals (Patton, 2002). When presenting qualitative content analysis results, you should strive for a balance between description and interpretation.[9]

[4] Joseph A. Maxwell, 'Using Qualitative Methods for Causal Explanation', *Field Methods* 16, no. 3 (2004), 258.

[5] Ibid., 12.

[6] Cane and Kritzer, *The Oxford Handbook of Empirical Legal Research*, 16.

[7] Ibid., 18.

[8] Ibid.

[9] Yan Zhang and Barbara M. Wildemuth, 'Qualitative Analysis of Content', in B. M. Wildemuth (ed.), *Applications of Social Research Methods to Questions in Information and Library Science* (Libraries Unlimited, 2009), 1–12.

While the other chapters provided a description of the problems in anti-dumping investigation procedures, the empirical research and qualitative content analysis in this chapter reveals the reality in practice.

> Qualitative research is fundamentally interpretive, and interpretation represents your personal and theoretical understanding of the phenomenon under study. An interesting and readable report 'provides sufficient description to allow the reader to understand the basis for an interpretation, and sufficient interpretation to allow the reader to understand the description' (Patton, 2002, p.503–504).[10]

The empirical findings are interpreted under the description of the issue so that the problem can be better analysed.

5.3 Data Collection Process

The primary data collection method is online surveys for the Chinese exporters and WTO lawyers. For the semi-structured interviews with investigating authorities, the email interview method was used. After determining the lists of exporters and law firms, the participants were asked to complete the survey within a month. The surveys included some open-ended questions and sub-questions, combining quantitative and qualitative elements. When needed, some of the participants were asked additional questions to obtain more detail. The additional questions were directed to participants according to the comments they provided on the questionnaires. The surveys devoted to the US and EU investigating authorities were designed after data collection from Chinese exporters. Email interviews were preferred over phone or face-to-face communication with the officials from MOFCOM. Regarding the Chinese exporters, when they face procedural barriers and cannot cooperate with investigating authorities, they suffer from high anti-dumping duties.[11] Therefore, Chinese exporters were targeted due to their likelihood of participation in the survey. As not all the problems in practice can be challenged before the WTO DSM, this empirical study is an opportunity for exporters to explain their positions. However, few exporters participated, which is also a sign of the underestimation of anti-dumping investigations.

[10] Ibid.

[11] Zhou and Percival, 'Debunking the Myth of "Particular Market Situation" in WTO Antidumping Law', 865.

Table 5.1 *Participant exporters and their industries*

Industry	Number of companies	Products
Textiles	2	Mattresses
Chemicals	1	Acesulfame potassium
Plastics/Rubber/Wood	3	Bus tyres, plywood
Machinery/Electronic equipment	4	Solar panels, e-bikes, aluminium radiators
Metals	2	Aluminium foil, wheels
Total	12	

5.4 Fieldwork on Anti-dumping Procedures of the US and the EU

Surveys were sent first to Chinese exporters, WTO lawyers and MOFCOM officials. According to the responses, additional surveys were designed for and addressed to the US and EU investigating authorities.

5.4.1 *Problems Faced by Chinese Exporters*

The top five industries cover around 80 per cent of the total anti-dumping measures; therefore, companies were selected among those industries. The breakdown of companies responding to the questionnaire is given in Table 5.1.

The following questions were sent to Chinese exporters through various channels.[12]

1) ***How many anti-dumping investigations were initiated against your company by the US or the EU from 2010 onwards?***

a) ***By the US:***
☐ *none*
☐ 1
☐ 2
☐ 3 or more

b) ***By the EU:***
☐ *none*
☐ *1*
☐ *2*
☐ *3 or more*

[12] Mail, phone call, WeChat, LinkedIn, etc.

2) ***In how many investigations did your company cooperate with the investigating authorities?***
   For the US investigations: Cooperated in _____ investigations out of _____ cases.
   For the EU investigations: Cooperated in _____ investigations out of _____ cases.

3) ***What procedural obstacles did your company face during these anti-dumping investigations? Please check all that apply.***

a) ***US investigations:***
☐ *calculation methods*
☐ *transparency (e.g., concerning investigation guidelines, non-confidential summaries, etc.)*
☐ *public notice/notification*
☐ *selection of samples*
☐ *submission of evidence*
☐ *access to non-confidential files*
☐ *hearing*
☐ *newcomer*
☐ *enforcement (e.g., concerning provisional duties, reviews, etc.)*
☐ *others? Please specify: _____*

b) ***EU investigations:***

☐ *calculation methods*
☐ *transparency (e.g., concerning investigation guidelines, non-confidential summaries, etc.)*
☐ *public notice/notification*
☐ *selection of samples*
☐ *submission of evidence*
☐ *access to non-confidential files*
☐ *hearing*
☐ *newcomer*
☐ *enforcement (e.g., concerning provisional duties, reviews, etc.)*
☐ *others? Please specify: _____*

4) ***Did you experience any difference in anti-dumping investigation procedures applied by the US and the EU?***

☐ *N/A (no previous investigation by the US or the EU)*
☐ *No*
☐ *Yes*

If yes, what were the differences? Please check all that apply.
☐ *calculation methods*
☐ *transparency (e.g., concerning investigation guidelines, non-confidential summaries, etc.)*
☐ *public notice/notification*

☐ *selection of samples*
☐ *submission of evidence*
☐ *access to non-confidential files*
☐ *hearing*
☐ *newcomer*
☐ *enforcement (e.g., concerning provisional duties, reviews, etc.)*
☐ *others? Please specify: _____*

Can you comment on the differences?

5) ***Can you specify the reasons why your company refused to cooperate in anti-dumping investigations? Please check all that apply.***

a) ***US investigations:***
☐ *N/A (never refused to cooperate)*
☐ *high expenses*
☐ *time-consuming*
☐ *government requiring confidential information*
☐ *procedural burdens, procedural differences*
☐ *submitted response but treated as a non-cooperating company by the investigating authority*
☐ *others? Please specify: _____*

b) ***EU investigations:***
☐ *N/A (never refused to cooperate)*
☐ *high expenses*
☐ *time-consuming*
☐ *government requiring confidential information*
☐ *procedural burdens, procedural differences*
☐ *submitted response but treated as a non-cooperating company by the investigating authority*
☐ *others? Please specify: _____*

6) ***What were the outcomes of non-cooperation for your company? Please check all that apply.***

☐ *N/A (never refused to cooperate)*
☐ *higher duties*
☐ *lower market share*
☐ *others? Please specify: _____*

7) ***Based on your experience, do you think that the US and EU investigators adopted stricter procedural rules against Chinese exporters vis-à-vis other exporters?***

a) ***US investigations:***

☐ *no*
☐ *yes*

If yes, what were the stricter procedural rules against Chinese exporters? Please check all that apply.

☐ *calculation methods*

☐ *transparency (e.g., concerning investigation guidelines, non-confidential summaries, etc.)*

☐ *public notice/notification*

☐ *selection of samples*

☐ *submission of evidence*

☐ *access to non-confidential files*

☐ *hearing*

☐ *newcomer*

☐ *enforcement (e.g., concerning provisional duties, reviews, etc.)*

☐ *others? Please specify:* _____

b) ***EU investigations:***

☐ *no*

☐ *yes*

If yes, what were the stricter procedural rules against Chinese exporters? Please check all that apply.

☐ *calculation methods*

☐ *transparency (e.g., concerning investigation guidelines, non-confidential summaries, etc.)*

☐ *public notice/notification*

☐ *selection of samples*

☐ *submission of evidence*

☐ *access to non-confidential files*

☐ *hearing*

☐ *newcomer*

☐ *enforcement (e.g., concerning provisional duties, reviews, etc.)*

☐ *others? Please specify:* _____

8) ***In your view, which of the following measures would encourage your company to cooperate with different investigating authorities? Please check all that apply.***

☐ *a standard anti-dumping questionnaire to be used by all countries*

☐ *raising the awareness of exporters about non-cooperation*

☐ *an NGO providing low-cost legal assistance for the exporters*

☐ *others? Please specify measures:* _______

9) ***Any additional comments on the US and EU anti-dumping investigations as regards how they can be improved?***

a) ***US investigations:*** ______

b) ***EU investigations:*** _______

Twelve companies that had been subject to anti-dumping duties by the US or EU responded to the questionnaires. The responses were grouped based on the company's experiences with the US and EU investigations.

The responses on US investigations included mattress manufacturers, which had faced one of the highest anti-dumping duties in the WTO's history. The US imposed rates of up to 1,700% for mattresses from China in 2019. The first mattress company's senior business manager completed the questionnaire and engaged in email communication. The company faced procedural burdens, such as calculation methods, transparency, public notices, hearings and being a newcomer. Also, the company's manager noted that the public notice and evidence submission were enforced strictly for Chinese exporters. The whole process was challenging for the company. He stressed that:

> I would love to add that I think the 'ruling mechanism' should also be studied closely – like, who makes the final decision on this? What is the basis for their decision? How do we make it more objective than subjective?
>
> Our company, for one, is simply not 'dumping' mattresses from Vietnam (where we've moved to now and are AGAIN facing Anti-dumping) and we were not doing so in China either.
>
> It's all very frustrating.
>
> We hired and spent significant dollars on ... [law firm] for our first defence in China – it was expensive and difficult, but they burdened a lot of that difficulty. However, we just simply aren't in a position to have covered those expenses again from Vietnam and so I was the one who personally filled out and submitted the ITC questionnaire on behalf of our company just this last week, in fact.

High rates restrict exports to a market, and the mattress investigation is an excellent example of this issue. A second mattress company commented:

> [O]f course, we have the affection from the trade war. But to us, the US market is not our main market for exporting. And as final result for the Anti-dumping Duty, our company is as 172.67%, there are total 36 companies are same as 172.67%, the others will be more than 1,100%. So, I think we are not too bad from this.

A corroborating finding comes from a Canada-based sofa bed manufacturer that was interviewed by the *Business in Vancouver* newsletter about anti-dumping duties on Chinese mattresses. The company cancelled all shipments of sofa beds from China. Normally, the company imported mattresses from China to Canada and used these products to manufacture sofa beds for export to the US. While an average sofa bed costs around $650 USD, after the US measures, the price of a sofa bed with a Chinese mattress rose to $11,000 USD according to the company's vice president.[13]

> I feel like overall our business may come out ahead. But our business is broken down into divisions and certain divisions are really going to lose hard.[14]

Thus, even for manufacturers located in Canada, the level of anti-dumping duty adversely affects the export of the finished product into the US.

Companies may even relocate due to high anti-dumping duties. A foreign trade manager working at a wooden cabinet manufacturer could not be reached, but on her LinkedIn profile, she explains:

> We are ... in VIETNAM AND CHINA. As anti-dumping in US, we suffered huge losses and had to move to Vietnam.[15]

Another company's sales manager's profile on LinkedIn highlights similar information:

> Our company has a history of 26 years and we mainly export 5 types of product, there are film faced plywood, engineered flooring, cabinet, plywood and cabinet part. Our product mainly exports to European, America, Korea, Australia, Canada.
>
> About cabinet, we have move to Malaysia cause the anti-dumping.[16]

A plywood exporter in China is also structured as an importer in the US. The company cooperated with two anti-dumping investigations. This company is also affected by the US–China trade war and the sudden escalation of tariffs:

> Anti-dumping duties were levied as a retaliatory action to Chinese import duties. US Court of International Trade (CIT) is contesting the assessment of the List 3 and List 4 tariffs that has been imposed under section 301 of the Trade Act of 1974. The law suit states that the tariffs were imposed untimely. Companies importing products from China were not given sufficient time to update their business models. Millions of

[13] Hayley Woodin, 'Burnaby Company Hit with 1,732% US Anti-Dumping Duties', accessed 18 July 2023, https://biv.com/article/2019/06/us-china-trade-war-pushes-burnaby-company-cancel-exports.

[14] Ibid.

[15] Profile available at www.linkedin.com/in/july-lee-b58b19134/, accessed 18 July 2023.

[16] Profile available at www.linkedin.com/in/abby-xu-892a02144/?originalSubdomain=cn, accessed 18 July 2023.

> businesses suffered financially yet they had to fulfil contractual obligations. Some businesses were agile enough to relocate to other countries or back to the US however the financial damage and lost business left scars that will take years to repair. In this case the US as an importing nation has been hurt. Businesses are still trying to relocate, hire staff, train workers and management teams in order to bring their business back to 2019 levels. Many businesses are struggling to achieve their manufacturing goals without off shore support of semi-processed parts and materials.

Regarding cooperation with the investigating authorities, the company explained:

> As the nature of anti-dumping tariffs levies, only a handful of companies are selected for investigation representing the industry. Selected companies have to cooperate and provide information per international trade mandate. However, companies that fall in the same category and are not being investigated receive an industry applied import rate. Usually, cooperation is required for contesting and testifying the court case for which the country of origin representing industry body organize companies and testify on their behalf. Companies with large volumes of business represent themselves and most others join an organization by the representing industry body of origin. The cost is not the hindrance for participating. Time, energy, fact collection and effort required is so much that most companies prefer to change business model instead of fighting the cause. So, the answer of the question is that most think that duties are applied for a reasonable cause therefore there is no need to fight the cause unless they are being investigated for special subsidies received.

Therefore, the cost of cooperation in terms of time and effort is not worth it, even if lower anti-dumping duties are applied. Companies simply prefer to change their business models, which includes investing in the importing country or circumventing duties. This company also explains the effects of trade remedies on a macroeconomic level:

> When anti-dumping actions are used for retaliatory purposes OR as a result of lobbyist political agenda, levies bring more harm than benefits. It is unfortunate that biased political views may go ahead of investigations and their force the application of actions in an untimely manner.

Lobbying industries are overprotected, without any examination of the effects on consumers or other industries. According to one econometric model, USITC is affected by political factors, and the rulings are especially biased against Chinese exporters.[17] Thus, for companies that face

[17] Wang et al., 'ITC Antidumping toward China Rulings', 1–17.

anti-dumping from the US, the procedures are complex and costly, and they cannot easily cooperate. Even when they do, they do not believe they are treated equally.

Turning to companies that faced anti-dumping investigations from the EU, their complaints focus more on a lack of transparency. An aluminium radiator producer stresses that they lost the whole EU market after the anti-dumping duty was imposed:

> No exports since the anti-dumping duty on aluminium radiators. Measure is in force for 8 years. EU wants to protect its own market, I understand that. But the measure is in force so long.

Another food chemical company also complained about the long duration of the anti-dumping measures:

> Our company had a separate rate which is lower than other companies. So, this is an advantage for us but the measure is in force for a long time. We are waiting it to be cancelled. Our costs are also increasing because of the environmental requirements of domestic government policies.

A tyre company argues that they were not sampled during the EU anti-dumping investigation:

> Our company cooperated with EU but not sampled after the anti-dumping measures, we have few orders from EU and US.

A bike manufacturer facing an EU anti-dumping investigation comments on a more general point as 'dumping is a result of global economic problems so it is very hard to solve'. After facing anti-dumping duties, the company jumped the tariffs and shifted manufacturing to Poland:

> We received an anti-dumping rate around 37%. Now we are partnering with a company in Poland so our buyers do not need to pay any anti-dumping. some parts are produced different countries such as Singapore or Taiwan but the factory is Poland so dumping is no more problem.

This response shows the willingness of companies to move the manufacturing process to avoid additional costs from the enterprise perspective and supports the tariff jump theory.

One aluminium foil manufacturer with a recent EU anti-dumping investigation experience asserts that they faced problems with access to non-confidential files and enforcement. The company supported the idea of a standard anti-dumping questionnaire to be used by all countries, raising awareness among exporters of non-cooperation, with an NGO providing low-cost legal assistance for exporters to improve their ability to cooperate. After these responses to the survey, additional explanations were requested from the company, particularly on non-confidential files and enforcement:

> At first, we didn't know where to get the information about non confidential files or enforcement, there was no instruction available, we have to find information by our own effort. So, we got late info and sometimes we were not sure if the info is correct, which confuse us at first stage.

Thus, even if exporters attempt to cooperate, they may find themselves excluded from the proceedings, which impedes meaningful participation. On the effects of anti-dumping duty on the company's exports to the EU, the company stated:

> It brought big impact, immediate impact is we lost all small-scale customers and many big clients. Subsequently, we lost a lot of biddings. As a result, our export to EU dropped significantly.

Moreover, the company was asked, 'Do you think you could defend yourself fairly during the investigation?'

> We understood it's unavoidable from the very beginning, what we can only do is minimum the anti-dumping duty to us.

To this exporter, the anti-dumping investigation is an unavoidable casualty. They sense that they will lose their export market, but they cannot avoid it. Another exporter with investigation experience of both jurisdictions mentioned differences in terms of calculation methods, transparency, public notice, selection of samples, and hearings. Furthermore, due to the high expenses and time required to engage in the investigation, the company did not cooperate with the US investigation. The company also mentioned the EU's procedural burdens EU as a barrier to cooperation. The company stressed that the US is treating Chinese exporters strictly compared to other exporters, whereas in EU anti-dumping investigations, this is not a concern. The company expects the US investigations 'to be more reasonable and more fair'. The company considers 'the EU is a bit more reasonable and fairer than the US but still has some space to get better'.

A tyre company facing an anti-dumping investigation from the US and EU could not cooperate in both cases. The reasons for not cooperating with the US investigating authorities were the high costs and the requirement of confidential information by the government, whereas for the EU investigation, the concern was the time required and also confidential information requirements. On the outcomes of non-cooperation, the company states that it 'cannot export to the EU or US anymore. We do not receive any orders anymore because of anti-dumping'.

A solar panel manufacturer faced investigations by both the US and EU. The company did not cooperate in either investigation.

> Anti-dumping has negative effects on our exports. Some shipping companies have a solution like exporting to other countries like Vietnam or Thailand and shipping to US and EU without anti-dumping.

This response supports the theory of circumvention, where the higher the duties are, the more likely they are to be circumvented. This is also why few companies are interested in dealing with complex and costly anti-dumping investigation procedures. Rather, they find that circumvention methods are faster and cheaper, without the need to share confidential information with overseas governments.

Another profile on LinkedIn explains the circumvention method explicitly in his profile:

> Hello, my name is ... I'm here to provide solutions for the export of Chinese products that encounter trade restrictions such as anti-dumping or high tariffs. To avoid these limitations,
>
> First of all, we will send the goods to a third country outside China. Then operate in a third country and issue the certificate of origin of the third country,
>
> Finally, the goods are exported to the final destination.
>
> This operation can save a lot of costs due to trade barriers.
>
> If you are interested in our business, please contact my wechat:. . .[18]

So, all these companies highlight how they lost market share after anti-dumping measures were imposed. This supports the argument that anti-dumping is used for overly protectionist purposes. Another Hong Kong-listed company, Hilong Holdings, was interviewed by the *South China Morning Post*, and the senior assistant to the Chairman shared similar views:

[18] Profile available at www.linkedin.com/in/%E6%B4%81%E4%BC%9F-%E9%99%88-49b36b146/, accessed 18 July 2023.

> Hilong has been subject to US anti-dumping duties on Chinese seamless steel pipes since 2009, so it has not been a major market for us for a while. . . . In recent years we have changed most of our US business from sales to leasing.[19]

Hilong has been subject to 25 per cent anti-dumping duties, and the company had to change its target markets. With the Belt and Road Initiative, the company expanded to new markets, such as Russia, Central Asia and the Middle East.[20] If the anti-dumping tool balances the price difference reasonably, these companies would still be competitive in export markets. However, especially for the US, the rates are way above balancing the real dumping margins, so, in theory, there is no way to export after the anti-dumping duties are imposed. The second common problem revealed by these comments is that most exporters do not have the financial and legal capacity to defend themselves in overseas jurisdictions. They find the procedures complicated and demanding, both financially and commercially.

Those two issues result in the circumvention of duties. Rather than paying a large amount of money to lawyers to cooperate, companies evaluate the benefits of not cooperating and circumventing the duty. Even if they cooperate and dedicate a considerable amount of money and time, they still face high anti-dumping duties. On the other hand, exporters can change export operations to avoid additional duties. Therefore, even if the act of circumvention is an offence in the importing country jurisdictions, there are profiles on social media explicitly stating how they circumvent anti-dumping or other trade remedies.

5.4.2 Problems Faced by Lawyers

The participants in this section represent a variety of anti-dumping practitioners in terms of location and investigation experience. Table 5.2 gives a simple breakdown of the lawyers who responded to the questions and their experience in US and EU anti-dumping investigations.

19 'How a Chinese Company Targeted by US Tariffs for the Last 10 Years Has Adapted and Thrived', *South China Morning Post*, accessed 18 July 2023, www.scmp.com/business/companies/article/3010378/how-chinese-company-targeted-us-tariffs-last-10-years-has.

20 Ibid.

Table 5.2 *Distribution of lawyers*

Location	Number of lawyers	Number of US anti-dumping investigation experiences	Number of EU anti-dumping investigation experiences
US	8	113	98
EU	7		
China	5		
Other	2		
Total	22		

The survey questions for WTO lawyers are as follows:

1) ***How many anti-dumping investigations did you advise on from 2010 onwards?***

a) ***US investigations:***

☐ none
☐ 1–4
☐ 5–10
☐ more than 10

b) ***EU investigations:***

☐ none
☐ 1–4
☐ 5–10
☐ more than 10

2) ***In how many investigations did your clients cooperate with the investigating authorities?***

For the US investigations: Cooperated in _____ investigations out of _____ cases
For the EU investigations: Cooperated in ______ investigations out of ____ cases

3) ***What procedural obstacles did you or your clients face during these anti-dumping investigations? Please check all that apply.***

a) ***US investigations:***
☐ *calculation methods*
☐ *transparency (e.g., concerning investigation guidelines, non-confidential summaries, etc.)*

☐ *public notice/notification*
☐ *selection of samples*
☐ *submission of evidence*
☐ *access to non-confidential files*
☐ *hearing*
☐ *newcomer*
☐ *enforcement (e.g., concerning provisional duties, reviews, etc.)*
☐ *others? Please specify: _____*

b) ***EU investigations:***
☐ *calculation methods*
☐ *transparency (e.g., concerning investigation guidelines, non-confidential summaries, etc.)*
☐ *public notice/notification*
☐ *selection of samples*
☐ *submission of evidence*
☐ *access to non-confidential files*
☐ *hearing*
☐ *newcomer*
☐ *enforcement (e.g., concerning provisional duties, reviews, etc.)*
☐ *others? Please specify: _____*

4) ***Did you experience any difference in anti-dumping investigation procedures applied by the US and the EU?***

☐ *N/A (no previous investigation by the US or the EU)*
☐ *No*
☐ *Yes*

If yes, what were the differences? Please check all that apply.
☐ *calculation methods*
☐ *transparency (e.g., concerning investigation guidelines, non-confidential summaries, etc.)*
☐ *public notice/notification*
☐ *selection of samples*
☐ *submission of evidence*
☐ *access to non-confidential files*
☐ *hearing*
☐ *newcomer*
☐ *enforcement (e.g., concerning provisional duties, reviews, etc.)*
☐ *others? Please specify: _____*

Can you comment on the differences?

____

5) ***Can you specify the reasons why your clients refused to cooperate with the US or EU investigating authorities? Please check all that apply.***

a) ***US investigations:***

☐ *N/A (never refused to cooperate)*
☐ *high expenses*
☐ *time-consuming*
☐ *government requiring confidential information*
☐ *procedural burdens, procedural differences*
☐ *submitted response but treated as a non-cooperating company by the investigating authority*
☐ *others? Please specify: _____*

b) ***EU investigations:***

☐ *N/A (never refused to cooperate)*
☐ *high expenses*
☐ *time-consuming*
☐ *government requiring confidential information*
☐ *procedural burdens, procedural differences*
☐ *submitted response but treated as a non-cooperating company by the investigating authority*
☐ *others? Please specify: _____*

6) ***What were the outcomes of non-cooperation for your clients? Please check all that apply.***

☐ *N/A (never refused to cooperate)*
☐ *higher duties*
☐ *lower market share*
☐ *others? Please specify: _____*

7) ***Based on your experience, do you think that the US and EU investigators adopted stricter procedural rules against Chinese exporters vis-à-vis other exporters?***

a) ***US investigations:***

☐ *no*
☐ *yes*

If yes, what were the stricter procedural rules against Chinese exporters? Please check all that apply.

☐ *calculation methods*
☐ *transparency (e.g., concerning investigation guidelines, non-confidential summaries, etc.)*
☐ *public notice/notification*
☐ *selection of samples*
☐ *submission of evidence*
☐ *access to non-confidential files*
☐ *hearing*
☐ *newcomer*
☐ *enforcement (e.g., concerning provisional duties, reviews, etc.)*
☐ *others? Please specify: _____*

b) ***EU investigations:***
☐ *no*
☐ *yes*

If yes, what were the stricter procedural rules against Chinese exporters? Please check all that apply.
☐ *calculation methods*
☐ *transparency (e.g., concerning investigation guidelines, non-confidential summaries, etc.)*
☐ *public notice/notification*
☐ *selection of samples*
☐ *submission of evidence*
☐ *access to non-confidential files*
☐ *hearing*
☐ *newcomer*
☐ *enforcement (e.g., concerning provisional duties, reviews, etc.)*
☐ *others? Please specify: _____*

8) ***In your view, which of the following measures would encourage your clients to cooperate with different investigating authorities? Please check all that apply.***

☐ *a standard anti-dumping questionnaire to be used by all countries*
☐ *raising the awareness of exporters about non-cooperation*
☐ *others? Please specify measures: _____*

9) ***Any additional comments on the US and EU anti-dumping investigations as regards how they can be improved?***

a) ***US investigations:*** _____
b) ***EU investigations:*** ______

Participants have engaged in many anti-dumping investigations in both jurisdictions, so their views reflect issues in practice. The responses show that the companies facing US anti-dumping investigations are less likely to cooperate compared to EU investigations. Calculation methods are the top problem in US investigations, whereas transparency is the main concern with the EU. Most of the lawyers agreed that the investigation procedures are different in the two jurisdictions, particularly with respect to the calculation methods and transparency. Regarding the reasons for non-cooperation, lawyers highlight the high cost and procedural burdens in both jurisdictions. Again, most lawyers said that non--cooperation results in higher anti-dumping duties. The majority of lawyers believe that US investigators adopt stricter procedural rules against Chinese exporters, especially in terms of calculation methods. On the other hand, the majority believe that the EU does not treat Chinese exporters more strictly than exporters from other countries. More than a third of lawyers agree that a standard anti-dumping questionnaire would improve the cooperation rate with the investigating authorities, while the same proportion opted for 'raising the awareness of exporters about non-cooperation'. The comments of the lawyers on anti-dumping investigations are presented below; the responses of lawyers are grouped according to the location.

Starting with the US-based lawyers, a US lawyer with almost thirty years of experience commented on the anti-dumping investigations in the US rather than filling out the survey. He said:

> The reason why the US system is less favorable for Chinese respondents is substantive not procedural. Chinese goods are subject to an entirely different methodology for establishing normal value – the NME system.
>
> Most Chinese respondents who have to make a decision about filling out a US questionnaire have an easy decision to make. They are not under consideration for full individual examination as mandatory respondents, and are (or may be) simply interested in qualifying for 'separate rate' status. The questionnaire relevant to that is pretty short and inexpensive to complete. Afterward, if found eligible for 'separate rate' status, you get an average result rather than the 'China-wide entity' result.
>
> Chinese companies who receive full questionnaires (because they have been selected for individual examination as mandatory respondents) have a different kind of decision to make. The normal reason for not participating (i.e., declining to answer questionnaires) is an understanding that the cost of participating, which may be very high, will exceed any benefit that might arise from participating. This is again not really a procedural

> problem but a substantive one. The data requirements are huge and often correspond to product definitions not separately tracked in the normal course of business. You have to devote a lot of internal accountant time and spend a lot on counsel. Unless you can foresee a good result, it may not be worthwhile.

The lawyer suggests that the NME system is a substantive issue. The classification of the Chinese market as a non-market economy is a key policy decision, but the calculation of anti-dumping duty based on the NME methodology is a procedural issue. There is not much detailed discussion about the classification of the calculation methods in the literature, but Horlick agrees that calculation methods are procedural matters.[21] The procedural burdens are heavier when they are combined with the NME methodology. Also, for the mandatory respondents, the costs in time and legal fees deter active participation. Even if an exporter cooperates and submits the questionnaire, it will be subject to an average rate rather than a fully individual anti-dumping duty. Therefore, the cost of participating is more than the cost of non-cooperation, according to him.

Another US lawyer, with twenty years of anti-dumping investigations experience, highlighted the time and cost burdens on exporters:

> Biggest barrier is the expense (time and money) of clients' participating. Nothing can be done about this, though. US govt. has a frankly protectionist bias, but this is a function of the law and the fact that foreigners have no say in the legislative process
>
> (e.g., the recent PMS explosion in US dumping cases).

Even if companies cooperate, a positive outcome is still not guaranteed. A US lawyer with twenty-five years of experience commented on the US's anti-dumping investigation system. According to him, only three out of ten companies cooperate with the US investigating authorities. He stresses that 'the US retroactive assessment system creates too much risk to participate'. Regarding improvements to the US anti-dumping investigation system, he points out that '"the all others rate" is nonsense, and retroactive assessment is fundamentally unfair. Do away with both'.

Another US-qualified international trade lawyer with more than twenty-five years of experience emphasised that cost and time burdens result in non-cooperation by exporters. According to him, non-

21 Horlick, 'Ten Major Problems in the United States'.

cooperating companies received the 'all others rate', which is higher than the individual anti-dumping duties in most cases. Both cooperating and non-cooperating exporters face strict procedural rules if they are from China. Calculation methods are stricter for Chinese exporters, and he asserts that the 'NME rate is a major problem. Also, some clients were not selected as a mandatory respondent and received the all-others rate.' The US procedures punish both exporters and importers:

> The US system of retrospectively conducting AD/CVD reviews continues to be a major issue for US importers, as does the NME method used for China, as it leads to ridiculously high and inaccurate margins.

Another US lawyer, with more than twenty years of Post Qualification Experience (PQE) and more than ten years of investigation experience, explained that even trivial errors are penalised, resulting in high anti-dumping duties. Calculation methods, submission of evidence and enforcement are procedural obstacles faced by his clients during US anti-dumping investigations. He did not agree that US investigators have adopted stricter procedural rules against Chinese exporters vis-à-vis other exporters. He explained:

> I have experience primarily with US AD cases, but I am familiar with EU AD cases from talking with colleagues who have handled those cases.
>
> The US and EU AD systems are very different and both have their inherent unfairness to respondents.
>
> For US cases, the DOC questionnaire process is exhaustive and detailed under tight deadlines. It is a hyper-objectified process that penalizes respondents for even tiny discrepancies or errors. Petitioners consistently request that DOC apply total adverse facts available (total AFA) in US cases for every possible discrepancy because it is the easiest way to get a complete knock-out blow (i.e., highest penalty rate applied). The US AD system has been consistently upheld by the US court system and even the WTO, so there really isn't much chance of arguing the unfairness of US AD system bc there is zero chance of it changing. It is what it is. DOC's determinations have been overturned by courts when DOC has provided inadequate justification for their decisions (e.g., cannot point to enough record evidence to support their decisions).
>
> But my clients who do choose to hire me are well aware of the burdens and unfairness of DOC's AD process. So, once they commit to participate, generally they participate as fully as possible and I try to guide my clients as to what kind of response is needed to meet DOC's requirements.

Subsequently, his position is that the US investigations are unfair in the sense that they penalise even minor errors. The courts rarely overturn the decisions of Commerce, and it is very difficult to change the US anti-dumping system. The existence of a system that makes cooperation so difficult endorses the protective bias argument.

The protective bias of the US investigating authorities was also mentioned by another US trade lawyer, with twenty-five years of experience. He stated:

> US proceedings are more transparent but US cases also have calculations that are more manipulated by the authorities to obtain results favorable to the domestic industry.

Regarding the reasons for non-cooperation with the US investigating authorities, he highlighted high expenses, time costs and submission of evidence, but being regarded as a non-cooperating company by the investigating authorities result in a huge loss of business. He also mentioned that 'Chinese companies being treated as owned or controlled by the Chinese government and thus being given a punitive rate regardless of the level of cooperation and information provided'. This implies prejudice and a biased attitude against Chinese exporters. As the investigating authorities assume Chinese exporters are subsidised, they are comfortable overprotecting local industries. Transparency was also highlighted as a procedural burden on exporters. He noted:

> In terms of transparency, I am pointing to the fact that the Department of Commerce often announces reasons for its determinations without having engaged the parties with a discussion of issues. i.e., parties are surprised to find that DOC has made critical decisions without discussion of the issues or letting the parties discuss the issues, and parties are surprised at the outcome when the final determination is released.

Another lawyer, with twenty-five years of experience on more than ten EU anti-dumping investigations, explained that, due to high expenses, the amount of time consumed and the government's requirement of confidential information, his clients cannot cooperate. The outcomes of non-cooperation, as expressed by him, are high anti-dumping duties and lower market shares. Nonetheless, he did not think that EU investigators adopt stricter procedural rules against Chinese exporters vis-à-vis other exporters. As to how the EU anti-dumping investigations system could be improved, he raised two suggestions:

1. Better judicial review, perhaps a specialised court like in the US, and
2. more transparency (the EU could take the US example re. the APO[22] and publication of all non-confidential submissions, incl. the complaint.)

A highly experienced Brussels lawyer who regularly lectures and writes on EU and international trade law matters commented that his clients face procedural burdens such as transparency, selection of samples, and access to non-confidential files during EU anti-dumping investigations. On the differences between US and EU investigations, he highlighted calculation methods, transparency, access to non-confidential files, and hearings as the main differences:

> US system provides for a greater level of transparency in both the dumping and injury determinations.

He further criticises the high expense, amount of time consumed and government requiring confidential information as discouraging exporters from cooperating with EU investigating authorities. The outcome of non-cooperation is higher duties. He also remarks that the US and EU investigating authorities adopt stricter procedural rules against Chinese exporters vis-à-vis other exporters in terms of calculation methods, transparency and submission of evidence. According to him, 'greater transparency; possibility of prompt and effective judicial review' would encourage exporters to cooperate with the investigating authorities. Also 'greater transparency during verification visits; possibility to record verification visits; stricter disciplines on the use of best information available' would improve the EU investigations.

Another top expert and scholar in international trade law responded to the questionnaire. He had advised on more than ten EU investigations across several sectors. His clients faced procedural burdens, such as calculation methods, transparency and access to non-confidential files

[22] Administrative Protective Order (APO) is defined thus:

> The APO is the mechanism under which the Department regulates and ensures the security of proprietary information released to APO authorized representatives involved in AD/CVD proceedings. The APO Unit within Operations Support can assist you with understanding the APO requirements contained and suggest procedures firms can employ internally to protect business proprietary information they receive under an administrative protective order ('APO') in the course of a proceeding.
>
> (https://legacy.trade.gov/enforcement/operations/)

during EU anti-dumping investigations. He commented that these three issues are also different between the US and EU jurisdictions. On the differences, he noted:

> EU undercutting and injury margin calculations are confidential. Non-confidential summaries are often meaningless. On the injury side, the disclosure is not transparent.

He also advised that the adoption of the APO system would improve the EU system. This suggestion also asserts that standardising the anti-dumping procedures would be beneficial for exporters from all WTO members.

A European lawyer who had advised on more than ten investigations listed procedural obstacles, such as calculation methods, transparency, submission of evidence, and enforcement. The lawyer commented that expense and time consumption lead to non-cooperation by exporters. Non-cooperation, on the other hand, causes higher anti-dumping duties. In practice, Chinese companies are disadvantaged due to the Commission's calculation methods and lack of transparency. He stated:

> [A] key problem in EU AD investigations is the absence of an APO akin to that in the US. A company only sees their own data, and if third country info is used (e.g., in the context of the old non-market economy methodology), not even the data used for your own calculations. On top of that, the EU Commission has, according to the CJEU, a wide margin of discretion, meaning they get the benefit of the doubt in any court case: only if the Commission made a manifest error, will the courts annul/invalidate an EU AD measure. From a dumping perspective, the problem is primarily for Chinese companies because of the methodology for calculating their normal value. From an injury perspective, the problem is everywhere. For instance, there is no way to check whether undercutting and underselling have been properly calculated – which, in the EU – is key, given that the EU applies a lesser duty rule that is based on the underselling margin. So, lawyers can focus on logical errors only (i.e., showing that a Commission decision/calculation is simply impossible), and the Commission gets away with errors that cannot be deduced.

Calculation of the normal value is within the discretion of the Commission, resulting in inflation of the anti-dumping duty. However, due to a lack of transparency, exporters are not able to see the calculations, thus preventing any challenges to the Commission's decision.

An international trade law practitioner who is also a Brussels lawyer and a professor of law, he has experience in both US and EU investigations. He highlighted calculation methods and submission of evidence as common procedural obstacles in both jurisdictions, although the calculation methods and submission of evidence are different.

Similar answers were submitted by other lawyers. One, with experience of both jurisdictions, stated that clients had cooperated in three out of four investigations with the US authorities, while clients in EU investigations had cooperated in two out of three. During the US investigations, clients faced procedural problems, namely calculation methods, selection of samples, and submission of evidence. With EU investigations, calculation methods and selection of samples were highlighted as procedural burdens. In terms of differences, this lawyer mentioned that transparency and calculation methods are different between these two jurisdictions. On the other hand, high expense, the amount of time needed, and procedural differences lead to exporters refraining from cooperating with both the US and EU investigating authorities.

The head of WTO and International Trade practice at an international law firm located in Brussels experienced two US and more than ten EU anti-dumping investigations. He remarked that calculation methods and submission of evidence are problematic in US investigations, whereas transparency and access to non-confidential files are the main concerns with EU investigations. On the differences, he echoed previous views that: 'The US system is way more transparent than the EU and way tougher in collecting evidence and level of detail.'

He also noted that, while the US investigating authorities are not strict towards Chinese exporters, EU investigators adopt stricter calculation methods and evidence collection procedures and are less transparent. He advised that the US should 'be more reasonable on the burden of proof, on level of detail of reporting and on the surrogate values used in the calculations'. The EU, on the other hand, needs 'more transparency, a more streamlined procedure across the various trade defence units' to improve.

Chinese international trade lawyers have investigative experience in both jurisdictions. A Chinese lawyer with twenty years of experience in international trade law, including an appointment to China's Mission to the WTO, also participated in the survey. He has experience in several investigations in both the US and EU. He agrees that calculation methods are a common procedural obstacle for both US and EU investigations, whereas transparency and access to non-confidential files are particular to the latter. He also highlighted calculation methods, transparency and access to non-confidential files as different between the two jurisdictions. He commented:

> The US procedure has higher transparency than EU procedure. The US lawyers cooperating with Chinese respondents are able to access the confidential version of the documents filed by other parties upon APO.

Given this response, an additional question was sent by mail exploring whether the procedure allowing only US lawyers access to confidential files constitutes a procedural burden. He replied:

> We see this issue from two levels, from the perspective of transparency, we think it shall be endorsed that lawyers from both parties may see the confidential information. But we agree that it creates high financial burden especially compared with other jurisdictions which prevent some mandatory exporters from cooperating in the investigation. Having said that, high transparency can significantly improve the efficiency and effect of the rebuttal preparation. Accordingly, once an exporter decides to participate a US investigation and cooperates with the authority as a mandatory respondent, it is definitely worth to retain the lawyers who can access to the confidential files.

Thus, allowing only US lawyers to access confidential files is a procedural burden for exporters in defending themselves overseas because of the high cost.

Another Chinese international trade counsel at an international law firm commented that the EU and US investigations are different in terms of calculation methods, transparency, public notice/notification, selection of samples, submission of evidence, access to non-confidential files, and hearings. He suggested that EU investigation procedures are much less complicated compared to the US. Apart from the procedural complexity, his clients do not cooperate with the US investigating authorities due to the high cost and the non-market economy status applied to Chinese exporters, which results in higher duties. Lastly, he advised that fairness and transparency should be improved for exporters.

A trade remedy lawyer with both US and EU anti-dumping investigation experience highlighted calculation methods and enforcement as procedural obstacles to US and EU investigations, respectively.

Another Chinese lawyer with both EU and US investigation experience agreed that calculation methods are different in those two jurisdictions, and they are applied strictly, mainly against Chinese exporters. To increase the level of cooperation, individual rates should be used more often according to him.

The head of a WTO and international trade law practice at an international Chinese law firm advised that the EU system challenges his clients regarding the calculation methods, transparency and submission of evidence. While commenting on the differences between the US and EU investigations, he emphasised:

> both apply non-market economy procedures; the US requests heavy and bulky evidence and documents; both have bias procedures against China; as far as companies from market economy countries, there is not much difference.

Having advised more than ten anti-dumping cases in both jurisdictions, he suggested that both EU and US investigations are biased against Chinese exporters. He also felt that improving the level of cooperation is challenging because of unfair rules rather than the absence of a standard anti-dumping questionnaire. He stated that improving the US and EU anti-dumping system is 'impossible because of the unfair rules and prejudice position adopted by the US against Chinese economic structure'.

Lawyers outside the three jurisdictions were also contacted to confirm the previous findings. One practitioner suggested that 'the USITC should increase transparency of its anti-dumping procedure'. Other participants also stressed the high financial costs. An in-house lawyer specialising in trade remedies explained:

> US and UE systems tend to be the best in terms of AD investigations. Other countries would need to catch up. But, US system, should allow to participate through making it not as expensive as it is today.

In terms of differences, he advises that 'the US uses a retroactive system for enforcement and applies the full margin of dumping. The EU has a prospective system and usually applies a "lesser duty rule"'.

There were some common points between the lawyers. First, there are procedural problems with both the US and EU anti-dumping investigations. Second, calculation methods and transparency are major issues with these two jurisdictions; EU procedures seem to be less transparent compared to the US system. Third, US procedures are biased and are aimed at protecting domestic industries, even though they provide greater transparency. However, transparency brings high legal costs, and so transparency is a problem faced by exporters in both jurisdictions. Fourth, non-cooperating companies face higher anti-dumping duties and mostly lose their market. Fifth, a standard anti-dumping questionnaire may be useful for improving procedural justice, but this would be hard to agree. Transparency would be another way of improving anti-dumping proceedings.

5.4.3 Problems Faced by MOFCOM

Questions were addressed to officials in MOFCOM to gain a deeper understanding of the procedures faced by Chinese exporters. Most of these questions were open-ended, so this section is formed through semi-structured interviews.

Rather than a phone call or a face-to-face interview, an email interview was preferred to collect data from officials of MOFCOM. An email interview has many advantages compared to phone or face-to-face interviews. From the ethical point of view, participants are more comfortable with emails than with techniques involving the researcher's presence.[23] Participants are also able to think more before writing down their answers.[24] Also, as opposed to other methods, the email interview method saves time and money in terms of transcription costs.[25] The questions were sent to two MOFCOM officials. One of the MOFCOM officials answered the following questions:

1) ***Can you specify the role of MOFCOM in anti-dumping investigations against Chinese exporters?***

2) ***Can you share some of your observations in terms of the anti-dumping investigations initiated by the:***

a) ***US:***

b) ***EU:***

3) ***Nearly 40 WTO members have taken anti-dumping measures against Chinese exporters. Do you think different investigation procedures are being applied to Chinese exporters vis-à-vis other exporters during the anti-dumping investigations?***

☐ No
☐ Yes

If yes, were the differences about:

☐ *calculation methods*

☐ *transparency (e.g., concerning investigation guidelines, non-confidential summaries, etc.)*

☐ *public notice/notification*

[23] Janice E. Hawkins, 'The Practical Utility and Suitability of Email Interviews in Qualitative Research', *Qual. Rep.* 23, no. 2 (2018), 494.

[24] Ibid.

[25] Ibid.

☐ *selection of samples*
☐ *submission of evidence*
☐ *access to non-confidential files*
☐ *hearing*
☐ *newcomer*
☐ *enforcement (e.g., concerning provisional duties, reviews, etc.)*
☐ *others? Please specify: _____*

4) ***In your view, what were the reasons for Chinese exporters' non-corporation with the US and EU investigating authorities?***
a) ***US:***
b) ***EU:***

5) ***How would you compare the outcomes of cooperation and non-cooperation for Chinese exporters?***

6) ***Do you think stricter procedural rules applied by the US and EU investigators (if any) create any problems at the global level and at the WTO (e.g., in terms of market access, non-transparency, dispute settlement, etc.)?***

7) ***In your view, which of the following measures would encourage Chinese exporters to cooperate with different investigating authorities? Please check all that apply.***

☐ *a standard anti-dumping questionnaire to be used by all countries*
☐ *raising the awareness of exporters about non-cooperation*
☐ *an NGO providing low-cost legal assistance for the exporters*
☐ *others? Please specify measures:*

Please explain why:

8) ***Any additional comments on the US and EU anti-dumping investigations as regards how they can be improved?***
a) ***US investigations: __________***
b) ***EU investigations: ___________***

The official mentioned that MOFCOM is monitoring the rules and practices of other WTO members and assisting Chinese exporters when they face anti-dumping investigations by WTO members. The concerns raised by the MOFCOM official are parallel to the ones highlighted by the lawyers. The official finds that the US is abusive in terms of the WTO's trade remedy rules, and the EU is more cautious compared to the US regarding these rules. The official did not think that different rules are being applied against Chinese exporters 'except the US and certain members who use surrogate methods in calculating normal value'. However, he agreed that stricter procedural rules are being applied against Chinese exporters by the US and EU investigating authorities. For the US investigations, the discriminatory procedures, especially for state-owned enterprises, prevent exporters from cooperating. For EU investigations, the 'burden of submitting questionnaire particular for SMEs' is the main concern. The official acknowledged that the duties vary widely between cooperating companies and non-cooperating companies. To increase the rate of cooperation, he advised that:

> lightening the burden of responding to questionnaires, reducing the cost of hiring legal assistance, as well as receiving a fair treatment are crucial for exporters to undertake cooperation.

Also, the official noted that the withdrawal of surrogate methods is essential for Chinese exporters. The official stressed that responding to anti-dumping questionnaires is a difficult task for exporters, especially SMEs. Hiring lawyers is expensive, and responding to questionnaires is burdensome. Legal costs are one of the main concerns in US investigations, whereas submission of evidence is a significant problem in EU investigations. Procedural justice needs to be improved to increase the level of cooperation. The official highlighted the need for simpler procedures in responding to questionnaires, lower legal costs, and fair treatment. These suggestions mirror those of WTO lawyers and Chinese exporters.

5.4.4 *Comments by the US Investigating Authorities*

The questions devoted to the US investigating authorities were shaped after analysis of the content of the previous responses. Since several responses suggested the use of procedures as barriers to deter cooperation, the book's hypothesis prevails. Particular attention was given to the seventh question, where the calculation methods were highlighted. There is enough empirical evidence to show that US calculation methods have a protective bias rather than provide an objective assessment. Also, due to high legal costs and time commitment, exporters cannot defend themselves properly before the US investigating authorities; this point is also directed as a specific question in the questionnaire. The email interview method was used to collect data from the US investigating authorities. The form below was sent to the US investigation authorities:

1) ***Can you specify the role of USITC/Commerce in anti-dumping investigations?***

2) ***Do you think different investigation procedures are being applied to Chinese exporters vis-à-vis other exporters during the anti-dumping investigations?***

3) ***In your view, what are the reasons for Chinese exporters' non-corporation with the US investigating authorities?***

4) ***How would you compare the outcomes of cooperation and non-cooperation for exporters?***

5) ***Do you think stricter procedural rules applied by the US investigators (if any) create any problems at the global level and at the WTO (e.g., in terms of market access, non-transparency, dispute settlement, etc.)?***

6) ***In your view, which of the following measures would encourage Chinese exporters to cooperate with the US investigating authorities? Please check all that apply:***

   ☐ *a standard anti-dumping questionnaire to be used by all countries*
   ☐ *raising the awareness of exporters about non-cooperation*
   ☐ *an NGO providing low-cost legal assistance for the exporters*
   ☐ *others? Please specify measures:*

   Please explain why:

7) ***Do you think the procedures regarding the following matters adopted by the US investigating authorities are compatible with the ADA and the Appellate Body reports? Please explain why:***

a) ***calculation methods:*** _________
b) ***submission of evidence:*** __________
c) ***transparency:*** ______________
d) ***access to non-confidential files:*** ____________

8) ***Do you consider any of the following matters as barriers against cooperation?***

a) ***high legal costs:*** _________
b) ***time spent on investigations:*** __________
c) ***procedural burdens:*** __________

9) ***Any additional comments on how the US anti-dumping investigations can be improved?***

10) ***Any additional comments on how the WTO's ADA can be improved?***

5.4.4.1 USITC

The USITC's office of external relations responded to the email and provided their handbook for reference:

> Unfortunately, it is not our practice to participate in surveys. However, if you are interested in our AD/CVD process, we do have a handbook that is available online at: www.usitc.gov/trade_remedy/documents/handbook.pdf.

A follow-up email was sent to the investigating authority asking for general comments on the US anti-dumping practices and their function in the US WTO policies. The following response was received:

> The Commission is not a policy-making agency. We conduct AD/CVD cases according to statute. If you are interested in a policy response, I recommend you contact the US Department of Commerce, or the US Trade Representative's Office.

The refusal to make any comment may be due to the workload but also raises some transparency concerns over the investigative procedures.

5.4.4.2 Commerce

The same questions were sent to Commerce, and no response was received.

5.4.5 Comments by the EU Investigating Authority

As the findings reveal abuse of investigation procedures, a questionnaire was directed to the EU investigating authorities. Most of the questions were similar to the US questionnaire, except the seventh question emphasised complaints about transparency in the EU's investigations. To collect data from the EU investigators, the email interview method was used:

1) ***Can you specify the role of European Commission in anti-dumping investigations?***
2) ***Do you think different investigation procedures are being applied to Chinese exporters vis-à-vis other exporters during the anti-dumping investigations?***
3) ***In your view, what are the reasons for exporters' non-corporation with the Commission?***

4) ***How would you compare the outcomes of cooperation and non-cooperation for exporters?***

5) ***Do you think stricter procedural rules applied by the EU investigators (if any) create any problems at the global level and at the WTO (e.g., in terms of market access, non-transparency, dispute settlement, etc.)?***

6) ***In your view, which of the following measures would encourage Chinese exporters to cooperate with the EU investigating authorities? Please check all that apply.***

☐ *a standard anti-dumping questionnaire to be used by all countries*
☐ *raising the awareness of exporters about non-cooperation*
☐ *an NGO providing low-cost legal assistance for the exporters*
☐ *others? Please specify measures:*

Please explain why:

7) ***Do you think the procedures regarding the following matters adopted by the European Commission are compatible with the ADA and the Appellate Body reports? Please explain why:***

a) ***transparency:*** ________
b) ***calculation methods:*** __________
c) ***enforcement:*** ______________
d) ***access to non-confidential files:*** ____________

8) ***Do you consider any of the following matters as barriers against cooperation?***
a) ***high legal costs:*** _________
b) ***time spent on investigations:*** __________
c) ***procedural burdens:*** __________

9) ***Any additional comments on how the EU anti-dumping investigations can be improved?***

10) ***Any additional comments on how the WTO's ADA can be improved?***

No response was received regarding this questionnaire.

5.5 Evaluation of the Findings and Causation

This chapter attempts to demonstrate practical knowledge about anti-dumping investigations by the US and EU. Compared with doctrinal research, empirical research adds a more practical perspective to the questions under consideration. The responses by practitioners and exporters reflect the latest policies and activities. To cover a wider range, a mixture of strategies was used, and three main groups were surveyed: WTO lawyers, Chinese exporters and investigating authorities. Sampling for each group was carried out according to particular needs, as the populations were diverse. Investigating authorities were contacted directly where a single response was considered sufficient. Regarding WTO lawyers, location and investigation experience were the main determinants, and samples were chosen from more senior lawyers, such as partners, to gain intimate knowledge. For the Chinese exporters, industries were the main determinant as the top five industries represent around 80 per cent of the anti-dumping measures globally. Also, the number of employees and the date of incorporation were used to filter exporters from business databases. This query returned around 32,000 exporters, which were sampled randomly, and emails were sent. However, few responses were received. Therefore, the method was changed to purposive sampling. Unlike quantitative research, qualitative research does not rely on a large amount of data and so, to draw accurate conclusions, sampling should be representative and sufficiently large.[26] Consequently, Chinese exporters were traced according to industry and official gazette announcements of anti-dumping measures.

Within the scope of this book, empirical research has reached the theoretical saturation point, which is where there are no new perspectives to be discovered.[27] Determination of the saturation point depends on the research design and data triangulation.[28] Data triangulation requires the adoption of several methods to reach theoretical saturation.[29] Several methods were adopted in this book to collect empirical data from different sources relating to anti-dumping investigations. For each category of data source, the study should reach saturation. Again, the question arises about the sample size and whether the number of responses is sufficient to saturate the qualitative research. Mathematical models show that six

26 Lisa Webley, 'Qualitative Approaches to Empirical Legal Research', in Peter Cane and Herbert Kritzer (eds.), *The Oxford Handbook of Empirical Legal Research* (Oxford University Press, 2010), 926–950.

27 John Bacon-Shone, *Introduction to Quantitative Research Methods* (Graduate School, The University of Hong Kong, 2013).

28 Patricia I. Fusch and Lawrence R. Ness, 'Are We There Yet? Data Saturation in Qualitative Research', *Qual. Rep.* 20, no. 9 (2015), 1408.

29 Ibid.

participants can uncover 80 per cent of a problem.[30] Also, twelve interviews can uncover 90 per cent.[31] If the selected group is homogeneous and the research's aim is to reveal general patterns for the research area, then twelve responses are generally considered adequate.[32]

The findings in this chapter support the view that the procedural rules are being used to discourage exporters from cooperating. Non-cooperation of exporters allows the investigating authorities to adopt higher anti-dumping duties without examining each exporter individually. The basic principle of the ADA is that anti-dumping duties are individual to exporters and sampling should be used in exceptional cases. However, if the investigating authorities adopt exceptions disproportionately, this empirically implies that members are benefitting from the gaps in the ADA. This phenomenon can be explained by the 'procedural effect' of anti-dumping investigations. Moreover, procedural justice could be a cure, balancing the overly protectionist usage of procedural rules. Responses from WTO lawyers imply that both jurisdictions enjoy a large amount of discretion. The US system is more transparent but the calculation methods favour domestic industries by overprotecting them. Procedural difficulties, such as high legal costs or access to non-confidential files, result in low rates of cooperation, and non-cooperating companies face high anti-dumping duties. Lawyers empirically indicate that EU investigations are not transparent, as parties cannot access the filing documents or calculation methods. The MOFCOM official framed the obstacles to cooperation with the US and EU investigations as: the long questionnaire, the cost of lawyers and being treated fairly. Chinese exporters' responses are similar in that they are mostly affected by the high legal costs and losing their market at the end of anti-dumping investigations. Chinese exporters find anti-dumping investigations frustrating in both jurisdictions and do not believe that they are treated fairly.

Therefore, the empirical findings from the major stakeholders of the anti-dumping investigation confirm that the procedural rules adopted by both the US and EU investigating authorities are problematic from various perspective. The exporters cannot defend themselves properly, and they believe they are treated unfairly.

[30] Greg Guest, Arwen Bunce and Laura Johnson, 'How Many Interviews Are Enough? An Experiment with Data Saturation and Variability', *Field Methods* 18, no. 1 (2006), 59–82.

[31] Ibid.

[32] Ibid.

5.6 Conclusion

As the WTO is a platform where governments are the main players, it is unlikely to reflect all the procedural obstacles faced by the exporters at this level. Thus, additional information has been collected from exporters, law firms, and officials of MOFCOM. Surveys and semi-structured interviews were prepared for these three groups of actors in anti-dumping investigations conducted by the US and the EU. The findings are helpful for readers to recognise procedural problems that exist in practice.

This chapter aims to clarify the link between procedural burdens and the level of cooperation in anti-dumping investigations. Empirical research may not fully ensure that strict procedural rules cause low levels of cooperation. However, some empirical findings reached in this chapter support the view that investigation procedures are biased. At least from most of the WTO lawyers and Chinese exporters' points of view, anti-dumping investigations are not procedurally or substantially transparent, objective, or fair. Some companies try to cooperate but still face high anti-dumping duties. Almost all the companies and WTO lawyers agree that, after the measures are imposed, business falls sharply. However, some companies disclosed that circumvention of anti-dumping duties is an easier solution. Again, the empirical findings in this chapter can only support the hypothesis of the study to some extent.

Furthermore, data collected from the field can also assist in answering the research questions up to a certain point. The empirical findings cannot answer whether the procedural rules are exclusively used for hidden trade protectionism purposes. Another notable conclusion about the data collection process is that, although hundreds of companies were contacted, few were interested in participating in empirical research. This shows that exporters evaluate anti-dumping as a problem without a solution. Exporters are right in the sense that their experience reminds them that even if they try to cooperate, their exports will be negatively affected by anti-dumping measures. However, there is strong evidence supporting the over-protectionist use of anti-dumping investigations by the US and EU, particularly against Chinese exporters. Exporters are struggling to cooperate with US and EU investigating authorities. For instance, solar panel or bus tyre manufacturers who faced investigations in both jurisdictions are not able to cooperate fully due to the lack of financial and legal capacity. The companies need to process completely different questionnaires and different procedures and, generally, even if they do cooperate, they are faced with an anti-dumping duty rather than an exemption. This is possibly the reason exporters approach other markets or try to circumvent the duties.

Based on the preliminary findings, additional surveys were prepared for the US and EU investigating authorities to seek their perception. However, no comments were received. There may be several reasons for this refusal to participate in empirical research. First, there is no obligation for the investigating authorities to participate in academic research. Second, even if officials would like to participate, they may feel that any unofficial statement would be used against their government, so they do not want to bear this risk, especially when there is no obligation to do so. Also, if the real intention behind complicated investigating procedures is to increase the level of protectionism, officials would not mention this explicitly. Furthermore, this book holds the view that if the propositions in the survey are completely groundless, the investigating authorities would attempt to refute them by showing some evidence. Therefore, as there was no objection or explanation from US and EU investigators, the hidden trade protectionism assumption behind anti-dumping investigation procedures is supported.

Overall, it is clear that there are problems in anti-dumping investigation methodologies, from calculation methods and transparency to high legal costs and time consumed. The fieldwork in this chapter builds connections between strict procedural rules and the level of cooperation. Exporters are unable to defend their interests under these circumstances, which damages procedural justice. The 'procedural effect' is a new concept introduced by this book, meaning that strict procedural rules make it hard to cooperate, and the investigating authorities can enforce inflated dumping margins by using the facts available clause under the ADA. In other words, if the procedural rules were more transparent and unbiased, the anti-dumping measures of the US and the EU would not be as restrictive as they are now, especially against China. These improvements would also require some revision of the ADA. Improving procedural justice would bring enhanced transparency and predictability while ensuring meaningful participation. Chinese exporters and WTO lawyers mostly agree that cooperation with the investigating authorities could be improved by use of standard questionnaires, with NGOs providing low-cost legal assistance and training exporters about the outcomes of non-cooperation. Otherwise, anti-dumping will be used to overprotect domestic industries and there will be an increased risk of circumvention.

6

Possible Solutions for Protectionist Anti-dumping Procedures

6.1 Introduction

Chapter 6 highlights the need for a modification of the anti-dumping mechanism, preferably through the revision of the ADA.[1] There are ongoing negotiations on the ADA; however, these negotiations seem to be going nowhere. There are several reasons for this, such as the deadlock of the Doha Development Round,[2] the advent of giant trade agreements, the unwillingness of top users of anti-dumping measures to agree, and the latest Appellate Body crisis at the WTO. Nonetheless, alternatives can be discussed to resolve these problems, which include the misuse of anti-dumping procedures.

The revision of the ADA has been on the table since the Doha Round Negotiations, but there are controversial issues on anti-dumping negotiations. During negotiations, the US proposed that zeroing should be permissible,[3] and some WTO members denounced others for abusing the ADA and called for clearer rules.[4] The need to revise the ADA is also highlighted by the literature,[5] but this study departs by prioritising

[1] This chapter has been previously published as two articles. I would like to thank Professor Michael Palmer for his valuable comments and his support during the publication process and to Institute of Advanced Legal Studies, which publishes the journal *Amicus Curiae*. Abdulkadir Yilmazcan, 'The Slow Train to Reforming Anti-Dumping Measures', *Amicus Curiae* 2. 3 (2022), 335. Abdulkadir Yilmazcan, 'The Slow Train to Reforming Anti-Dumping Measures: Concrete Solutions for the Future', *Amicus Curiae* 2 3 (2022), 517.

[2] Doha Round was held between 2001 and 2003. The deadlock was more due to the disagreement between developing and developed members on the liberalisation on agricultural goods. For more details on Doha Deadlock please see www.wto.org/english/forums_e/public_forum12_e/art_pf12_e/art19.htm.

[3] Chaisse and Chakraborty, 'Normative Obsolescence of the WTO', p. 236.

[4] Hongsong Liu, 'China's Proposing Behavior in Global Governance: The Cases of the WTO Doha Round Negotiation and G-20 Process', *Rev. Bras. Polít. Int.* 57, no. SPE (2014), 129.

[5] Michael Andrews, 'The Facts Available on "Facts Available": An Analysis of Article 6.8 and Annex II of the WTO Anti-Dumping Agreement', *N.Z. J. Public & Int'l L.* 6 (2008), 40; Chaisse and Chakraborty, 'Normative Obsolescence of the WTO', 263.

procedural revisions rather than substantive modifications. The study proposes improvements from procedural justice in anti-dumping procedures before reforming the substantial rules. A standard anti-dumping investigation questionnaire to be used by all members would be helpful to solve most of the procedural problems arising from different enforcement by WTO members. The idea of a standard questionnaire is also considered helpful given the responses collected during the empirical research described in Chapter 5. An exporter can defend itself accurately against different anti-dumping investigations and would cooperate with investigating authorities more readily if each member adopted the same anti-dumping questionnaire. Also, a detailed handbook or guideline on procedures could be added as an annex to the ADA to prevent problems. Furthermore, an NGO providing low-cost legal assistance was felt to be useful by exporters and WTO lawyers. This chapter aims to highlight the normative solutions, constraints and possible practical solutions to avoid the hidden trade protectionism behind anti-dumping investigations. These alternatives may improve procedural justice without a revision of the ADA and would limit the level of discretion by investigating authorities.

6.2 General Suggestions for a Comprehensive Reform of the ADA

Previous chapters in this study attempt to show that the anti-dumping mechanism is no longer serving its original design purposes. It is the most disputed issue under the DSM. Regarding the cases analysed in Chapter 3, there are several inconsistencies to the ADA, as well as grey areas, such as zeroing. Zeroing is not explicitly prohibited by the ADA, but the Appellate Body considers this practice to be inconsistent with the fair comparison of prices under Article 2.4.

Furthermore, the empirical findings in Chapter 5 show that anti-dumping procedures are not transparent, objective or fair, especially for Chinese exporters, when companies cooperate with investigating authorities and defend interests. Empirical findings also show that investigating authorities are biased and overprotect local industries; therefore, exporters do not stand to gain even if they bear high legal costs and spend days preparing submissions. Rather, some companies choose to circumvent the duties, which eliminates the expected balancing effect of anti-dumping duties. In this context, the revision of ADA is the first option to be addressed.

6.2.1 Current Negotiations

The current negotiations on anti-dumping matters are led by the Negotiating Group on Rules (NGR), which was established in 2002 at the Doha Ministerial Conference. The Doha Development Agenda of 2001 was a deadlock in many ways due to busy negotiating schedules, tight deadlines and the single undertaking model.[6] Apart from the technical side, agriculture was the main concern of developing members who argued that concessions agreed on at the Uruguay Round had not been fulfilled.[7] As several attempts failed to conclude the Agenda, the Nairobi Ministerial Declaration officially ended the Doha Development Agenda.[8] The Nairobi Package of 2015 brought some momentum to the ongoing negotiations, especially on export competition and agricultural subsidies.[9] However, dumping issues were not mentioned in the closing statement or in the Ministerial Declaration. In 2017, the Buenos Aires Ministerial Conference ended with some decisions on fisheries subsidies, e-commerce, TRIPS and work programme on small economies.[10] The twelfth Ministerial Conference was planned to be held in Kazakhstan in June 2020, but was cancelled due to the COVID-19 pandemic.

There are evident problems with the WTO and the ADA, and these need to be fixed. GATT has been successful for more than seventy years, but due to the well-known spaghetti bowl phenomenon, the WTO's relevance is questioned by members such as the US.[11] Free trade agreements and customs unions are exceptions to the general principles of the GATT, as regulated under Article XXIV.[12] However, the use of Article XXIV's exceptions exceeds all expectations while harming the multilateral trading system. As Panezi states:

6 Antoine Martin and Bryan Mercurio, 'Doha Dead and Buried in Nairobi: Lessons for the WTO', *J. Int'l Trade L. Pol'y* 16, no. 1 (2017), 49–66.

7 Ibid., 51.

8 Erin Hannah, James Scott and Rorden Wilkinson, 'The WTO in Buenos Aires: The Outcome and Its Significance for the Future of the Multilateral Trading System', *World Econ.* 41, no. 10 (2018), 2578–2598.

9 Martin and Mercurio, 'Doha Dead and Buried in Nairobi', 49.

10 Eleventh WTO Ministerial Conference, WTO, accessed 18 July 2023, www.wto.org/english/thewto_e/minist_e/mc11_e/mc11_e.htm.

11 Maria Panezi, 'The WTO and the Spaghetti Bowl of Free Trade Agreements: Four Proposals for Moving Forward', CIGI Papers No. 87 (2016), 5.

12 Full text of GATT 47 available at www.wto.org/english/docs_e/legal_e/gatt47_02_e.htm#articleXXIV, accessed 18 July 2023.

> WTO members should seriously consider formally adopting a more assertive approach that allows FTAs, RTAs and PTAs to continue to exist, although not to the detriment of multilateral rights and duties, especially for developing and least-developed countries.[13]

With the recent crisis at the WTO, the Director-General was re-elected in 2021. Depending on the direction of the deglobalisation trend, the negotiation agenda may primarily be aimed at saving the gains of the rules-based system. Revising the agenda for anti-dumping rules may seem a secondary matter, but there is a need for revision. If the new agenda can be determined according to the most disputed areas, then anti-dumping should be the first issue discussed.

Canada proposed that problematic areas should be identified first; and dumping comes first. In this context, the rules and negotiations are not only proposing an important role for an improved ADA but also the WTO as a whole.

The NGR discusses two main topics: anti-dumping and subsidies on fisheries. The mandate related to the anti-dumping negotiations states:

> In the light of experience and of the increasing application of these instruments by Members, we agree to negotiations aimed at clarifying and improving disciplines under the Agreements on Implementation of Article VI of the GATT 1994 ... while preserving the basic concepts, principles and effectiveness of these Agreements and their instruments and objectives, and taking into account the needs of developing and least-developed participants.[14]

The reason for the anti-dumping matters to be on the Doha Agenda was that many WTO Members denounced abuse in anti-dumping investigations.[15] Therefore, these members acknowledge the need for improving discipline under the ADA, but the problem is how to achieve this goal. The NGR also has a Technical Group where members exchange ideas in an informal setting.[16] The negotiations under the NGR take place among three groups. The first group, FANs, consists of several WTO members pushing for more transparency and due process.[17] FANs

13 Panezi, 'The WTO and the Spaghetti Bowl of Free Trade Agreements', 5.

14 Doha WTO Ministerial 2001: Ministerial Declaration, WT/MIN(01)/DEC/1, accessed 18 July 2023, www.wto.org/english/thewto_e/minist_e/min01_e/mindecl_e.htm.

15 Liu, 'China's Proposing Behavior in Global Governance', 129.

16 The Rules Negotiations, WTO, accessed 18 July 2023, www.wto.org/english/tratop_e/rulesneg_e/rulesneg_e.htm.

17 Chile, Colombia, Costa Rica, Hong Kong China, Israel, Japan, Korea, Norway, Singapore, Switzerland, Chinese Taipei and Thailand. WTO, 'FANs Push Transparency, Due

argues that the ADA is being abused and, therefore, their aim is to fill the gaps in the ADA with clearer rules.[18] The second group consists of developed countries, such as the US, which aims to maintain the status quo.[19] China, Egypt and India, as the third group, call for developing countries' concerns to be taken into consideration while revising the ADA.[20] China has submitted relatively few proposals, although it is the most affected member as the top anti-dumping target.[21] Apart from these groups, members such as the EU, Canada or Australia agree on the revision but do not agree to amend their domestic laws.[22]

Driven by these interest groups, the NGR managed to announce its first draft in 2007.[23] The draft consists of procedural amendments, such as the clarification of the exchange rate source, limitation of the anti-dumping measures to ten years, and legalisation of the zeroing methodology.[24] The majority of members opposed the draft due to the legalisation of zeroing. FANs submitted a statement specifically on zeroing:

> The Chair's text, as it now stands, permits the practice of zeroing, thus running counter to the above. Zeroing is a biased and partial method for calculating the margin of dumping and inflates antidumping duties. If the use of such practice prevails in the future, it could nullify the results of trade liberalization efforts. In Marrakesh, Ministers expressed their determination to resist protectionist pressure of all kinds. They believed that trade liberalisation and strengthened rules achieved in the Uruguay Round would lead to a progressively more open world trading environment. We call upon all Members to ensure that the Multilateral Trading System is not undermined through zeroing.[25]

Process, but Members Reluctant to Engage in Rules Negotiations', accessed 18 July 2023, www.wto.org/english/news_e/news15_e/rule_25jun15_e.htm.

[18] Yi Lu, 'Exploring Aggressive Legalism: Is Now a Good Time to Promote This Approach in Greater Asia?', *Asian J. L. Econ.* 6, no. 1 (2015), 85–123; Won-mog Choi, 'People's Republic of China's Proposals for Anti-dumping in WTO/DDA Rules Negotiations', *Asian J. WTO & Int'l Health L. & Pol'y* 2 (2007), 25.

[19] Choi, 'People's Republic of China's Proposals for Anti-dumping in WTO/DDA Rules Negotiations'.

[20] Ibid.

[21] Julia Ya Qin, 'China, India, and the Law of the World Trade Organization', *Asian J. Comp. L.* 3 (2008), 20.

[22] Ibid.

[23] Jun Kazeki, 'Anti-dumping Negotiations under the WTO and FANs', *J. World Trade* 44, no. 5 (2010), 931–965, p. 940.

[24] Draft Consolidated Chair Texts of the AD and SCM Agreements, WTO, accessed 18 July 2023, www.wto.org/english/tratop_e/rulesneg_e/rules_chair_text_nov07_e.htm.

[25] Negotiating Group on Rules, 2007, Statement on 'Zeroing' in the Anti-Dumping Negotiations, Statement of Brazil; Chile; China; Costa Rica; Hong Kong, China; India;

Thus, FANs believe that the draft did not adopt a balanced view, contrary to their expectations. The US, as a supporter of zeroing, was dissatisfied with other revisions of the ADA. The second text was circulated by the chairman in 2008 and the latest in 2011. The 2011 draft text includes bracketed issues just like the 2008 text.[26] The bracketed issues are controversial in the draft where the final amendment is left to further negotiation: zeroing, causation of injury, material retardation, the product under consideration, information requests to affiliated parties, public interest, lesser duty, anti-circumvention, sunset review, third-country dumping, and technical assistance for developing countries.[27] On zeroing, the chairman comments:

> [ZEROING: This issue remains among the most divisive in the anti-dumping negotiations, and there have been few signs of convergence. Positions range from insistence on a total prohibition on zeroing irrespective of the comparison methodology used and in respect of all proceedings to a demand that zeroing be specifically authorised in all contexts. Some delegations however hold more nuanced positions, and there is openness among some delegations to undertake a technical examination of this issue in particular contexts, such as for example the third ('targeted dumping') methodology provided for in Article 2.4.2.][28]

It is mostly procedural issues that divide WTO members into at least two groups. China's position is that the ADA is being abused, and this harms efforts on trade liberalisation.[29] China suggests revising the ADA to avoid misuse of anti-dumping measures.[30] The EU also supports reform of the ADA to keep the rules-based system working[31] and wants new approaches in negotiations to hasten progress.[32] The following presents the main positions under the NGR regarding procedural matters.

Japan; Korea, Rep. of; Mexico; Norway; Singapore; Switzerland; Separate Customs Territory of Taiwan, Penghu, Kinmen and Matsu; and Thailand, TN/RL/W/214, 1.

26 Negotiating Group on Rules, Communication from the Chairman, TN/RL/W/254.

27 Ibid.

28 Ibid., 6.

29 Choi, 'People's Republic of China's Proposals for Anti-dumping in WTO/DDA Rules Negotiations', 52.

30 Ibid.

31 Shi Yan, 'The EU's Push for WTO Reform: Proposals, Paths and Impacts', *China Int'l Stud.* 76 (2019), 65.

32 Ibid.

6.2.2 *Reform of the WTO ADA*

The ADA has been an agenda item since the Doha Declaration, where it was expected that negotiations would improve disciplines while protecting the basic concepts and principles of the ADA.[33] In this context, several proposals were submitted, but negotiations have not been successful since the establishment of the NGR in 2002. This is mainly because users and target members take different positions in terms of regulation or deregulation of the ADA. Some proposals submitted by the members are presented below.

6.2.2.1 The EU

Early on, in 2002, the EU acknowledged the need to revise the ADA, stating:

> The EC would be ready to engage in discussions on the issues outlined below as well as other issues that may be presented by Members in this context.
>
> –Disclosure and access to non-confidential documents are key procedural rights for interested parties, in particular exporters and domestic industries. . . .
>
> –In the experience of the EC, a mandatory lesser duty rule leads to stronger disciplines. It significantly limits the level of the measures to what is strictly necessary for removing injury to the domestic industry.
>
> –A public interest test (in terms of an examination of the impact on economic operators), even if discretionary in nature, provides for a wider and more complete analysis of the situation on the domestic importing market. Linked with appropriate substantive and procedural provisions the public interest test could be a useful additional condition before measures can be imposed.
>
> –Provisions governing the settlement of disputes lead to long delays before disputes are settled and measures modified. The very initiation of an investigation can already put a heavy burden on exporters, importers and ultimately the domestic user industry. Consequently, a reflection could be made as to whether and under which conditions initiations of investigations could be made subject to a swift dispute settlement mechanism, taking into due account the relevant provisions and practice under the Understanding on the Settlement of Disputes.
>
> –A strengthening of the disciplines could also, by definition, reduce the costs of investigations. Indeed, a major problem of today's anti-

33 WTO Negotiations on the Agreement on Anti-Dumping Practices, ITC (2005), accessed 18 July 2023, https://ticaret.gov.tr/data/5b8ee73113b8761b8471c2c4/wtonegotiations.pdf.

> dumping practice, identified in particular by developing countries, is the cost which firms incur when they want to cooperate effectively in such proceedings. It could be explored whether a further and beneficial improvement could be achieved by screening all procedural aspects with a view to identifying those areas where changes can bring about a reduction in the cost of cooperation while at the same time maintaining the quality of the investigation. Areas such as simplifying and standardising information collection, particularly at the initial stages of the investigations, could be a further issue to be discussed under this heading.[34]

The submission of the EU is objective and accurate in that the procedural burdens on the exporters are recognised. In terms of access to non-confidential files, the EU is criticised, and even the EU ombudsman decided against the Commission.[35] Delay in the dispute settlement system is also another reality with anti-dumping measures related to transparency. In a more recent communication, the EU suggested that increased transparency is beneficial from a common-sense perspective and may reduce the number of disputes at the DSM.[36] The public interest test is not mandatory under the ADA but, nonetheless, the EU adopts the test before imposing anti-dumping measures so any additional duties do not only serve the interests of domestic industries. The EU, therefore, suggests that the public interest test should be covered by the ADA.[37] Another remarkable point in the submission is that the EU acknowledges the cost of cooperation for exporters and suggests screening all procedures and revising those that are burdensome and costly. One concrete suggestion is the standardisation of the information collection method at the early stages of the investigation, which could be accomplished with a standard questionnaire for all members as proposed in this study.

In 2003, the EU called for model/standard questionnaires to be used by all members.[38] The EU sorts the benefits of standard questionnaires as time and money saving, as well as easier preparation of

[34] Negotiating Group on Rules, Submission from the European Communities Concerning the Agreement on Implementation of Article VI of GATT 1994 (Anti-Dumping Agreement), TN/RL/W/13, (2002), 2–3.

[35] Maurizio Gambardella, 'Transparency in EU Antidumping Investigations: The European Ombudsman Perspective', *Glob. Trade Cust. J.* 6, no. 3 (2011), 157–163.

[36] Negotiating Group on Rules, 2015, Rules Negotiations: Transparency, Communication from the European Union, TN/RL/W/260, 2.

[37] Ibid.

[38] Negotiating Group on Rules, Proposals on Cost Saving in Anti-Dumping Proceedings, Submission from the European Communities and Japan, TN/RL/W/138 (2003).

submissions.[39] This would increase the level of cooperation and reduce the discretion of investigating authorities. In 2006, the EU sought procedural improvements, stating that the information required, verification visits, and the selected language create uncertainty during investigations,[40] which discourages exporters from cooperating. Since limited number of companies cooperate, breaches of the ADA cannot be monitored effectively, and the anti-dumping mechanism is more likely to be abused by investigating authorities.[41] The EU also contends that the DSM is not able to handle all of these issues in practice, just as discussed in Chapter 5.[42]

In this context, the EU proposes a review mechanism to ensure transparency in anti-dumping investigations.[43] Given that there is a more general review mechanism (Trade Policy Review Mechanism) that also covers anti-dumping matters, this additional review mechanism would be burdensome unless it was empowered to enforce sanctions on violating members.

A document circulated in 2018 by the EU Commission reflecting the EU's position is called the 'WTO Modernization – Introduction to Future EU Proposals'.[44] The paper highlights the lack of a review mechanism for anti-dumping investigations that results in inefficient notification of subsidies, a growing number of state-owned enterprises, and trade-distorting measures.[45] The need for improved transparency is also once more suggested in the document.[46]

The EU's suggestions seem ambitious compared to its practice, as it has been challenged in several disputes, such as *DS405*. In several submissions, the EU has highlighted the need for improved transparency but, in *DS405*, the EU was found to be violating Article 6.5.1 of the ADA by failing to disclose non-confidential summaries to interested parties who submit confidential information.[47]

39 Ibid.

40 Negotiating Group on Rules, Transparency of Anti-Dumping Activity, Submission from the European Union, TN/RL/GEN/110, 1.

41 Ibid.

42 Ibid.

43 Ibid.

44 European Commission Presents Comprehensive Approach for the Modernisation of the World Trade Organization, EU (2018), accessed 18 July 2023, http://trade.ec.europa.eu/doclib/press/index.cfm?id=1908.

45 Yan, 'The EU's Push for WTO Reform', 2.

46 Ibid.

47 DS405, European Union – Anti-Dumping Measures on Certain Footwear from China, Report of Panel, 282.

6.2.2.2 The US

As a frequent user, the position of the US is to amend Articles 2.4 and 9.3 of the ADA to legalise the use of the zeroing methodology.[48] FANs strongly oppose the US's proposals in this regard.[49] The US's submission in 2002 acknowledged that procedures differ widely among WTO members.[50] The US also mentioned that procedural justice is a key principle of the ADA, and some issues should be discussed under the NGR.[51] The outcomes of disputes heard by the DSM, especially on zeroing, indicate that the US's position during the negotiations contradicts its actual practice. The contradiction also appears in other ADA Articles.

Regarding ADA Article 6.4, the US argued that interested parties should have timely opportunities to see all non-confidential information used by the investigating authorities.[52] The US offered a public record system of non-confidential files to be accessible by all interested parties to promote public accountability, consistency and predictability.[53]

The US finds the language of Article 12 of the ADA unsatisfactory as the requirement for 'sufficient detail' to be disclosed on public notices is not clearly defined.[54] Therefore, the US calls for the inclusion of more information in public notices, such as calculation methods. The US is considered to be more transparent than the EU in allowing parties to access confidential information and the calculation method.[55]

Regarding Article 6.7 and Annex I of the ADA, the results of verification visits should be made available but the level of detail in this disclosure is not clear. Therefore, the US suggests revising these Articles and setting clearer verification procedures, especially concerning verification reports,[56] which are considered internal documents and confidential by many WTO members. However, non-disclosure of these documents by

[48] Sungjoon Cho, 'No More Zeroing?: The United States Changes Its Antidumping Policy to Comply with the WTO', *Am. Soc. Int'l L.* 16, no. 8 (2012).

[49] Ibid.

[50] Negotiating Group on Rules, Investigatory Procedures under the Anti-Dumping and Subsidies Agreements Submission by the United States, 2002, TN/RL/W/35.

[51] Ibid.

[52] Ibid.

[53] Ibid.

[54] Ibid.

[55] 'An Introduction to Anti-Dumping Law of EU and US as It Applies to Seafood', 31.

[56] Negotiating Group on Rules, Investigatory Procedures under the Anti-Dumping and Subsidies Agreements Submission by the United States.

the parties subject to verification visits obstructs exporters from meaningfully participating in the procedure.[57]

In terms of Article 18 of the ADA, domestic regulations should conform to the ADA. The US suggested detailed local regulations and administrative guidelines in order to improve predictability and due process.[58] The US recognises the need to reduce the costs of investigations as a requirement of procedural fairness. Such detailed domestic regulations would increase the predictability, but, on the other hand, if each member regulates detailed anti-dumping provisions, it would be more burdensome for exporters to cooperate in anti-dumping investigations. They need to comply with more detailed rules in different jurisdictions, which would discourage them from cooperating with each investigation. Instead of regulating anti-dumping procedures domestically, it would be more practical and beneficial to harmonise procedures globally so that exporters do not face different rules in each investigation. In that regard, the EU's model/standard questionnaire proposal is more practical and solution-oriented than the US's proposals.

6.2.2.3 China

Since its accession to the WTO in 2001, China has submitted many proposals to revise the ADA, as it is the top target for other members. The overall position of China on anti-dumping is that members enjoy room for discretion, so they arbitrarily abuse the anti-dumping mechanism that harms free trade.[59]

In 2003, China proposed reassessing some of the issues regarding the ADA. China expressed concern about back-to-back anti-dumping investigations and proposed adding a provision to Article 5 of the ADA in order to prevent new anti-dumping investigation initiation if the previous initiation resulted in a negative finding.[60] This suggestion would be helpful to prevent the abuse of anti-dumping because, otherwise, exporters would face questionnaires regularly and, if they fail to cooperate, the outcome would be positive. China also suggests that some terms, such as 'product under investigation', 'particular market situation' or 'major

[57] Horlick and Vermulst, 'The 10 Major Problems with the Anti-dumping Instrument: An Attempt at Synthesis', 68.

[58] Negotiating Group on Rules, Investigatory Procedures under the Anti-Dumping and Subsidies Agreements Submission by the United States.

[59] Liu, 'China's Proposing Behavior in Global Governance', 129.

[60] Negotiating Group on Rules, Proposal of the People's Republic of China on the Negotiation on Anti-Dumping, 2003, TN/RL/W/66.

proportion' need to be defined clearly in order to limit the discretion of the investigating authorities.[61] China also suggested that Article 2.4.2 of the ADA highlights the prohibition of 'zeroing'.[62] One of the main concerns in the submission from China is the 'non-market economy clause'. China argued that Article 2.7 and the second Supplementary Provision to Paragraph 1 of Article VI in Annex I to GATT 1994 acknowledge that members may not be able to compare domestic prices due to monopoly or state-fixed prices.[63] Under these clauses, members are able to compare third-country or surrogate prices with export prices. China argued that while selecting the surrogate country, members enjoy room of discretion and generally choose the countries at a more advanced level with higher costs and prices.[64] This inflates anti-dumping duties and overprotects domestic industries. China also expressed concern that, under the ADA, exporters do not have the right to respond to the initiation of an anti-dumping investigation.[65] Therefore, China suggested a twenty-day response period before initiation.[66]

In 2007, China also suggested revisions to limit the discretion of members. One of the suggestions was to limit sunset reviews to one so that the total duration of an anti-dumping duty would be limited to ten years.[67] In the current setting, anti-dumping measures can be in force as long as the investigating authority renews them as a sunset review. China also suggested special and differentiated treatment for developing members in anti-dumping investigations.[68]

In 2008, China joined other members in a statement supporting the prohibition of zeroing.[69] China and other members took the view that the zeroing issue should be addressed clearly to avoid long-lasting

[61] Ibid.

[62] Ibid.

[63] Ibid.

[64] Ibid.

[65] Choi, 'People's Republic of China's Proposals for Anti-dumping in WTO/DDA Rules Negotiations', 37.

[66] Ibid.

[67] Liu, 'China's Proposing Behavior in Global Governance', 129.

[68] Ibid. Negotiating Group on Rules, Proposal on Trade Remedies, Submission by China, 2007, TN/RL/GEN/185.

[69] Negotiating Group on Rules, Prohibition of Zeroing, Statement of Brazil; Chile; China; Colombia; Costa Rica; Hong Kong, China; India; Indonesia, Israel; Japan; Korea, Rep. of; Mexico; Norway; Pakistan; Singapore; South Africa; Switzerland; Separate Customs Territory of Taiwan, Penghu, Kinmen and Matsu; Thailand; and Viet Nam (2008) TN/RL/W/215.

problems. The position of the submission can be summarised by the following statement: 'We believe continued disputes between Members on zeroing should be avoided by clearly codifying the prohibition of zeroing at all stages of procedures under the DDA.'[70] In 2008, China, Hong Kong and Pakistan submitted a separate communication about the anti-circumvention provision on the Chair's Consolidated Text in ADA.[71] Currently, anti-circumvention is not regulated under the ADA, which results in local regulations to combat circumvention of anti-dumping duties. However, as there are no uniform rules on anti-circumvention, members enjoy discretion on how to respond to circumvention. Also, circumvention is more likely to occur where anti-dumping measures are used excessively to protect domestic industries. Empirical findings from Chapter 5 also support this view.

A proposal by China in 2017 on trade remedies highlighted five issues: enhancing transparency and strengthening due process, preventing anti-dumping measures from becoming 'permanent', preventing anti-dumping measures from 'overreaching', special consideration and treatment of SMEs and transplanting similar provisions from the ADA to the Agreement on SCM.[72] In this context, China proposed certain revisions, such as the introduction of a notice before the initiation of an investigation, standardisation of evidence for subsidy accusations, and limiting sunset reviews.[73]

6.2.2.4 FANs

FANs have submitted several papers to the NGR. Three papers by FANs were submitted in 2002 stressing the 'abusive interpretation of the current AD Agreement'.[74] The first paper calls for clearer guidelines for procedural issues, such as constructed value, zeroing, facts available and public interest.[75] In the second paper, FANs emphasised the ambiguous definition of the like product, the lax standards of initiation, grey areas on

70 Ibid.

71 Negotiating Group on Rules, Proposed Provision of Anti-Circumvention, Statement of China; Hong Kong, China; Pakistan, 2008, TN/RL/W/216.

72 Negotiating Group on Rules, Proposal on Trade Remedies, Submission by China, 2017, TN/RL/GEN/185.

73 Ibid.

74 Negotiating Group on Rules, Anti-Dumping: Illustrative Major Issues Paper from Brazil; Chile; Colombia; Costa Rica; Hong Kong, China; Israel; Japan; Korea; Mexico; Norway; Singapore; Switzerland; Thailand and Turkey, 2002, TN/RL/W/6.

75 Ibid.

sunset reviews, abusive calculation methods for constructed value, implementation of all others rate and cost data.[76] The third paper of 2002 also underlined transparency in public notices regarding Article 12.1 of the ADA.[77] FANs used the words 'procedural fairness' in the 2005 submission, stating:

> The FANs suggested in this paper a transparency provision for this purpose, and may consider to propose, in the course of negotiations, to expand this type of discipline on procedural fairness and transparency to a broader context of the Agreement, inter alia, to other provisions that contain the word 'normally'.[78]

The suggestion is to improve the 'procedural fairness' by adding the word 'normally' to Article 9.6.[79] However, the word 'normally' is ambiguous and may leave more room for discretion. Members would claim that the conditions were not 'normal' for the case.

In addition to the above submissions, FANs also proposed another communication in 2005.[80] Six objectives were identified to prevent the abusive use of anti-dumping: mitigating the excessive effects of anti-

[76] Negotiating Group on Rules, Second Contribution to Discussion of the Negotiating Group on Rules on Anti-Dumping Measures, Paper by Brazil; Chile; Colombia; Costa Rica; Hong Kong, China; Israel; Japan; Korea; Norway; Separate Customs Territory of Taiwan, Penghu, Kinmen and Matsu; Singapore; Switzerland; and Thailand, 2002, TN/RL/W/10.

[77] Negotiating Group on Rules, Third Contribution to Discussion of the Negotiating Group on Rules on Anti-Dumping Measures, Paper from Brazil; Chile; Colombia; Costa Rica; Hong Kong, China; Japan; Korea; Norway; Separate Customs Territory of Taiwan, Penghu, Kinmen and Matsu; Singapore; Switzerland; Thailand; and Turkey, 2002, TN/RL/W/29.

[78] Negotiating Group on Rules, Further Submission on Proposals on Proceedings under Article 9, Paper from Chile; Costa Rica; Hong Kong, China; Japan; Korea, Rep. of; Norway; Switzerland; Separate Customs Territory of Taiwan, Penghu, Kinmen and Matsu; Thailand; and Turkey, 2005, TN/RL/GEN/44, 2.

[79] FANs suggestion is:

> The provisions of Article 2 shall apply to all determinations pursuant to paragraphs 3 and 5 of this Article. The authorities shall normally use the same methodologies consistently in determining a margin of dumping in an investigation initiated pursuant to Article 5 and in subsequent determinations pursuant to paragraph 3. If the authorities use a different methodology, the parties concerned shall be provided with opportunities to make comments, and a full explanation shall be given why such different methodology was used.
>
> (Ibid.)

[80] Negotiating Group on Rules, Senior Officials' Statement, 2005, TN/RL/W/171.

dumping, preventing anti-dumping measures from becoming 'permanent', strengthening due process and enhancing the transparency of proceedings, reducing costs for authorities and respondents, terminating unwarranted and unnecessary investigations at an early stage, and providing discipline to improve and clarify substantive rules for dumping and injury.[81] These objectives reflect the previous submissions by FANs urging members to agree to clearer rules. The objectives summarise anti-dumping today as the problem has only increased since then. Zeroing, for instance, became a chronic disease among WTO members leading to several cases.[82] More than thirty Panel or Appellate Body reports have found the zeroing methodology to be inconsistent with the ADA.[83] As one of the top zeroing practitioners, the US lost several disputes over zeroing. Consequently, these defeats before the Appellate Body triggered the US to criticise the Appellate Body of judicial overreach and block the appointment of Appellate Body members.[84] Therefore, either way, zeroing should be the first issue to be revised under the ADA. Other procedural improvements are also essential as underlined by FANs, such as the burden of participating in anti-dumping investigations, especially for SMEs.[85] Thus, procedural justice should be improved for a fair, transparent and cost-effective anti-dumping mechanism.

There has not been much change in the position of FANs after ten years. In 2015, FANS proposed that:

> Transparency of AD investigation procedures and due process rights are fundamental and are critical aspects for improving the disciplines, principles and effectiveness of the AD regime while preserving basic concepts. Transparency and due process are vital to interested parties. Parties need information and reasonable procedures in order to participate effectively in an investigation and defend their interests. This will be impossible unless the parties are kept fully informed of all individual steps and procedures undertaken by the authority from the initiation of the investigation until the imposition of AD duty, have the opportunity to access all

81 Ibid.

82 There are eighteen disputes filtered by the subject of 'zeroing' according to the WTO database. Available at www.wto.org/english/tratop_e/dispu_e/dispu_subjects_index_e.htm, accessed 18 July 2023.

83 Petros C. Mavroidis and Thomas J. Prusa, 'Die Another Day: Zeroing in on Targeted Dumping: Did the AB Hit the Mark in US–*Washing Machines*?' *World Trade Rev.* 17, no. 2 (2018), 239–264; Yilmazcan, 'The Role of Anti-Dumping in the US–China Trade War', 8.

84 Jeffrey J. Schott and Euijin Jung, The WTO's Existential Crisis: How to Salvage Its Ability to Settle Trade Disputes, No. PB19-19 (2019).

85 Negotiating Group on Rules, Senior Officials' Statement, 2005, TN/RL/W/171.

> public/non-confidential information on the record of an investigation in a timely manner, are given sufficient time to prepare their factual and legal submissions, and are provided with an explanation (either in a published notice or a separate report) which provides details on the authority's assessment of the evidence and its consideration of comments from interested parties.[86]

FANs also emphasised that if a certified translation is required by the investigating authorities, then additional time should be granted to the participants to respond to questionnaires.[87] The issues touched upon are subject to several disputes. FANs believe by improving transparency and due process, the DSM will need to handle fewer cases so both interested parties and investigating authorities would benefit. FANs also support the view that the lack of clear rules causes arbitrary use of ADA provisions.

6.2.2.5 Other Members

Other members also contribute to discussions by pointing out similar views on how to revise the ADA. As a FANs member, Japan individually stresses the importance of transparency and procedural fairness.[88] South Africa also emphasises the importance of meaningful participation in anti-dumping proceedings[89] and believes this can be achieved by improving the transparency and predictability of the proceedings.[90] South Africa has also highlighted the adverse effects of detailed questionnaires on the level of cooperation and proposed amendment of Article 6 of the ADA to guarantee a reasonable opportunity to complete the submission.[91]

Mexico recommended that price undertakings should be used more efficiently, as bilateral trade is adversely affected by anti-dumping investigations.[92] The ADA, in Article 8, allows members to use price undertakings as an alternative to final anti-dumping measures.

86 Negotiating Group on Rules, Anti-Dumping: Issues of Transparency and Due Process Communication from Chile; Colombia; Costa Rica; Hong Kong, China; Israel; Japan; Korea, Rep. of; Norway; Singapore; Switzerland; The Separate Customs Territory of Taiwan, Penghu, Kinmen and Matsu; and Thailand, 2021, TN/RL/W/257, 2.

87 Ibid., 2.

88 Negotiating Group on Rules, Anti-Dumping Follow-up Paper on the Issues of Transparency and Due Process, Communication from Japan, 2015, TN/RL/W/265, 3.

89 Negotiating Group on Rules, Proposals on Issues Relating to the Anti-Dumping Agreement Paper from South Africa, 2006, TN/RL/GEN/137, 4.

90 Ibid.

91 Ibid., 5.

92 Negotiating Group on Rules, Price Undertakings, Communication from Mexico, 2005, TN/RL/GEN/76, 1.

Canada put two approaches to the negotiations: determining the problematic provisions of the ADA and developing practices to avoid injurious dumping while considering both developed and developing countries.[93] Canada further acknowledged that existing rules on transparency and procedural fairness should be improved, especially regarding the initiation standards, disclosure of information, public hearings and sufficient explanation of determinations.[94] Also, clarification is needed for some terms, such as the ordinary course of trade, such as product, domestic industries, sunset reviews, and divergences between the ADA and SCM.[95]

India, as the top user of anti-dumping, has also demanded clarification of ADA provisions.[96] India highlighted the unfair use of back-to-back anti-dumping investigations, which dilute the gains from free trade.[97] India also noted the need for more favourable provisions for developing members, such as mandatory application of the lesser duty rule or increasing the *de minimis* margin.[98]

Australia has concerns about providing timely opportunities to establish transparency, as regulated under Article 6.4.[99] Australia further shared its own practice of transparency during the investigation, where all non-confidential information and correspondence are publicised.[100] Egypt similarly emphasised that 'the active participation of all parties concerned, including the respondents, in an AD proceeding is essential to ensure transparency and fairness of the system'.[101]

Norway holds the view that Article 6.9 of the ADA is not clear in defining the disclosure requirement for preliminary determinations of final anti-dumping measures as well as provisional measures.[102] Norway agrees that due process requires disclosure of all relevant factors leading to the final and provisional measures and proposed a twenty-day period for commenting on the factual considerations before the adoption of final

93 Negotiating Group on Rules, Submission from Canada, 2003, TN/RL/W/47.
94 Ibid.
95 Ibid.
96 Negotiating Group on Rules, Proposals on Implementation Related Issues and Concerns, 2002, TN/RL/W/4.
97 Ibid.
98 Ibid.
99 Negotiating Group on Rules, Submission by Australia, 2003, TN/RL/W/43.
100 Ibid.
101 Negotiating Group on Rules, Submission by Australia, 2003, TN/RL/W/56.
102 Negotiating Group on Rules, Further Proposal on Issues Relating to Article 6.9 of the ADA, Paper from Norway, 2005, TN/RL/GEN/87.

or provisional measures.[103] This approach was also suggested by China and can be helpful to provide meaningful participation of the relevant parties to the investigation.

Some members jointly proposed amendments to the ADA covering the inclusion of a public interest clause.[104] As well as being a part of the previous submission, Hong Kong separately stated that:

> members should strike a balance between concerns of 'administrative burden' and the merits of the issue at hand. Ultimately, the proposal is about good governance: due process, procedural fairness, proportionality and public accountability. Due regard should be given to these objectives.[105]

In addition to members, the International Chamber of Commerce (ICC) holds the position that the current ADA leaves room for discretion to investigating authorities.[106] The ICC suggested that investigating authorities should have less discretion in calculating constructed normal values, zeroing should be prohibited, injury margin calculation should be standardised, and a mandatory lesser duty rule should be introduced.[107] The ICC paper concluded that:

> Antidumping duties should in no case exceed the dumping margin and should not exceed the injury margin. Disproportionate information requirements and inadequate procedural rules increase prohibitively the costs of cooperation in anti-dumping investigations. These increased costs are particularly hurtful to parties in developing nations where resources are scarce, to small and medium size enterprises, and to exporting producers that only ship relatively small quantities.[108]

Other members and the ICC generally support revising the ADA by clarifying problematic provisions, such as zeroing and enhanced transparency. These revisions, in turn, will prevent the abuse of the anti-dumping mechanism and develop procedural justice thus reducing the number of disputes at the global level.

[103] Ibid.

[104] Negotiating Group on Rules Original: Public Interest Paper from Chile; Costa Rica; Hong Kong, China; Israel; Japan; Korea, Rep. of; Norway; Singapore; Switzerland; the Separate Customs Territory of Taiwan, Penghu, Kinmen and Matsu; and Thailand, 2005, TN/RL/W/174/Rev.1.

[105] Negotiating Group on Rules, Further Explanation of the Public Interest Proposal, Paper from Hong Kong, China, 2005, TN/RL/W/194, 6.

[106] Anti-dumping in the Doha Development Agenda, ICC, accessed 18 July 2023, https://iccwbo.org/publication/anti-dumping-in-the-doha-development-agenda/.

[107] Ibid.

[108] Ibid.

6.2.3 *Discussion on a Comprehensive Reform of the ADA*

The reform of the ADA has been discussed in the WTO as well as in the literature for many years. The previous section presented the main arguments and submissions by WTO members to reform the ADA. While most of the literature discusses WTO reform as a whole, some studies focus on reform of the ADA. Kazeki examined the negotiations about the ADA from the FANs perspective.[109] Chaisse and Chakraborty contend that the increasing use of anti-dumping investigations by developing countries underlines the misuse of grey areas in the ADA and call for reform of the ADA rather than its abolition.[110] Thus, both literature and policymakers agree on the idea of reforming the ADA.

Furthermore, as supported by empirical evidence in Chapter 5, exporters encounter difficulties due to procedural burdens reducing the motivation to cooperate. For instance, one company mentioned that, 'we understood it's unavoidable from the very beginning, what we can only do is [achieve the] minimum the anti-dumping duty to us'. Another company representative believes that anti-dumping has a macro perspective, which is problematic enough. The company asserted that 'dumping is a result of global economic problems so it is very hard to solve'. A similar macro-scale analysis was set out by an exporter: 'When anti-dumping actions are used for retaliatory purposes or as a result of lobbyist political agenda, levies bring more harm than benefits. Unfortunately, biased political views may go ahead of investigations and their force the application of actions in an untimely manner.' On collection of empirical data about these problems, the US and EU investigation authorities were asked for their comments on a possible revision of the ADA; however, neither provided responses to the surveys.

The need for revision of the ADA is obvious, but it not so easy to achieve. Reform proposals include the revision of the provisions, attaching standard questionnaires for anti-dumping investigations to the ADA and adopting best practice guidelines. A paper by the ICC is a useful summary suggesting that standard/model questionnaires drafted by the WTO anti-dumping committee would be helpful for exporters to defend their interests.[111] The need for a clear prohibition of mandatory

[109] Kazeki, 'Anti-dumping Negotiations Under the WTO and FANs'.
[110] Chaisse and Chakraborty, 'Normative Obsolescence of the WTO'.
[111] Anti-dumping in the Doha Development Agenda, ICC.

representation by lawyers is stressed.[112] This suggestion would be particularly helpful for Chinese exporters to cooperate in US investigations. A revision of the timelines has also been suggested, in order to provide a short investigation procedure while ensuring enough time for participants; however, it is not clear how to balance these two requirements.[113] Limiting the time span of anti-dumping measures through sunset reviews is another point to improve.[114] Currently, there is no time limit for an anti-dumping measure, which means that some members use anti-dumping measures as long-term trade policies.

There is a need for clarification of several Articles, and many proposals have been submitted to improve the rules. The submissions aim to re-establish the original rationale of the anti-dumping tool, which is to provide a level playing field by prohibiting predatory pricing and price discrimination between markets.[115] On the other hand, more regulation may not limit the discretion of investigating authorities as expected, especially the 'facts available' provisions.[116] The current 'facts available' provisions are descriptive and designed in a way that investigating authorities are authorized to use the information in support of the investigation.[117] The selection of the information creates room for discretion resulting in the misuse of the ADA provisions.

To prevent abusive use, the public interest clause in the ADA could be made mandatory.[118] This would limit the lobbying effect by businesses while supporting the interests of the consumers and other industries. Furthermore, circumvention can be defined under the ADA to guide WTO members against fraudulent practices that avoid anti-dumping duties.[119] Transparency, predictability and consistency are key issues supporting the better functioning of the ADA:

> The anti-dumping negotiations present a difficult challenge as WTO members will have to find a delicate balance between transparency and protecting confidentiality. Furthermore, flexibility and the desire for complete accuracy need to be balanced against practicality and the desire to reduce administrative costs and minimize the burden on companies

112 Ibid.
113 Ibid.
114 Ibid.
115 Andrews, 'The Facts Available on "Facts Available"', 34.
116 Ibid.
117 Ibid.
118 Anti-dumping in the Doha Development Agenda, ICC.
119 Ibid.

> subject to an anti-dumping investigation. ICC hopes that adoption of the above recommendations by WTO members will help achieve an appropriate balance and encourage a more harmonized, disciplined and transparent approach in the implementation of the ADA.[120]

To summarise the normative revisions on the ADA: zeroing should be explicitly prohibited (Article 2.4.2), a public interest test should be mandatory, circumvention of anti-dumping duties should be regulated, modal/standard anti-dumping investigation questionnaires should be introduced, additional review mechanism for transparency should be regulated, timely opportunities to access non-confidential files should be included (Article 6.4), the term 'sufficient detail' should be clarified under Article 12, clearer verification methods should be introduced under Article 6.7 and Annex I, back-to-back investigations should be prohibited under Article 5, the non-market economy methodology under Article 2.7 should be limited, transparency in public notices under Article 12.1 should be improved as should the disclosure requirement under Article 6.9. These revisions would strengthen the reliability of the anti-dumping mechanism.

6.3 Practical Constraints on Possible Reforms

Certainly, revising the ADA is not an easy task as different players are trying to use the ADA to further their interests. Also, negotiation and revision procedures are complicated and slow. Regarding the complexities of the revision, the Chairman of the NGR in 2011 urged members to adopt a pragmatic, flexible and less doctrinal approach during the negotiations.[121] In doing so, there should be a balance between effectively restoring the injury caused by dumping and unduly harsh trade restriction.[122]

Preserving the level playing field and avoiding too much room for discretion is a challenging task, and achieving this through negotiations at the WTO is also a distant goal. Andrews explains:

> [F]or any reform of the Anti-Dumping Agreement to be warranted, the proposed reform should help reduce the gap between the objective or goal of the Anti-Dumping Agreement and its instruments of preventing discriminatory, below cost and predatory pricing behaviour and the Agreement's actual practice.[123]

120 Ibid.

121 Stephen W. Hartman, 'The WTO, the Doha Round Impasse, PTAs, and FTAs/RTAs', *Int'l Trade J.* 27, no. 5 (2013), 411–430.

122 Anti-dumping in the Doha Development Agenda, ICC.

123 Andrews, 'The Facts Available on "Facts Available"', 21.

Furthermore, current US policies represent a threat to further progress in the anti-dumping negotiations. The recent policy shift of the US after forty years from special protection, such as anti-dumping, countervailing or safeguard measures, into unilateral tariffs against China constitutes a serious threat to the rule-based WTO.[124] The US formerly protected its domestic industries with traditional measures, such as anti-dumping, but Chinese subsidies and the Appellate Body's unfavourable reports triggered the US government to take actions that led to a crisis with China and the WTO.[125] On bilateral trade, the US has increased tariffs since 2018, resulting in retaliation from China. Countries using escalating tariffs in a retaliatory manner in a trade war, rather than using other negotiation mechanisms, have been shown empirically to be harming their economies.[126] On the WTO side, the US blocked the appointment of the new Appellate Body Members, which paralysed the appealing body of the DSM.[127] The first blockade was against the reappointment of the Korean Appellate Body member in 2016.[128] The US accuses the WTO's Appellate Body of judicial overreach, especially regarding several reports finding that the zeroing practice violates the ADA.[129] This move has been criticised, as the system may return to the pre-GATT 94 era.[130]

Regarding DSM reforms, Hoekman and Mavroidis classify negotiators into four types. The hawks are the US, requesting a severe modification of the current system, especially on deadlines or the elimination of the formation of panels.[131] The US's proposals are triggered by the lobbies, such as steel, seeking more protectionism.[132] Therefore, the US's proposals are not aimed at promoting the predictability or objectivity of the

[124] Chad P. Bown, 'The 2018 US–China Trade Conflict after 40 Years of Special Protection', *China Econ. J.* 12, no. 2 (2019), 109–136.

[125] Ibid.

[126] Thiemo Fetzer and Carlo Schwarz, 'Tariffs and Politics: Evidence from Trump's Trade Wars', *Econ. J.* 131, no. 636 (2021), 1717–1741.

[127] Jennifer Hillman, 'Three Approaches to Fixing the World Trade Organization's Appellate Body: The Good, the Bad, and the Ugly', *IIEL Issue Briefs* (2018).

[128] James Bacchus, 'Might Unmakes Right: The American Assault on the Rule of Law in World Trade', CIGI Papers No. 173 (2018).

[129] Ernst-Ulrich Petersmann, 'The 2018 Trade Wars as a Threat to the World Trading System and Constitutional Democracies', *Trade L. & Dev.* 10 (2018), 185.

[130] Chad P. Bown, 'The 2018 Trade War and the End of Dispute Settlement as We Knew It', in Meredith A. Crowley (ed.), Trade War the Clash of Economic Systems Endangering Global Prosperity (CEPR Press, 2019), 21.

[131] Hoekman and Mavroidis, 'Burning Down the House?',, 5.

[132] Panezi, 'The WTO and the Spaghetti Bowl of Free Trade Agreements', 5.

WTO.[133] The doves, Japan and Korea, do not seek to change what was accomplished with the GATT.[134] Hawkish doves, such as Australia and Canada, follow the US to some extent.[135] The dovish hawk, the EU, currently plays an objective mediator role, aiming to sustain the rules-based system in favour of both developed and developing countries.[136] The EU's constructive role in the rules-based system can also be traced to the proposed initiative interim appeal arrangement for WTO disputes after the US blockade of the Appellate Body.

Ensuring an objective and fair revision of the ADA also depends on other areas, such as the DSM, SCM and even GATT 94 as a whole. Furthermore, WTO members take different positions regarding these issues. The same challenges existed before GATT 47 and GATT 94, so multilateral compromise is needed again to gain the advantages of free and fair trade.

Another major limitation to revising the ADA is the problems faced during negotiations. Unlike the Bali and Nairobi Ministerial Conferences, Buenos Aires did not result in any commitment.[137] Several factors can be linked to this dysfunctionality, such as developments in international trade and the shift in the balance of power in global trading.[138] One year after Buenos Aires, the US–China trade war broke out. In 2020, the WTO faced a serious crisis due to the US blockade of Appellate Body members and the stepping down of the Director-General.

In this context, serious challenges lie ahead for the reform of the WTO and the ADA. There are polarised views about how to reform the ADA. US foreign trade policy is the greatest threat to clear and more transparent rules in the ADA. The selection of the new DG of the WTO and a new US President might give a fresh impetus to trade liberalisation. Also, China announced that its subsidies to the steel sector have been reduced.[139] China is also purchasing US goods, as agreed on in 2020,

133 Ibid.

134 Hoekman and Mavroidis, 'Burning Down the House?'.

135 Ibid.

136 Ibid.

137 Anna Wróbel, 'The Functionality and Dysfunctionality of Global Trade Governance: The European Union Perspective', in Marek Rewizorski, Karina Jędrzejowska and Anna Wróbel (eds.), *The Future of Global Economic Governance* (Springer, 2020), 161–175.

138 Ibid.

139 Keith Tan et al., China Removes VAT Rebate on Steel Exports, Cuts Tax on Raw Material Imports to Zero (2021), accessed 18 July 2023, www.spglobal.com/platts/en/market-insights/latest-news/metals/042821-china-removes-vat-rebate-on-steel-exports-cuts-tax-on-raw-material-imports-to-zero.

during the trade war.[140] These developments should help reduce the rivalry between top economies and ease the tension at the WTO level. Perhaps it should once more be acknowledged by all WTO members that the rules-based system provides a greater benefit to the global economy than do power-based trade policies. At this point, changing the approach to negotiations is essential. Rather than discussing both the substantive and procedural rules of the ADA, perhaps it would be more practical to focus first on procedural rules. Improved procedural rules would limit room for discretion and reduce the number of disputes. Also, other suggestions need to be considered that do not require a revision of the ADA.

6.4 Concrete Solutions for the Future

6.4.1 Publishing Best Practice Guidelines

The general tendency of exporters is to avoid cooperation with investigating authorities. One exporter noted: 'Time, energy, fact collection and effort required is so much that most companies prefer to change business model instead of fighting the cause.' Similar views were raised in the empirical research in Chapter 5. Thus, there is a need for best practice guidelines that would benefit both exporters and investigating authorities.

New Zealand suggested publishing best practice guidelines, particularly for the transparency provisions of the ADA,[141] especially Articles 5 and 6. If such guidelines could be produced only for these two articles, it would still significantly improve the practice of anti-dumping investigations. From a macro perspective, anti-dumping investigations are complicated and costly for exporters from the beginning to the end. Therefore, developing best practice guidelines would clarify the ADA as a whole and bring benefits to the investigating authorities and exporters.[142] Besides these benefits, best practice guidelines would also prevent the abuse of ADA provisions.[143]

[140] Chad P. Bown, US-China Phase One Tracker: China's Purchases of US Goods, Peterson Institute for International Economics, 2021, accessed 18 July 2023, www.piie.com/research/piie-charts/us-china-phase-one-tracker-chinas-purchases-us-goods.

[141] Negotiating Group on Rules, The Role of Transparency in the Anti-Dumping Agreement, Submission by New Zealand, 2003, TN/RL/W/137.

[142] Negotiating Group on Rules, Summary Report of the Meeting Held on 21–22 July 2003, Note by the Secretariat, 2003, TN/RL/M/11, 2.

[143] Andrews, 'The Facts Available on "Facts Available"', 36.

Currently, the task of developing such guidelines is assigned to the Committee on Anti-Dumping Practices, which operates as a subsidiary of the Council on Trade in Goods. The Committee works on the guidelines through its Working Group on Implementation.[144] The Working Group is supposed to suggest to the Committee a concrete draft that can be discussed by all members at the Committee meetings.[145] Since the task was assigned to the Committee, the Working Group has not been able to develop a general guideline for the anti-dumping investigations.

6.4.2 A Standardised Questionnaire

As there is no standardised questionnaire defined under the ADA, investigating authorities adopt their own. The empirical study in Chapter 5 suggests that a standard questionnaire would benefit exporters, improving transparency and predictability and thus increasing the opportunity for them to defend their rights. The MOFCOM official, several WTO lawyers, and exporters supported the idea of having a standard anti-dumping questionnaire to be adopted by all WTO members. One lawyer stated: 'For US cases, the DOC questionnaire process is exhaustive and detailed under tight deadlines. It is a hyper-objectified process that penalises respondents for even tiny discrepancies or errors.'

A standard questionnaire would increase the legal capacity of exporters and increase their chance to cooperate. This point was also made during the negotiations in the NGR:

> While broad support was expressed for the idea of standardized questionnaires, several participants cautioned that development of a model might best be left to technical bodies. It was noted that a model should serve only as a starting point, to be modified based on the needs of a given investigation, and that no arbitrary limit should be paced on length. It was queried whether any discussion of standardised questionnaires should be accompanied by discussion of whether dispute settlement claims based on an argument that the record contained insufficient information on a particular point should be barred if such information was not requested in the standard questionnaire.[146]

[144] Ibid.
[145] Ibid.
[146] Negotiating Group on Rules, Summary Report of the Meeting Held on 21–22 July 2003, Note by the Secretariat, TN/RL/M/11.

A standard questionnaire would therefore reduce the abuse of ADA rules. The aim of an anti-dumping measure should be to balance the unfair trade practice of dumping. With the different questionnaires used by WTO members, it is a challenge for exporters to cooperate with the investigating authorities. Andrews suggests that such a standard questionnaire could be developed by the WTO Rules Division.[147] Currently, members have the discretion to design the questionnaires in a way that exporters are not able to defend their rights properly during investigations.[148] By adopting a standard questionnaire, the compliance costs would be significantly reduced for exporters.[149] Reducing the legal costs of anti-dumping investigations is beneficial for SMEs, which would also support sustainable development.

The adoption of a standard questionnaire may not be possible through reform of the ADA because there are other issues to be addressed during a revision. Therefore, the adoption of a standard questionnaire could be achieved through an independent initiative led by a WTO working group or other international organisations, such as ACWL. On the other hand, the mega FTAs could provide an opportunity for WTO plus rules to be applied in several jurisdictions. FTAs are allowed to do so under Article XXIV of the GATT, although this violates the most favoured nation principle. In many FTAs, there are rules on anti-dumping investigations improving transparency, such as notification obligations. In this sense, mega FTAs covering several jurisdictions offer opportunities for the adoption of standard anti-dumping questionnaires. This option seems more likely to occur compared to the adoption of a standard anti-dumping questionnaire under the ADA. The harmonisation of the questionnaire could begin with FTAs and spread to the ADA.

6.4.3 Dispute Settlement Mechanism

One US lawyer stated:

> The US AD system has been consistently upheld by the US court system and even the WTO, so there really isn't much chance of arguing the unfairness of US AD system bc there is zero chance of it changing. It is what it is. DOC's determinations have been overturned by courts when

[147] Andrews, 'The Facts Available on "Facts Available"', 38.
[148] Ibid.
[149] Ibid.

- DOC has provided inadequate justification for their decisions (e.g., cannot point to enough record evidence to support their decisions).

It was argued in Chapter 3 that the DSM is not effective in settling disputes in its current form. However, DSM decisions are strong indicators of members' compliance level with WTO agreements. One of the most controversial issues in anti-dumping is the zeroing methodology applied by the US. The Appellate Body found zeroing to be inconsistent with the ADA in several disputes. The position of the US is that it lost trade remedy cases unjustly.[150] This is one of the reasons the US blocked the appointments of Appellate Body members, which caused the shutdown of the Appellate Body in late 2019. The US has blocked the reappointment of Appellate Body members in the past. In 2011, US national Ms Hillman was not reappointed by the US since she was not supporting the US positions.[151] The Appellate Body stated that linking the reappointment of a member to a specific dispute would harm impartiality and trust in the Appellate Body.[152] However, the constant blocking of Appellate Body members resulted in the 2019 shutdown. This blockade harms the WTO's well-respected DSM.

Previous proposals to amend the WTO's DSB are still under consideration, such as the length of reviews and annual meetings between the Appellate Body and the DSB. For panel reports after December 2019, Pauwelyn draws four possible scenarios.[153] First, under Article 16.4 of the DSU, the DSB can adopt reports after they are appealed.[154] In this regard, panel reports are practically non-executable since they do not have a chance to be adopted by the DSB.[155] The second scenario is that parties to the dispute do not appeal the panel report, but this is very unlikely due to the dissatisfaction of at least one party.[156] The third scenario involves the EU's recent proposal to use Article 25 of the DSU to sustain a two-

[150] Jens Lehne, *Crisis at the WTO: Is the Blocking of Appointments to the WTO Appellate Body by the United States Legally Justified?* (Carl Grossmann Verlag, 2019), 113.

[151] Markus Wagner, 'The Impending Demise of the WTO Appellate Body: From Centrepiece to Historical Relic?', in Chang-fa Lo, Junji Nakagawa and Tsai-fang Chen (eds.), *The Appellate Body of the WTO and Its Reform* (Springer, 2020), 67–90.

[152] Ibid.

[153] Joost Pauwelyn, 'WTO Dispute Settlement Post 2019: What to Expect?', *J. Int'l Econ. L.* 22, no. 3 (2019), 297–321.

[154] Article 16.4 of the DSU: 'If a party has notified its decision to appeal, the report by the panel shall not be considered for adoption by the DSB until after completion of the appeal.'

[155] Pauwelyn, 'WTO Dispute Settlement Post 2019'.

[156] Ibid.

level dispute settlement mechanism.[157] The EU and twenty-two WTO members have agreed to implement an interim arbitration mechanism.[158] This arrangement allows participating members to access a binding and impartial dispute settlement mechanism until the Appellate Body can function again.[159] Other WTO members would join if the deadlock with the Appellate Body continues. The US, however, contends that the blockade of appointments is made to push DSB reform.[160] The last scenario is that the panel reports will neither be adopted nor appealed by the Appellate Body.[161] In that case, panel reports will be used during the negotiations of trade disputes.[162]

Therefore, reform is also needed at the DSM, especially after the crisis caused by the US. The reforms should strengthen the member-driven nature of the WTO rather than a single member-driven scenario.[163] A stronger DSM would also avoid the misuse of anti-dumping measures to overprotect local industries.

6.4.4 Raising Awareness among Exporters

As mentioned by the MOFCOM official, 'lightening the burden of responding to questionnaires, reducing the cost of hiring legal assistance, as well as receiving fair treatment are crucial for exporters to undertake cooperation'. Exporters are generally unprepared for anti-dumping investigations. Under Article 6.1.1 of the ADA, exporters have no more than thirty days to submit their responses after they receive the questionnaires.[164] The notification is deemed to be received seven days after the questionnaires are sent to the diplomatic missions of the exporting

[157] Ibid.

[158] European Commission, The WTO Multi-party Interim Appeal Arrangement Gets Operational, accessed 18 July 2023, https://trade.ec.europa.eu/doclib/press/index.cfm?id=2176.

[159] Ibid.

[160] Pauwelyn, 'WTO Dispute Settlement Post 2019'.

[161] Ibid.

[162] Ibid.

[163] Chang-fa Lo, 'A Proper Balance between WTO's Members-Driven Nature and the Appellate Body's Role as an Adjudicator: Careful Exercise of Judicial Activism', in Chang-fa Lo, Junji Nakagawa and Tsai-fang Chen (eds.), *The Appellate Body of the WTO and Its Reform* (Springer, 2020), 125–139.

[164] Article 6.1.1 available at www.wto.org/english/docs_e/legal_e/19-adp_01_e.htm#article VI, accessed 18 July 2023.

country.[165] In this regard, the exporting country should immediately warn exporters about the investigation. This is not an obligation under the ADA, as stated by the Appellate Body in DS295, Mexico – Anti-Dumping Measures on Rice.[166] The importing country officially announces the initiation of the investigation in the official gazette and notifies diplomatic missions, but notification to exporters and importers is controversial. Mexico argues that there is no obligation for the investigating authorities to find exporters and foreign producers under the ADA.[167] The Appellate Body agreed that in reading Article 6.1, it cannot be clearly understood that the investigating authority or the exporting country has an obligation to find exporters and importers and notify them directly. In practice, exporters are not expected to follow the official gazettes of their exporting markets. Therefore, they may not be aware of an anti-dumping investigation shortly after its initiation. In this sense, even though it is not an explicit obligation of the exporting countries to notify exporters, it would be beneficial. If exporters are late in the submission of responses, it is highly likely that they will face higher anti-dumping duties.

Apart from coordination between the exporting country's government and the exporters, it is also beneficial that exporters are trained about the anti-dumping investigations and their consequences. Exporters' associations can offer regular training sessions to their members, which would encourage exporters to cooperate with the investigating authorities in order to avoid high anti-dumping duties.

6.4.5 Improving the Accounting System of Chinese Companies

Globalisation enhanced capital flow from one market to another. Regulators were motivated to achieve greater harmonisation of International Financial Reporting Standards (IFRS).[168] IFRS reduces information asymmetries between markets and, therefore, encourages

[165] Ibid., footnote 15 of the ADA.

[166] DS295, Mexico – Definitive Anti-Dumping Measures on Beef and Rice, Report of the Appellate Body, WT/DS295/AB/R, 2005, accessed 18 July 2023, www.wto.org/english/tratop_e/dispu_e/cases_e/ds295_e.htm.

[167] Ibid., 14.

[168] Judge William, Shaomin Li and Robert Pinsker, 'National Adoption of International Accounting Standards: An Institutional Perspective', *Corp. Gov. Int'l Rev.* 18, no. 3 (2010), 161–174.

foreign direct investment.[169] In 2007, China introduced IFRS to increase FDI and gain an advantage in exports to overseas markets. However, this was mandatory only for publicly listed companies.[170] For domestic companies, the IFRS is still not mandatory.[171] Considering the majority of exporters subject to anti-dumping investigations are not listed companies, accounting systems constitute a barrier to cooperation. With the difficulties overseas, there is resistance to give full compliance with IFRS standards by Chinese regulators and scholars.[172] An empirical study of accounting standards supports this perspective.

> . . . (full) adoption of IFRS may send the wrong political signal to people: How can we just copy from another country and completely Westernize? In addition to direct copying, what about the operationalization of IFRS? Some of them may not suit Chinese circumstances.[173]

On the other hand, this view may change, bearing in mind the high anti-dumping duties levied on Chinese exporters. Both the US and EU anti-dumping investigation questionnaires include detailed questions about the accounting systems of exporters.[174] In this sense, accounting plays an evidentiary role in responding to anti-dumping investigations. However, Chinese exporters are not fully capable of submitting satisfactory accounting information. First, many exporters do not have a competent accounting team.[175] Therefore, the accounting files are not classified, ordered or archived. This makes it difficult to respond to the questionnaire within thirty-seven days. Also, many Chinese exporters use

169 Sun Shuwei, Hailong Zhao, Xianjie He and Ying Zhang, 'The Impact of Accounting Standards Convergence on Chinese Firms' Overseas Mergers and Acquisitions', *China J. Account. Res.* 12, no. 3 (2019), 231–250.

170 Liu Chunhui, Lee J. Yao, Nan Hu and Ling Liu, 'The Impact of IFRS on Accounting Quality in a Regulated Market: An Empirical Study of China', *J. Account. Audit. & Finance* 26, no. 4 (2011), 659–676.

171 IFRS, Who Uses IFRS Standards?.

172 Mahmoud Ezzamel and Jason Zezhong Xiao, 'The Development of Accounting Regulations for Foreign Invested Firms in China: The Role of Chinese Characteristics', *Account. Organ. Soc.* 44 (2015), 60–84.

173 Ibid.

174 EU Questionnaire, accessed 18 July 2023, https://trade.ec.europa.eu/doclib/docs/2013/december/tradoc_151932.pdf; Generic US Commerce Questionnaire, accessed 18 July 2023, https://enforcement.trade.gov/questionnaires/nme/20131101/q-inv-nme-20131101.pdf.

175 Wu Guocan and Gong Yifei, 'The Accounting Information Support and Accounting Tactics of Protecting Rights and Interests in the Anti-Dumping Responding', in *2010 2nd IEEE International Conference on Information Management and Engineering*, IEEE (2010), 177–181.

a costing system according to the market they sell into, not the product itself.[176] Factory overheads are not classified so the composition of cost for each product type is hard to track.[177] Thus, in many cases, the accounting information is not regarded as accurate, reliable or integrated to international standards.[178] International accounting standards are not mandatory in responding to US or EU investigations but, without such standards, it is likely that the information submitted will be disregarded.

6.4.6 *Support Tool for Exporters (Similar to ACWL)*

As expressed by WTO lawyers and Chinese exporters, the financial costs of cooperation and the lack of legal capacity are serious obstacles to cooperation. Even if the exporters are aware of initiation, it is challenging for them to prepare a response within thirty-seven days. In the empirical research, one company stated:

> At first, we didn't know where to get the information about non confidential files or enforcement, there was no instruction available, we have to find information by our own effort. So, we got late info and sometimes we were not sure if the info is correct, which confuse us at first stage.

The legal capacity and cost problems are also concerns of the least-developed and developing countries. Therefore, in 2001, ACWL was established independently of the WTO.[179] ACWL provides legal assistance to developing and least-developed WTO members who plan to file cases before the WTO DSM. Former WTO Director-General Lamy states:

> [B]y ensuring that the legal benefits of the WTO are shared among all Members, the ACWL contributes to the effectiveness of the WTO legal system, in particular its dispute settlement procedures, and to the realisation of the WTO's development objectives.[180]

Without the ACWL, numerous disadvantaged WTO members would lose or would not even be able to file a case against developed members. Thus, ACWL is playing a balancing role in terms of legal capacity for

[176] Ibid.
[177] Ibid.
[178] Ibid.
[179] The ACWL's Mission, available at www.acwl.ch/acwl-mission/, accessed 17 July 2023.
[180] Ibid.

these countries. Therefore, another international organisation or a department under the ACWL could support exporters facing anti-dumping investigations at the micro-level. This organisation would offer low-cost assistance while employing anti-dumping consultants, thus improving legal capacity in developing or least-developed members. This, in turn, will increase the rate of cooperation and meaningful participation, promoting procedural justice in anti-dumping investigations.

6.4.7 *Software to Assist Exporters to Fill in Questionnaires*

Another idea to improve the level of cooperation would be developing software to fill in the questionnaires sent by investigating authorities. There is currently no technology to help complete anti-dumping questionnaires. Lawyers, consultancy firms or in-house accountants prepare the submissions. After the submission, investigating authorities conduct on-the-spot investigations to cross-check the information in the response with the exporters' ERP systems. Investigating authorities are strict in finding mistakes and generally do not allow corrections, even for simple calculation errors. As a result of these strict procedural rules, investigating authorities classify exporters as non-cooperating companies, which results in the adoption of higher anti-dumping measures.

Software, on the other hand, may digitalise the whole process. The time spent in filling in the questionnaires could be significantly reduced so that the company has more time for cross-checking. Also, software may even be able to automatically file the questionnaire and transfer information to the government using blockchain technology. This may help exporters to defend themselves more objectively, so they face lower anti-dumping duties. The transfer of information by blockchain at the same time will reassure governments that exporters have not altered the submitted information. Thus, this solution may simplify a complex compliance procedure by reducing the costs and time consumed by all parties involved. In this scenario, procedural justice would be improved without the need for any revision at the ADA. The WTO or its members pursuing greater transparency could adopt a similar initiative.

6.5 Conclusion

This chapter covers two issues. First, it examines the ongoing negotiations on the ADA through the NGR. The negotiations on anti-dumping started in 2002 with the mandate to establish the NGR. Three main groups have different interests and take different positions in the ADA negotiations. FANs push for transparency and more regulation. The second group of developed members tries to protect existing rules so that the investigating authorities can enjoy more discretion. The third group consists of several members that echo developing countries' concerns. Thus, even though there are very useful suggestions for improving the ADA and addressing procedural problems, due to the multipolar positioning of members, meaningful revision may not be possible in the short term. Furthermore, the Ministerial Conference in Buenos Aires was not successful and, afterwards, the rules-based system of the WTO was damaged by US foreign trade policies, which include the trade war with China and the blockade of appointments of Appellate Body members. Revision of the ADA is the best solution to avoid the misuse of anti--dumping investigations. However, due to the malfunctioning of the WTO negotiations, this does not seem to be achievable in the short term. The main players in global trade, notably the US and China, have opposing views on issues such as the zeroing methodology. Zeroing is the key issue to be solved, as it is behind most of the disputes between WTO members. It is a procedural issue with substantive effects because significantly impacts the level of anti-dumping duty. The EU could play a balancing role in the case of zeroing. Although it opposed an explicit prohibition of zeroing during the negotiations of the Uruguay Round, after losing two disputes, the EU stopped practising zeroing in its anti-dumping investigations.[181] The EU has also taken a constructive role in trying to solve the Appellate Body crisis.[182] Therefore, currently, the EU is the most suitable candidate to negotiate between the US and China in order to protect the rules-based system of the WTO and reduce tension. Considering the consistent rulings of the Appellate Body and Panels, it is more acceptable to prohibit zeroing in line with the fair comparison requirement of the ADA. As fair comparison is a general principle, a revision of the ADA should consider previous interpretations by the Appellate Body and Panels as guidance and prohibit zeroing. Consequently, other revisions to promote transparency and objectivity would follow. While this would be an ideal solution for the most litigated topic under WTO adjudication, it is unlikely to happen soon. Therefore, other solutions might be more practical.

[181] Hoekman and Mavroidis, 'Burning Down the House?'.
[182] Sharma, 'WTO Appellate Body at Cross Roads'.

In this context, this chapter also attempts to set out possible solutions to overcome the hidden trade protectionism in anti-dumping investigations. First, increasing awareness among exporters to encourage them to cooperate would reduce room for discretion. A support tool for exporters could also increase their legal capacity, especially SMEs. Software that would integrate with the ERP systems and automatically file the questionnaires could also significantly reduce time and costs. One of the most useful improvements in legal capacity would be the standardisation of the anti-dumping questionnaires. This idea has already been proposed by some members and scholars, so there is precedent to this idea. As anti-dumping questionnaires are different in each jurisdiction, the ability of exporters to cooperate effectively in each investigation is limited. With this solution, exporters would cooperate with jurisdictions, such as the solar panel, tyre or aluminium foil manufacturers who faced the US and EU investigations around the same time. As mentioned, if the investigation procedures are burdensome for exporters, they avoid cooperation and attempt to circumvent the duties. Given the current tensions at the WTO, it is unlikely that a standardised questionnaire will be accepted anytime soon. However, mega FTAs would be a good starting point to harmonise anti-dumping questionnaires. There are many promising articles under the RCEP that improve the transparency and objectivity of anti-dumping investigation procedures. After a concrete attempt to harmonise anti-dumping questionnaires, it would be easier to adopt a worldwide recognised questionnaire. These practical measures would reduce the hidden trade protectionism behind the anti-dumping investigations.

7

Conclusion

This chapter consolidates previous ideas and findings after presenting the issues and challenges in contemporary trade. These issues, such as the US–China trade war, Brexit, the WTO crisis, and mega free trade agreements are then linked to anti-dumping measures in order to highlight its role and impact on global trade. The problems in relation to anti-dumping investigations and possible solutions are revisited with the concluding remarks at the end of this chapter.

7.1 Issues and Challenges in Contemporary Trade

The ADA allows investigating authorities to use the facts available in case exporters do not cooperate. Facts available and other procedural methods result in substantially higher anti-dumping duties compared to methods relying on the information provided by exporters. This recalls the hypothesis that anti-dumping procedures can be abused to overprotect local industries. Thus, this book examined whether anti-dumping procedures could be used as a form of hidden trade protectionism and whether US and EU investigations against China support this assumption. By examining US and EU investigations against Chinese exporters, it is possible to conclude that anti-dumping investigation procedures can be a tool for hidden trade protectionism. In this regard, the last question addressed in this book is whether procedural justice would avoid the hidden trade protectionism. After an analysis of current negotiations at the WTO, DSB rulings and empirical findings, it can be concluded that improving procedural justice in anti-dumping investigations would limit the discretion of investigating authorities and enable exporters to better defend their interests, which would lead to lower anti-dumping duties and fewer investigations. Before going into more detail, it is best to take a broader perspective to link anti-dumping investigations with the recent trade issues.

International trade has witnessed unexpected challenges in the last few years. The US–China trade war, the crisis at the WTO, Brexit, COVID-19, blockchain technologies and mega FTAs such as RCEP, have shaped the contemporary trade framework. These issues will direct the way forward for international trade and the WTO, including the anti-dumping investigations.

With the election of President Trump, US–China relations became tense. Trump gave the first signs of a commercial policy change towards China during his campaign in 2016.[1] In 2017, the Office of the United States Trade Representative was ordered to investigate steel/aluminium imports in terms of national security. The Trump administration relied on national security or Section 232 tariffs more than previous administrations.[2] Consequently, trade talks failed between the US and China in the same year.[3] In 2018, there was another phase in which the US started to hit Chinese solar panels, washing machines, steel and aluminium exports with additional tariffs.[4] While the measures taken by the US against other countries, such as Canada and Mexico, were mostly settled by negotiation, China retaliated with tariff increases on more than a hundred US products. At the end of 2018, the US took additional measures affecting $200 billion USD worth of Chinese exports, while China retaliated with tariff increases on US exports worth $60 billion USD. This increase resulted in 12 and 18 per cent average tariffs in the US and China, respectively.[5] After talks between the US and China, tariffs were reduced slightly in the first half of 2019. However, in the second half, the US adopted measures of up to $300 billion USD, while Chinese measures hit $75 billion USD,[6] thus increasing the average tariff

[1] Yilmazcan, 'The Role of Anti-Dumping in the US–China Trade War', 19.

[2] The Trump administration was criticised for abusing section 232 tariffs and using them for protectionist purposes rather than national security, and similar to anti-dumping laws, a public interest clause and elimination of procedural loopholes were suggested by scholars. Scott Lincicome and Inu Manak, 'Protectionism or National Security? The Use and Abuse of Section 232', Policy Analysis 912 (2021).

[3] Timeline: Key Dates in the US–China Trade War, accessed 17 July 2023, www.reuters.com/article/us-usa-trade-china-timeline/timeline-key-dates-in-the-u-s-china-trade-war-idUSKBN1ZE1AA.

[4] Ibid.

[5] Chad P. Bown, US–China Trade War Tariffs: An Up-to-Date Chart, PIIE Charts (14 February 2020 [20 September 2019]) www.piie.com/research/piie-charts/us-china-trade-war-tariffs-date-chart [last updated on 6 April 2023 as: China and the United States Change Their Tariffs].

[6] Ibid.

by around 21 per cent.[7] The phase one trade deal in February 2020 slightly reduced the averages.[8]

Although President Biden has opposing views to most of President Trump's policies, it is unlikely that the tariffs will be loosened in the short term.[9] In terms of the ongoing crisis with the DSM, the new administration and the new Director-General of the WTO, Ms Ngozi, could make a positive impact. As of 2024, panel reports cannot be appealed to the Appellate Body due to the US blockade of new members. This is a serious problem ahead of the global trade system.[10]

Turning back to the trade war and its implications, it is devastating. According to economic regression models for exports, employment and consumption have been reduced because of the US–China trade war.[11] This causes welfare loss.[12] Also, as some of the additional duties have been levied upon raw materials, such as aluminium and steel, costs to manufacturers have risen, such as the automobile industry in the US. Trade also diverts, as is the case with other bilateral protectionist measures, with manufacturing capacity shifts from China to other countries such as Vietnam.[13] However, since some factories cannot be easily moved to other countries, as with textile or plastic manufacture, tariffs can be expected to be circumvented.[14] US Commerce has already proposed tightening anti-dumping regulations to avoid circumvention of duties.[15] Vietnam is also a hot spot for Chinese manufacturers because the FTA

7 Ibid.

8 Ibid. Yilmazcan, 'The Role of Anti-Dumping in the US–China Trade War', 7–36.

9 M. D. Habib Alam, 'Next Steps Might Be Considered by Joe Biden for the Development of International Trade Law', *Eur. J. Eng. Res. Sci.* 5, no. 11 (2020), 1372–1375.

10 Stuart S. Malawer, 'Biden, National Security, Law & Global Trade: Less Subterfuge & More Strategy in the New Era of Crisis', *China WTO Rev.* 7, no. 1 (2021), 189.

11 Michael E. Waugh, The Consumption Response to Trade Shocks: Evidence from the US–China Trade War, No. w26353 (National Bureau of Economic Research, 2019).

12 Yilmazcan, 'The Role of Anti-Dumping in the US–China Trade War', 17.

13 Lucy Colback, How to Navigate the US–China Trade War, *Financial Times* (2020), www.ft.com/content/6124beb8-5724-11ea-abe5-8e03987b7b20.

14 Ibid.

15 Sydney H. Mintzer, Duane W. Layton and Timothy C. Lee, Proposed Changes to Antidumping and Countervailing Duty Regulations Would Make Proceedings More Efficient and Create New Enforcement Mechanisms (2020), www.mayerbrown.com/en/perspectives-events/publications/2020/08/proposed-changes-to-antidumping-and-countervailing-duty-regulations-would-make-proceedings-more-efficient-and-create-new-enforcement-mechanisms.

between the EU and Vietnam was signed in early 2020.[16] Apart from the trade diversion effects, investment rates will also decline due to uncertainty, and company divorce rates will increase due to national security concerns.[17]

Hong Kong is another area with economic consequences. Hong Kong's draft bill on extradition of offenders with China resulted in pro-democracy protests, starting in the summer of 2019, and in public unrest. The US used the situation to undermine China in the international arena, politically and economically. As of August 2020, Hong Kong lost the special trading status granted by the US under the US–Hong Kong Policy Act of 1992. The impact of this move is that Hong Kong will no longer be able to enjoy its special status and will be treated like China in terms of customs rules. In this regard, the US first banned the export of dual-use products to Hong Kong and then required Hong Kong exports to be labelled 'Made in China'.[18] The logistics sector will be negatively affected by the US–China trade war as Hong Kong plays a crucial role in the re-export of products to the US.[19]

Overall, the economic effects of the trade war are negative for both sides, but the US is affected more deeply.[20] US companies in China and Hong Kong will be negatively affected, just like Chinese companies in the US. It is also notable that the US has had a trade deficit for many years not only with China but also with several other countries.[21] The trade balance between the US and China over the years turned against the US.[22] Furthermore, the core inflation rate increased sharply in the US, whereas China managed to maintain lower inflation.[23] In terms of GDP growth rates in the early 2020s, both economies saw a slowdown.

16 European Commission, *Countries and Regions*, accessed 17 June 2023, https://ec.europa.eu/trade/policy/countries-andregions/countries/vietnam/#:~:text=The%20European%20Union%20and%20Vietnam,Council%20on%2030%20March%202020.

17 Ibid. Yilmazcan, 'The Role of Anti-Dumping in the US–China Trade War', 7–36.

18 Guidance on Marking of Goods of Hong Kong – Executive Order 13936, US Customs and Border Protection, accessed 18 July 2023, https://www.cbp.gov/trade/rulings/frequently-asked-questions-guidance-marking-goods-hong-kong-executive-order-13936?_ga=2.69427856.1287851153.1597626421-308187796.1597626421 (last modified 6 October 2020).

19 Edwin L.-C. Lai, 'The US–China Trade War, the American Public Opinions and Its Effects on China', *Econ. Pol. Stud.* 7, no. 2 (2019), 169–184. Yilmazcan, 'The Role of Anti-Dumping in the US–China Trade War', 7–36.

20 Yilmazcan, 'The Role of Anti-Dumping in the US–China Trade War', 21.

21 Dan Steinbock, 'US–China Trade War and Its Global Impacts', *China Q. Int. Strateg. Stud.* 4, no. 4 (2018), 515–542.

22 TradeMap.

23 Available at https://tradingeconomics.com, accessed 18 July 2023.

However, in the second quarter of 2020, while China recovered, the US economy suffered a reduction of 30 per cent.[24] The reason for the sharp decline in GDP was the lockdown in both economies due to the COVID-19 pandemic.

Before more details on COVID-19's impact, another deglobalisation policy to be addressed is the UK exiting the EU, also known as the Brexit. Dent asserts, 'Brexit's economic nationalism also possesses protectionist elements, although this primarily relating to the labour market, immigration and economic policy regulations.'[25] The UK voted to separate from the EU in 2016, meaning that it would also leave the single market. After long negotiations, the EU–UK Trade and Cooperation Agreement was signed in January 2021. The agreement includes an FTA framing trade and services as well as other trade-related issues such as investment, competition, state aid, tax transparency, air and road transport, energy and sustainability, fisheries, data protection, and social security coordination.[26] Like Trump's policies, Brexit is another example of populist nationalism.[27]

On top of rising populism, COVID-19 hit supply, demand, manufacturing and trade hard.[28] In response to the pandemic, members took immediate measures, such as elimination of import tariffs or restriction of exports, to secure enough medical supplies.[29] Also, due to the complete lockdowns, manufacturing stopped suddenly in several countries. The lockdown in China resulted in supply shocks in other countries.[30] For instance, automobile industries around the world needed to shut down due to delays and uncertainties in supply chains.[31] Even if production continued, the demand-side had shrunk dramatically. As mentioned

[24] Ibid.

[25] Christopher M. Dent, 'Brexit, Trump and Trade: Back to a Late Nineteenth Century Future?', *Compet. Change* 24, nos. 3–4 (2020), 338–357.

[26] European Commission, The EU-UK Trade and Cooperation Agreement, available at https://commission.europa.eu/strategy-and-policy/relations-non-eu-countries/relations-united-kingdom/eu-uk-trade-and-cooperation-agreement_en, accessed 19 July 2023.

[27] Dent, 'Brexit, Trump and Trade'.

[28] Richard Baldwin and Eiichi Tomiura, 'Thinking Ahead about the Trade Impact of COVID-19', in R. Baldwin and B. Weder di Mauro (eds.), *Economics in the Time of COVID-19* (CEPR Press, 2020), 59.

[29] WTO, COVID-19: Measures Affecting Trade in Goods, accessed 19 July 2023, www.wto.org/english/tratop_e/covid19_e/trade_related_goods_measure_e.htm.

[30] Richard Baldwin and B. Weder Di Mauro, Introduction, *Economics in the Time of COVID-19: A New eBook* (VOX CEPR Policy Portal, 2020), 18.

[31] Ibid.

by Cochrane, 'shutting down the economy is not like shutting down a light bulb. It's more like shutting down a nuclear reactor. You need to do it slowly and carefully or it melts down'.[32] The WTO foresaw a fall in world goods merchandise trade of around 9.2 per cent in 2020 due to the pandemic.[33] For services, the situation is worse, as the fall is predicted to be 27 per cent.[34] World Bank research estimated that the decline in global GDP would be around 2.1 per cent due to COVID-19. According to one calculation, the cost of COVID-19 to the global economy amounts to $11.7 trillion USD.[35] All elements of the global economy – namely goods, services, people, financial capital, foreign direct investment, international banking, and exchange rates – were adversely affected.[36] This also triggered deglobalisation as well as digitalisation. A recent study suggests that in the short term, COVID-19 caused a significant decrease in GDP but still did not cause a significant increase in anti-dumping investigations in the EU.[37] However, it is expected that the number of anti-dumping measures will increase in the long term in several jurisdictions.

Blockchain is 'a decentralized, distributed record or "ledger" of transactions in which the transactions are stored in a permanent and near inalterable way using cryptographic techniques'.[38] Compared to conventional digital transfer methods, blockchain is much more secure and traceable. The application of blockchain in international trade is evolving rapidly and is used in the following areas of international trade: (1) supply chain finance, (2) trade finance, (3) know your customer, (4) insurance, (5) distributed ledger technology digitisation of trade documents, (6) shipping and logistics/supply chain and (7) others.[39] Billions of dollars are being invested in blockchain projects due to the benefits.

[32] Ibid.

[33] WTO, COVID-19 and World Trade, accessed 19 July 2023, www.wto.org/english/tratop_e/covid19_e/faqcovid19_e.htm.

[34] Ibid.

[35] OXFAM, 2.7 Billion People Have Had No Social Protection to Cope with Covid-19 Economic Crisis (2020), accessed 19 July 2023, www.oxfam.org/en/press-releases/27-billion-people-have-had-no-social-protection-cope-covid-19-economic-crisis.

[36] Ibid.

[37] Henrich Juhás and Zuzana Kittová, 'Antidumping Investigations of the European Union in the Time of Pandemic COVID-19', *Twenty-first International Joint Conference Central and Eastern Europe in the Changing Business Environment* (2021).

[38] Emmanuelle Ganne, *Can Blockchain Revolutionize International Trade?* (World Trade Organization, 2018).

[39] Deepesh Patel and Emmanuelle Ganne, 'Blockchain & DLT in Trade: Where Do We Stand?', *Trade Finance Global* (2020), 52, www.wto.org/english/res_e/booksp_e/blockchainanddlt_e.pdf.

According to one study, 'blockchain could reduce banks' infrastructure costs attributable to cross-border payments, securities trading and regulatory compliance by the US $15–20 billion per annum by 2022'.[40]

Mega FTAs is another agenda item in contemporary trade to be monitored. Fifteen countries signed RCEP in 2020, covering 2.2 billion people and 30 per cent of the global GDP.[41] Apart from trade in goods and services, RCEP includes issues such as investment, e-commerce, IP, competition, SMEs, economic and technical cooperation, and public procurement as well as trade remedies.[42] The Comprehensive and Progressive Agreement for Trans-Pacific Partnership (CPTPP) is another mega FTA that covers around 13 per cent of global GDP and 14 per cent of trade.[43] CPTPP evolved from TPP, which was annulled after the withdrawal of the US in 2017.[44] TPP was signed between the remaining members, but CPTPP also refers to TPP so both agreements should be read together.[45] The agreement also has provisions for higher transparency standards beyond the ADA, which is discussed in Section 7.2.

The Russian invasion of Ukraine also had significant impact on global trade. Since the initiation of the military campaign in 2022, G7 countries and the EU announced sanctions against Russia. Those sanctions include financial, individual, import, export, travel and trade-related restriction aiming to cut the finances and goods supply to Russia and to force a halt to the operation. In terms of dual-use goods and technology, exports are restricted for the Russian end users as a rule. The US, for instance, imposed strict bans on the export of oil and gas exploration-related goods and technology for Russian end users. The US also granted some general exceptions for medicine and food or consumer communication commodities and technology.[46] The current measures against Russia are

[40] Ganne, *Can Blockchain Revolutionize International Trade*, 53.

[41] Niall McCarthy, 15 Countries Sign World's Biggest Free Trade Deal, Statista, 2020, accessed 19 July 2023, www.statista.com/chart/23497/key-facts-about-the-regional-comprehensive-economic-partnership/.

[42] Regional Comprehensive Economic Partnership Agreement, accessed 19 July 2023, https://rcepsec.org/legal-text/.

[43] CPTPP Text and Associated Documents, accessed 19 July 2023, www.dfat.gov.au/trade/agreements/in-force/cptpp/official-documents.

[44] The United States Officially Withdraws from the Trans-Pacific Partnership, accessed 19 July 2023, https://ustr.gov/about-us/policy-offices/press-office/press-releases/2017/january/US-Withdraws-From-TPP.

[45] CPTPP Text.

[46] U.S. Department of Commerce, Bureau of Industry and Security, Resources on Export Controls Implemented in Response to Russia's Invasion of Ukraine, Updated

not as strict as embargoes but still, the complexity of the sanctions and secondary sanctions prevent businesses from conducting any kind of transaction related to Russia.

7.2 What Has Anti-dumping to Do with These Trade Issues?

Anti-dumping measures have played either a direct or indirect role in the recent developments in contemporary trade. Some issues are affected by anti-dumping and, in some cases, it is the outcome. Putting aside the political and economic triggers, the problems caused by the anti-dumping mechanism may be one of the underlying reasons for the US–China trade war. Anti-dumping measures are designed to balance unfair pricing strategies, but the US is misusing the measures conventionally to address the trade deficit with China. The supporting evidence for the US's abuse of anti-dumping duties is the crisis at the WTO. The US is not satisfied with the rulings of the DSM. To be more specific, the US has lost 86 per cent of the cases before the DSM.[47] In many of these disputes, the US has been found to be adopting inconsistent measures, especially regarding zeroing. As mentioned in previous chapters, zeroing allows investigating authorities to calculate a lower export price, and this increases the level of anti-dumping duty calculated. In several disputes, the DSM required the US government to recalculate and lower the margins in question in compliance with the fair comparison principle in Article 2 of the ADA. However, rather than complying with the Appellate Body rulings, the US has blocked the appointment of new members since late 2019 to paralyse the DSM. The EU proposed the Interim Appeal Arbitration pursuant to Article 25 DSU, to settle disputes until the Appellate Body is functioning again.[48] This proposal became effective with some members' participation but it cannot be effective in the cases involving the US as a respondent. Therefore, the US currently cannot be challenged regarding its trade practices at the WTO level.

3 March 2023, accessed 19 July 2023, www.bis.doc.gov/index.php/policy-guidance/country-guidance/russia-belarus.

[47] Marianne Schneider-Petsinger, Dispute Settlement in Crisis, in Reforming the World Trade Organization Prospects for Transatlantic Cooperation and the Global Trade System, Chatham House Research Paper (2020), accessed 19 July 2023, www.chathamhouse.org/2020/09/reforming-world-trade-organization/04-dispute-settlement-crisis.

[48] Sharma, 'WTO Appellate Body at Cross Roads'.

Due to the shift from rule-based to power-based policies, the global trading system is being harmed, and more WTO members are following protectionist policies. The political risk in Asia is increasing as the US is also threatening to use the measures against Vietnam. This trend leads to de-globalisation rather than globalisation.[49] After a period of liberalisation, currently, domestic policies direct regulatory protection. These domestic policies aim at cost-raising, behind-the-door measures or hidden trade protectionism.[50] With the new US administration and a new Director-General of the WTO, there is increasing confidence in rebuilding the rule-based framework for international trade.

It may still be early to correlate COVID-19 and anti-dumping. However, the response to COVID-19 is protectionist measures, and one of the popular tools of protectionism is anti-dumping. Between 2017 and 2019, the average anti-dumping initiations for all WTO members were 221.[51] In just the first six months of 2020, the initiations reached 188, which means there will be a significant increase when the annual data is available. For instance, the US initiated fifty-eight anti-dumping investigations in the first six months of 2020, whereas in 2019, only thirty-three were initiated in the whole year.[52] Indian initiations over six months also reached the annual level. In terms of sectoral distribution of initiations from all WTO members, chemicals and base metals surged or almost reached the annual levels in six months.[53]

After Brexit, the UK and EU have signed an FTA that also covers rules on anti-dumping. Article GOODS.17: Trade Remedies states:

> 3. Each Party shall apply anti-dumping and countervailing measures in accordance with the requirements of the Anti-Dumping Agreement and the SCM Agreement, and pursuant to a fair and transparent process.
> 4. Provided it does not unnecessarily delay the conduct of the investigation, each interested party in an anti-dumping or countervailing investigation shall be granted a full opportunity to defend its interests.
> 5. Each Party's investigating authority may, in accordance with the Party's law, consider whether the amount of the anti-dumping duty to be imposed shall be the full margin of dumping or a lesser amount.

49 Alicia Herrero, 'From Globalization to Deglobalization: Zooming into Trade', *Las claves de la globalizacion* 4 (2019), 33–52. Yilmazcan, 'The Role of Anti-Dumping in the US–China Trade War', 7–36.

50 Richard Baldwin, 'Regulatory Protectionism, Developing Nations and a Two-Tier World Trade System', in *Brookings Trade Forum* (Brookings Institution Press, 2000), 237–293.

51 WTO, Anti-dumping Statistics.

52 Ibid.

53 Ibid.

6. Each Party's investigating authority shall, in accordance with the Party's law, consider information provided as to whether imposing an anti-dumping or a countervailing duty would not be in the public interest.

These articles reflect the need for improved transparency around the ADA framework. By highlighting the need for an opportunity to defend one's interests, parties agree that the ADA fails to provide such a guarantee. The public interest will be also taken into consideration before the imposition of an anti-dumping duty, which is beyond the ADA.[54] Therefore, anti-dumping is an agenda item in free trade agreements.

RCEP has a section on trade remedies, covering safeguards and anti-dumping. There are specific provisions that improve procedural justice in anti-dumping proceedings. Article 7.11.2 of the RCEP requires seven days' advance notice of an on-the-spot investigation to the respondent for proper preparation. Article 7.12 also requires seven days' advance notice before the initiation of an anti-dumping investigation, which is parallel with the Chinese submission at the WTO. Article 7.11.3 enables interested parties to receive a hard or soft copy of a non-confidential file. Article 7.13 explicitly forbids zeroing, which is being negotiated at the WTO as well.[55] The agreement, in that sense, shows that during any reform of the ADA, the US's proposal to permit zeroing will not be easily accepted. Article 7.14 requires signatories to disclose all essential facts at least ten days before the final determination, which improves transparency.[56] Interested parties are also able to comment on essential facts that should be taken into consideration in the final determination. One downside of the agreement is that under the RCEP, there is a dispute settlement mechanism. However, this is not applicable to trade remedies, meaning that disputes arising from anti-dumping should be settled before the DSM. Still, RCEP offers a great opportunity to develop an anti-dumping framework at the multilateral level. RCEP is a perfectly appropriate mechanism for adopting a standard questionnaire. If such a questionnaire is established and adopted by the fifteen signatories, this

[54] Trade and Cooperation Agreement between the European Union and the European Atomic Energy Community, of the One Part, and the United Kingdom of Great Britain and Northern Ireland, of the Other Part, OJ L 444, 31 December 2020, P. 14–1462, EurLex, accessed 19 July 2023, https://eur-lex.europa.eu/legal-content/EN/TXT/?uri=uriserv%3AOJ.L_.2020.444.01.0014.01.ENG.

[55] Legal Text of the RCEP Agreement, available at https://rcepsec.org/legal-text/, accessed 19 July 2023.

[56] Ibid.

would support the benefit of procedural justice and make a positive impact, with fewer disputes.

The text of CPTPP is relatively short for a mega FTA as it incorporates TPP except for a few articles. In this regard, TPP has a section on anti-dumping. In order to promote transparency, TPP requires parties to notify other parties seven days before the initiation of an anti-dumping investigation. Also, as with the RCEP, TPP requires notification ten days before an on-the-spot investigation between parties.[57] Unlike RCEP, TPP does not prohibit zeroing,[58] mainly because the US was a party to the TPP. Nonetheless, as it has wide coverage in terms of trade and GDP, a standard questionnaire could also be adopted by the signatories, and this would increase the legal capacity of exporters. The adoption of a standard questionnaire in RCEP or CPTPP could easily spread to the others, as some members, such as Japan, Australia and Malaysia, are signatories to both agreements.

Furthermore, mega FTAs provide opportunities for other suggestions, as mentioned in Chapter 6. The signatories to RCEP, CPTPP or other FTAs could agree on preparing best practice guidelines regarding anti-dumping investigations. This would contribute to the harmonisation of anti-dumping procedures. Also, as both agreements cover administrative and institutional provisions, a support tool for exporters could be established under these agreements. This tool would increase the legal capacity of exporters, especially against anti-dumping investigations initiated by third countries. It is also possible to increase the awareness of exporters by means of government-led knowledge-exchange events, such as workshops or seminars. These joint measures would also help to develop a common position during WTO negotiations. Therefore, starting with more practical measures, procedural justice could be improved, and mega FTAs are perfectly suitable to achieve consensus with some members and implement WTO plus rules. There are existing common policies towards more objectivity and transparency, such as the prohibition of zeroing under the RCEP. Therefore, there is potential to develop and implement new measures to improve procedural justice.

Blockchain technology is revolutionising international trade. Consequently, blockchain will affect anti-dumping investigations at some

[57] Text of the Comprehensive and Progressive Agreement for Trans-Pacific Partnership (CPTPP), available at www.dfat.gov.au/sites/default/files/6-trade-remedies.pdf, accessed 19 July 2023.

[58] Ibid.

point. As suggested in Chapter 6, software to assist exporters or WTO lawyers with the anti-dumping questionnaires is highly achievable. This would improve the possibility of cooperation with investigating authorities and the legal capacity of exporters. Investigating authorities would also benefit from blockchain technology while verifying the information submitted to them. Conventionally, investigating authorities conduct on-the-spot investigations to verify the responses by the exporters. Blockchain could ensure that the data submitted by the exporters was genuine.

7.3 The Relevance of This Book and Its Findings to Contemporary Trade

Dumping is exporting at a lower price compared to the normal value of the goods. This practice is considered to be unfair in the context of WTO law.[59] WTO members can initiate anti-dumping investigations and adopt anti-dumping measures if they find dumping, material injury and causal links between these two. The ADA regulates the general principles and procedures of anti-dumping investigations to some extent. It is one of the most technical agreements under the GATT, and there are grey areas about the procedures leaving room for discretion. This book hypothesised that investigation procedures are being used to adopt overprotective anti-dumping measures.

By definition, regulatory protection 'raises the costs of foreign suppliers (or the domestic importers with whom they deal) by inducing an expenditure of resources for no purpose (or with no effect) other than to raise the price of imported goods'.[60] Regulations also cover unwritten rules and norms so long as they are general and prospective, according to WTO case law.[61] In this sense, procedural obstacles can be used to increase the costs to exporting companies in two ways. First, it is costly to participate in an investigation as a cooperating company. Second, according to the empirical findings, even if companies cooperate with investigating authorities, they face high anti-dumping duties which

[59] Peter Van den Bossche and Denise Prévost, 'Rules on Unfair Trade', in Peter Van den Bossche and Denise Prévost (eds.), *Essentials of WTO Law* (Cambridge University Press, 2016), 141–177.

[60] Sykes, 'Regulatory Protectionism and the Law of International Tradé', 1–46.

[61] Appellate Body Reports DS244, DS294, DS471, 'Dispute Settlement', WTO, accessed 30 June 2023, www.wto.org/english/tratop_e/dispu_e/dispu_e.htm.

increase the cost of imported goods. In other words, exporters facing anti-dumping duties lose business.

This book attempts to clarify three specific issues. The main question is to what extent the procedural rules of anti-dumping investigations can be used as a form of hidden trade protectionism in favour of domestic industries. In seeking an answer to this question, particular attention was paid to the relationships between the US, EU and China. Within the scope of this research, it was further questioned whether anti-dumping investigation procedures used by the US and EU support the hidden trade protectionism assumption, particularly against China. Third, it was argued that procedural justice would to some extent avoid the hidden trade protectionism in anti-dumping investigations.

In terms of the theoretical context, it should be acknowledged that the rationale behind anti-dumping measures is to balance unfair trade. Dumping is regarded as an unfair trading practice due to its negative effect on competition and local manufacturers. Predatory pricing is commonly accepted as a trigger for anti-dumping regulations. Anti-dumping measures are used to avoid monopolies by addressing predatory pricing strategies. In terms of competition, avoidance of monopolies is a legitimate goal. However, competition laws prioritise consumers, unlike anti-dumping laws. Anti-dumping laws are triggered by the interests of local manufacturers and are therefore criticised in terms of efficiency and the welfare effects on consumers. Anti-dumping measures are considered to be market distortions that reduce efficiency and welfare. Circumvention is another risk to the efficiency of public policies, and the empirical research in this book suggests that exporters and importers tend to find ways to circumvent anti-dumping duties.

It is notable that almost a hundred years ago, the clash of interests between local industries and consumers was being discussed just like today:

> Washington, April 22 – Declaring that the anti-dumping bill recently passed by the House would prevent American consumers from reducing living costs by buying cheaper European wares, Senator Thomas of Colorado and Nugent of Idaho, Democrats, filed a minority report today urging defeat of the measure. They charged that the moving force behind the bill was the selfish interests of American manufacturers, who desired to hold a monopoly of the domestic market.[62]

[62] Oppose Anti-Dumping Bill, *New York Times*, ProQuest Historical Newspapers (1920).

Regarding fairness arguments, some find anti-dumping measures are beneficial to levelling the playing field. The motivation for anti-dumping derives from avoiding the negative effects of subsidies granted by the exporting country. Through anti-dumping measures, exporters and importers are expected to be levelled with local manufacturers. However, the grey areas in the ADA give considerable discretion to investigating authorities. In addition, due to the lobbying by domestic industries, anti-dumping turns into an overly protectionist tool. Dumping is an unfair trade practice and anti-dumping measures should balance it to the extent of the dumping. If the amount of levelling exceeds the dumping, it creates over protectionism.

In terms of political arguments, without anti-dumping measures, negotiations for GATT 47 and 94 would not have succeeded. Developed members rely on trade remedies as safety valves against a sudden increase from developing countries. The safety valve argument is widely recognised but, on the other hand, the WTO's main objective is liberalisation and trade facilitation. Although fair trade is respected more than free trade, fairness should operate both ways. Exporting members should not subsidise exporters and importing members should not overprotect local manufacturers. Therefore, anti-dumping is a controversial tool in the WTO ecosystem and many oppose it due to its abusive use in practice. Consequently, anti-dumping is the most disputed issue under the WTO's DSB.

Given the political realities of the WTO framework, anti-dumping laws cannot be abolished. The arguments for anti-dumping laws are not entirely convincing, and the arguments against anti-dumping have more grounds in terms of economics, fairness and politics. However, the solution lies in the determination of a justifiable level of anti-dumping law.[63]

The solution offered by this book is ensuring procedural justice during anti-dumping investigations. Procedural justice is achieved when the procedures are trustworthy, respected, and neutral and allow input.[64] While guaranteeing the transparency of the process, procedural justice also limits the discretion of investigating authorities. This would also allow standard procedures in different jurisdictions, which would also secure improved opportunities for companies to defend themselves.

[63] See Chapter 2 and Table 2.1 for a detailed discussion of the arguments regarding anti-dumping.

[64] Barkworth and Murphy, 'Procedural Justice Policing and Citizen Compliance Behaviour'.

Greater participation in anti-dumping procedures may enhance the principles of fairness and reduce the political tension between members. Greater participation or input would also reduce the number of disputes about anti-dumping before WTO adjudication. Another positive outcome of improved procedural justice would be that exporters may comply with the investigating authorities rather than attempt to circumvent duties. Social psychological studies show that 'when people are treated with trust, respect, neutrality and are given an opportunity to express their views – all aspects of procedural justice – they are more likely to comply with directives, rules and laws and are more likely to voluntarily cooperate with authorities'.[65] In this sense, procedural justice improves regulatory compliance, and this would also reduce unfair trade practices by exporters. Thus, a justifiable level of anti-dumping is possible with improved procedural justice. Otherwise, attempts to reform the ADA substantially may not achieve consensus. This approach also increases tension between members and triggers retaliation and strict procedural rules causing more protectionism. The underestimation of procedural justice in anti-dumping therefore results in inefficiency or missed opportunities for gains from trade. This assumption is tested throughout the study by means of doctrinal and empirical research.

Turning to WTO disputes on anti-dumping in Chapter 3, it is clear that the DSM is ineffective in some cases. For instance, several DSM reports prohibit the use of the zeroing methodology, and constant adoption of non-compliant procedures implies that non-compliance with the DSB reports can be advantageous. The first reason is that DSM proceedings take a long time to restore the violation. It is generally too late for businesses to wait for the DSB report and its outcomes. Importers generally find alternative suppliers upon the initiation of an investigation. The decrease in the import of the goods after the initiation of an investigation is referred to as the 'investigation effect'.[66] Even if there are no duties in the end, the investigation effect is used to reduce imports for a certain period. Second, it is costly to take disputes before the DSM, so members cannot present all issues. In Chapter 3, all disputes related to anti-dumping procedures were examined and classified. There are several categories of procedural rule that are challenged before the DSM, indicating that members adopt regulatory protection by means of procedural rules to hamper exporters and overprotect local manufacturers more

[65] Ibid.

[66] Staiger and Wolak, *Measuring Industry Specific Protection*.

than is allowed by the ADA. DSM is designed to protect the proper enforcement of WTO agreements but, as it is not as effective as it seems on paper, it cannot guarantee procedural justice in anti-dumping investigations.

To return to the research questions, the book focuses on US and EU investigations, particularly against Chinese exporters, to find out whether anti-dumping investigation procedures are being used to overprotect local industries. The findings also allow the reader to evaluate whether improving procedural justice in anti-dumping investigations would help to prevent hidden trade protectionism. Therefore, after the discussion of the theoretical framework of anti-dumping investigations, this book attempts to highlight the key features of US and EU investigation procedures, as well as the position of China as the top target of those investigations. Chapter 4 discusses the investigation procedures of the US and EU, as well as the position of China, but does not discuss whether Chinese exporters are receiving subsidies or adopting dumping strategies. Being the top anti-dumping target implies that Chinese exporters' prices are aggressive and may be predatory. However, anti-dumping measures should balance this price differentiation fairly to the extent of the real difference between markets. Focusing on the investigation procedures of the US and EU, the level of discretion becomes clear. For instance, the EU shifted from 'non-market economy' terminology into 'market distortion' and 'surrogate country'. EU public information suggests that while normal calculation methods lead to anti-dumping duties of around 10 per cent on average, the surrogate country method increases the average to around 40 per cent.[67] The US also has procedures that limit the meaningful participation of exporters. For instance, even if companies cooperate, the US investigating authorities choose a few as mandatory respondents, and the rest of the cooperating companies are subject to all other rates, which are likely to be higher than the individual rates. The key findings in Chapter 3 are that investigating authorities adopt different procedures, such as calculation methods, sampling, verification visits, and lesser duty rules. However, in addition to differences, both jurisdictions have their shortcomings in terms of allowing exporters to cooperate. This, in turn, may be used to inflate the final measures.

While Chapters 3 and 4 reveal that the DSM cannot guarantee procedural justice in anti-dumping investigations, two more steps were

[67] 'Calculation of Dumping Margins'.

pursued in the subsequent chapters. Chapter 5 provided further information on procedural problems by discussing empirical research. Chapter 6 concentrated on the ongoing negotiations at the WTO to modify the ADA and examined alternative ways of securing procedural justice.

In Chapter 5, additional information was collected from exporters, law firms and officials in MOFCOM. Empirical research cannot fully demonstrate that strict procedural rules result in low levels of cooperation. However, some empirical findings reached in this chapter support the view that investigation procedures are biased. Empirical findings from WTO lawyers and Chinese exporters confirm that anti-dumping investigations are not transparent, objective or fair. Most find cooperation unreasonable due to high cost and the absence of gains at the end of the investigation. In any case, exports fall dramatically. Some exporters, therefore, attempt circumvention to avoid the adverse effects of anti-dumping investigations. The data collected from the field can only support the view that procedural rules are being used for purposes of hidden trade protectionism. It is not possible to know the exact intention of investigating authorities in adopting procedural rules. However, the different procedures adopted by the US and EU anti-dumping investigating authorities create burdens for Chinese exporters. Companies are obliged to submit completely different questionnaires and are subject to different procedures.

Chapter 6 addresses general suggestions for a comprehensive reform of the ADA. This section examined the negotiations on the ADA in the NGR. As members are polarised in terms of regulation or deregulation, it is not an easy task to agree on the future of the ADA in the short term. Above all, the failure of the last Ministerial Conference and the US policies of blocking the DSM are the main concerns related to constructive negotiations. Due to these constraints, comprehensive reform of the ADA may not be possible. Therefore, other options were also discussed, such as publishing best practice guidelines, standard questionnaires, raising awareness of exporters, a support tool for exporters, and software to assist exporters in completing questionnaires.

The implications of these findings can guide future attempts to revise the anti-dumping mechanism. It should be borne in mind that anti-dumping is a highly controversial matter under the WTO, and it is very unlikely to be abolished completely. On the contrary, increasingly, developing countries are adopting anti-dumping measures, just like developed countries. However, the number of disputes before the DSM indicates that anti-dumping is an ill-defined and abused tool. The opinions of WTO lawyers and Chinese exporters are valuable in showing the impact of anti-dumping investigations on a microeconomic level.

One of the remarkable implications is that Chinese exporters are either unaware of investigations or they simply choose not to cooperate. There are several reasons for this. First, cooperating with the investigating authorities is costly and time-consuming. Second, the vast amount of information requested by the investigating authorities raises concerns over commercial secrets. Third, even if companies cooperate, it is likely that they will face high anti-dumping duties. Finally, companies are aware that they can circumvent the duties until the investigating authorities detect this unfair trading practice. Circumvention of duties can be placed at a higher level among other unfair trade practices because dumping is a pricing strategy that is not prohibited by competition laws, whereas circumvention is intentional tax fraud. This point reflects the importance of uniform rules on anti-circumvention under the ADA. Therefore, over protection of local industries with anti-dumping duties can lead to circumvention, which avoids the remedial effect of anti-dumping and results in a tax loss for the importing country.

Anti-dumping is the most popular trade remedy, and its effects are remarkable in terms of bilateral and global trade. At the micro-level, local manufacturers are lobbying for more anti-dumping duties whereas exporters respond by circumventing or lobbying their governments to take the case before the DSM. In doing so, local manufacturers restrict foreign competition and increase their market share. Exporters and importers, on the other hand, seek ways to avoid anti-dumping duties. Regardless, considering the time allocated for the investigation and the time needed to settle disputes before the DSM, initiation of an anti-dumping investigation adversely affects trade.

From a macro perspective, non-tariff barriers increased significantly after the success in trade liberalisation. With lower tariffs, WTO members needed more protection and anti-dumping became a popular way to restrict imports. Although anti-dumping is designed as a balancing tool, the gaps in the ADA allow WTO members to adopt strict procedural rules and higher anti-dumping duties. This can be explained by the asymmetric information that the importing governments have.[68]

[68] Xenia Matschke and Anja Schöttner, 'Antidumping as Strategic Trade Policy under Asymmetric Information', CESifo Working Paper Series No. 2536 (2009).

However, from examining the investigation methods, it is clear that the aim is not to determine the normal value of products reflecting true costs.

Adopting high anti-dumping duties benefits the importing countries in several ways. First, demands from local manufacturers are met so the government can argue that additional jobs are created. Second, it attracts foreign direct investment as, in some cases, exporters relocate production to the importing country for tariff jumping purposes. Third, if the high duties can be collected, this improves the budget performance. Fourth, the adoption of high anti-dumping duties creates tension with the exporting country and can be used as means of obtaining concessions. On the other hand, there are disadvantages to anti-dumping duties, including welfare loss, especially for consumers, and the risk of circumvention.

7.4 Concluding Remarks

The contemporary trade framework changes rapidly. Most recent issues – such as the US–China trade war, Brexit, and COVID-19 – are caused by protectionism or trigger more of it. Anti-dumping is a common trade remedy that can be abused easily to apply greater protection. This study sought to answer the question whether anti-dumping investigation procedures are used to overprotect local industries. To zoom in from the broad question, the anti-dumping investigation procedures of the US and EU towards Chinese exporters were examined. Due to the uncertainties of the ADA, WTO members have discretion in adopting national anti-dumping laws and rules. Some of the procedures, such as zeroing, are prohibited by the DSM. However, the efficiency of the DSB is questionable in terms of timing, cost and enforceability; therefore, members may not comply with rulings. The US is a good example of a strategically motivated infringer of the DSM. Some DSB rulings are not implemented, even six years after the initiation of the dispute. This also supports the view that members can be motivated to increase burdens rather than comply with DSB rulings. Thus, regulatory protection or hidden trade protectionism may occur, either by adopting strict procedural rules where the ADA leaves grey areas or by slowing down the dispute settlement process.

In this regard, the first finding of the book is that due to the grey areas in the ADA, WTO members have considerable discretion on anti-dumping investigation procedures, which leads to diverse anti-dumping investigation procedures used by WTO members. Exporters and importers subject to investigation need to submit extremely detailed information and pass through a complex process. For instance, solar panels or bus tyre manufacturers in China needed to handle anti-dumping investigation procedures by the US and EU around the same period. Exporters need to comply with US and EU investigations separately and, as the procedures have their own characteristics or complexities, it is extremely burdensome to cooperate with both investigating authorities.

Second, empirical findings support the view that anti-dumping procedures are neither transparent, objective nor fair. It is generally unreasonable to attempt to cooperate with the investigating authorities because of high expenses and the absence of gains at the end of the investigation. That is how hidden trade protectionism achieves its objective. As a result of requests for extremely detailed information within a relatively short period of time, exporters generally have no option but to avoid the investigation and face high anti-dumping duties. Consequently, a drastic decrease in exports is inevitable.

Third, improving procedural justice in anti-dumping investigations could limit the misuse of the anti-dumping mechanism. In their current state, anti-dumping procedures serve as non-tariff barriers to trade more than they should. If exporters had a chance to defend themselves in overseas jurisdictions, normal value calculations would be closer to reality. In practice, the investigating authorities set complex procedural rules so only a few companies can cooperate. The rest of the exporters are subject to anti-dumping duties, which are calculated according to constructed normal values.

In terms of accuracy, there are certain limitations to this book. First, empirical research is directed to practitioners and enterprises. Their views are generally negative towards the US and EU investigation procedures. The reason is that, on one side, there are exporters and importers and, on the other side, there are the investigating authorities and local manufacturers, so there is a clash of interests. This also results in a negative attitude towards the investigating authorities' procedures. In other words, the participants in this study, namely WTO lawyers, Chinese exporters and MOFCOM officials, are not objective. They have suffered from those procedures, so they contend that there are problems with US and EU anti-dumping investigations. Second, these comments only can support the hypothesis about hidden trade protectionism. The empirical evidence through the WTO lawyers or Chinese exporters cannot prove that there is hidden trade protectionism behind anti-dumping investigations. Third, finding the actual intention of protectionism behind the investigating authorities' procedures is not possible unless decision-makers explicitly state that they design procedures with this goal in mind. Surveys were directed to EU and the US investigating authorities, but no response was received, except that USITC commented that it is an enforcing body rather than a policymaking department. This may also imply that there is an agenda beneath the investigation procedures. Furthermore, even if US and EU officials had participated in the surveys, it is very unlikely that they would admit to hidden trade protectionism motivations behind the anti-dumping investigation procedures, as this would be a violation of the ADA Article 2.4.

This highlights the need for further research in this field. Some further questions can be addressed by the literature in future in order to reveal more facts about anti-dumping investigations. These questions would be: How do policymaking agencies decide on anti-dumping or trade remedy policies? What are the motivations behind anti-dumping policies? How do policymaking agencies react when they receive an Appellate Body report highlighting inconsistencies in their practices? Do the investigating authorities monitor and track the performance of domestic industries after the investigation? Do sunset reviews objectively evaluate the effects of anti-dumping duties on local industries or are they used as a tool to extend the adopted duty? Also, as the study focuses on three jurisdictions – namely the US, EU and China – further research could be conducted on a larger scale to test the conclusions, especially with the new frequent users such as India, Brazil, Mexico and Turkey.

The book focuses on US and EU anti-dumping procedures, particularly against China, as this combination covers a large proportion of anti-dumping measures. This work does not elaborate on the foreign trade practices of Chinese economic operators regarding subsidies or dumping. These practices are mostly unfair and constitute a violation of WTO agreements. The problem focused on in this book is whether unfair trading practices are remedied justly and without the abuse of WTO agreements. Also, there are tensions between these two poles on political and economic grounds. Therefore, the practices of the US and EU against Chinese exporters would allow the readers to recognise how the procedures can be used to overprotect local industries. However, as mentioned, further research is needed to see if the conclusions are valid for other WTO members. Anti-dumping was designed as a balancing tool and a safety valve in order to promote tariff liberalisation during the GATT negotiations. However, as there are grey areas in the ADA, investigating authorities adopt procedural burdens to limit the level of cooperation.

Less cooperation results in higher anti-dumping duties. This book systematically explains the theories of anti-dumping, the investigation procedures of the US and EU, the position of China, the disputes at the WTO, the empirical findings of the procedural burdens and possible solutions to avoid hidden trade protectionism through anti-dumping investigations.

Regarding the way anti-dumping turned into the most popular trade remedy, one should recap globalisation since the 1940s. Average tariffs were around 20 to 30 per cent in 1947, whereas in 1996, tariffs had been reduced to 11.1 per cent.[69] As of 2019, average tariffs were around 9 per cent.[70] Anti-dumping and other trade remedies played a vital role in this liberalisation process to secure developed countries participation in the GATT 94. Consequently, world trade levels increased around 300 times from the 1950s to 2019.[71] However, the safety valves, especially anti-dumping, became so popular that they turned into a mechanism to overprotect local industries rather than fight unfair trade practices. Therefore, anti-dumping is the most litigated issue before the DSM. It was initially a weapon used by developed countries, but developing countries are also adopting anti-dumping duties.

A company facing an anti-dumping investigation is unlikely to find cooperation a useful strategy. The company must allocate days and hundreds of thousands of dollars just to meet the submission requirements. Considering that the cost structure of the company includes confidential information, managers tend not to share this information with foreign governments. Cooperation is viable if the importing market makes up the largest share of a company's exports. Nonetheless, cooperation does not guarantee low anti-dumping duties. In the exceptional US mattress investigation, the USITC enforced 57 to 192 per cent anti-dumping duties against selected companies, whereas the China-wide entity rate was 1,731 per cent.[72] Therefore, as supported by the empirical findings in this book, companies may prefer to circumvent high anti-

[69] Evolution of Trade under the WTO: Handy Statistics, WTO, accessed 19 July 2023, www.wto.org/english/res_e/statis_e/trade_evolution_e/evolution_trade_wto_e.htm.

[70] Ibid.

[71] Ibid.

[72] USITC, Mattresses from the People's Republic of China: Antidumping Duty Order, A Notice by the International Trade Administration on 16 December 2019, accessed 19 July 2023, www.federalregister.gov/documents/2019/12/16/2019-27166/mattresses-from-the-peoples-republic-of-china-antidumping-duty-order.

dumping duties rather than try to cooperate. Also, studies based on econometric models show that if anti-dumping is justified to restore unfair trade practices, evasion of anti-dumping duties can harm welfare.[73] However, if anti-dumping is considered a protection tool for local industries, circumvention still harms efficiency in transportation of goods.[74] There are no uniform rules on anti-circumvention under WTO law, so tackling of circumvention activities also differs, which allows investigating authorities to enjoy discretion and multiply the effects of anti-dumping duties. Regardless, complex anti-dumping procedures discourage companies from cooperating and thus trade decreases or circumvention activities increase.

With this in mind, anti-dumping can be addressed as a necessary evil for international trade. It cannot be abolished or replaced with competition laws, but there are clear signs that reform is needed. Considering the negotiations held by the NGR, even if a substantial reform is hard to achieve, some steps could be taken in order to improve procedural justice. Procedural justice is needed to achieve substantive equality. By improving procedural justice, accuracy, cost-balancing and meaningful participation are secured. Exporters should be more able to defend their interests during anti-dumping investigations. By improving procedural justice, anti-dumping investigations would be more objective and less abusive, less protectionist. In other words, improved procedural justice in anti-dumping investigations would result in fewer anti-dumping measures and lower rates. Thus, the number of disputes under the DSM would see a significant decline.

Aside from reforming the ADA, there are practical measures to improve procedural justice in anti-dumping investigations. These measures can be classified in two groups: the measures already offered and the measures offered by this book. Publishing best practice guidelines was offered at Negotiating Group on Rules in 2003. Adopting a standard questionnaire to be used by all WTO members was offered by Andrews in 2008. A model questionnaire would have a positive impact on procedural justice and the predictability of investigations. Therefore, a standard questionnaire substantially lowers room for discretion and avoids overly protectionist use of investigation procedures. This book revisits those two measures and argues that Mega FTAs such as RCEP of CPTPP would be

[73] Liu Xuepeng and Huimin Shi, 'Anti-dumping Duty Circumvention through Trade Rerouting: Evidence from Chinese Exporters', *World Econ.* 42, no. 5 (2019), 1427–1466.
[74] Ibid.

an opportunity to adopt this kind of documents. The second group of measures offered by this study would also improve the procedural justice in anti-dumping investigations. Raising awareness among exporters of the outcomes of non-cooperation and encouraging them to react quickly would be a decent option to improve meaningful participation. Linking to this, a support tool similar to the ACWL would be established to assist SMEs in participating in anti-dumping procedures and improve their legal capacity at low cost. This mechanism was supported by participants in the empirical research part of this book. In the case of China, accounting standards constitute a barrier to cooperation with the investigations initiated by the US or the EU. If China improves accounting standards according to international standards, Chinese exporters would benefit in due course from anti-dumping investigations. Another project would be to develop software to assist exporters in automatically filling out the questionnaires used by the US, EU or other WTO members, thus allowing more time for the companies to double-check and prepare other required documents and meet tight deadlines. With the recent developments in technology, there are countless opportunities to facilitate complex procedures of anti-dumping investigations.

In conclusion, anti-dumping is at the core of contemporary trade issues. The book hypothesised that anti-dumping investigation procedures are used as a form of hidden trade protectionism. The case of US and EU investigations against Chinese exporters supports this hypothesis. By conducting empirical research with WTO lawyers, MOFCOM officials and Chinese exporters, it was revealed that anti-dumping investigation procedures discourage exporters from cooperating. This can be regarded as the procedural effect of anti-dumping investigations. Investigating authorities enjoy a high level of discretion that puts exporters in an asymmetric position. Exporters believe they cannot defend their interests fairly and objectively due to procedural obstacles and high costs. Therefore, improving procedural justice in anti-dumping proceedings could play a vital role in the future of global trade. A revision of the ADA would offer opportunities to develop and harmonise diverse practices in anti-dumping investigations. The negotiations at the WTO should prioritise the procedural aspects. Even if it is challenging to reach a conclusion at the WTO level, mega FTAs, such as RCEP and CPTPP, can be a great opportunity to trigger procedural justice initiatives. Thus, compartmentalisation of the problem by prioritising procedural issues and taking harmonisation measures under the FTAs would help to reduce the burden of the DSM.

SELECT BIBLIOGRAPHY

Primary Sources

Statues, Agreements, Government Documents and Cases

19 USC § 1677(18) A, accessed 17 June 2023, www.law.cornell.edu/uscode/text/19/1677.

Agreement on Rules of Origin.

Council Regulation (EC) No 1225/2009, accessed 15 July 2023, https://publications.europa.eu/en/publication-detail/-/publication/81daf628-e6ca-49e6-a41c-05aebdf017fe/language-en.

European Commission v. Xinyi PV Products (Anhui) Holdings Ltd, Judgement of the Court, accessed 15 July 2023, http://curia.europa.eu/juris/document/document.jsf?docid=199765&mode=req&pageIndex=1&dir=&occ=first&part=1&text=distortion%2Bchina&doclang=EN&cid=698897#ctx1.

GATT 47, accessed 18 July 2023, www.wto.org/english/docs_e/legal_e/gatt47_02_e.htm#articleXXIV.

Matsushita Elec. Ind. Co. v. Zenith Radio Corp., 475 US 574, 588–93 (1986).

Regulation 2016/1036, accessed 15 July 2023, https://eur-lex.europa.eu/legal-content/EN/TXT/?qid=1556980299597&uri= CELEX:02016R1036–20180608.

Report of the Panel, China – Countervailing and Anti-Dumping Duties on Grain Oriented Flat-Rolled Electrical Steel from the United States, WT/DS414/R, 2014.

SCM Agreement, accessed 16 July 2023, www.wto.org/english/docs_e/legal_e/24-scm_01_e.htm.

Shanxi Taigang Stainless Steel Co. Ltd v. European Commission, Judgement of the Court (Tenth Chamber) of 29 July 2019, accessed 15 July 2023, https://eur-lex.europa.eu/legal-content/EN/TXT/?uri=CELEX%3A62018CJ0436.

Special Import Measures Act of Canada, accessed 16 July 2023, http://laws-lois.justice.gc.ca/PDF/S-15.pdf.

The Tariff Act of 1930, 19 USCS § 1677 35 (B) (1995).

The Technical Barriers to Trade (TBT) Agreement, accessed 21 December 2021, www.wto.org/english/docs_e/legal_e/17-tbt_e.htm.

Trade and Cooperation Agreement between the European Union and the European Atomic Energy Community, of the One Part, and the United Kingdom of Great Britain and Northern Ireland, of the Other Part, OJ L 444, 31 December 2020, EurLex, accessed 19 July 2023, https://eur-lex.europa.eu/legal-content/EN/TXT/?uri=uriserv%3AOJ.L_.2020.444.01.0014.01.ENG.

WTO Disputes

DS8, Japan – Taxes on Alcoholic Beverages, www.wto.org/english/tratop_e/dispu_e/cases_e/ds8_e.htm.

DS99, United States – Anti-Dumping Duty on Dynamic Random Access Memory Semiconductors (DRAMS) of One Megabit or above from Korea, Panel Report, www.wto.org/english/tratop_e/dispu_e/cases_e/ds99_e.htm.

DS141, European Communities – Anti-Dumping Duties on Imports of Cotton-Type Bed Linen from India, Appellate Body Report, www.wto.org/english/tratop_e/dispu_e/cases_e/ds141_e.htm.

DS178R, United States – Safeguard Measure on Imports of Fresh, Chilled or Frozen Lamb from Australia, www.wto.org/english/tratop_e/dispu_e/cases_e/ds177_e.htm.

DS179, United States – Anti-Dumping measures on Stainless Steel Plate in Coils and Stainless Steel Sheet and Strip from Korea, Panel Report, www.wto.org/english/tratop_e/dispu_e/cases_e/ds179_e.htm.

DS184, United States – Anti-Dumping Measures on Certain Hot-Rolled Steel Products from Japan, Panel Report, www.wto.org/english/tratop_e/dispu_e/cases_e/ds184_e.htm.

DS189, Argentina – Definitive Anti-Dumping Measures on Carton-Board Imports from Germany and Definitive Anti-Dumping Measures on Imports of Ceramic Tiles from Italy, Panel Report, www.wto.org/english/tratop_e/dispu_e/cases_e/ds189_e.htm.

DS219, European Communities – Anti-Dumping Duties on Malleable Cast Iron Tube or Pipe Fittings from Brazil, Panel Report, Appellate Body Report, www.wto.org/english/tratop_e/dispu_e/cases_e/ds219_e.htm.

DS264, United States – Final Dumping Determination on Softwood Lumber from Canada, www.wto.org/english/tratop_e/dispu_e/cases_e/ds264_e.htm.

DS294, United States – Laws, Regulations and Methodology for Calculating Dumping Margins (Zeroing), Appellate Body Report, www.wto.org/english/tratop_e/dispu_e/cases_e/ds294_e.htm.

DS295, Mexico – Definitive Anti-Dumping Measures on Beef and Rice, Report of the Appellate Body, WT/DS295/AB/R, 2005, accessed 18 July 2023, www.wto.org/english/tratop_e/dispu_e/cases_e/ds295_e.htm.

DS322, United States – Measures Relating to Zeroing and Sunset Reviews, Appellate Body Report, www.wto.org/english/tratop_e/dispu_e/cases_e/ds322_e.htm.

DS337, European Communities – Anti-Dumping Measure on Farmed Salmon from Norway, Panel Report, Adopted on 17 November 2007, accessed 30 June 2023, www.wto.org/english/tratop_e/dispu_e/cases_e/ds337_e.htm.

DS350, United States – Continued Existence and Application of Zeroing Methodology, www.wto.org/english/tratop_e/dispu_e/cases_e/ds350_e.htm.

DS371, Thailand – Customs and Fiscal Measures on Cigarettes from the Philippines, www.wto.org/english/tratop_e/dispu_e/cases_e/ds371_e.htm.

DS379, United States – Definitive Anti-Dumping and Countervailing Duties on Certain Products from China, Appellate Body Report, accessed 15 July 2023, https://docs.wto.org/dol2fe/Pages/SS/directdoc.aspx?filename=Q:/WT/DS/379ABR.pdf&Open=True.

DS402, United States – Use of Zeroing in Anti-Dumping Measures Involving Products from Korea, www.wto.org/english/tratop_e/dispu_e/cases_e/ds402_e.htm.

DS405, European Union – Anti-Dumping Measures on Certain Footwear from China, Panel Report, www.wto.org/english/tratop_e/dispu_e/cases_e/ds405_e.htm.

DS425, China – Definitive Anti-Dumping Duties on X-Ray Security Inspection Equipment from the European Union, Report of Panel, Addendum, www.wto.org/english/tratop_e/dispu_e/cases_e/ds425_e.htm.

DS460, China – Measures Imposing Anti-Dumping Duties on High-Performance Stainless Steel Seamless Tubes ("Hp-Ssst") from the European Union, Report of Panel, www.wto.org/english/tratop_e/dispu_e/cases_e/ds460_e.htm.

DS464, United States – Anti-Dumping and Countervailing Measures on Large Residential Washers from Korea, www.wto.org/english/tratop_e/dispu_e/cases_e/ds464_e.htm.

DS471, United States – Certain Methodologies and Their Application to Anti-Dumping Proceedings Involving China, Panel Report, accessed 15 July 2023, www.wto.org/english/tratop_e/dispu_e/cases_e/ds471_e.htm.

DS488, United States – Anti-Dumping Measures on Certain Oil Country Tubular Goods from Korea, Panel Report, accessed 15 July 2023, www.wto.org/english/tratop_e/dispu_e/cases_e/ds488_e.htm.

DS516, European Union – Measures Related to Price Comparison Methodologies, accessed 15 July 2023, www.wto.org/english/tratop_e/dispu_e/cases_e/ds516_e.htm.

DS534, United States – Anti-Dumping Measures Applying Differential Pricing Methodology to Softwood Lumber from Canada, www.wto.org/english/tratop_e/dispu_e/cases_e/ds534_e.htm.

Secondary Sources

Books, Book Chapters and Journal Articles

Aggarwal, Aradhna, 'Trade Effects of Anti-dumping in India: Who Benefits?', *Int'l Trade J.* 25, no. 1 (2010), 112–158.

Alam, M. H., 'Next Steps Might Be Considered by Joe Biden for the Development of International Trade Law', *Eur. J. Eng. Res. Sci.* 5, no. 11 (2020), 1372–1375.

Andrews, Michael, 'The Facts Available on "Facts Available": An Analysis of Article 6.8 and Annex II of the WTO Anti-dumping Agreement', *N.Z. J. Public & Int'l L.* 6, no. 2 (2008), 11–42.

Aranoff, Shara L., Sonam Patel and Molly J. Doggett, 'A Review of the Court of International Trade's 2015 Decisions Addressing Trade Remedy Determinations of the US International Trade Commission and the Court's Decisions Pursuant to 28 USC 1581 (i)', *Geo. J. Int'l L.* 48 (2016), 7–68.

Areeda, Philip and Donald F. Turner, 'Predatory Pricing and Related Practices under Section 2 of the Sherman Act', *J. Reprints Antitrust L. & Econ.* 6 (1975), 697–733.

d'Aspremont, Claude, David Encaoua and Jean-Pierre Ponssard, 'Competition Policy and Game Theory: Reflections Based on the Cement Industry Case', in George Norman (ed.), *Market Structure and Competition Policy: Game Theoretical Approaches* (Cambridge University Press, 2000), 9–30.

Bacon-Shone, John, *Introduction to Quantitative Research Methods* (Graduate School, The University of Hong Kong, 2013).

Bagwell, Kyle, Chad Bown and Robert W. Staiger, 'Is the WTO Passé?', *J. Econ. Lit.* 54, no. 4 (2016), 1125–1231.

Baldwin, Richard, 'Regulatory Protectionism, Developing Nations and a Two-Tier World Trade System', in *Brookings Trade Forum* (Brookings Institution Press, 2000), 237–293.

Baldwin, Richard and Beatrice W. Di Mauro, *Economics in the Time of COVID-19: A New eBook* (VOX, CEPR Policy Portal, 2020).

Baldwin, Richard and Eiichi Tomiura, 'Thinking Ahead about the Trade Impact of COVID-19', in R. Baldwin and B. Weder di Mauro (eds.), *Economics in the Time of COVID-19* (CEPR Press, 2020), 59.

Bao, Xiaohua and Larry D. Qiu, 'Is China's Antidumping More Retaliatory than That of the US?', *Rev. Int'l Econ.* 19, no. 2 (2011), 374–389.

Barkworth, Julie M. and Kristina Murphy, 'Procedural Justice Policing and Citizen Compliance Behaviour: The Importance of Emotion', *Psychol. Crime & L.* 21, no. 3 (2015), 254–273.

Benedetto, John, Lauren Gamache, James Holbein and Craig Thomsen, 'Summary of the US International Trade Commission Centennial Proceedings', *J. Int'l Com. & Econ.* 2017 (2017), 1–23.

Beshkar, Mostafa and Adam S. Chilton, 'Revisiting Procedure and Precedent in the WTO: An Analysis of US–Countervailing and Anti-dumping Measures (China)', *World Trade Rev.* 15, no. 2 (2016), 375–395.

Bi, Ying, 'Is Dumping Still Harmful? New Thinking on Anti-dumping in the Global Free Trade', *JE Asia & Int'l L.* 6 (2013), 29–51.

Bork, Robert H., *The Antitrust Paradox* (Basic Books, 1978).

Bouët, Antonie and Jeanne Métivier, 'Is the Dispute Settlement System, "Jewel in the WTO's Crown", beyond Reach of Developing Countries?', *Rev. World Econ.* 156 (2020), 1–38.

Bown, Chad P., 'The 2018 Trade War and the End of Dispute Settlement as We Knew It', in Meredith A. Crowley (ed.), *Trade War: The Clash of Economic Systems Endangering Global Prosperity* (CEPR Press, 2019), 21–32.

'The 2018 US–China Trade Conflict after 40 Years of Special Protection.' *Chin. Econ. J.* 12, no. 2 (2019), 109–136.

'Antidumping and Other Trade Disputes', in Shenggen Fan, Kanbur Ravi, Shang-Jin Wei and Xiaobo Zhang (eds.), *The Oxford Companion to the Economics of China* (Oxford University Press, 2014), 114–119.

Bown, Chad P., Bernard Hoekman and Caglar Ozden, 'The Pattern of US Antidumping: The Path from Initial Filing to WTO Dispute Settlement', *World Trade Rev.* 2, no. 3 (2003), 349–371.

Brander, James and Paul Krugman, 'A "Reciprocal Dumping" Model of International Trade', *J. Int'l Econ.* 15, nos. 3–4 (1983), 320–321.

Brander, James and Barbara Spencer, 'Tariff Protection and Imperfect Competition', in G. M. Grossman (ed.), *Imperfect Competition and International Trade* (MIT Press, 1992), 107–119.

Brewster, Rachel, 'The Remedy Gap: Institutional Design, Retaliation, and Trade Law Enforcement', *Geo. Wash. L. Rev.* 80, no. 1 (2011), 102–158. Accessed 17 June 2023, https://ssrn.com/abstract=2146121.

Broncken, Marco and McNelis Natalie, 'Rethinking the "Like Product" Definition in WTO Antidumping Law', *J. World Trade* 33, no. 3 (1999), 73–91.

Brooks, Stephen G. and William C. Wohlforth, 'The Once and Future Superpower: Why China Won't Overtake the United States', *Foreign Aff.* 95 (2016), 91–104.

Bruton, Samuel V., 'Teaching the Golden Rule', *J. Bus. Ethics* 49, no. 2 (2004), 179–187.

Busch, Marc L., Eric Reinhardt and Gregory Shaffer, 'Does Legal Capacity Matter? A Survey of WTO Members', *World Trade Rev.* 8, no. 4 (2009), 559–577.

Cane, Peter and Herbert Kritzer, eds., *The Oxford Handbook of Empirical Legal Research* (Oxford University Press, 2010).

Cann, Wesley A., 'Internationalizing Our Views toward Recoupment and Market Power: Attacking the Anti-dumping/Antitrust Dichotomy through WTO-Consistent Global Welfare Theory', *U. Pa. J. Int'l Econ. L.* 17 (1996), 69–231.

Carmody, Chios, 'A Theory of WTO Law', *J. Int'l Econ. L.* 11, no. 3 (2008), 527–557.

Chaisse, Julien and Chakraborty Debashis, 'Normative Obsolescence of the WTO Anti-dumping Agreement: Topography of the Global Use and Misuse of Initiations and Measures', *Asian J. Int'l L.* 6, no. 2 (2016), 233–263.

Chan, Kam C. and Hung-gay Fung, eds., *China's Capital Markets: Challenges from WTO Membership* (Edward Elgar, 2007).

Chemerinsky, Erwin, *Constitutional Law* (Aspen, 2019).

Chen, Chien-Hsun, Chao-Cheng Mai and Hui-Chuan Yu, 'The Effect of Export Tax Rebates on Export Performance: Theory and Evidence from China', *China Econ. Rev.* 17, no. 2 (2006), 226–235.

Chen, Yusong, 'Laws and Implementation in China: A 16 Years Review after Accession to the WTO', in Marc Bungenberg, Michael Hahn, Christoph Herrmann and Till Müller-Ibold (eds.), *The Future of Trade Defence Instruments* (Springer, 2018), 283–294.

Cheng, Wenting and Peter Drahos, 'How China Built the World's Biggest Patent Office: The Pressure Driving Mechanism', *Int. Rev. Intellect. Prop. Compet. L.* 49, no. 1 (2018), 5–40.

Chilton, Adam S. and Ryan W. Davis, 'Equality, Procedural Justice, and the World Trade Organization', *Intercultural Hum. Rts. L. Rev.* 7 (2012), 277–327.

Cho, Sungjoon, 'No More Zeroing?: The United States Changes Its Antidumping Policy to Comply with the WTO', *Am. Soc'y Int'l L.* 16, no. 8 (2012).

Choi, Won-mog, 'People's Republic of China's Proposals for Anti-dumping in WTO/DDA Rules Negotiations', *Asian J. WTO & Int'l Health L & Pol'y* 2 (2007), 25–64.

Chunhui, Liu, Lee J. Yao, Nan Hu and Ling Liu, 'The Impact of IFRS on Accounting Quality in a Regulated Market: An Empirical Study of China', *J. Account. Audit. & Finance* 26, no. 4 (2011), 659–676.

Colantone, Italo and Piero Stanig, 'The Trade Origins of Economic Nationalism: Import Competition and Voting Behavior in Western Europe', *Am. J. Pol. Sci.* 62, no. 4 (2018), 936–953.

Cook, Graham, 'Confidentiality and Transparency in the WTO's Party-Centric Dispute Settlement System', in J. Huerta-Goldman and Marco Tulio Molina-Tejeda (eds.), *Practical Aspects of WTO Litigation* (Wolters Kluwer, 2019), 1–23.

Corr, Christopher F., 'Trade Protection in the New Millennium: The Ascendancy of Anti-dumping Measures', *Nw. J. Int'l L. & Bus.* 18 (1997), 49-110.

Croley, Steven P. and Jack H. Jackson, 'WTO Dispute Procedures, Standard of Review, and Deference to National Governments', *Am. J. Int'l Law* 90, no. 2 (1996), 193–213.

Czako, Judith, Human Johann and Miranda Jorge, *A Handbook on Anti-Dumping Investigations* (Cambridge University Press, 2003).

Daly, Gemma, 'Should Truth Commissions Be Viewed as Second-Best Alternatives to Prosecutions', *SOAS L.J.* 2 (2015) 176.

Dani, Rodrik, 'Has Globalization Gone Too Far?', *Challenge* 41, no. 2 (1998), 81–94.

Davey, William J., 'The WTO and Rules-Based Dispute Settlement: Historical Evolution, Operational Success, and Future Challenges', *J. Int'l Econ. L.* 17, no. 3 (2014), 679–700.

Deardorff, Alan V., 'Economic Perspectives on Dumping Law', in John H. Jackson and Edwin A. Vermulst (eds.), *Anti-dumping Law and Practice: A Comparative Study* (The University of Michigan Press, 1989), 23–39.

Debroy, Bibek and Chakraborty Debashis, eds., *Anti-Dumping: Global Abuse of a Trade Policy Instrument* (Academic Foundation, 2007).

Dent, Christopher M., 'Brexit, Trump and Trade: Back to a Late Nineteenth Century Future?', *Compet. Change* 24, nos. 3–4 (2020), 338–357.

Denton, Ross, "(Why) Should Nations Utilize Anti-dumping Measures?', *Mich. J. Int'l L.* 11 (1989), 224-272.

Fuchs, Richard, Peter Alexander, Brown Calum, Frances Cossar, Roslyn C. Henry and Mark Rounsevell, 'Why the US–China Trade War Spells Disaster for the Amazon', *Nature* 567, no. 7749 (2019), 451–454.

Edlin, Aeron S., 'Stopping Above-Cost Predatory Pricing', *Yale L. J.* 111, no. 4 (2002), 941–991.

Effron, Robin J., 'Reason Giving and Rule Making in Procedural Law', *Ala. L. Rev.* 65 (2013), 683–733.

Ehlermann, Claus-Dieter and Nicolas Lockhart, 'Standard of Review in WTO Law', *J. Int'l Econ. Law* 7, no. 3 (2004), 491–521.

Endriss, Ulle, 'Logic and Social Choice Theory', *Log. Philos. Today* 2 (2011), 2–38.

Erixon, Fredrik, 'Anti-dumping in the European Union', in B. Debroy and Debashis Chakraborty (eds.), *Anti-Dumping: Global Abuse of a Trade Policy Instrument* (Academic Foundation, 2007), 139–142.

Ezzamel, Mahmoud and Jason Zezhong Xiao, 'The Development of Accounting Regulations for Foreign Invested Firms in China: The Role of Chinese Characteristics', *Account. Organ. Soc.* 44 (2015), 60–84.

Falkner, Robert, *International Political Economy* (University of London Press, 2005).

Fan, Shenggen, Kanbur Ravi, Shang-Jin Wei and Xiaobo Zhang, eds., *The Oxford Companion to the Economics of China* (Oxford University Press, 2014).

Feenstra, Robert C., *Advanced International Trade: Theory and Evidence* (Princeton University Press, 2015).

Feinberg, Robert M. and Kara M. Reynolds, 'How Do Countries Respond to Anti-dumping Filings? Dispute Settlement and Retaliatory Anti-dumping', *World Econ.* 41, no. 5 (2018), 1251–1268.

Fetzer, Thiemo and Carlo Schwarz, 'Tariffs and Politics: Evidence from Trump's Trade Wars', *Econ. J.* 131, no. 636 (2021), 1717–1741.

Fontanelli, Filippo and Paolo Busco, 'The Function of Procedural Justice in International Adjudication', *Law Pract. Internat'l Court. Trib.* 15, no. 1 (2016), 1–23.

Fox, Eleanor M., 'Competition Law and the Agenda for the WTO: Forging the Links of Competition and Trade', *Pac. Rim L. & Pol'y J.* 4 (1995), 1.

Francois, Joseph, 'Subsidies and Countervailing Measures: Determining the Benefits of Subsidies' in Kyle W. Bagwell, George A. Bermann and Petros C. Mavroidis (eds.), *Law and Economics of Contingent Protection in International Trade* (Cambridge University Press, 2009), 113–115.

Fusch, Patricia I. and Lawrence R. Ness, 'Are We There Yet? Data Saturation in Qualitative Research', *Qual. Rep.* 20, no. 9 (2015), 1408–1416.

Gaffney, John P., 'Due Process in the World Trade Organization: The Need for Procedural Justice in the Dispute Settlement System', *Am. U. Int'l L. Rev.* 14 (1998), 1179–1221.

Gallo, Andres, 'Trade Policy and Protectionism in Argentina', *Econ. Affairs* 32, no. 1 (2012), 55–59.

Gambardella, Maurizio, 'Transparency in EU Antidumping Investigations: The European Ombudsman Perspective', *Glob. Trade Cust. J.* 6, no. 3 (2011), 157–163.

Garner, Bryan A., *Black's Law Dictionary* (West Group, 1999).

Garrity-Rokous, Gates and Raymond H. Brescia, 'Procedural Justice and International Human Rights: Towards a Procedural Jurisprudence for Human Rights Tribunals', *Yale J. Int'l L.* 18 (1993), 559–603.

Gaudin, Germain and Despoina Mantzari, 'Margin Squeeze: An Above-Cost Predatory Pricing Approach', *J. Comp. L. & Econ.* 12, no. 1 (2016), 151–179.

Gong, Xun and Cortese Corinne, 'A Socialist Market Economy with Chinese Characteristics: The Accounting Annual Report of China Mobile', *Account. Forum* 41, no. 3 (2017), 206–220.

Green, Andrew and Michael Trebilcock, 'Enforcing WTO Obligations: What Can We Learn from Export Subsidies?', *J. Int'l Econ. Law* 10, no. 3 (2007), 653–683.

Guest, Greg, Arwen Bunce and Laura Johnson, 'How Many Interviews Are Enough? An Experiment with Data Saturation and Variability', *Field Methods* 18, no. 1 (2006), 59–82.

Gwartney, James D., Richard L. Stroup, Russel S. Sobel and David A. Macpherson, *Economics: Private and Public Choice* (Cengage Learning, 2016).

Halverson, Karen, 'China's WTO Accession: Economic, Legal, and Political Implications', *BC Int'l & Comp. L. Rev.* 27 (2004), 319–370.

Han, Baoqing, 'Analyzing China's Litigation Costs in the WTO: Problems and Solutions', *J. WTO China* 3, no. 4 (2013), 119–128.

Hannah, Erin, James Scott and Rorden Wilkinson, 'The WTO in Buenos Aires: The Outcome and Its Significance for the Future of the Multilateral Trading System', *World Econ.* 41, no. 10 (2018), 2578–2598.

Hartman, Stephen W., 'The WTO, the Doha Round Impasse, PTAs, and FTAs/RTAs', *Int'l Trade J.* 27, no. 5 (2013), 411–430.

Hawkins, Janice E., 'The Practical Utility and Suitability of Email Interviews in Qualitative Research', *Qual. Rep.* 23, no. 2 (2018), 493–501.

Hoekman, Bernard M. and Michael M. Kostecki, *The Political Economy of the World Trading System: The WTO and Beyond* (Oxford University Press, 2009).

Hoekman, Bernard M. and Petros C. Mavroidis, *World Trade Organization (WTO): Law, Economics, and Politics* (Routledge, 2007).

Hollander-Blumoff, Rebecca and Tom R. Tyler, 'Procedural Justice and the Rule of Law: Fostering Legitimacy in Alternative Dispute Resolution', *J. Disp. Resol.* 1, no. 1 (2011), 1–20.

Horlick, Gary, 'Ten Major Problems with the Anti-Dumping Instrument in the United States', *J. World Trade* 39, no. 1 (2005), 169–179.

Horlick, Gary and Edwin Vermulst, 'Ten Major Problems with the Anti-Dumping Instrument: An Attempt at Synthesis', *J. World Trade* 39 (2005), 67–73.

Hovenkamp, Herbert, 'The Areeda–Turner Test for Exclusionary Pricing: A Critical Journal', *Rev. Indust. Org.* 46, no. 3 (2015), 209–228.

Howse, Robert and Trebilcock Michael, *The Regulation of International Trade* (Routledge, 2005).

Hua, Xiuping, Ying Jiang, Qian Sun and Xinyi Xing. 'Do Antidumping Measures Affect Chinese Export-Related Firms?', *Rev. Quant. Finance Account.* 52 (2019), 891–900.

Hudec, Robert E., 'Differences in National Environmental Standards: The Level-Playing-Field Dimension', *Minn. J. Global Trade* 5 (1996), 1–28.

Hutton, Susan and Michael Trebilcock, 'An Empirical Study of the Application of Canadian Anti-Dumping Laws: A Search for Normative Rationales,' *J. World Trade* 24 (1990), 123–146.

Jensen, Bradford J., Dennis P. Quinn and Stephen Weymouth, 'The Influence of Firm Global Supply Chains and Foreign Currency Undervaluations on US Trade Disputes', *Int'l Org.* 69, no. 4 (2015), 913–947.

Kazeki, Jun, 'Anti-dumping Negotiations under the WTO and FANs', *J. World Trade* 44, no. 5 (2010), 931–965.

Kennedy, D. and Joseph E. Stiglitz, eds., *Law and Economics with Chinese Characteristics: Institutions for Promoting Development in the Twenty-First Century* (Oxford University Press, 2013).

Kerr, William A., 'Dumping–One of Those Economic Myths', *Estey Centre J. Int'l L. Trade Pol'y* 2, no. 2 (2001), 211–220.

Khan, Owais Hasan, 'Interface between Antidumping and Competition Law: A Critical Analysis', *Interface* 123 (2016), 123–138.

Kissinger, Henry, *On China* (Penguin Press, 2010).

Krishna, Raj, *Anti-Dumping in Law and Practice* (The World Bank, The World Bank E-Library, 1999).

Kroeber, Arthur R., *China's Economy: What Everyone Needs to Know* (Oxford University Press, 2016).

Kwok, Kelvin, 'The New Hong Kong Competition Law: Anomalies and Challenges', *World Comp.* 37, no. 4 (2014), 541–567.

Kyounghwa, Kim and Dukgeun Ahn, 'To Be or Not to Be with Targeted Dumping', *J. Int'l Econ. L.*21, no. 3 (2018), 567–598.

Lai, Chung-Fu and Xi-Tsz Lee, 'The Effects of Anti-Dumping Duties in a New Open Economy Macroeconomics Model', *Int'l J. Econ. Fin. Issues* 6, no. 3 (2016), 837–844.

Lai, Edwin, 'The US–China Trade War, the American Public Opinions and Its Effects on China', *Econ. Pol. Stud.* 7, no. 2 (2019), 169–184.

Langlois, John D., 'The WTO and China's Financial System', *China Quart.* 167 (2001), 610–629.

Leclerc, Jean-Mark, 'Reforming Anti-dumping Law: Balancing the Interests of Consumers and Domestic Industries', *McGill L.J.* 44 (1998), 111–140.

Lee, Pierce, 'Rethinking the Rhetoric of Anti-dumping: A Response to Mark Wu's Reform Proposal', *Ga. J. Int'l & Comp. L.* 42 (2013), 459–488.

Lehne, Jens, *Crisis at the WTO: Is the Blocking of Appointments to the WTO Appellate Body by the United States Legally Justified?* (Carl Grossmann Verlag, 2019).

Lekfuangfu, Nam-Ake, 'Rethinking the WTO Anti-Dumping Agreement from a Fairness Perspective', *Cambridge Student L. Rev.* 4 (2008), 300.

Lenway, Stefanie, Morck Randall and Yeung Bernard, 'Rent Seeking, Protectionism and Innovation in the American Steel Industry', *Econ. J.* 106 (1996), 410–421.

Liu, Hongsong, 'China's Proposing Behavior in Global Governance: The Cases of the WTO Doha Round Negotiation and G-20 Process', *Rev. Bras. Polít. Int.* 57, no. SPE (2014), 121–137.

Liu, Tao and Wing Thye Woo, 'Understanding the US–China Trade War', *China Econ. J.* 11, no. 3 (2018), 319–340.

Liu, Xuepeng and Huimin Shi, 'Anti-dumping Duty Circumvention through Trade Rerouting: Evidence from Chinese Exporters', *World Econ.* 42, no. 5 (2019), 1427–1466.

Lichtman, Marilyn, *Qualitative Research for the Social Sciences* (SAGE Publications, 2013).

Lindsey, Brink and Ikenson Daniel, *Antidumping 101: The Devilish Details of 'Unfair Trade' Law* (Center for Trade Policy Studies, Cato Institute, 2002).

'The Rhetoric and Reality of US Anti-dumping Law', in Bibek Debroy and Debashis Chakraborty (eds.), *Anti-dumping: Global Abuse of a Trade Policy Instrument* (Academic Foundation, 2007), 101–118.

Lo, Chung-fa, 'A Proper Balance between WTO's Members-Driven Nature and the Appellate Body's Role as an Adjudicator: Careful Exercise of Judicial

Activism', in Chang-fa Lo, Junji Nakagawa and Tsai-fang Chen (eds.), *The Appellate Body of the WTO and Its Reform* (Springer, 2020), 125–139.

Lu, Yi, 'Exploring Aggressive Legalism: Is Now a Good Time to Promote This Approach in Greater Asia?', *Asian J. L. Econ.* 6, no. 1 (2015), 85–123.

Luo, Yan, *Anti-dumping in the WTO, the EU, and China: The Rise of Legalization in the Trade Regime and Its Consequences*, Vol. 69 (Kluwer Law International BV, 2010).

Lynn, Preece S. and Bart M. McMillan, 'Free Trade Does Not Equal Freedom from Red Tape: Practitioner Thoughts on FTAA Rules of Origin', *Int'l L. Rev.* 1 (2003), 159.

Malawer, Stuart S., 'Biden, National Security, Law & Global Trade: Less Subterfuge & More Strategy in the New Era of Crisis', *China WTO Rev.* 7, no. 1 (2021), 185–198.

Margolis, Stephen E., 'Two Definitions of Efficiency in Law and Economics', *J. Legal Stud.* 16, no. 2 (1987), 471–482.

Marsh, Sarah J., 'Creating Barriers for Foreign Competitors: A Study of the Impact of Anti-dumping Actions on the Performance of US Firms', *Strateg. Manag. J.* 19, no. 1 (1998), 25–37.

Martin, Antoine and Mercurio Bryan, 'Doha Dead and Buried in Nairobi: Lessons for the WTO', *J. Int'l Trade L. Pol'y* 16, no. 1 (2017), 49–66.

Martyn, Taylor D., *International Competition Law: A New Dimension for the WTO?* (Cambridge University Press, 2006).

Matsushita, Mitsuo, 'Basic Principles of the WTO and the Role of Competition Policy', *Wash. U. Global Stud. L. Rev.* 3 (2004), 363–385.

Matsushita, Mitsuo, Thomas J. Schoenbaum, Petros C. Mavroidis and Michael Hahn, *The World Trade Organization: Law, Practice, and Policy* (Oxford University Press, 2015).

Mavroidis, Petros C., Patrick A. Messerlin and Jasper M. Wauters, *The Law and Economics of Contingent Protection in the WTO* (Edward Elgar, 2008).

Mavroidis, Petros C. and Thomas J. Prusa, 'Die Another Day: Zeroing in on Targeted Dumping: Did the AB Hit the Mark in US–*Washing Machines*?', *World Trade Rev.* 17, no. 2 (2018), 239–264.

Maxwell, Joseph A., 'Using Qualitative Methods for Causal Explanation', *Field Methods* 16, no. 3 (2004), 243–264.

Messerlin, Patrick A., 'Anti-Dumping Regulations or Pro-Cartel Law? The EC Chemical Cases', *World Econ.* 13, no. 4 (1990), 465–492.

'China in the World Trade Organization: Antidumping and Safeguards', *World Bank Econ. Rev.* 18, no. 1 (2004), 105–130.

Miranda, Jorge, 'Implementation of the 'Shift in Burden of Proof' Approach to Interpreting Paragraph 15 of China's Protocol of Accession', *Glob. Trade Cust. J.* 11, no. 10 (2016), 447–453.

Mitchell, Andrew D., Muthucumaraswamy Sornarajah and Voon Tania, eds., *Good Faith and International Economic Law* (Oxford University Press, 2015).

Mokrov, Gennady, Raisa V. Kamanina, Valentina V. Pavlova, Katerina V. Isaeva and Leonid D. Bashkatov, 'Antidumping Investigation: Calculation of the Dumping Margin', *Indian J. Sci. Technol.* 9, no. 42 (2016), 104276, 1-11.

Moore, O. Michael, 'US Facts–Available Antidumping Decisions: An Empirical Analysis', *Eur. J. Pol. Econ.* 22, no. 3 (2006), 639–652.

Moore, O. Michael and Zanardi Maurizio, 'Does Anti-dumping Use Contribute to Trade Liberalization in Developing Countries?', *Can. J. Econ./Rev. Can. d'Econ.* 42, no. 2 (2009), 469–495.

Morgan, Clarisse, 'Competition Policy and Anti-Dumping', *J. World Trade* 30 (1996), 61–88.

Niels, Gunnar and Adriaan T. Kate, 'Anti-dumping Protection in a Liberalising Country: Mexico's Anti-dumping Policy and Practice', *World Econ.* 27, no. 7 (2004), 967–983.

Nielsen, Ulff-Moller Jorgen and Gert Tinggaard Svendsen, 'EU Lobbying and Anti-dumping Policy', *J. World Trade* 46 (2012), 187–211.

Oesch, Matthias, 'Standards of Review in WTO Panel Proceedings', *J. Int'l Econ. L.* 6, no. 3 (2005), 635–659.

Pauwelyn, Joost, 'WTO Dispute Settlement Post 2019: What to Expect?', *J. Int'l Econ. L.* 22, no. 3 (2019), 297–321.

Petersmann, Ernst U., 'The 2018 Trade Wars as a Threat to the World Trading System and Constitutional Democracies', *Trade L. & Dev.* 10 (2018), 179–225.

Porter, Michael, *Competitive Advantage of Nations: Creating and Sustaining Superior Performance*, Vol. 2. (Simon & Schuster, 2011).

Prost, Oliver, 'Confidentiality Issues under the DSU: Fact-finding Process versus Confidentiality', in Rufus Yerxa and Bruce Wilson (eds.), *Key Issues in WTO Dispute Settlement* (Cambridge University Press, 2005), 190–203.

Prusa, Thomas J., 'Anti-dumping: A Growing Problem in International Trade', *World Econ.* 28, no. 5 (2005), 683–700.

Prusa, Thomas J. and Edwin Vermulst, 'United States – Certain Methodologies and Their Application to Anti-Dumping Proceedings Involving China: Nails in the Coffin of Unfair Dumping Margin Calculation Methodologies', *World Trade Rev.* 18, no. 2 (2019), 1–21.

Prusa, Thomas J. and Edwin Vermulst, 'United States – Continued Existence and Application of Zeroing Methodology: The End of Zeroing?', *World Trade Rev.* 10, no. 1 (2011), 45–61.

Qin, Julia Ya, 'China, India, and the Law of the World Trade Organization', *Asian J. Comp. L.* 3 (2008), 1–43.

'Trade, Investment and Beyond: The Impact of WTO Accession on China's Legal System', in Perry Keller (ed.), *Law and the Market Economy in China* (Routledge, 2017), 720–741.

Quartner, David, 'Public Choice Theory, Protectionism and the Case of NAFTA', *Econ. Aff.* 26, no. 1 (2006), 59–60.

Raju, K. D., 'India's Involvement in Anti-Dumping Cases in the First Decade of WTO', in Dibek Debroy and Debahsis Chakraborty (eds.), *Anti-Dumping: Global Abuse of a Trade Policy Instrument* (Academic Foundation, 2007), 31–47.

Ramírez, Rafael S. Espinosa, 'Reciprocal Dumping and Environmental Polices', *Panor. Econ.* 3, no. 6 (2017), 7–33.

Reich, Arie, 'The Effectiveness of the WTO Dispute Settlement System: A Statistical Analysis', in Toshiyuki Kono, Mary Hiscock and Arie Reich (eds.), *Transnational Commercial and Consumer Law* (Springer, 2018), 1–43.

Resnick, David, 'Due Process and Procedural Justice', *NOMOS Am. Soc'y Pol. Legal Phil.* 18 (1977), 206–228.

Rodrik, Dani, 'Political Economy of Trade Policy', in G. M. Grossman and Kenneth Rogoff (eds.), *Handbook of International Economics*, Vol. 3 (Elsevier Science BV, 1995), 1457–1494.

Romano, Alessandro and Peachya Thammapitagkul, 'Anti-dumping: A Public Interest Not So Much in the Public Interest', *Manchester J. Int'l Econ. L.* 10 (2013), 59–77.

Rovegno, Laura, 'Trade Protection and Market Power: Evidence from US Anti-Dumping and Countervailing Duties', *Rev. World Econ.* 149, no. 3 (2013), 443–476.

Ruttley, Philip R., Iain Macvay and Mark Weisberger, *Due Process in WTO Dispute Settlement* (Cameron May, 2001).

Schneider, Andrea K., 'Not Quite a World without Trials: Why International Dispute Resolution Is Increasingly Judicialized', *J. Disp. Resol.* 2006 (2006), 119–129.

Seo Dong, Woo, 'Material Retardation Standard in the US Anti-dumping Law', *Law & Pol'y Int'l Bus.* 24 (1992), 835–914.

Shadikhodjaev, Sherzod, 'Non-Market Economies, Significant Market Distortions, and the 2017 EU Anti-Dumping Amendment', *J. Int'l Econ. L.* 21, no. 4 (2018), 885–905.

Sharma, Rajesh, *WTO Appellate Body at Cross Roads: Options and Alternatives*, in Chang-fa Lo, Junji Nakagawa and Tsai-fang Chen (eds.), *The Appellate Body of the WTO and Its Reform* (Springer, 2020), 239–254.

Slater, Valerie A. and Lisa W. Ross, 'Judicial Review of the International Trade Commission's Determinations in Antidumping and Countervailing Duty Proceedings: An Overview of Decisions in 2006', *Geo. J. Int'l L.* 39 (2007), 69.

Smith, Stephen C. and Yao Pan, 'US–China Economic Relations', in Shenggen Fan, Kanbur Ravi, Shang-Jin Wei and Xiaobo Zhang (eds.), *The Oxford Companion to the Economics of China* (Oxford University Press, 2014), 119–124.

Solum, Lawrence B., 'Procedural Justice', *S. Cal. L. Rev.* 78 (2004), 181–320.

Spamann, Holger, 'Standard of Review for World Trade Organization Panels in Trade Remedy Cases: A Critical Analysis', *J. World Trade* 38 (2004), 509–555.

Stancil, Paul, 'Substantive Equality and Procedural Justice', *Iowa L. Rev.* 102 (2016), 1635–1690.

Steinbach, Armin, 'Price Undertakings in EU Anti-dumping Proceedings – An Instrument of the Past?', *J. Econ. Integr.* 29, no. 1 (2014), 165–187.

Steinbock, Dan, 'US–China Trade War and Its Global Impacts', *China Q. Int. Strateg. Stud.* 4, no. 4 (2018), 515–542.

Stemler, Steve, 'An Overview of Content Analysis', *Pract. Assess. Res. Eval.* 7, no. 17 (2001), 137–146.

Stewart, TerenceP., 'US–Japan Economic Disputes: The Role of Anti-Dumping and Countervailing Duty Laws', *Ariz. J. Int'l & Comp. L.* 16 (1999), 689–750.

Sun, Shuwei, Hailong Zhao, Xianjie He and Ying Zhang, 'The Impact of Accounting Standards Convergence on Chinese Firms' Overseas Mergers and Acquisitions', *China J. Account. Res.* 12, no. 3 (2019), 231–250.

Suranovic, M. Steven, 'A Positive Analysis of Fairness with Applications to International Trade', *World Econ.* 23, no. 3 (2000), 283–307.

Sykes, Alan O., 'Regulatory Protectionism and the Law of International Trade', *Univ. Chi. L. Rev.* 66 (1999), 1–46.

Telep, Jeffrey M. and Richard C. Lutz, 'China's Long Road to Market Economy Status', *Geo. J. Int'l L.* 49 (2017), 693–708.

Tharakan, P. K. Mathew, 'Is Anti-Dumping Here to Stay?', *World Econ.* 22, no. 2 (1999), 179–206.

Trommer, Silke Melanie, 'Special Market Economy: Undermining the Principles of the WTO?', *Chin. J. Int'l L.* 6, no. 3 (2007), 565–599.

Tyler, Tom R., 'What Is Procedural Justice? Criteria Used by Citizens to Assess the Fairness of Legal Procedures', *Law & Soc'y Rev.* 22 (1988), 103–136.

Updegraff, Ragan, 'Striking a Balance between Necessity and Fairness: The Use of Adverse Facts Available in Dumping and Subsidies Investigations', *Geo. J. Int'l L.* 49 (2017), 710–787.

Van Bael, Ivo and Jean-François Bellis, *EU Anti-Dumping and Other Trade Defence Instruments* (Kluwer Law International, 2011).

Van den Bossche, Peter and Prévost Denise, 'Rules on Unfair Trade', in Peter Van den Bossche and Denise Prévost (eds.), *Essentials of WTO Law* (Cambridge University Press, 2016), 141–177.

Van den Bossche, Peter and Werner Zdouc, *The Law and Policy of the World Trade Organization: Text, Cases and Materials* (Cambridge University Press, 2017).

Vermulst, Edwin, 'Ten Major Problems with the Anti-Dumping Instrument in the European Community', *J. World Trade* 39 (2005), 67–73.

Vermulst, Edwin and Ikenson Daniel, 'Zeroing under the WTO Anti-Dumping Agreement: Where Do We Stand?', *Glob. Trade Cust. J.* 2, no. 6 (2007), 231–242.

Vermulst, Edwin and Brian Gatta, 'Concurrent Trade Defense Investigations in the EU, the EU's New Anti-Subsidy Practice against China, and the Future of Both', *World Trade Rev.* 11 (2012), 527–553.

Vermulst, Edwin and Juhi Dion Sud, 'The New Rules Adopted by the European Union to Address "Significant Distortions" in the Anti-Dumping Context', in Marc Bungenberg, Michael Hahn, Christoph Herrmann and Till Müller-Ibold (eds.), *The Future of Trade Defence Instruments* (Springer, 2018), 63–87.

Viner, Jacob, 'The Prevalence of Dumping in International Trade: I', *J. Pol. Econ.* 30, no. 5 (1922), 655–680.

'The Prevalence of Dumping in International Trade: II', *J. Pol. Econ.* 30, no. 6 (1922), 796–826.

Voon, Tania, 'Eliminating Trade Remedies from the WTO: Lessons from Regional Trade Agreements', *Int'l & Comp. L. Q.* 59, no. 3 (2010), 625–667.

Wagner, Markus, 'The Impending Demise of the WTO Appellate Body: From Centrepiece to Historical Relic?', in Chang-fa Lo, Junji Nakagawa and Tsai-fang Chen (eds.), *The Appellate Body of the WTO and Its Reform* (Springer, 2020), 67–90.

Wang, Xiaosong, Jack Hou and Faqin Lin, 'ITC Antidumping toward China Rulings: Is Political Factor Overwhelming?', *Bull. Econ. Res.* 74, no. 1 (2021), 106–122.

Wang, Xiasong, Zhexi Liu, Lu Yue and Chunming Zhao, 'Trade Barriers and Participation in the Global Value Chain: An Empirical Study Based on Anti-dumping toward China', *China World Econ.* 27, no. 2 (2019), 86–106.

Washington, Andre J., 'Not So Fast, China: Non-Market Economy Status Is Not Necessary for the Surrogate Country Method', *Chi. J. Int'l L.* 19 (2018), 260–294.

Webley, Lisa, 'Qualitative Approaches to Empirical Legal Research,' in Peter Cane and Herbert Kritzer (eds.), *The Oxford Handbook of Empirical Legal Research* (Oxford University Press, 2010), 1–21.

Whalley, John and Jing Wang, 'Using Tax-Based Instruments for Innovative China's Trade Rebalancing,' in Shenggen Fan, Kanbur Ravi, Shang-Jin Wei and Xiaobo Zhang (eds.), *The Oxford Companion to the Economics of China* (Oxford University Press, 2014), 145–149.

William, Judge, Shaomin Li and Robert Pinsker, 'National Adoption of International Accounting Standards: An Institutional Perspective', *Corp. Gov. Int'l Rev.* 18, no. 3 (2010), 161–174.

Williams, Adam, 'What a Dump! The Current State of Antidumping Duty Calculations in Non-Market Economy Cases', *Emory Int'l L. Rev.* 32 (2017), 433–465.

Willems, Arnould R. and Matilda J. Brolin, 'The Unhappy Marriage of Customs and Anti-Dumping Legislation: Tensions Relating to Product Description and Origin', *Leg. Issues Econ. Integration* 45, no. 3 (2018), 229–251.

Williams, Mark, *Competition Policy and Law in China, Hong Kong and Taiwan* (Cambridge University Press, 2005).

Willig, Robert D., 'Economic Effects of Antidumping Policy', in Robert Lawrence (ed.), *Brookings Trade Forum* (Brookings Institution Press, 1998), 57–79.

Wooton, Ian and Maurizio Zanardi, 'Trade and Competition Policy: Anti-Dumping versus Anti-trust', University of Glasgow Discussion Paper in Economics No. 02-06 (2002).

Wood, Diane P., '"Unfair" Trade Injury: A Competition-Based Approach', *Stan. L. Rev.* 41, no. 5 (1989), 1153–1200.

World Trade Organization, *Dispute Settlement Reports 2001: Volume 8, Pages 3303–4047*, Vol. 8 (Cambridge University Press, 2004).

A Handbook on the WTO Dispute Settlement System (Cambridge University Press, 2017).

Wróbel, Anna, 'The Functionality and Dysfunctionality of Global Trade Governance: The European Union Perspective', in Marek Rewizorski, Karina Jędrzejowska and Anna Wróbel (eds.), *The Future of Global Economic Governance* (Springer, 2020), 161–175.

Wruuck, Patricia, *The Political Economy of Anti-dumping Protection* (Springer, 2015).

Wu, Mark, 'Anti-dumping in Asia's Emerging Giants', *Harv. Int'l L.J.* 53 (2012), 1–72.

Xu, Bin, 'Trade Policy Reform and Trade Reform', in Shenggen Fan, Ravi Kanbur, Shang-Jin Wei and Xiaobo Zhang (eds.), *The Oxford Companion to the Economics of China* (Oxford University Press, 2014), 156–160.

Xun, Gong and Corinne Cortese. 'A Socialist Market Economy with Chinese Characteristics: The Accounting Annual Report of China Mobile', *Account. Forum* 41, no. 3 (2017), 206–220.

Yan, Shi, 'The EU's Push for WTO Reform: Proposals, Paths and Impacts', *China Int'l Stud.* 76 (2019), 60.

Yang, Dennis Tao, 'China's Agricultural Crisis and Famine of 1959–1961: A Survey and Comparison to Soviet Famines', *Comp. Econ. Stud.* 50, no. 1 (2008), 1–29.

Yilmazcan, Abdulkadir, 'The Role of Anti-Dumping in the US–China Trade War', *China & WTO Rev.* 2021, no. 1 (2021), 7–36.

'The Slow Train to Reforming Anti-Dumping Measures', Series 2, Vol. 3 *Amicus Curiae* (2022), 335–360.

'The Slow Train to Reforming Anti-Dumping Measures: Concrete Solutions for the Future', Series 2, Vol. 3 Amicus Curiae (2022), 517–531.

Yong, Liu and Xie Yiyi, 'Analysis of the EU's New Surrogate Country System for External Anti-Dumping and Its Illegality', *J. WTO & China* 10 (2020), 52.

Yu, Chen, 'Currency Manipulation and WTO Laws: Should the Anti-Dumping Mechanism Be Entirely Dumped?', *J. World Invest. Trade* 20, no. 6 (2019), 891–915.

Yu, Tian, 'The 10 Major Problems with the Anti-Dumping Instrument in The People's Republic of China', *J. World Trade* 39, no. 1 (2005), 97–103.

Yu, Yongding, 'Can China and the United States Avoid a Full-Blown Trade War?', in Ha Jiming and Adam S. Posen (eds.), *US–China Economic Relations: From Conflict to Solutions* (PIIE, 2019), 41–57.

Zeng, Lingliang, 'Non-market Economy Issues in Sino-EU Relations: A Purely Technical Matter or Beyond?', in An Chen (ed.), *Contemporary International Law and China's Peaceful Development* (Springer, 2021), 577–597.

Zhang, Yan and Barbara M. Wildemuth, 'Qualitative Analysis of Content', in B. M. Wildemuth (ed.), *Applications of Social Research Methods to Questions in Information and Library Science* (Libraries Unlimited, 2009), 53–70.

Zhao, Yun, ed., *International Governance and the Rule of Law in China under the Belt and Road Initiative* (Cambridge University Press, 2018).

Zheng, Wentong, 'Reforming Trade Remedies', *Mich. J. Int'l L.* 34 (2012), 151.

Zhou, Weihuan, 'China's Litigation on Non-Market Economy Treatment at the WTO: A Preliminary Assessment', *Chin. J. Comp. L.* 5, no. 2 (2017), 345–364.

Zhou, Weihuan and Percival Andrew, 'Debunking the Myth of "Particular Market Situation" in WTO Antidumping Law', *J. Int'l Econ. L.* 19, no. 4 (2016), 863–892.

Zhou, Weihuan and Peng Delei, 'EU–Price Comparison Methodologies (DS516): Challenging the Non-Market Economy Methodology in Light of the Negotiating History of Article 15 of China's WTO Accession Protocol', *J. World Trade* 52, no. 3 (2018), 505–533.

Zhou, Weihuan and Shu Zhang, 'Anti-dumping Practices and China's Implementation of WTO Rulings', *China Quart.* 230 (2017), 512–527.

Zimmermann, Claus D., 'The Neglected Link between the Legal Nature of WTO Rules, the Political Filtering of WTO Disputes, and the Absence of Retrospective WTO Remedies', *Trade L. & Dev.* 4, no. 1 (Summer 2012), 251–267.

Papers and Reports

37th Annual Report from the Commission to the Council and the European Parliament on the EU's Anti-Dumping, Anti-Subsidy and Safeguard Activities and the Use of Trade Defence Instruments by Third Countries Targeting the EU in 2018, EU Commission, accessed 17 June 2023, http://trade.ec.europa.eu/doclib/docs/2019/march/tradoc_157810.pdf.

'Anti-dumping in the Doha Development Agenda', ICC, accessed 17 June 2023, https://iccwbo.org/publication/anti-dumping-in-the-doha-development-agenda/.

Bacchus, James, 'Might Unmakes Right: The American Assault on the Rule of Law in World Trade', CIGI Papers No. 173 (2018).

Bown, Chad P., 'Temporary Trade Barriers Database: Update through 2013', World Bank, 2014, accessed 17 June 2023, http://econ.worldbank.org/ttbd/.

'China's Market Economy Status and Antidumping: A $100 Billion, $10 Billion, or $1 Billion Dispute? Part 2', Peterson Institute for International Economics (8 June 2016), accessed 1 June 2022, https://piie.com/blogs/trade-investment-policy-watch/chinas-market-economy-status-and-antidumping-100-billion-10-0.

'Should the United States Recognize China as a Market Economy?' No. PB16–24 (2016).

Trade Remedies and World Trade Organization Dispute Settlement: Why Are So Few Challenged? (The World Bank, 2005).

'US–China Phase One Tracker: China's Purchases of US Goods', Peterson Institute for International Economics (2021), accessed 18 July 2023, www.piie.com/research/piie-charts/us-china-phase-one-tracker-chinas-purchases-us-goods.

US–China Trade War Tariffs: An Up-to-Date Chart, PIIE Charts (14 February 2020 [20 September 2019]) www.piie.com/research/piie-charts/us-china-trade-war-tariffs-date-chart [last updated on 6 April 2023 as: China and the United States Change Their Tariffs].

Bown, Chad P. and Thomas J. Prusa, 'US Antidumping: Much Ado About Zeroing', The World Bank Research Working Paper (2010).

Bown, Chad P. and Yiwen Zhang, Measuring Trump's 2018 Trade Protection: Five Takeaways, Technical Report, Peterson Institute for International Economics (2019).

China, The World Factbook, accessed 15 July 2023, www.cia.gov/library/publications/the-world-factbook/geos/ch.html.

Chow, Gregory, 'The Impact of Joining WTO on China's Economic', Legal and Political Institutions (2001), accessed 15 July 2023, http://econwpa.wustl.edu.

Eechout, Piet, 'Administrative Procedures in EU External Trade Law' (2011), accessed 10 July 2023, www.europarl.europa.eu/RegData/etudes/note/join/2011/432758/IPOL-JURI_NT(2011)432758_EN.pdf.

European Commission, Report from the Commission to the European Parliament and the Council (2019), accessed 15 July 2023, https://trade.ec.europa.eu/doclib/docs/2020/may/tradoc_158733.PDF

Ganne, Emmanualle, Can Blockchain Revolutionize International Trade? (World Trade Organization, 2018).

Global Trade Alert, Total Number of Implemented Interventions since November (2008), www.globaltradealert.org/global_dynamics.

Hansen, Jørgen Drud and Jørgen Ulff-Møller Nielsen. 'The Puzzle of Simultaneous Anti-dumping and Anti-subsidy Measures', draft, at 4 (2011).

Herrero, Alicia, 'From Globalization to Deglobalization: Zooming into Trade', *Las Claves de la Globalizacion*, 33–52 (2019).

Hillman, J., 'Three Approaches to Fixing the World Trade Organization's Appellate Body: The Good, the Bad, and the Ugly', *IIEL Issue Briefs* (2018).

Hoekman, Bernard, Competition Policy and the Global Trading System: A Developing-Country Perspective (The World Bank, 1999).

Hoekman, Bernard and Petros C. Mavroidis, 'Burning Down the House? The Appellate Body in the Centre of the WTO Crisis', *The Appellate Body in the Centre of the WTO Crisis*, Robert Schuman Centre for Advanced Studies Research Paper No. RSCAS 56 (2019).

'An Introduction to Anti-Dumping Law of EU and US as It Applies to Seafood' (2010), accessed 14 June 2022, www.hambreyconsulting.co.uk/Documents/Course-handbook-eng.pdf.

Juhás, Henrich and Kittová Zuzana, 'Antidumping Investigations of the European Union in the Time of Pandemic COVID-19', *21st International Joint Conference Central and Eastern Europe in the Changing Business Environment* (2021).

Krugman, Paul R., 'Industrial Organization and International Trade', *Handb. Ind. Organ.* 2 (1989), 1179–1223.

Li, Yuefen, 'Why Is China the World's Number One Anti-Dumping Target?', *China in a Globalizing World* (2005).

Lincicome, Scott and Inu Manak, 'Protectionism or National Security? The Use and Abuse of Section 232', Policy Analysis 912 (2021).

Matschke, Xenia and Anja Schöttner, 'Antidumping as Strategic Trade Policy under Asymmetric Information', CESifo Working Paper Series No. 2536 (2009).

McGee, Robert, 'Some Ethical Aspects of Antidumping Laws' (2000), available at SSRN, accessed 16 July 2023, https://ssrn.com/abstract=242412 or http://dx.doi.org/10.2139/ssrn.242412.

Michalopoulos, Constantine, Developing Countries' Participation in the World Trade Organization (The World Bank, 1999).

Neufeld, Nora I., Anti-dumping and Countervailing Procedures: Use or Abuse?: Implications for Developing Countries (UN, 2001).

OECD, Competition Policy, 'General Distribution OCDE/GD (96) 59' (OECD, 1996).

Palmeter, David N., 'The Antidumping Law: A Legal and Administrative Nontariff Barrier', Down in the Dumps: Administration of the Unfair Trade Laws (Brooking Institution, Washington, 1991), 65–89.

Panezi, Maria, 'The WTO and the Spaghetti Bowl of Free Trade Agreements: Four Proposals for Moving Forward', CIGI Policy Brief No. 87 (2016).

Puccio, Laura, 'Granting Market Economy Status to China: An Analysis of WTO Law and of Selected WTO Members' Policy', European Parliamentary Research Service, November-PE 571 (2015).

Report from the Commission to the European Parliament and the Council, European Commission (31 July 2018), accessed 17 July 2023, https://eur-lex.europa.eu/LexUriServ/LexUriServ.do?uri=COM:2018:0561: FIN:EN:PDF.

Sanjay Kumar, Pandey and Mansi Bahal, 'International Trade: Dumping and Its Impact on Competition', Competition Commission of India (2012).

Schneider-Petsinger, M., Dispute Settlement in Crisis, in Reforming the World Trade Organization Prospects for Transatlantic Cooperation and the Global Trade System, Chatham House Research Paper (2020), accessed 19 July 2023, www.chathamhouse.org/2020/09/reforming-world-trade-organization/04-dispute-settlement-crisis.

Schott, Jeffrey J. and Jung Eujin, The WTO's Existential Crisis: How to Salvage Its Ability to Settle Trade Disputes, No. PB19–19 (2019).

Staiger, Robert W. and Frank A. Wolak, Measuring Industry Specific Protection: Anti-Dumping in the United States, No. W4696 (National Bureau of Economic Research, 1994).

Trade and Competition: Frictions after the Uruguay Round, OECD Economics Department Working Papers No. 165 (1996), accessed 17 July 2023, www.oecd-ilibrary.org/docserver/448346818265.pdf?expires=1614743590&id=id&accname=guest&checksum=09E0B528B657F096315B9466E2760DE4.

Trade Policy Review Report by the Secretariat China, WTO, 2018, WT/TPR/S/375, accessed 16 July 2023, https://docs.wto.org/dol2fe/Pages/SS/directdoc.aspx?filename=q:/ WT/TPR/S375. pdf&Open=True.

Van Li Thi, T. and Sarah Y. Tong, 'China and Anti-dumping: Regulations, Practices and Responses', East Asia Institute National University of Singapore Working Paper 149 (2009).

Waugh, Michael E., The Consumption Response to Trade Shocks: Evidence from the US-China Trade War, No. w26353, National Bureau of Economic Research (2019).

World Trade Statistical Review, Statistics on Anti-Dumping (2021), accessed 15 July 2023, www.wto.org/english/res_e/statis_e/wts2021_e/wts2021_e.pdf.

Wrobel, Ralph, 'The "China Effect": Changes in International Trade Patterns as Reasons for Rising Anti-Globalism', No. 2020-1. Ordnungspolitische Diskurse (2020).

Yandle, Bruce and Elizabeth M. Young, 'Dumping, Anti-dumping and Efficiency', World Bank Internal Discussion Paper, http://documents.worldbank.org/curated/en/163311468914400721/pdf/multi0page.pdf.

Webpages, Newspapers and Others

Administrative Protective Order, accessed 16 July 2023, www.usitc.gov/secretary/apo_forms_and_redbook.htm.

Bandyopadhyay, N., 'Anti-dumping Investigation in Agriculture: Issues of Trade Diversion-Named vs Non-named Countries', LSU Master's Theses (2008).

Bown, Chad P., Paola Conconi, Aksel Erbahar and Lorenzo Trimarchi, 'Trade Protection along Supply Chains: The Negative Effects of Tariffs on Downstream Sectors', USApp–American Politics and Policy (2021), accessed 16 July 2023, http://eprints.lse.ac.uk/109194/1/usappblog_2021_02_10_trade_protection_along_supply_chains_how.pdf.

Calculation of Dumping Margins: EU and US Rules and Practices in Light of the Debate on China's Market Economy Status, European Parliament (2016) accessed 30 June 2023, www.europarl.europa.eu/RegData/etudes/IDAN/2016/ 583794/EPRS_IDA(2016)583794_EN.pdf.

Cambridge Dictionary, 'a level playing field', accessed 16 July 2023, https://dictionary.cambridge.org/dictionary/english/a-level-playing-field.

Carmody, Chios, 'Fairness in International Economic Law and Relations', SSRN (13 February 2013), https://ssrn.com/abstract=2161623.

China December Trade Data Bad, but Likely to Get Worse This Year (2019), accessed 15 July 2023, www.scmp.com/economy/china-economy/article/2181951/china-trade-data-worse-expected-bad-news-economy.

China-EU – International Trade in Goods Statistics, accessed 17 June 2023, https://ec.europa.eu/eurostat/statistics-explained/index.php?title=Main_Page.

Chronological List of Disputes Cases, WTO, accessed 16 July 2023, www.wto.org/english/tratop_e/dispu_e/dispu_status_e.htm.

Claims Are Made That Parts for E-bikes Imported from Mainland China Face Unwarranted Anti-dumping Tariffs, HKTDC Research (2019), accessed 15 July 2023, https://hkmb.hktdc.com/en/1X0AH7IX/hktdc-research/Claims-Are-Made-That-Parts-for-E-bikes-Imported-from-Mainland-China-Face-Unwarranted-Anti-dumping-Tariffs.

Colback, Lucy, How to Navigate the US–China Trade War, *Financial Times* (2020), www.ft.com/content/6124beb8-5724-11ea-abe5-8e03987b7b20.

Commerce Questionnaires, accessed 15 July 2023, https://enforcement.trade.gov/questionnaires/questionnaires-ad.html.

Country Report on China (2017), accessed 15 June 2022, http://trade.ec.europa.eu/doclib/docs/2017/december/tradoc_156474.pdf.

Cunningham, Edward, What Is the Future of China's Private Sector?, Harvard Kennedy School (2022), accessed 17 June 2023, www.hks.harvard.edu/faculty-research/policy-topics/international-relations-security/what-future-chinas-private-sector.

Dao, Toan, 'US Court of Appeals Upholds Anti-dumping Duties on Shrimp from Vietnam' (2018), accessed 15 July 2023, www.seafoodsource.com/news/supply-trade/us-court-of-appeals-upholds-anti-dumping-duties-on-shrimp-from-vietnam.

Dispute Settlement: Legal Text, Understanding on Rules and Procedures Governing the Settlement of Disputes, accessed 16 July 2023, www.wto.org/english/tratop_e/dispu_e/dsu_e.htm#12.

European Commission, Countries and Regions, accessed 17 June 2023, https://ec.europa.eu/trade/policy/countries-and-regions/countries/vietnam/#: ~:text=The%20European%20Union%20and%20Vietnam,Council%20on%2030%20March%202020.

The EU-UK Trade and Cooperation Agreement, accessed 19 July 2023, https://ec.europa.eu/info/relations-united-kingdom/eu-uk-trade-and-cooperation-agreement_en.

European Commission Presents Comprehensive Approach for the Modernisation of the World Trade Organisation, 2018, EU, accessed 17 June 2023, http://trade.ec.europa.eu/doclib/press/index.cfm?id=1908.

Greater Bay Area Overview, accessed 15 July 2023, www.bayarea.gov.hk/en/about/overview.html.

Guidance on Marking of Goods of Hong Kong – Executive Order 13936, US Customs and Border Protection, accessed 18 July 2023, www.cbp.gov/trade/rulings/frequently-asked-questions-guidance-marking-goods-hong-kong-executive-order-13936?_ga=2.69427856.1287851153.1597626421-308187796.1597626421 (last modified 6 October 2020).

Guocan, Wu and Gong Yifei, 'The Accounting Information Support and Accounting Tactics of Protecting Rights and Interests in the Anti-Dumping Responding', in *2010 2nd IEEE International Conference on Information Management and Engineering* (IEEE, 2010).

Hancock, Tom, 'China's Relentless Export Machine Moves Up the Value Chain', *Financial Times* (2018), accessed 17 June 2023, www.ft.com/content/cdc53aee-bc2e-11e8-94b2-17176fbf93f5, www.worldtradelaw.net/, https://rcepsec.org/, https://tradingeconomics.com.

'How a Chinese Company Targeted by US Tariffs for the Last 10 Years Has Adapted and Thrived', *South China Morning Post* (2019), accessed 25 April 2020, www.scmp.com/business/companies/article/3010378/how-chinese-company-targeted-us-tariffs-last-10-years-has.

Keith, Tan et al., China Removes VAT Rebate on Steel Exports, Cuts Tax on Raw Material Imports to Zero (2021), accessed 17 June 2023, www.spglobal.com/platts/en/market-insights/latest-news/metals/042821-china-removes-vat-rebate-on-steel-exports-cuts-tax-on-raw-material-imports-to-zero.

KPMG, *China: Country VAT Essentials Guide* (2017).

McCarthy, Nail, 15 Countries Sign World's Biggest Free Trade Deal, Statista (2020), accessed 19 July 2023, www.statista.com/chart/23497/key-facts-about-the-regional-comprehensive-economic-partnership/.

Mintzer, Sydney H., Duane W. Layton and Timoty C. Lee, Proposed Changes to Antidumping and Countervailing Duty Regulations Would Make Proceedings More Efficient and Create New Enforcement Mechanisms (2020), www.mayerbrown.com/en/perspectives-events/publications/2020/08/proposed-changes-to-antidumping-and-countervailing-duty-regulations-would-make-proceedings-more-efficient-and-create-new-enforcement-mechanisms.

MOFCOM, Decree No. 12, 2006, Promulgating the Provisions on Responding to Actions of Anti-dumping of Export Products (2006), http://english.mofcom.gov.cn/.

Mwathi, Njeri, Types of Zeroing Methods in Dumping Margin Calculations, LinkedIn, accessed 17 June 2023, www.linkedin.com/pulse/types-zeroing-methods-dumping-margin-calculations-njeri-mwathi/.

Oppose Anti-Dumping Bill, *New York Times*, ProQuest Historical Newspapers (1920).

OXFAM, 2.7 Billion People Have Had No Social Protection to Cope with Covid-19 Economic Crisis (2020), accessed 19 July 2023, www.oxfam.org/en/press-releases/27-billion-people-have-had-no-social-protection-cope-covid-19-economic-crisis.

Patel, Deepesh and Emmanuelle Ganne, 'Blockchain & DLT in Trade: Where Do We Stand', Trade Finance Global (2020), www.wto.org/english/res_e/booksp_e/blockchainanddlt_e.pdf.

Timeline: Key Dates in the US–China Trade War (2020), accessed 17 June 2023, www.reuters.com/article/us-usa-trade-china-timeline/timeline-key-dates-in-the-u-s-china-trade-war-idUSKBN1ZE1AA.

TradeMap, accessed 15 July 2023, www.trademap.org/.

Training Module on the WTO Agreement on Anti-Dumping, UNCTAD (2006), accessed 16 July 2023, https://unctad.org/system/files/official-document/ditctncd20046_en.pdf.

UNCTAD, World Investment Report 2018 (2018), accessed 17 June 2023, https://unctad.org/en/PublicationsLibrary/wir2018_en.pdf.

US International Trade Commission (USITC), *Antidumping and Countervailing Duty Handbook*, 14th ed. (2015).

USITC, Generic Questionnaires, accessed 17 June 2023, www.usitc.gov/trade_remedy/question.htm.

Mattresses from the People's Republic of China: Antidumping Duty Order, A Notice by the International Trade Administration on 16 December 2019, accessed 17 June 2023, www.federalregister.gov/documents/2019/12/16/2019-27166/mattresses-from-the-peoples-republic-of-china-antidumping-duty-order.

'Understanding Antidumping & Countervailing Duty Investigations', accessed 17 June 2023, www.usitc.gov/press_room/usad.htm.

Who Uses IFRS Standards?, accessed 15 July 2023, www.ifrs.org/use-around-the-world/use-of-ifrs-standards-by-jurisdiction/.

Woodin, Hayley, 'Burnaby Company Hit with 1,732% US Anti-Dumping Duties' (2019), accessed 18 July 2023, https://biv.com/article/2019/06/us-china-trade-war-pushes-burnaby-company-cancel-exports.

The World Bank Data, accessed 17 June 2023, https://data.worldbank.org/indicator/TM.TAX.MRCH.WM.AR.ZS?locations=CN

WTO Negotiations on the Agreement on Anti-Dumping Practices, ITC (2005), accessed 17 June 2023, https://ticaret.gov.tr/data/5b8ee73113b8761b8471c2c4/wtonegotiations.pdf, www.wto.org, www.brainyquote.com.

WTO Tariff Analysis Online System, accessed 16 July 2023, http://tao.wto.org/.

INDEX